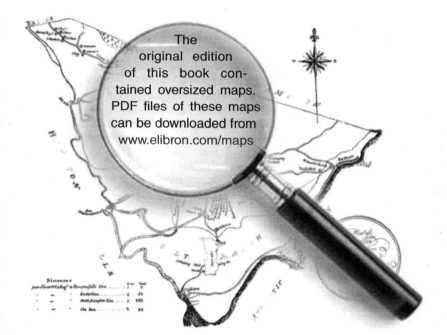

John Nisbet

BURMA UNDER BRITISH RULE - AND BEFORE

VOLUME I

Elibron Classics
www.elibron.com

London Borough of Lambeth	
LM 1175684 5	
Askews	04-Feb-2009
	£41.00

Elibron Classics series.

© 2005 Adamant Media Corporation.

ISBN 1-4021-5294-9 (paperback)
ISBN 1-4212-9509-1 (hardcover)

This Elibron Classics Replica Edition is an unabridged facsimile
of the edition published in 1901 by Archibald Constable & Co., Ltd.,
Westminster.

BURMA UNDER BRITISH RULE
—AND BEFORE

A BURMESE VILLAGE (SĔYWA, THARRAWADY DISTRICT).

VOL. I.

BURMA UNDER BRITISH RULE—AND BEFORE

BY JOHN NISBET D.ŒC

LATE CONSERVATOR OF FORESTS, BURMA
AUTHOR OF "BRITISH FOREST TREES"
"STUDIES IN FORESTRY" "OUR
FORESTS AND WOOD-
LANDS" ETC

IN TWO VOLUMES
WITH MAPS
VOL I

WESTMINSTER
ARCHIBALD CONSTABLE & CO Ltd
2 WHITEHALL GARDENS
1901

Butler & Tanner,
The Selwood Printing Works,
Frome, and London.

To

SIR FREDERIC WILLIAM RICHARDS FRYER K.C.S.I

THE LAST OF MANY EMINENT CHIEF COMMISSIONERS AND THE

FIRST LIEUTENANT - GOVERNOR OF BURMA

THIS ENDEAVOUR TO DESCRIBE THE GREAT

PROVINCE ENTRUSTED TO HIS CHARGE

ITS INTERESTING PEOPLE AND

THE RAPID PROGRESS OF

BURMA UNDER BRITISH RULE

IS DEDICATED

Preface

MANY books are now written about distant lands by those who have only a very slight acquaintance with them, and such usually form very pleasant reading. Burma has received a fair share of this sort of attention from casual visitors, but the present work is not one of these books written in lighter vein. It is intended to be a comprehensive treatise on one of the richest provinces of our Indian Empire, and it embodies knowledge and experience acquired there in a service extending over nearly twenty-five years.

During that time great political, commercial, and social changes have taken place throughout Burma and among the Burmese, and the main objects of this book are to describe these, and to show how they have already affected and are bound still more to affect the land and the people. It tries to describe the latter as they were, and as they now are. The historical sketch of Burma has been confined solely to what is necessary in order to understand the position of affairs at different times.

The author feels that some explanation is needed for the appearance of these volumes. The work was undertaken for the simple reason that no comprehensive book has been published about Burma since it came entirely under British rule in 1886, although the record of the material progress achieved seems well worthy of being submitted to the public in some such convenient form. Matters affecting the life and habits of the Burmese have also been treated in a way which it is hoped may be of use to those going to spend the best years of their lives in Burma, and this is the reason why so many Burmese terms have been introduced and explained. An endeavour has at the same time been made to indicate various commercial openings for investment of capital, because the development of a rich Indian province ought surely to be worthy of consideration by British capitalists.

PREFACE

The plan of the book was sketched early in 1896, and several chapters of it were then written, but press of official work prevented its completion till the leisure of furlough from 1898–1900. In the meantime the official Gazetteer of Upper Burma has been published, which also deals with many of the matters here treated of. The two works, however, cannot in any way clash. The one is an official record, the other is an independent publication meant for such of the general public as may feel an interest in Burma or in its administration by the British. If there be any similarity between portions of the two books with regard to matters specially affecting Upper Burma, this can only be due to the fact that the actual historical data have been obtained from the same sources, because neither author has yet seen the work of the other.

The scheme which has been followed was to treat each subject comprehensively in a chapter by itself. One drawback to this method is the necessity for occasional repetitions and references to previous pages, but the advantages seemed to outweigh this disadvantage.

The French position in Indo-China has of course been dealt with at considerable length. But even since the chapter dealing with "Britain and France in Further India and Western China" has been passed for press, matters affecting French railway enterprise in south-western China have again advanced. The latest account of the existing position will be found in an article on "The French Railway into Yun-nan" in the *Times* of July 22, 1901, to which the attention of those specially interested in this subject may be drawn.

A book of this description can hardly appeal to any large circle of readers, and it is not at all likely to command anything but a very limited sale. It is therefore in no small degree owing to assistance kindly guaranteed by the leading steamship companies and the merchants of Rangoon that its publication has been assured, and the author gladly takes this opportunity of thanking them for the encouragement thus given.

LONDON, *August* 15, 1901.

CONTENTS

CONTENTS

LIST OF
MAPS AND ILLUSTRATIONS

Chapter I

ESSENTIAL FACTS IN THE HISTORY OF BURMA DOWN TO THE SECOND BURMESE WAR (1852)

THE early history of Burma is wrapped in the mists of traditional legends, which afterwards became crystallised in the *Yazawin* or Royal Chronicles. Formed by the fusion and union of Mongol tribes, the Burmese probably drove the earlier settlers out of the valleys into the mountain fastnesses, where they form the wild hill-tribes of the present day.

Successive waves of immigration seem to have burst in from the north-west, due to incursions from Upper India, each fresh immigration forcing southwards towards the sea those who had established themselves in the fertile valley of the Irrawaddy river.

In course of time various independent kingdoms sprang up, ⌜so that when the truly historical epoch was reached separate nations, with dynasties of their own, held sway in different parts of the country.⌟ Thus there arose the petty kingdoms of Arakan, Pegu, and Tavoy along the coastline, of Prome and Toungoo in Central Burma, and of Burma proper in the upper portion of the Irrawaddy valley.

Internecine warfare was habitual among these various petty kingdoms, though Arakan and Tavoy, thanks to their geographical position, suffered much less on this account than the central principalities occupying different portions of the Irrawaddy valley.

Arakan formed a separate kingdom over which various dynasties are supposed to have ruled in an unbroken line of succession from 2666 B.C. down to 1784 A.D., when Thamada, who ruled at the city of Myauku (or Myohaung), was conquered and taken prisoner by Bodaw Payá, king of Ava. Tavoy, colonised from Arakan, was soon absorbed into the Peguan kingdom, though it long formed a bone of contention between the rulers of Pegu and Siam, now being held by one and again by the other. The central kingdoms of Prome and Toungoo appear to have been, respectively, merely a very early dynasty and a comparatively recent off-shoot from the kingdom of Burma, into which they were subsequently again merged. The Prome dynasty was established at Thare Kettará by Maha Thambawá, in 483 B.C., and terminated with the death of Thu Pinyá in 95 A.D., shortly after which a new dynasty was founded at Pagán, in 108 A.D., by Thamôkdarit. Later on, it assumed independence from time to time, before it was finally absorbed into the kingdom of Burma. The Toungoo off-shoot, however, played a much more important part in the general history of the country.

While Duttiya Min Kaung ruled over Burma he conferred independence on his tributary Min Kyi Nyo of Toungoo about 1480 A.D. The latter was succeeded in 1530 by his son, Min Tayá Shweti, better known as Tabin Shweti. Ten years later, by the time he was only twenty-six years of age, Tabin Shweti had made himself master of Pegu, and had been appointed king, according to the ancient ceremonies, in the capital. To celebrate this event he placed new *Ti* on the great national pagodas at Pegu and Dagôn (now Rangoon). Ousting the Shan usurpers from Ava he next had himself solemnly consecrated there, in 1544, as "king of kings" or emperor of all Burma, and he appointed tributary kings for the government of Ava, Prome, Toungoo, and Martaban. In 1546 he invaded Arakan, but was obliged to discontinue operations owing to disturbances in his eastern territories. He was now master of all Burma, except Arakan, and would probably also have conquered and added to his dominions the whole of the Shan States and Northern Siam, as happened during the second half of the sixteenth century, had he not given way to debauchery rendering him incapable of ruling. In 1550, when only thirty-six years of age, this able, but cruel and unscrupulous monarch was murdered by a scion of the late royal race of Pegu.

MYTHICAL AND LEGENDARY HISTORY

In considering the history of Burma, even broadly and briefly without going into details, the two main factors most deserving of consideration are the Burmese kingdom in the upper portion of the Irrawaddy, and the Môn kingdom occupying the lower portions of the Irrawaddy and Sittang valleys, as well as the whole of the southern sea-coast. To prevent confusion, the rulers of these kingdoms will invariably be respectively referred to throughout this chapter as the kings of Burma and of Pegu, while their subjects will be called by their correct distinctive names, Burmese and Môn.

The Burmese kingdom seems to have been originally established by a dynasty which came from India. That portion of the Royal Chronicle which may be classed as purely mythical gives a list of thirty-three kings who reigned at Tagaung (Hastinapura), and of seventeen more who had their capital at Mauroya and Tagaung. The last king, Thado Damma Raja, was dethroned at the time of an invasion from the east.

The legendary portion of the Burmese Chronicles may be regarded as commencing about 483 B.C., when Maha Thambawá established a new dynasty at Prome (Thare Kettará). Here twenty-seven kings reigned till the close of the first century A.D., when, after the death of King Thu Pinyá, his nephew, Thamôkdarit, removed the capital to Pagán. Forty kings reigned at Pagán before what may be regarded as the actually historic epoch began with the accession of King Anawratazaw to the throne, about 1010 A.D. Even this period possesses, however, so little of interest for the general reader that the course of events in Burma may be lightly skimmed, only the essential facts being noted, till the last dynasty was founded in 1755 by Alaung Payá.

The Pagán dynasty came to an end in 1279 A.D., when King Kyawswa was deposed and afterwards killed by three Shan brothers. Previous to this, there had been a Mongol invasion, caused by the Emperor of China enforcing his claim to receive tribute and homage from Burma. The army consisted more probably of Shans and Shan-Chinese than of Chinese proper; for men of Shan race had long been gradually overrunning the country and

3

acquiring positions of great influence through royal favour. This was not the first time the Shans had spread over the country. Centuries before they had swarmed into Burma, and had even pushed northwards so far as to found the Shan or Ahom kingdom of Assam.

In 1298 A.D. a Shan dynasty was founded in Burma, which reigned for about seventy years with Myinzaing, Panyá, and Sagaing as the capitals. In 1364, however, a new Burmese dynasty was founded by Thado Minbya, who dethroned the contemporaneous rulers at Panya and Sagaing, and established his capital at Ava. Said to be a descendant of the ancient kings of Tagaung, Thado Minbya was of Shan extraction on his mother's side; and all the seventeen kings of his dynasty, which held the reins of government till 1554, were mainly of Shan descent. On the last king of this line being conquered and deposed by Bayin Naung, of the Toungoo dynasty, King of Pegu, the kingdom of Burma was held as a tributary of the kingdom of Pegu.

The ancient Môn Chronicles give a list of fifty-nine kings of Pegu, who reigned at Suvarna Bhûmi or Thatôn. The first of these, Thiha Raja, came from India, and died in 543 B.C., the year in which Gaudama attained Buddhahood; and the last of the long line, Manúha, was conquered and carried off as a prisoner to Pagán by Anawratazaw, in 1057 A.D.

An off-shoot from this direct line had, however, long before this been sent to establish itself to the west of Thatôn; and this resulted in the foundation of the city of Pegu (Hanthawadi) in 573 A.D. Between then and 781 A.D. seventeen kings reigned here; but after that there is a blank of about 500 years in the Pegu chronicles, during which the names of the rulers are not given. This may perhaps in part be explained by the religious strife existing between the Brahminists and the Buddhists, which extended over about 300 years; for each monkish party would naturally tamper with the chronicles whenever they gained the ascendancy for the time being.

After the conquest of the kingdom of Pegu, including both Thatôn and Hanthawadi, Pegu became subject to

4

EXTENSION OF BURMESE EMPIRE

Burma for about 230 years, until a Shan chief called Wareyu established a dynasty in 1287 A.D., with the seat of government at Muttama (Martaban). About sixty years later, however, the capital was transferred to the ancient city of Hanthawadi, which remained the stronghold of the dynasty till Takárutbi was conquered and deposed by Tabin Shweti, King of Toungoo, in 1540 A.D.

The dynasty founded by Tabin Shweti, a king of Burmese race to whom reference has already been made, was but of short duration. It ended in 1599, when Nanda Bayin, the eldest son of Bayin Naung, was dethroned and put to death by his tributary, the King of Toungoo.

From 1599, when the Nyaung Yan Min, a younger son of Bayin Naung, ascended the throne of the "king of kings," the Toungoo dynasty reigned at Ava, and at Pegu, holding sway throughout the whole of the present province, with the exception of Arakan. This was the first time the kingdoms of Burma and Pegu had ever been united under one sovereign. At the same time, the eastern frontiers of the Burmese empire had been pushed forward so as to include large tracts in Western China, all the Shan and Siamese-Shan States, and the greater portion of Siam.

In 1740, however, the Môn, who had never relinquished their aspirations for national independence, again revolted, and elected as King of Pegu a monk of Shan origin, who took the title of Budda Ketti. Six years later he abandoned the throne in favour of another Shan, who assumed the title of Binya Dala, a name famous in Môn history. Successful in arms against the King of Burma, he conquered Ava in 1751 and burned it to the ground, taking prisoner Maha Damma Raja Dibuti, who was sent to Pegu and there executed two years later.

Binya Dala's sway over the re-united kingdoms of Pegu and Burma, this time under a ruler of Shan descent, was but of short duration. In 1757 he was conquered and taken prisoner by Alaung Payá, the founder of the last ruling dynasty in Burma, which was

5

overthrown for ever in 1885. Binya Dala ultimately met the same fate as he had meted out to Maha Damma Raja, for he was publicly executed by Sinpyuyin, son of Alaung Payá, in 1775, when the Burmese king held great religious festival at the Shwe Dagôn pagoda in Rangoon.

Alaung Payá, or Alompra as he was called by the English, was perhaps the greatest of all the rulers of Ava. Born in 1714 at Môksóbo, "the hunter's cooking place," he was first of all the subordinate of a village headman and then became headman of the town. Through his craft and his personal influence, aided no doubt among so superstitious a people by his auspicious name, Maung Aung Zeya, or "conquering victory," he raised a petty local revolt against the Môn power, then paramount in Burma. This proving successful, large numbers flocked to his rebel band, and he was at last able to score important victories against the forces of the King of Pegu.

In 1754 Ava fell before him, and he carried the war southwards to the delta, occupying Bassein, at that time the chief seaport of the country. It was then, in 1755, that he proclaimed himself King of Burma and Pegu, assuming the pretentious title of Alaung Payá, "the incarnation of a Buddha," and conferring royal titles upon his two eldest sons. He established his capital at Môksóbo, now called Shwebo.

He died in 1760, at the early age of forty-six years. During the short space of seven years he not only freed his country from the yoke of the Môn, whom he degraded to be the *Talaing* or "down-trodden" race, and raised himself to the throne, but he also extended the boundaries of his kingdom from Manipur in the north-west to Siam in the south and east. And while thus engaged in successful warlike operations, he likewise did much for the improvement of internal administration throughout his dominions. He prohibited gambling and the sale of intoxicating drink, and he purified the judicial system by enforcing the trial of cases in public and the registration of every judicial order that was passed. It was a misfortune for Burma that

ALAUNG PAYÁ'S DYNASTY, 1755–1885

the sway of so competent a ruler only lasted between five and six years,—for he died in 1760, while laying siege to Ayódyá, then the capital of Siam.

In the following genealogical tree of this dynasty it will be seen how the succession varied by the national custom of nominating the heir-apparent and successor, in place of following any distinct rule like that of primogeniture :—

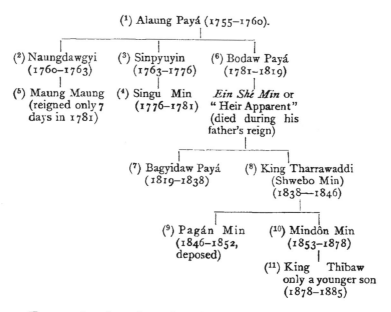

From shortly after the date of the foundation of Alaung Payá's dynasty the history of Burma becomes gradually more closely interwoven than was previously the case with that of British India until, after partial dismemberments in 1826 and 1852, the kingdom of Ava was finally and completely absorbed into the British Indian Empire on 1st January, 1886.

Down to the close of Alaung Payá's reign the influences of foreign countries on Burma, so far as territorial possessions were concerned, were confined to those emanating from the other Mongol kingdoms, China and Siam, lying further to the east, and nothing had yet been felt of the irresistible pressure which was finally to be exerted from the west. A Chinese or Shan-Chinese invasion from Yunnan had taken place in 1659, but the invaders were repulsed in their attack on Ava, the capital. Siam (Ayódyá) had been conquered and made a tributary province of Bayin Naung in 1564, and Zimmè was dealt with in the same manner in 1578, while the northern Shan States were also brought to the condition of subordinate tributaries. Siam soon after freed itself from the Burmese yoke, and even invaded Pegu. Alaung Payá's war of 1759 against Siam was caused by offended vanity, the King of Siam having refused to give him one of his daughters in marriage as a minor queen.

Alaung Payá had six sons by his chief wife, and he expressed the wish that the succession to the throne should devolve upon each of these in turn. Looked upon as a sort of dynastic order, this unfortunate and rather unreasonable wish later on proved the cause of much bloodshed.

The first king to succeed Alaung Payá was his eldest son, who took the title of Naungdawgyi. Transferring his capital to Sagaing, then the chief town in his dominions, his short reign of only three years was chiefly occupied in putting down an insurrection in Ava, and quelling minor disturbances in various parts of the large empire to which he had fallen heir.

On being succeeded in 1763 by his brother, who assumed the grandiloquent regal name of Sinpyuyin or "Lord of the White Elephant," the capital was immediately removed from Sagaing to Môksóbo. Dissatisfied with this change as soon as it had been effected, the King consulted his astrologers, who advised him to select Ava once more as the capital. Accordingly he re-transferred the seat of government to Ava.

Naturally ambitious, Sinpyuyin invaded and annexed Manipur in 1764, reduced Zimmè and the Shan States to obedience, and subsequently invaded Siam in 1765. Ayódyá, the capital, was taken, and was destroyed by fire early in 1767, when the victorious king found himself compelled to return to Ava to defend his own

BURMESE WARS WITH CHINA

proper dominions against a threatened Chinese invasion. This incursion arose out of purely commercial causes.

In the spring of 1765 a Chinese trader had been interfered with when approaching Bhamo, and was taken into custody and sent to Ava. Being there released, he found some of his goods were missing when he got to Bhamo. Similar friction having frequently been caused by misconduct of Burmese officials at various points along the eastern frontier, a Shan-Chinese incursion was made into the southern Shan States.

This was soon easily quelled, but Sinpyuyin became uneasy about his relations with China when he heard, early in the following year, that a large army was being massed on the frontier near Momein. In 1767 the Chinese troops invaded Burma and occupied Bhamo, while a southern column marched by the trade route through the northern Shan State of Theinni to threaten the capital. The Burmese, however, succeeded in routing and driving back again the northern column, and in forcing the southern also to retreat. The net result of the contest proved advantageous for Burma, as it definitely gained certain Shan States in the extreme north which really belonged to China, though they had from time to time been under Burmese suzerainty.

Furious at one he considered an upstart and a petty barbarian daring to resist an army of the son of heaven, the Emperor of China again sent troops across the Shan hills towards the close of 1767. Defeating one of the Burmese columns in the Thibaw State, it pushed on towards the edge of the plateau overlooking the valley of the Irrawaddy, but was then defeated and forced to retreat from Burmese territory. The Chinese entrenchments or camping grounds (*Tarôk Sakán*) then formed are still to be found dotted all along the line of march from Maymyo, through Thibaw and Lashio, eastwards. But from the size of even the largest of these entrenchments, it seems evident that only small bodies of troops could have been employed, and not the large army of 50,000 men whose inglorious defeat the Burmese Chronicle boastfully narrates.

Rumours of troops being massed in still larger numbers

9

beyond the frontiers soon again troubled the King, and the earthquakes of 1769, which rent asunder pagodas and threw down the golden *Ti*, or "umbrella" pinnacle of the great Shwe Dagôn pagoda in Rangoon, were viewed as omens of direst import, presaging national disaster. Religious frenzy seized hold of the people and of their King. Vast treasures were lavished in repairing and beautifying the great pagodas throughout the land, and thousands of gold and silver images were enshrined in order to gain sufficient *Kútho*, or "religious merit," to avert disaster.

Hardly had these great works of religious merit been accomplished before the storm broke from the north-east, in the early part of the autumn of 1769. Decimated by malarious fever, the Chinese were easily overpowered by the Burmese ; and before the close of the year peace was established by a convention signed at Bhamo. This was the last time war actually occurred between Burma and China. Shortly after this the Siamese revolted, and in 1771 a Burmese force was sent against them. It consisted mainly of Talaings, who mutinied, massacred their Burmese fellow-soldiers, and, retracing their steps, invested Rangoon, the new metropolis of the sea-board. This uprising was soon suppressed locally, but it was not till the beginning of 1774 that the Burmese authority was completely re-established throughout Pegu. To celebrate this happy issue and the victories of Burmese arms in Manipur and Kachar, as well as to consolidate his power in Pegu, Sinpyuyin placed a new golden *Ti* on the summit of the Shwe Dagôn pagoda in 1774 ; and then, full of what he probably considered good deeds, he passed away in 1776, being succeeded by his son, the Singu Min.

When Singu Min ascended the throne, Burma was again embroiled in a Siamese war. After the complete destruction of Ayódyá by fire, and the carrying off of the Siamese royal family as prisoners by Sinpyuyin's army in 1767, a man named Payá Tak, of Chinese descent, obtained a following, and inflicted heavy losses on the retreating Burmese. Assuming the title of king, he founded a new capital at Bangkôk. It was not till 1774

that Sinpyuyin found himself in a position to conduct
fresh operations against Siam, and these had not been
concluded when he died. Meanwhile, it was not going
well in Siam with the Burmese arms. So the new king
determined to put an end to the conflict, and ordered the
withdrawal of his troops, both from Ayódyá and from
the Zimmè and Upper Menam territories, where they
could no longer stay with safety.

Internal disturbances connected with the succession now
began as a direct consequence of Alaung Payá's desire
that each of the six sons of his chief queen should in
their turn succeed to the throne, as it became vacant.
The Singu Min was the son of Sinpyuyin. If Alaung
Payá's death-bed wish were to be regarded as the law of
succession, then the eldest surviving son was the rightful
heir to the throne ; while, if otherwise, then a prince
named Maung Maung, son of King Naungdawgyi, was
by some held to have stronger claims to the throne than
the Singu Min. These ideas were probably only formu-
lated about a couple of years after the latter had obtained
regal power, and even then only because he turned out
a cruel, dissolute, and brutal monster.

Suspicious of plots that began to be whispered in 1779,
he had his two most favoured rivals killed. These were
a younger brother of his own and his uncle, the fourth
son of Alaung Payá ; and a short time after that, in a fit
of jealousy, he drowned his favourite queen. Another
uncle, Badún Min, the fifth son of Alaung Payá, an astute
prince, who had so conducted himself as to be considered
almost outside the pale of rivalry for the throne, escaped
death, but was sent to Sagaing, and there kept under
close supervision.

In 1781, however, a band of conspirators seized the
palace while the King was absent from Ava on a royal
progress, and proclaimed as king Maung Maung, who
was then a lad of eighteen. Returning to the palace, the
Singu Min was allowed to enter the inner precincts, where
he was slain by the father of his murdered queen. At
once seizing the opportunity, the Badún Min cited Alaung
Payá's dying wish, that his sons should succeed him according to their seniority, as the dynastic law of succes-

sion, and Maung Maung, who only reigned a week, was at once put to death, the Badún Min being now proclaimed the rightful king.

The new king from time to time adopted various titles, one of them being "lord of many white elephants," but he is best known to the English by the name of Bodaw Payá, although the Burmese themselves usually refer to him as Min Tayágyi, "the great lawgiver."

To seat himself more securely on the throne, he put to death many of those who had secured the power for Maung Maung. About a year later an attempt was made to seize the palace for a scion of the old Burmese royal family ; but, this proving unsuccessful, the assailants were put to death. And to prevent conspiracies in future, a holocaust was made of all the inhabitants of the village of Paungha, where the plot was hatched. Men, even including monks, and women to the number of over a hundred are said to have been burned alive on huge piles of wood, while their houses were razed to the ground, their fruit trees cut down, and their fields allowed to revert to jungle. A revolt about the same time occurred among the Talaing near Rangoon, which was also crushed with characteristic cruelty, more than 500 of the malcontents being put to the sword.

Having thus crushed organised opposition to his kingship, Bodaw Payá at once proceeded to wash away the blood-stains with which his life-account had become blotted and beflecked. He built a vast pagoda near Sagaing, and, following the advice of his astrologers, founded a new capital at Amárapura, about six miles to the north-east of Ava, which was occupied in 1783. That same year he caused a sort of Domesday Book to be compiled, giving the financial resources of each district throughout his kingdom, but the first use he made of this was to demand an extraordinary contribution from each town and village for the repairing and restoration of pagodas, and for other royal works of religious merit.

On the foundation of the new capital, Bodaw Payá at the same time determined the succession to the throne in favour of his eldest son, whom he appointed *Ein Shé Min*, or "heir apparent." On Pandali Thakin, the sixth son of Alaung Payá, quoting the dynastic wish which the King had enforced in dethroning Maung Maung, Bodaw Payá now pooh-poohed that as a silly idea. The younger brother then becoming troublesome, he was disposed of in what was considered the really orthodox and proper way of doing a royal prince to death : he was tied in a red velvet sack and thrown into the Irrawaddy river.

Impelled partly by lust of territory, and partly by religious desire to possess the great sacred image of Arakan, Bodaw Payá waged war against that kingdom in 1783, and annexed it in 1784. Elated with his easy success in this enterprise, he conceived the ambitious design of conquering the whole of Further India.

In pursuit of this object, Bodaw Payá began by invading Siam in 1785. Placing himself at the head of an army, he demanded tribute asserted to be due, and intimated his intention to avenge the defeats inflicted by Payá Tak on the Burmese arms. Junk Ceylon was taken, but was soon after regained by the Siamese ; and Bodaw Payá precipitately retreated to Rangoon.

In the following year a fresh invasion of Siam was embarked on, but the Burmese troops were cut to pieces near the frontiers of Tavoy and Mergui. Bodaw Payá fled back to Martaban, and thence proceeded to his own capital, there to engage his attention with further works of religious merit, so that future undertakings might be more auspicious.

During 1791 the Siamese established themselves at Tavoy, but the town was in 1792 regained by the Burmese, and peace between the two countries was declared in 1793. But many of the Shan chiefs had meanwhile been incited to throw off their allegiance to Burma, and to become tributaries of Siam ; and these tributaries were retained by the Siamese.

Foiled in his aspirations as to the conquest of Siam, Bodaw Payá resigned all thoughts of invading and over-running China. But he still devoted attention to the extension of his frontiers towards the north and west. Dissensions, intrigues, and difficulties about the succession gave him the opportunities he desired both in Manipur and in Assam. After the death of Alaung Payá, Manipur, with British assistance from Bengal, had been enabled to free itself again from the Burmese yoke, but in 1813 Bodaw Payá was appealed to for the purpose of settling a disputed succession. Citing the occupant of the throne before him, in order to settle the dispute, the Raja refused to appear ; so Burmese troops overran Manipur in 1813, the prince who had sought the intervention of Bodaw Payá was placed on the throne, and the Kubo valley was annexed to Burma.

Similarly, in Assam, a dispute about the succession to the throne led to one candidate beseeching the intervention of the King of Burma, and troops were sent there in 1816. But before anything definite had resulted from this ready interference in the internal affairs of Assam, Bodaw Payá died in 1819. Cruel and ferocious, he drew fearful bills of mortality on the Burmese nation. Though he was almost constantly engaged in warfare, yet the tale of men killed in cold blood by his inhuman orders was even greater than the total of those that fell in the field. Conscious of his blood-guiltiness, he tried to wipe out the debit balance standing to his life-account, and to earn a surplus of religious merit by lavish expenditure of money, labour, and life—all wrung from his people without consideration, payment, or return of any sort—on pagodas, irrigation tanks, and sacred shrines. Bodaw Payá's impulse towards creating works of religious merit gradually became a passion, and finally developed into a mania. As such, it was probably a premonitory symptom of the more pronounced insanity with which his grandsons, who succeeded him on the throne, were subsequently afflicted. But the crowning glory of his reign was, in his own estimation, the possession of a perfect white male elephant, caught in the Pegu forests, which was received at Court with more than regal honours, and which was greatly venerated during the fifty years it lived at the capital.

Bodaw Payá was succeeded by his grandson, Sagaing Min, who had been appointed heir-apparent on his father's death in 1809, and who now took the title of Bagyidaw.

Although his accession to the throne was unopposed,

he soon made himself a terror by executing two of his uncles, the Princes of Prome and Toungoo, together with a large number of public officers whom he suspected of conspiring against him. Early in Bagyidaw's reign an evil omen made itself seen, for a vulture one day alighted on the spire of the palace. Soon after this, too, the spire itself, along with other portions of the palace buildings, the court of justice, and a large part of the city were destroyed by fire. So it was resolved to re-establish Ava as the capital. Preparations were at once begun, though it was not till 1823 that the move was ultimately made.

In matters of foreign policy, Bagyidaw followed in the footsteps of his predecessor. Marjit, Raja of Manipur, who had been placed on the throne by Bodaw Payá in 1813, was summoned to do homage to his new suzerain along with the other tributary princes in 1819, but merely made excuses in place of putting in his appearance. This, coupled with offences against the Burmese sumptuary laws as to the number of roofs on the spire above his palace,[1] and the amount of gilding in it, was made an excuse for despatching troops against him. These occupied the capital, and the Burmese garrison was retained at Manipur during 1820.

In Assam, too, Chandra Kanta, who was seated on the throne by the troops sent by Bodaw Payá, soon showed a desire to be free from Burmese control and interference. Additional troops were therefore sent under a commander named Maung Yit, who, through his successes in Manipur and Assam, gained the title of "Maha Bandúla," after a mighty warrior who did great deeds according to the Burmese legends. This general afterwards commanded the troops fighting against the British. The result of this Burmese invasion was that Chandra Kanta was defeated and fled into British territory, and Assam was declared a Burmese province in 1821.

The extension of the frontiers to the north and west,

[1] The roofs of the spire above the king's chief throne, and of those above the four main gates of the royal capital, were nine in number; and monasteries may also have the same number. But even the most powerful tributary princes were only allowed seven roofs on the palace spire surmounting their throne.

beyond the mountain ranges forming the western watershed of the Irrawaddy valley, proved a source of friction with British India. The situations which in this manner arose from time to time were the preponderating causes of both the first and the second Burmese wars. And, as neither of these very severe lessons could teach the Burmese Court that the British Empire in India was of a more solid and resisting nature than any of the countries mentioned in the Royal Chronicles, similar causes in course of time led directly to the total extinction of the Burmese monarchy and of national independence.

The earliest contact of Burma with western nations was extremely limited, and was purely of a commercial character. Brief reference to the details of this is therefore more appropriately made in the beginning of the chapter on " Trade and Commerce " (chap. XIV.).

The annexation of Arakan by Bodaw Payá in 1784 had already brought Burma into collision with the British in Chittagong. The British territory was utilised as a sanctuary by some thousands of Arakanese refugees, who made raids from time to time and harassed the Burmese garrison. In place of representing that, as would only have been just, the British authorities should take measures to put a stop to these incursions, the Burmese demanded that the raiders should be given up to them. This being refused, they followed the outlaws into British territory. The friction thus caused led to an Envoy, Captain Symes, of H.M. 76th Regiment, being sent to Rangoon in 1795. He was treated with great indignity, but received what seemed to be a treaty. In accordance with this, Captain Hiram Cox was sent in the following year as Resident at Amárapura. Received only once in audience by the King, he was afterwards treated with great insult, and finally withdrew during 1798. Difficulties soon again arose on the Arakan frontier, and the Envoy of 1795, now Lieut.-Col. Symes, was once more sent to negotiate a treaty. This time he was treated even more insultingly than before, being made to halt and reside for forty days on an "accursed" island where criminals were executed, and cremations and burials were carried out. After waiting for nearly eighteen months, he returned to India, without having attained the desired objects of his mission. Another mission, sent in 1809, under Captain Canning, also returned in 1810 without having effected its object.

Troubles again occurring on the Chittagong frontier, Captain Canning was once more sent on a mission to Rangoon in 1811, but had to return in 1812 with as unsatisfactory a result as before. In 1813 a Burmese Envoy was sent to Calcutta to demand the extradition of the Arakanese fugitives in Chittagong, which was refused.

During the next few years matters gradually drifted from bad to worse, and the Burmese began to intrigue with the Mahrattas and the Court of Lahore, intending to enter the confederacy against the British then being arranged by the Peishwa—a plan which was frustrated by the victory at Kirki and the routing of the Pindari hordes.

On the death of Bodaw Payá, in 1819, affairs had fallen into a chronic state of trouble all along the frontiers of Arakan, Manipur, and Assam; and they were soon forced by the Burmese into a more acute stage. On the borders of Chittagong aggressions were almost uninterrupted. From Manipur and from Assam a Burmese force marched in two columns into Kachar, which had been taken under British protection to check any advance of the Burmese towards Sylhet. The column from Assam was driven back from the Surma river; while that from Manipur also retired, but not until after it had stubbornly and successfully beaten off a British attack on a strong stockade on the bank of the Barák river.

While these skirmishes were going on further north, a *casus belli* had evolved itself on the Náf river, the boundary between Arakan and Chittagong. On 23rd September, 1823, an armed party of Burmese attacked a British guard on Shapuri, an island close to the Chittagong side, killing and wounding six of the guard. During November the island was re-occupied by a detachment of British sepoys; but Bagyidaw was bent on war. Confident of victory, he sent Maha Bandúla, in January, 1824, with 6,000 men, to assume command of the troops in Arakan, and to march on Chittagong.

BURMA UNDER BRITISH RULE

On 5th March, 1824, war was formally declared by the British against Burma. Recognising that any attempt to reach the Burmese capital through one or other of the frontier districts would be attended with enormous difficulties, the plan of attack on Ava was made by sea and up the Irrawaddy river. Troops were massed at Calcutta and Madras to the number of about 11,500 men, and the chief command was entrusted to General Sir Archibald Campbell, K.C.B. But other troops operated also in Assam under Brigadier-General McMorine, and in Kachar under Brigadier-General Shuldham.

On 11th May Rangoon was occupied without opposition, and shortly after that two strong stockades, thrown up at Kemmendine, now a north-western suburb, were captured. Some petty successes had been gained by the Burmese at the Náf, but these could not be followed up, while the Burmese troops were also withdrawn from Assam and Kachar.

The advance up the Irrawaddy was delayed through want of adequate transport, and as the rainy season set in the British troops suffered severely from sickness. Later on, finding it still impossible to operate in the Irrawaddy valley, expeditions were sent to Tavoy, Mergui, Martaban, and Pegu, all of which places were occupied by November.

Maha Bandúla had meanwhile been recalled from Arakan, and placed in chief command of the troops, said to number 60,000, opposing the advance of the British on the capital. Occupying as his base Danúbyu a town on the right bank of the Irrawaddy, about sixty miles north-west of Rangoon, he crossed the river and marched on Rangoon. But, before the close of the year, the attacks of the Burmese had been repulsed with so much slaughter that they found themselves forced to retreat, the greater part of the force breaking up and dispersing itself.

Owing to the unforeseen difficulties about transport in the Irrawaddy valley, another British army, of about 11,000 men, was assembled at Chittagong under General Morrison, and sent, partly by sea and partly by land, into Arakan. Little opposition was encountered in occupying the districts, but the climate proved deadly during the rains. As the Arakan Yoma, forming the western watershed of the Irrawaddy, proved impracticable for the transport of heavy guns, the idea of attacking Ava from Arakan had to be abandoned. By the end of the dry season, in the spring of 1825, the Burmese had been driven from all the places they had previously occupied in Assam, Kachar, Manipur, and Arakan, while the British held the chief towns along the sea-coast, and were preparing to advance in strength up the Irrawaddy to Ava. Sickness had, however, sapped the strength of the troops to such an extent that only 1,300 Europeans and 2,500 native soldiers were fit for duty at the time of Bandúla laying siege to Rangoon in December.

Reinforcements having been received, Sir Archibald Campbell marched north. His force was divided into two columns, one of which proceeded by land and the other by the river. The Burmese were found occupying a strongly fortified position at Danúbyu. Siege being laid, an assault was fixed for 2nd April, when it was found that the fort had been evacuated during the previous night. Maha Bandúla had been killed on 1st April by a portion of a shell, and with his death all resistance collapsed. Resuming the onward march, the British occupied Prome without opposition, and went into cantonment there for the rainy season.

When news of Bandúla's death and the advance on Prome reached Ava, the King and his courtiers were filled with dismay; yet the astrologers continued to predict success. During the latter part of the rains, the Burmese proposed and obtained an armistice, but the terms of peace offered were not accepted. As soon as the rains came to an end the advance on Ava was resumed. Some opposition was encountered about ten miles to the north of Prome, and again at Malún, about fifty miles further north, which was taken after renewed negotiations for the conclusion of hostilities had been again futile.

On 3rd January, 1826, the terms of a treaty for peace being signed, fifteen days were allowed for its ratification; but, as this did not arrive, the advance was continued. Pagán was taken on 8th February after some little fighting, and on the 16th the British encamped at Yandabú, only four marches from Ava. Intimation was then forthcoming that the treaty would be duly ratified, and it was signed without further discussion on the 24th. Under its provisions Assam, Arakan, and all Tenasserim lying east of the Salween river were ceded to the British, while the Burmese agreed to abstain from interference of any sort in Manipur, Kachar and Jyntia. An indemnity of a crore of rupees, or about £1,000,000, was paid towards the British military expenditure, which had exceeded five times that amount. Provision was also made for the arrangement of a commercial treaty, which was subsequently concluded in November, 1826, though no British Resident went to Ava till 1830, when Major Burney was sent there. Thus their first war with the British ended with a vast loss of territory and such a crushing blow to their national pride and prestige as the Burmese had never before received.

Ba-gyi-daw soon grew subject to melancholy fits, which finally led to insanity. The palace then became the scene of continual intrigues, until at last, in February, 1837, the Prince of Tharrawaddi, who presided over the State Council, somewhat in the manner of a Regent, deposed his brother and seized the throne for himself, assuming the name of King Tharrawaddi. The dethroned monarch was not made away with, but lived under restraint till 1845.

Meanwhile the British Resident to the Burmese Court had to put up with many indignities. Finding that he was thwarted in every way, and could do no good by remaining, Major Burney withdrew in 1837, for King Tharrawaddi simply refused to receive him or to consider himself bound by the treaty made by his brother, the late king. But the Governor-General, Lord Auckland, disapproved of this step, and in 1838 sent Colonel Benson to Amárapura as Resident. Him, too, the King declined to receive; and after enduring many indignities Colonel Benson also withdrew in 1839, leaving his subordinate, Captain Macleod, in charge of affairs. Early in 1840 Macleod was ordered to return, as the Government of India had now at length become convinced that diplomatic relations could only be opened and maintained by armed force.

Removing his capital to Amárapura, King Tharrawaddi reigned for nine years. But, shortly after his usurpation of the throne, he also exhibited symptoms of insanity. Gradually becoming worse, he finally became subject to fits of ungovernable fury, during which he committed acts of inhuman cruelty. One of his amusements at such times was to order any courtier near by to kneel down while he scored a chessboard on the poor fellow's back with a sword. More than once he was put under restraint by his sons, and he died in confinement in 1846, being most probably done to death secretly.

On Tharrawaddi's demise the throne was occupied by his eldest son, the Pagán Min, who had already assumed charge of the government when it became necessary to place his father under restraint. The new king followed his father's example in ignoring the provisions of the treaty of 1826; and, feeling sure of not being interfered with from Amárapura, the Governors of Pegu recommenced the course of exactions from British traders which had so often called for the remonstrance of the Resident. After the withdrawal of the Governor-General's Agent in 1840, things of course gradually went from bad to worse, until at last in 1851 matters came to a head through two more than usually outrageous cases of extortion.

King Pagán was cursed with the heritage of his father's vicious and cruel disposition, but was not endowed with any of his better or redeeming qualities. Avaricious to a degree, the King contrived to enrich himself by the deaths of well-to-do subjects, of whom he massacred about two thousand within a couple of years, some being secretly murdered, and others even executed in public.

Now Maung Ôk, who was appointed Governor of Pegu in 1846, followed his royal master's example— "like master, like man"—as closely as he dared in Rangoon. But at last he went too far. In July, 1851, he caused the master of a British barque, the *Monarch*, to be arrested on a false charge of murdering his pilot. Liberated on security, fined, re-arrested, and again fined, his crew arrested, ill-used, and fined, and not allowed to clear the port till payment of other money had been extorted, the master, Mr. Sheppard, reported the matter to the British Commissioner in Tenasserim, and made a claim of ten thousand rupees (£1,000) against the Burmese Government. A month later Mr. Lewis, master of the barque *Champion*, was treated in a very similar manner. Proceeding to Calcutta, he laid his complaint before Government and made a claim of nine thousand two hundred rupees (£920) against the Burmese authorities.

The amounts claimed by Messrs. Sheppard and Lewis being reduced to what were considered reasonable limits, Lord Dalhousie, the Governor-General, on 17th November, 1851, sent a letter to the King of Burma by H.M.S. *Fox* (Commodore Lambert), accompanied by three other ships, bringing to his notice the many complaints received concerning Maung Ôk's conduct, desiring that compensation should be given in these two particular cases, and also that Maung Ôk should be removed from the Governorship of Pegu, where he was causing friction and breaking the provisions of the commercial treaty of 1826.

Maung Ôk was superseded, but the new Governor sent to Rangoon was accompanied by a large army, while very large bodies of troops were also moved down to Bassein, the western seaport, and to Martaban on the east, almost opposite Moulmein. The new Governor at once proved himself just the same sort of man as his predecessor in his attitude towards the British subjects, who were permanently or temporarily resident in Rangoon.

In January, 1852, Commander Fishbourne was sent ashore by the Commodore with a letter to the Governor requesting that honourable reception might be accorded to him as British Agent along with a guard of fifty men, as provided for under Article VII. of the Treaty of Yandabú. But he was grossly insulted, and not even allowed to present the letter he had brought.

SECOND BURMESE WAR, 1852

A blockade of the port was therefore declared, and some fighting took place : then Commodore Lambert returned to Calcutta in order to confer with Government as to the further course to be pursued.

Measures were at once taken to pour reinforcements into Arakan and Tenasserim. Before proceeding to extremities, however, Lord Dalhousie, in February, gave the Burmese Court another chance of settling matters without recourse to arms, but in vain. The tone of the letter was certainly most peremptory, yet King Pagán never for a moment believed that the British would really follow up even a letter like this with immediate declaration of war. Consequently no special preparations were made for defence. The ultimatum was received at Amárapura on 15th March, and hostile operations were to be commenced if full compliance with all demands were not agreed to by the 1st April. Meanwhile a force consisting of 8,100 troops had been despatched to Rangoon under the command of General Godwin, C.B., while Commodore Lambert commanded the naval contingent.

No reply being vouchsafed to this letter, the first blow of the second Burmese war was struck by the British on 5th April, 1852, when Martaban was taken. Rangoon town was occupied on the 12th, and the Shwe Dagôn pagoda on the 16th, after heavy fighting, when the Burmese army retired northwards. Bassein was seized on the 17th May, and Pegu was taken on 3rd June after some sharp fighting around the Shwe-maw-daw pagoda.

During the rainy season the approval of the Court of Directors and of the British Government was obtained to the annexation of the lower portion of the Irrawaddy valley as the only feasible measure of adequate redress and of security against recurrence of past friction, and it was further approved that the line of annexation should be drawn so as to include the town of Prome within the new British territory. Lord Dalhousie visited Rangoon in July and August, and discussed the whole situation with the civil, military, and naval authorities. The result of this visit was that, in September, General Godwin advanced on Prome, which he occupied after but slight resistance on 9th October, while the Shwesandaw pagoda and stockades were captured during the course of the following week.

Thinking that the time had now come for terminating the war, Lord Dalhousie early in December appointed Captain (afterwards Sir Arthur) Phayre to the Commissionership of Pegu, and forwarded a letter to the King of Burma informing him that after what had occurred the province of Pegu should henceforth be a portion of the British territories in India. It also added that any Burmese troops still in Pegu or Martaban would be expelled, and warned the King that if he attempted to interfere with the British possessions in Pegu hostilities would be continued and His Majesty's kingdom inevitably and utterly extinguished. On 20th December, 1852, this proclamation was issued, the frontier from Arakan to the Salween being drawn along the parallel of $19\frac{1}{2}°$ north latitude. And thus the second Burmese war was brought to a close without any treaty being made.

The pacification of Pegu and its reduction to order occupied about ten years of constant work. But the second half of this period included the years of the Indian Mutiny, when all available troops were required to quell that uprising and to re-establish order throughout Upper India.

Even before this humiliating termination of the war was known at Amárapura, a rebellion had broken out there. King Pagán, conscious of being not only disreputable but also very unpopular, had of late been regarding two half-brothers of his own with marked jealousy. One of these, who found himself the special object of suspicion, the Mindôn Prince, at last felt his life to be unsafe; so on 17th December he fled, accompanied by his brother, the Mindat Prince, to Môksóbo, the dynastic stronghold. This, on the part of any prince of the house of Alaung Payá, was ever a sign of revolt and of aspiration to the throne.

Within a few days the princes had a sufficient number of adherents to march on the capital. This was done, although the Mindôn Prince remained behind in Môksóbo,

24

the very plausible reason given being that he, a most pious Buddhist, was averse to the shedding of blood. Even though there was but little real fighting, yet a considerable quantity of blood was spilled before the Pagán Min was dethroned on 18th February, 1853, when one of his half-brothers ascended the throne as the Mindôn Min. With remarkable humanity in a Burmese king, Mindôn permitted the dethroned monarch to reside in honourable confinement. There he held a small court of his own, while in other matters he was treated with much respect, until he at length died a natural death after outliving his successor on the throne.

Chapter II

AMONG other terms ratified in the Yandabú treaty
of 1826, with which the first Burmese war was concluded, a stipulation was made that at the Court of each
Government an accredited Minister should be placed by
the other State and requisite facility given for providing
him with a suitable guard and residence. Subsidiary to
this treaty a commercial agreement was also made in the
same year; but it soon became apparent that the Burmese Government had no real intention of carrying out
such conventions in the spirit of civilised nations. After
repeated failures the Government of India at last, in
1840, abandoned the attempt to maintain any representative at Amárapura. After the second Burmese war of
1852, when the kingdom of Ava was shorn of all its
coast-line and cut off from the sea so as to become a
purely inland territory, a special mission was sent to
Amárapura, where it was suitably received. But anything like regular diplomatic representation of the
Government of India, which had been suspended in
1840, was not resumed till many years afterwards.

In 1862 Sir Arthur Phayre, the first Chief Commissioner of British Burma, negotiated a new commercial
treaty with King Mindôn at Mandalay, and left an Agent
there to see that due observance was paid to the clauses
relating to free navigation of the Irrawaddy and to customs dues. Under this convention traders from British
territory were to be allowed, without let or hindrance
from the Burmese authorities, to travel in such manner
as they pleased throughout the whole extent of the Irra-

waddy river and to purchase whatever they required, while similar advantages were secured to Burmese traders along the lower portion of the Irrawaddy in British Burma. To promote trade the British abolished certain customs duties levied on the southern side of the frontier, but the Burmese indefinitely delayed performance of their part of the agreement. Royal monopolies acted very prejudicially for the development of trade, and altogether the working of the treaty was not successful, although considerable sacrifices had been made by the Government of India to foster trade and to ensure freedom from arbitrary interference. At the time of their abolition, in 1863, the British frontier duties yielded over £60,000 a year, while foreign goods imported through Rangoon for consumption in Upper Burma were chargeable with a nominal duty of only one per cent., although upon such goods imported for use in British Burma a duty of five per cent. was levied (except as regarded spirits, upon which the duty amounted to about 100 per cent.). This concession alone amounted to about another £30,000 annually. But a further privilege existed as regards rice, of which Upper Burma required large supplies. Its export up the Irrawaddy was allowed free of charge, whereas all exports by sea were chargeable with a duty of about five rupees a ton (or about ten shillings at that time).

Matters had again become so unsatisfactory by 1867 that the Government of India intimated to the Court of Ava their intention to restore the frontier duties unless negotiations were entered into for a new and more satisfactory treaty. A new commercial treaty was accordingly concluded by Colonel Fytche in 1867. Notwithstanding certain defects, this new convention, while confirming the agreement of 1862, pledged the Government of Ava to several valuable commercial arrangements, one of which was the restriction of the trade monopolies retained in the hands of the king. It likewise conferred upon the British Resident recognised powers to watch over British interests, by securing for him certain civil jurisdiction over cases concerning British subjects in Avan territory; and it provided for a political agent, subordinate to the Resident at Mandalay, being stationed at Bhamo, the town in the north through which the bulk of the trade with Yunnan was carried on.

From 1867 to 1879 the Government of India were continuously represented by a Resident at Mandalay, and the political and commercial arrangements between the two countries were placed upon a basis of reciprocity which was accepted in theory, though evaded in practice, by the Court of Ava. But questions of various sorts arose from time to time, some of which were settled temporarily and provisionally, while others were allowed to drag on without any attempt at a settlement being made by the Upper Burmese authorities. To neglect obligations whenever possible, and to temporise merely when brought to book, were of course the only tactics that could be expected of such a nation. Apart from the facts that the principal concessions secured by treaty for British traders were only temporary, for a period of ten years, and had never been carried out, while guarantees for their proper observance were altogether inadequate, the other three main causes of friction referred, firstly, to "the Shoe Question," or the want of a proper system of diplomatic intercourse ; secondly, to the proper treatment of British subjects in Upper Burmese territory ; and, thirdly, to certain territorial discussions. These four questions of importance varied in urgency, but, towards the close of King Mindôn's reign, they had all assumed the status of pending cases which it was necessary to bring to some practical issue. The hope of solving them by means of friendly negotiation was futile. The attitude of the Government of India, reluctant to proceed to force, merely encouraged the Court of Ava to assume and maintain an attitude of indifference with regard to proposals and remonstrances made in a spirit of forbearance, and repeatedly renewed.

As the commercial treaties of 1862 and 1867 were found to require revision, overtures were made with this view in 1877, and repeated in the following year : but they proved unsuccessful. King Mindôn was then approaching his end, and the Government of India hoped that his successor might feel inclined to inaugurate his reign by adopting a new and more conciliatory policy. For about five years previous to Mindôn's death, in 1878, all overtures and remonstrances on the part of the Government of India were ignored and disregarded by the Court of Ava; and it became perfectly clear that, unless they were urged in peremptory terms, and enforced by other pressure if necessary, the mere arrangement of a new commercial agreement would of itself not improve the state of affairs then existing.

The way in which King Mindôn managed to evade the spirit of the treaties was ingenious, though unscrupulous. Previous to the treaty of 1867, the Burmese Government would, from time to time, arbitrarily proscribe particular articles of commerce, and notify the trade in them throughout Upper Burma to be a royal monopoly. The effect of this was to debar private traders from purchasing any of these proscribed articles direct from the producer. The producer had to sell these classes of goods at fixed rates to the king's agents, who vended them at high profits to other traders. The treaty of 1867 stipulated for the royal monopolies being confined to teak-timber, earth-oil, and precious stones, while all other goods and merchandise were, throughout a period of ten years, to be subject to a duty of five per cent. *ad valorem*, leviable at the Burmese custom-houses. The object of this was to confine the old system of monopolies to the three products specifically named, and it was expected that the large and steadily increasing general commerce between Lower and Upper Burma would only be interfered with by the Burmese Government in so far as was necessary for the levy of the stipulated customs duty. But the king was by far the largest produce-merchant in Upper Burma, and, until his requirements had been fully met, none of his subjects were able to transact business with other traders. Thus, while the royal monopolies were nominally reduced to timber, petroleum, rubies, and jade, so that traders were at liberty to buy and sell freely, and without restriction, whatever they wanted, yet the fact remained that all purchases had practically to be made from the king or from the *Pwèza*, his brokers or agents. By these means the spirit of the treaty was circumvented, and its main object frustrated, without the king being directly chargeable with actual violation or infraction of the verbal terms.

Again, in the case of goods imported from Lower into Upper Burma, the European merchants in Rangoon represented to the Government of India that pressure was brought to bear upon independent dealers to induce them to sell goods preferentially to the royal brokers, from whom alone the king's subjects were allowed to buy. All of these unwarrantable proceedings tended to reduce the trade in staple products between Lower and Upper Burma to practical monopolies in the hands of the king, and of those who dealt with him on his own terms. The effect of this cramping system was to interfere with the action of private traders, both as to the remunerative sale of goods imported from Lower Burma and the purchase of articles for export from Upper Burma.

The "Shoe Question" was an indignity of long standing. The British Envoy or the Minister at Mandalay had always submitted, on the occasion of official visits to the palace, to the enforcement of a ceremonial requiring him to take off his shoes before entering the royal presence, and to sit upon the floor before the king. It is the custom in Burma that an inferior should sit before a superior in such manner that his feet should not be visible, for the feet are, in more than one sense, considered an inferior part of the body. Hence the respectful position amounts to kneeling down on the floor and sitting upon one's feet—a form of making obeisance called *Shekó*. When Sir Douglas Forsyth was sent upon a mission to Mandalay, in 1875, he was instructed to use his own discretion as to following past precedent in his interview with King Mindôn, but not to let such mere questions of form militate against the success of his negotiations; and he accordingly complied with the past usage by divesting himself of sword and shoes before entering the palace, and seating himself on the floor with his feet tucked in behind him, in the posture of a supplicant before the king. But, when his mission had been concluded, Sir Douglas Forsyth raised in his report the question of continuing to submit to a ceremonial so degrading to a British Envoy. A further opportunity of discussing this point was simultaneously obtained at the end of that year, when the King of Ava sent an Envoy to Calcutta to greet His Royal Highness the Prince of Wales, then making his tour in India. Intimation was given to the Envoy that as the Government of India had assumed direct relations with the Burmese Court, it was necessary that the British Resident should be received in a manner suitable to his high rank, and should in this respect receive similar treatment to that accorded to the Envoy by the Viceroy. / When the members of the mission from Ava obtained audience from the Viceroy a few days later, they wore head-covering and shoes, and they were accommodated with chairs. The Envoy was then verbally informed by Lord Northbrook that it was impossible the custom observed at the Court of Mandalay should continue any longer, and that it must cease, although the matter would not be pressed in a manner distasteful to the king. At the same time Colonel Duncan, then Resident at Mandalay, was instructed not to take off his shoes or to sit on the floor when received in audience by the king; but Mindôn tacitly declined to comply with this request. The consequence was, that from then till the final withdrawal of the British representatives from Mandalay, in October, 1879, no British Resident was ever again received in audience, business between the latter and the Court being conducted through the Burmese Ministers.

This suspension of direct personal intercourse was directly inimical to British influence, for it often happened that, under such an absolutely autocratic monarchy, the success of diplomatic representations ultimately depended entirely on the influence and arguments which the Resident could personally bring to bear on the king. Among the ministers were some who, besides being untrustworthy as to general character, had their own special and peculiar interests to look after: hence the Resident could never rely upon matters being correctly represented to the king. Upon critical occasions he could not act promptly and energetically without having the right of royal audience.

Whenever this "Shoe Question" was broached by the Resident, the Ministers of the Court of Ava were markedly averse to discuss it, and it became very plain that the resolute determination existed not to yield to ordinary diplomatic pressure upon the point. That it was necessary to terminate this degrading ceremony, and to insist on more civilised treatment for their accredited Minister, was equally clear to the Government of India; but it seems to have been a mistake to make the intimation that the taking off of shoes and making *Shekó* by the British Resident was not to be continued without the Government of India being prepared to insist both on a suitable form of reception being arranged, and on full privilege of access to the king being secured to their representative. It was a weak policy, because it led Government into a not altogether creditable *impasse* for the last three years of King Mindôn's reign; and, when Thibaw succeeded him, the opportunity was lost of insisting on an improved status of the diplomatic situation at Mandalay.

The treatment of British subjects under Burmese jurisdiction, and the disparity between the laws and the official usages of Lower and Upper Burma, were also among the chief matters calling for consideration. In 1878 a variety of cases occurred in which British subjects were barbarously treated and subjected to wanton indignities. Only two typical instances need be mentioned by way of illustration. In one of these, two *dhobi* or washermen, who had been assisting the Burmese police in catching some thieves and conveying them to the guard-house, were seized by some other police while returning home, and charged with being out after dark without a lantern. In place of merely being confined till the facts of the case could be ascertained, the two unfortunate washermen were thrown into the stocks, which were raised so high by pegs as to threaten dislocation of the ankles. While in this position a bribe of six rupees was demanded, and the two men had to give up their turbans as a pledge for the bribe in order to be relieved of further torture. Simultaneously with this, Captain Doyle, of the Irrawaddy Flotilla Company's steamer *Chindwin,* unintentionally trespassed on the river bund at Mandalay by crossing it to avoid a muddy bit of road. The path he took was a beaten track across the bund, and there was nothing to indicate that its use was prohibited. When challenged by the Burmese police he at once came down from the bund, but was seized, thrown into the stocks, and exhibited there to the public gaze for two hours, till relieved at the instance of Mr. Andreino, the Company's agent.

These cases were reported to the Minister by the British Resident on 4th September, 1878. Presuming them to be the unauthorized acts of the lowest classes of officials, it was pointed out that prompt and sufficient punishment would be taken as a proof of the Burmese Government being actuated by friendly feelings for the British. A couple of months later, on 5th November, the underlings concerned in the *dhobi* case were condemned to ten stripes and restitution of twice the sum extorted; while in Doyle's case the captain of the town-gate, where the indignity was perpetrated, was degraded from his post and imprisoned.

Mandalay was at that time in a very bad state. During the month of September King Mindôn lay dying. The palace was a hot-bed of intrigue, and the Ministers whose influence worked for good were thwarted and interfered with by those who were bent on evil. On 21st September the Thibaw Prince was declared heir-apparent to the Burmese throne, and on 1st October, after many false rumours, authentic intelligence was at last received of the King's death. His body lay in state for seven days, and then he was buried between the mausoleums of two of his queens near the great council chamber, outside of the main gate of the palace enclosure.

The British Resident was authorized to intimate to the Court of Ava that general recognition and support of King Thibaw by the Government of India would be proportionate to his adopting a more friendly policy towards them and their subjects, and that evidences of this would be expected in greater consideration for the position and influence of the Resident and in according him free access to the King. One of the first evidences of the spirit which ruled in the palace occurred on the 31st October, in connexion with the Irrawaddy Flotilla Company's steamer *Yankintaung*, under Captain Paterson. Before leaving Mandalay the steamer was boarded, and certain passengers were demanded to be given up for the purpose of being taken away. As no written authority was produced, the Captain refused to allow his passengers to be abducted in this manner, and left his moorings. On arrival at Myingyan, about eighty miles down stream, the Company's agent received a note from the Governor, which appeared to be a telegram from Mandalay, directing the seizure of thirty of the passengers; but a reply was given that the Governor's warrant or written order was necessary before the Captain could be required to deliver over the men. During the night over a hundred armed men, under two officials, boarded the steamer and forcibly abducted the passengers in question. It must be remembered that this was a steamer carrying Her Majesty's mails and flying the British flag.

But for the patience of the British Government and the various political events which were then peremptorily claiming their attention in other portions of the empire at this particular juncture, these acts of injustice and indignity must have ended in open rupture with the Court of Ava. As it was, the procedure adopted was to ask, through the Resident, for explanation and redress, which were never conceded without unnecessary delays deliberately made with the intention of showing that the King considered himself, and wished to exhibit himself in the eyes of his subjects, as strong enough to heap indignities and even inflict barbarous tortures on British subjects without fear of disastrous consequences to himself. The manifestation of this spirit of bravado had been increasing during the last years of Mindôn's reign, but it culminated when he lay stricken with fatal illness and then passed away, leaving the kingdom to his successor and to the practical guidance of the ignorant, barbarous, and unscrupulous men whose influence was greatest in the Council of the State.

Even in purely judicial matters great difficulty was experienced in obtaining any remedy for injustice to British subjects, for the careless indifference or intentional *lâches* of the Mandalay officials led to interminable delays in the law courts and in the definite settlement of suits instituted. As there was little reason to hope for reforms in the judicial administration of Upper Burma the Government of India, though naturally unwilling to interfere with the Burmese jurisdiction, found themselves forced to face the question of securing adequate protection for their subjects by insisting on the enforcement of extra-territorial rights for them and for the establishment of British Courts of Justice for the settlement of cases affecting British subjects. Such extra-territorial judicial rights and courts were no novelty in oriental countries.

The territorial questions in debate were also by no means unimportant. After the second Burmese war of 1852, the King of Burma refused to cede any portion of the territory conquered by the British, and all attempts to negotiate a treaty proved ineffectual. The matter was soon settled, however, by the Viceroy, Lord Dalhousie, defining as the northern boundary of the British province a line drawn along the parallel of latitude six miles north of the fort at Myedè, from the crest of the Arakan hill range on the west to the Salween river on the east. As the coast territories of Arakan and Tenasserim had been ceded under the treaty of Yandabú in 1826, on the conclusion of the first Burmese war, this prompt and powerful action of Lord Dalhousie added all the coast of Pegu to the British possessions and completely shut off the kingdom of Ava from the coast-line. The loss of Rangoon, then little more than a mere fishing village on a swampy tidal bank where each ebb of the water laid bare long black stretches of oozy mud, was not so much felt by the King as that of the port of Bassein situated on the Ngawun river, the extreme western branch of the Irrawaddy delta, near Cape Negrais.

BURMA UNDER BRITISH RULE

During the whole of the twenty-five years of King Mindôn's reign he never ceased cherishing the hope that he might one day get back this port as part of his possessions.

In pursuance of the Viceroy's orders, a survey party, accompanied by a suitable military escort, proceeded to clear the boundary line and demarcate it with suitable pillars. The work was under the charge of Major Allan—whose name still exists in Allanmyo, the old frontier customs' station on the Irrawaddy. For the most part the line had to be carried through dense woodlands and thick jungles offering considerable material difficulties to rapid progress. From west of the Irrawaddy across the Pegu range of hills, and beyond the Sittang river, the work was duly performed ; but before the cleared line could reach its eastern limit on the Salween river, the survey officers had to suspend operations in Western Karenni, whose inhabitants claimed recognition of their independence on the ground that this had always been respected by the Kings of Burma. On the matter being referred to Lord Dalhousie, he agreed to respect their alleged independence, subject to the proviso that, if any future attempt should be made by the Court of Ava to obtain possession of this tract, the British Government would interpose to defeat it. As Western Karenni was surrounded on the north by Upper Burmese territory, the officials in the latter habitually endeavoured to ferment trouble on our frontier by instigating the Karenni to annoyances. In 1873 King Mindôn took a farther step in claiming suzerainty over Western Karenni on the ground that it had always paid tribute to him. Two years having been wasted in correspondence and representations about the matter, Lord Northbrook finally ordered military preparations for repelling, if necessary, further interference by the Upper Burmese in Western Karenni. This was the main cause of Sir Douglas Forsyth's special mission to Mandalay in 1875, which resulted in an amicable agreement that Western Karenni was to be recognized and to remain a separate and independent State. The demarcation of the

A FRONTIER INCIDENT

boundary between Western Karenni and Upper Burma was thereupon undertaken by the British authorities, the Court of Ava tacitly declining when invited to co-operate in carrying it out. Intimation was at the same time given that the British Government reserved to themselves the right of prolonging their boundary eastwards to the Salween river in accordance with Lord Dalhousie's dictum of 1853, whenever this might seem desirable. This arrangement was in many ways unsatisfactory. Free from control, the Karenni country became a sort of sanctuary for lawless characters and a source of constant disturbance to the tranquillity of the British frontier.

On the western boundary of Upper Burma another territorial difficulty sprang up, during the closing years of Mindôn's reign, through the advancement and erection of a Burmese outpost on land which was known to be within the frontier of the Arakan Commissionership of Lower Burma. Requests for the removal of this outpost were practically ignored, beyond the casual expression of a doubt as to the validity of the Yandabú treaty of 1826, which the Burmese alleged to be now obsolete and out of date. While the Government of India could not afford to permit any doubt to exist as to the validity of this treaty, which formed the permanent deed of settlement regarding the cession of the territory in Arakan, this little frontier incident was obviously a matter for friendly agreement by laying down the boundary and demarcating it in a permanent manner. But this was just what the Burmese declined to do. They would neither comply with legitimate demands, nor adjust the disputed questions in a friendly manner. Obviously, the proper step to take under such circumstances was to notify to the Court of Ava that, if the obnoxious outpost were not withdrawn within a reasonable time, it would be removed by the British Government; but as this was in itself only a minor matter, it was merged in the general list of outstanding questions requiring settlement between the Governments of India and Upper Burma.

Up to this time, and till some years later, the external

relations of the Court of Ava with other nations than the British did not occasion much concern to the Government of India. A Treaty of Commerce between France and Upper Burma had been signed in Paris, on 24th January, 1873, and its ratification was authorized by the French National Assembly; but such ratification was not effected till April, 1884, when another Burmese embassy visited Paris to undertake fresh negotiations, which will be referred to later on. It need only be remarked here that, in order to arrange the question of the ratification with Ava, a M. de Rochechouart was sent to Mandalay. Instead of insisting upon the confirmation of the Convention already concluded at Paris, he took upon himself to sign another Treaty as a substitute for or a supplement to it. This new Treaty contained such objectionable clauses (*inter alia*, giving Upper Burma certain facilities for purchasing arms) that objections were raised by the British Cabinet and a promise was obtained from the French Government that this Treaty should not be ratified.

As the interests affected by the relations between Upper Burma and India in 1878 were mainly commercial rather than political, the political position of the Court of Ava with reference to other foreign countries had not yet assumed the importance they were subsequently to acquire a few years later. What concerned the Government of India most were the unsatisfactory commercial relations, the treatment of British subjects, the want of satisfactory judicial arrangements, the settlement of pending territorial questions, and the status of the Resident at Mandalay.

On King Mindôn's death it was felt that the time had come for collecting all these various questions and submitting them to the Secretary of State for decision as to a settled policy in dealing with the existing state of affairs. It was plainly pointed out, in forwarding for approval the proposals of the Government of India, that there seemed absolutely no hope of any adequate settlement of the pending questions unless a marked improvement of the position of the British Resident was to be insisted on. His extremely unsatisfactory position was the primary obstacle to success in placing British relations with Upper Burma on a footing more consistent with the dignity of the Government of India, and more conducive to the protection and the development of the interests committed to their charge. But no steps could be taken by the Government of India to ensure proper treatment unless the British Cabinet were prepared to authorize armed force being used, if necessary, to secure compliance with the demands once it was decided to formulate and present them.

When King Mindôn died, in 1878, it was hoped that the very unsatisfactory condition of these relations might perhaps spontaneously become improved. It was known that the late King felt strong personal reluctance to sign or to recognize any Treaty recording the cession of any portion of his territories, and it was believed that this sentiment strengthened his dislike of anything in the shape of a treaty adjusting and regulating commercial and political relations. Moreover, the strong trading instincts which led him to extend and abuse the system of monopolies were also regarded as probably personal idiosyncrasies from which his successor might perhaps be free. But it soon became evident that no such spontaneous action was to be expected from King Thibaw, and that no overtures he might make to the Government of India for the improvement of existing relations could possibly be accepted as sincere; while the massacres with which his reign was inaugurated, and his seat on the throne secured, rendered it impossible for the Government of India to take the first steps in making amicable overtures to the Court of Ava. What was insisted on at this juncture was the right, under the Treaty of Yandabú, to furnish the Resident with a suitable guard, which the disturbed condition of Upper Burma rendered absolutely necessary. This proposal was opposed by the King's Ministers, and they only yielded to strong and persistent pressure from the Government of India.

In the kingdom of Ava succession to the throne did not necessarily go by primogeniture, but by the exercise of royal prerogative. It was the custom of the country that an *Einshé Min*, or heir apparent, a "prince in front of the house," was formally elected by the King, and was thereafter associated with him in the government. He became vice-president of the State Council, and was *ex officio* regent at Mandalay whenever the King might be absent. The heir apparent, the King's brother, who had been elected early in his reign by Mindôn, was killed in 1866, when two of Mindôn's elder sons, displeased on that account, endeavoured to assassinate their father and uncle. King Mindôn had in all about thirty sons; but, as they grew up, he delayed till his last moments to carry out the duty of formally appointing his successor. In this he was actuated partly, no doubt, by fear of his own assassination, but also by the knowledge that the nomination of an heir apparent might probably lead to civil war. Each of his four principal sons aspired to the succession, and each of them had a political following. Of these the Nyaungyan Prince, of whose legitimacy there was no doubt, was the most popular, while he was the most esteemed and trusted by the King on account of his intellectual qualities and humane disposition. It was generally believed that Mindôn had frequently indicated his intention of nominating this favourite son as his successor; it is said that, in order to save the country from the horrors of civil war, a family compact had been signed by all the thirty royal princes mutually pledging themselves to respect the claims of him upon whom the King's choice might fall.

While on his death-bed, in September, 1878, King Mindôn sent for the Nyaungyan Prince for the purpose of conferring upon him the status of heir apparent; but in the meanwhile the mother of the Thibaw Prince, the youngest of the four principal sons then in Mandalay, had made herself mistress of the palace. Apprehensive of treachery, the Nyaungyan Prince delayed compliance with the royal summons, and shortly afterwards, during the third week in September, an announcement was made that the Thibaw Prince had been elected heir apparent. The mother of this Prince was one of the Queens of pure royal blood, but there were supposed to be grave doubts respecting the paternity, and it was said that King Mindôn had often expressed his determination not to select Thibaw to be his successor. Other accounts represent him as the favourite of the King, and it is certain that a very gorgeous and beautiful miniature *Kyaung*, or monastery, had been specially built near the State Council Chamber for the purpose of the young Thibaw Prince therein performing his obligatory duties in withdrawing for a period from the world and living the life of a yellow-robed religious mendicant, as prescribed for every male Burmese. But Thibaw, then a lad of twenty years of age, had there performed more than the usual prescribed religious duties in this respect. He devoted himself with exemplary zeal to the religious life, studied hard, and attained the high rank of a *Patama Byan* for distinguished excellence in knowledge of Buddhist literature at a competitive examination held by royal order in Mandalay. Both from apparent habit of mind and from religious training it might therefore have been anticipated that Thibaw's prospective reign would be inaugurated otherwise than by bloodthirsty and wholesale massacres. Meanwhile all news of the King's state of health was carefully kept secret, although rumours were already afloat that he was dead. The city of Mandalay was in a state of alarm and unrest, and the Nyaungyan Prince had, with his younger brother, the Nyaungôk Prince, to seek refuge in the British Residency, alleging that their lives were in danger. On the 1st October authentic intimation of the King's death was at last received by the Resident, and he was desired by the Minister to deliver up the two refugees. Declining to do this, he was then requested to have them deported to India, on account of the danger and disturbance to which the new King might otherwise be exposed from their presence in any part of Burma. This request was complied with, and, in maintaining these two Princes as pensioners in Calcutta, the Government of India substantially assisted in seating King Thibaw on his throne.

The Burmese Government were, however, apprehensive of British interference in the matter of succession, and moved troops southwards to the frontier of Lower Burma. Nor had the Government of India been idle in taking precautionary measures with regard to trouble on the frontier, or danger to the Resident at Mandalay. In view of the contingency of disputes as to the succession, and of lawlessness sure to become epidemic if a civil war broke out, the armament of the Indian Marine steamer *Irrawaddy* had been strengthened, and she lay at the military frontier station of Thayetmyo ready to proceed at once to Mandalay with troops to strengthen the guard at the Residency whenever a summons to this effect might come from the Resident.

For some time these arrangements and the fear of further military preparations kept the palace authorities in restraint, but this was only a temporary lull before the storm of horrors soon to burst over Mandalay. After the flight of the two Princes to the British Residency, all the other Princes and the Princesses of the royal blood were confined within the palace. According to hereditary custom, Thibaw was married to a half-sister of his own, Supayálat, the daughter of one of Mindôn's chief Queens. Ignorant, domineering, and lustful of power, she had great influence over him, and persuaded him that, to secure his position, it was necessary to make a holocaust of all those of the blood royal who were in confinement. Thibaw's mother urged the same policy. This horrible suggestion met with opposition from the majority of the Ministers. Two of these, the Yenangyaung Mingyi and the Magwe Mingyi, were deposed from office in order to weaken the opposition of the Ministry to their barbarous measure; but the scheme had the support of the notorious Taingda Mingyi, a military chief lately promoted to high rank and a great favourite with the King, of the Taingda's son, the Governor of the South Gate, and of the *Myowun*, or Governor of Mandalay. Despite the more humane counsels of the Kinwun Mingyi, the Prime Minister, and a few others among the high officials, orders were given by the King for the massacre of the majority of his relatives. The administration was disorganized; the chief executive power had for the time being passed from the constitutionally responsible Ministers into the hands of the violent and reckless party headed by the Taingda Mingyi.

On the night of the 15th February, 1879, the jail to the west of the main palace buildings was cleared for the reception of the political prisoners, and a large hole was dug in the jail precincts. The massacre was begun on that night under the superintendence of the personal followers of the King, and was continued on the following nights, the executioners being the worst among certain ruffians who had just been released from the jail in order to prepare it for being the scene of this crime. Excited with drink, they killed their victims with bludgeons, and strangled with their hands those who still had strength left to utter cries. The bodies of the women and children were thrown into the pit prepared in the jail, while on the following night eight cartloads of the corpses of the Princes were removed from the city by the western gate, and thrown into the Irrawaddy, according to custom. The massacre was continued during the nights of the 16th and the 17th; and on the 19th Mr. Shaw, the Resident, having meanwhile received confirmation of the horrors perpetrated, intimated to the Ministers that if any further slaughter occurred he would haul down the British flag, and break off all relations with the Court. Among those who were saved by this remonstrance were the mother of the Nyaungyan and the Mingun Princes living under British protection in Calcutta, the Princess Salin Supya, a favourite daughter of the late King, and some children of the heir apparent who was killed in 1866. The number of those thus done to death is supposed to have amounted to about eighty, amongst whom were most of the near relatives of the popular Nyaungyan Prince. In defiance of anything like international usage, emissaries were sent from Mandalay to Calcutta to attempt the life of the latter; but, on receiving intimation that they were under police supervision, they returned without effecting their object. No conspiracy or other provocation was ever put forward as a plea in justification of either the massacres at Mandalay or the attempted assassination in Calcutta. The remonstrances of the Resident as to the brutal massacres received the reply on the following day, prepared under direct instructions from the King, that it was his right as an independent sovereign to take such measures as seemed fit to prevent disturbance in his own country. The Resident then requested that, as a favour to the British Government, the lives of the remaining political prisoners, and especially of women and children, might be spared; and he offered to take charge of, and to convey beyond reach of doing harm, any such from whom disturbance to the kingdom might be feared. This friendly offer was tacitly declined by the King and his advisers. Remonstrances had also been made by the Italian consul.

The Chief Commissioner of British Burma, Mr. (afterwards Sir Charles) Aitchison, asked for a reinforcement of the troops in Burma, as a camp had been established outside Mandalay, and the garrison of the river forts had been increased, while the Resident telegraphed that the violent party in power, headed by the Taingda Mingyi, desired a rupture with the British Government, and wanted an excuse for overruling the moderate party of the Prime Minister. Levies were demanded from seven of the Shan chiefs, the officers of the army were completely changed, and troops were being drilled and despatched to the frontier, after being armed with rifles from the palace and undergoing the most unusual experience of receiving a month's pay in advance. With the King in an excitable condition from his own barbarities, and perhaps also from alarm at the possible consequences of his defiance of the Resident's remonstrances, some display of military strength on the British frontier was necessary to maintain peace within our own territory, and to support the Resident in his critical position. This measure secured its immediate objects, and put a stop to massacres for the time being. The military preparations brought home to the minds of the Court party that it had now become less a question of their attacking the British, than of the British proceeding against Mandalay. They could not disguise their uneasiness, and earnestly requested that the reinforcements might be withdrawn. Throughout both Lower and

Upper Burma it was everywhere believed that the Government of India were contemplating some early and decisive change in their policy of reserve and precaution.

Simultaneously with these military preparations the Government of India impressed on the Secretary of State the necessity of taking an early occasion for conveying to King Thibaw a clear exposition of their views and expectations with regard to a revision of treaty arrangements, to the improvement of existing commercial and political relations, to the settlement of pending differences and grievances, and to a change in his policy towards the British. But the British Government decided, early in April, 1879, that the grievances which had been tolerated from Mindôn had not yet been aggravated by King Thibaw, and that the time for such a decided intimation of policy as the Government of India desired would not be well chosen while the young King was surrounded by the worst of counsellors. Consequently no ultimatum was sent, and the Resident remained at his post in Mandalay.

This tone of extreme forbearance on the part of the British Cabinet would seem astoundingly weak if the circumstances of the spring of 1879 were not borne in mind. The Afghan war had been entered on in November, 1878, and the Zulu war had commenced in January, 1879, with disaster to British troops at Isandhlwana on the 22nd of that month. On Major-General Knox Gore, then in military command of Burma, being asked if he were prepared to march on Mandalay with the troops under him, he replied to the effect that he would guarantee to take Mandalay with 500 men, but that he would require 5,000 more than the recent reinforcements of the Burma garrison to enable him to pacify Upper Burma when once he had possessed himself of the capital. This settled the matter. Troops could not possibly be spared; they were wanted badly both in South Africa and in Afghanistan. Hence the British Government's rejection of the stronger policy advocated by the Government of India.

Looking back now, with the knowledge of subsequent events, there is much reason for congratulation at the turn events took. The Zulu war continued till Cetewayo's total defeat and capture in July, 1880; and the Afghan war was only brought to an end late in the same year, after a serious reverse had been sustained by the British arms at Maiwand in July, 1880. The experiences from 1886 to 1890 in Upper Burma make it extremely improbable that General Knox Gore's estimate of the strength required to pacify the country after the fall of the capital would have been sufficient; and it would have been a matter of rather serious difficulty to provide large numbers of trained British troops for Burma, in addition to the special demands of South Africa and Afghanistan. Moreover, if war had then been waged against Upper Burma, it would only have been for the purpose of deposing Thibaw and placing the Nyaung-yan Prince on the throne in his stead; whereas the ultimate annexation of Ava on 1st January, 1886, completely settled all political and commercial grievances, and added to the British Empire in India vast territories rich in material wealth, and far richer still in future possibilities.

The respite thus given to Thibaw, and the tidings of reverse to the British troops in Zululand, stimulated him and his ignorant advisers to further acts of discourtesy and injustice to the British, despite a certain feeling of disquietude at the maintenance of military preparations along the British frontier. In the middle of April a fracas took place at Sinbyugyun on board the Irrawaddy Flotilla Company's steamer *Shinsawbu*, owing to the local coolies insisting on piling loads of *Ngápi*, or fish pickled with salt, a favourite condiment having a vile smell, on the bedding and luggage of the passengers, and then belabouring these latter with bamboos and billets of firewood on their objecting to their personal effects being thus defiled. When the Commander tried to cause the combatants to separate by ordering the mooring-line to be cast off, the coolies on shore prevented his order being carried out; and when this interference was circumvented by cutting the hawser on board the steamer, the irate coolies seized the Company's lascars, who were discharging salt from a flat near by which had been left by a previous steamer. This was apparently done under the direction of an official mounted on a pony. About the same time another of the Company's steamers had to cast off suddenly from Myingyan, without completing the landing of her cargo, on account of the violence of the coolies. Towards the end of May the Assistant-Resident at Mandalay, Mr. Phayre, whilst returning from an early morning ride, was jeered at and reviled with insulting terms when passing a group of young Burmese, although he was attended by a small retinue bearing the usual large umbrella and fan forming the customary insignia of an official, and by two of the police guard furnished by the Burmese Government. Treatment of this sort had become not unusual, but it was often difficult to ascertain the offender; and in this case the Minister was asked to see that suitable punishment should be given to put a stop to such conduct. These were all very trifling and petty matters in themselves, but they distinctly showed the drift of popular opinion throughout the capital of the country as a reflection of the attitude of the Court and the feelings which were known to exist there.

Barbarities at the same time were again inflicted on the remaining political prisoners within the palace. The mother and the sister of the Nyaungyan Prince were loaded with irons and placed in closer confinement within a cell bricked upon all sides with the exception of a hole just big enough to admit a man. Here they were imprisoned along with three other ex-Queens at a time of the year when the thermometer usually registers about 105° in the shade during the daytime. They existed on alms of money sent secretly from the Residency; but the go-between becoming alarmed and fleeing to Rangoon, the prisoners became dependent on doles of food sent to them by one of the Queen-mothers. Orders were issued for their execution, but they were saved by the joint intercession of the mothers of the King and the Queen, prompted thereto by the Prime Minister, the Kinwun Mingyi. Some Princesses who endeavoured to escape by boat into Lower Burma were caught not far from the frontier, and were at once thrown into the river and drowned.

Whilst matters were still in a state of extreme tension

the British Resident at Mandalay, Mr. R. B. Shaw, died on the 15th June, 1879, and his duties were taken temporarily by Colonel Horace Browne, Commissioner of Pegu, who was sent up to Mandalay on deputation. As it was feared that the formal appointment of a successor to Mr. Shaw would be misconstrued and taken as a sign that the British were content to let both commercial and political matters drift on as they had been doing, and might be misinterpreted into a condonation of the disregard shown to the remonstrances made regarding the massacres in Mandalay, the Government of India determined not to fill the vacancy thus caused. It was considered that Mr. St. Barbe, a junior civil servant then acting as political agent at Bhamo, would be quite competent to transact ordinary business with the Burmese officials upon the footing to which the intercourse between the Residency and the Ministers had now been reduced. On 29th August, Colonel Browne accordingly left Mandalay, leaving Mr. St. Barbe as *Chargé d'affaires*, with Mr. Phayre as Assistant Resident. Out of regard for the safety of those he was leaving behind him, Colonel Browne refrained from saying or doing anything prior to leaving which might be likely to arouse hostility within the Court. No notice of his departure was taken by the Burmese authorities, although he had given them five days' informal and three days' formal notice of his intention to leave.

On the 4th September, 1879, Sir Louis Cavagnari, the English Envoy to Cabul, was murdered; and the Government of India naturally became apprehensive of the safety of their representatives in Upper Burma. Authority was therefore promptly given to the Chief Commissioner of Burma to withdraw the whole Mandalay agency and escort whenever he should consider this step advisable, or when any suitable opportunity occurred; but it was pointed out that this should not be done in any manner liable to misinterpretation as hasty or unnecessary. Apart from considerations regarding the welfare of Messrs. St. Barbe and Phayre, the withdrawal of British representatives from Mandalay was viewed by the Government of India with no reluctance; for relations

BRITISH RESIDENT WITHDRAWN

with the Court of Ava had latterly been such as to leave little hope of advantage, and much risk of disadvantage, from maintaining the Residency at Mandalay. By a strange coincidence these last representatives of British diplomacy at Mandalay were unfortunately the first two civilians to lose their lives in the operations after the annexation in 1886—Mr. St. Barbe (March, 1886) while attacking dacoits in the Bassein district (Lower Burma), and Mr. Phayre (June, 1886) while operating against Bo Shwe in the Minhla jungles.

Meanwhile rumours grew rife in Mandalay of conspiracies in favour of the Nyaungyan Prince, who was reported to be on the point of coming to Upper Burma. Large numbers of men and women were arrested in connexion with these supposed plots, and some were put to death. The pay of troops was now in arrears, and it was feared that advantage of the discontent among the soldiery might be taken by the Taingda Mingyi to overthrow the Prime Minister's party, which alone restrained the King and his bloodthirsty crew from massacring the inhabitants of the Residency. On several occasions in 1879 designs had been deliberately formed and preliminary preparations made with this object; and it was mainly due to the still existing authority of the Prime Minister that such designs had not actually been carried out. The Government of India therefore ordered the withdrawal of the officers, escort, and records from the Residency. Notice thereof was duly given to the Burmese Ministers and to all Europeans and British subjects residing in Mandalay or in Bhamo; and the withdrawal was quietly effected on 7th October, 1879, without the occurrence of any untoward incident.

The first move of the Burmese Government after this was to despatch an Ambassador on 23rd October with a letter and presents to the Viceroy of India. On arrival at the British frontier station of Thayetmyo, the Embassy was detained to ascertain its objects and the rank and powers of the Ambassador. As the inquiries regarding these points proved unsatisfactory, the Envoy was informed that the Government of India were not disposed, under existing circumstances, to receive a mission of ceremony, with nothing more than mere formal assurances of friendship from the King of Ava. The Envoy was afterwards duly empowered to discuss preliminaries for a new Treaty, but the proposals were entirely inadequate. He had consequently to be informed that, unless more substantial overtures could be expected, his remaining indefinitely at Thayetmyo was inconvenient and generally undesirable. After being hospitably entertained as a guest for more than six months at Thayetmyo without making any reasonable proposals for adjusting differences, he at length returned to Mandalay. But, before doing so, he sent to the Chief Commissioner of Burma a letter which was so improper both in tone and in matter that it was returned to him.

The frontier districts of Thayetmyo and Toungoo, with their strong garrisons, remained quiet and tranquil; but emissaries from Upper Burma began to sow the seeds of sedition among some of the Lower Burmese township officials, more particularly in the western districts of the Irrawaddy delta, from Danúbyu to Bassein, which had always remained rather disaffected ever since their annexation in 1853. The workshops of Mandalay were busy with the manufacture of rifles and torpedoes, while further troops were raised and fortifications erected near Minhla. Within the palace massacres still continued from time to time with unabated cruelty. Five sisters of the Thôngzè Prince, the eldest of the Princes murdered on 15th February, 1879, were executed, nominally for being in correspondence with the Nyaungyan Prince in Calcutta, but really because they had incurred the jealousy of the chief Queen Supayálat. Supayágyi, her elder sister and nominal chief Queen, became involved in an attempt to poison Thibaw and Supayálat, which cost not only her own life but also the lives of two Punnas or Manipuri Brahmans, a sect much venerated as soothsayers, and of their three Burmese attendants. The palace had in fact become a pandemonium.

On 13th November, 1879, a fracas and riotous assault took place on board the Irrawaddy Flotilla Company's steamer *Shwemyo* at Myingyan. Similar in nature to those which had in April occurred here and at Sinbyugyun, it was, however, more serious in degree, and the Government of India demanded adequate redress and punishment of offenders on account of infringement of the protection provided for British subjects under the existing commercial Treaties of 1862 and 1867. Failing satisfaction within a reasonable time, they urged the denouncement of these Treaties; but, before taking such a step, they desired to know the decision of the British Government as to the future measures which might be adopted. With their hands full in South Africa and Afghanistan, it was almost a foregone conclusion that the British Cabinet should temporize; hence they questioned the expediency of denouncing the treaties, and requested first of all to be informed how the Burmese Government replied to the demand for redress. After an interval of over three months the reply came from Mandalay in the form of a curt intimation that the case had been decided by the Governor of Myingyan to the satisfaction of both parties, and that under such circumstances it was not the custom to try petty cases afresh. The main points at issue were absolutely ignored. But Mr. Gladstone's Cabinet had taken office on 28th April, 1880; and their policy was peace at any price. The Government of India could not push matters without the consent and approval of the British Government. They did what they could in a despatch dated 1st June, 1880, which contained the following very emphatic statement of their position, and of the policy they urged:

"All further proceedings upon the Burmese Minister's letter are necessarily stayed until Her Majesty's Government shall have considered it; and, in submitting the papers for orders, we may observe that, unless the Government of India are eventually authorized to deal with the case as an infringement of treaty, it must, in our opinion, be silently dropped. But we consider that such a conclusion would be very prejudicial to the honour and interests of the British Government, and that the reasons upon which we determined that a demand must be made now prevail manifestly with redoubled strength on the side of prosecuting it to some distant issue, or at least to some understanding in regard to the future. . . . We still adhere to the view that the affair cannot be creditably passed over; while we still desire to point out to Her Majesty's Government that a plain, reasonable, and advantageous course of action can be found in the procedure which . . . we had the honour to recommend to Her Majesty's Government. It may be that the original affair is not, of itself, sufficiently important to form the basis for a dissolution of our commercial engagements; but we wish to represent, what in previous despatches has already been brought to the notice of Her Majesty's Government, that ever since the accession to the throne of the present King the attitude of his Government towards us has been one of open unfriendliness and of frequent disregard of treaty obligations. And since we have every reason to apprehend, from long experience of the conduct and character of the Burmese Government, from the recent behaviour in particular of the King and his Ministers, and from the fact of our having no representative at Mandalay for the protection of British subjects, that the Burmese Government cannot safely be encouraged either in discourtesy to our Government or in disregard to their engagements, we are most reluctant to leave this reply without some substantial rejoinder.

"We desire, therefore, permission from Her Majesty's Government to inform the Mandalay Court that the answer given to our demand is considered unsatisfactory, both in tone and substance; that the case is regarded as affecting our treaty relations; and that, having regard to the whole state of our present relations with the King, we consider that the honour and interests of the British Government require us to withdraw altogether from our existing engagements with Upper Burma. We propose, however, . . . to allow the Burmese Government an opportunity of fully considering the consequences that will follow our demand for redress."

While this despatch was being prepared in Simla, the British mail steamer *Yunnan* was, early on 26th May, forcibly seized and detained by the Governor of Salé-myo, the starting-gear being unshipped and an armed guard of twenty men placed on board the ship. On the evening of the following day the starting-gear was returned and the guard withdrawn. Demands were made, in the least exacting manner possible, for an explanation of the affair; but the reply from the Court of Ava was so evasive and unsatisfactory as to preclude any prospect of advantage from further correspondence on the subject. It was not until after receiving further information that the Secretary of State (Lord Hartington) in September intimated to the Viceroy (Lord Lytton) the reluctant approval of the British Government in the words that they were "*not prepared to dissent from the course*" which had been adopted by the Government of India. This cold consent, far from amounting to even lukewarm approval, was accompanied with the intimation that the Secretary of State "*was in the first instance disposed to doubt whether the absolute rejection of the Burmese over-*

tures, resulting in the return of the Embassy to its own country, was altogether judicious."

Using the outrage on the *Yunnan* and the Burmese treatment of the demand for redress as a suitable opportunity for once more urging their policy, the Government of India, on 9th November, 1880, again asked for the authority of Her Majesty's Government to denounce the commercial Treaties of 1862 and 1867; and in reply thereto the Secretary of State could only " *express the regret of Her Majesty's Government that, after full deliberation, they feel unable at present to accord their sanction to it. . . . They do not gather that trade has, as yet, been materially prejudiced by any action of the Burmese Government, or that any political question of urgency is pending at Mandalay. In these circumstances Her Majesty's Government consider that the attitude of forbearance lately observed towards the King may be maintained for the present, and that the Government of India should be slow to precipitate a crisis by measures of which neither the political nor commercial effect can be estimated with certainty."* This definitely settled the matter for the time being; for it was clear that the reasonable requirements of the Government of India as to commercial protection for British subjects and suitable reception and treatment of a Resident at Mandalay could only be secured in the event of Britain being prepared to enforce these demands at the point of the bayonet.

The Zulu war closed in the summer of 1880, and the Afghan war in the autumn of the same year; but, before the year 1880 closed, Britain had again become embroiled in warfare in South Africa through a rebellion of the Boers in the Transvaal, which had been annexed in April, 1877. The short campaign which followed was disastrous, the British arms sustaining three several defeats before peace was concluded on 22nd March, 1881, on an armistice proposed by the Boers. It was a humiliating instance of the impotence of Great Britain at the moment; but the Boers of the Transvaal and Mr. Gladstone's Cabinet saved King Thibaw, and maintained him on the throne from which he was five years later to fall with such a crash.

Chapter III

POLITICAL AND COMMERCIAL RELATIONS BETWEEN
BRITISH INDIA AND UPPER BURMA FROM 1881 TO
1885: THE CAUSES OF THE THIRD BURMESE WAR

THE incidents narrated in the latter portion of the
previous chapter may be summarized in a few
words as an introduction to the trend of affairs gradually
leading to the third Burmese war.   After the withdrawal
of the British mission from Mandalay in October, 1879,
the attitude of King Thibaw's Government grew more
hostile.   Unprovoked attacks were twice made upon
British mail steamers on the Irrawaddy river, and demands for redress were replied to in so curt and dis-
courteous a manner, that the Government of India
recommended the renunciation of all treaty engagements
with the Court of Ava.   The British Cabinet, however,
already embroiled in an inglorious war with the Boers of
the Transvaal within a few months of the conclusion of
the Zulu and the Afghan wars, were unable to accept the
policy urged by the Government of India, and deprecated
the precipitation of a crisis by means of which neither the
political nor the commercial effect could be accurately
gauged.   Meanwhile the relations between the Governments of India and Ava were at a deadlock.   Upper
Burma became completely disorganized, bands of armed
robbers roaming about at will and raiding at times into
British territory, and fresh atrocities occurring within the
King's palace.

In the spring of 1882 an Envoy from the Court of
Ava, bearing proposals for a new treaty, was permitted
to proceed to Simla.   Notwithstanding the occurrences
which had characterized the proceedings of an abortive
mission that remained at the frontier of British Burma

for over six months in 1880, without being able to make suitable proposals as a basis for negotiations, a most friendly reception was accorded to the Embassy by the Viceroy, Lord Ripon, while the utmost trouble and pains were taken to bring the negotiations to a successful and satisfactory issue. But the expectations thus raised of a renewal of friendly intercourse between the two Powers were frustrated by King Thibaw suddenly recalling his Envoy.

Commercial progress was retarded and trade intercourse interfered with by the King following the policy of his predecessor in the matter of creating monopolies. During the year 1881–82 the value of the international traffic fell off greatly from this cause, but it recovered again when the monopolies were restricted in compliance with representations made by the Government of India. In other matters also the attitude assumed by the Burmese Government continued to be unmistakably unfriendly, and even menacing. The hostility gradually became more marked, and it was stimulated by the intrigues and machinations of foreign agents.

This policy of hostility in May, 1883, led the Court of Ava to despatch a mission to Europe, ostensibly with the object of gathering information relating to industrial arts and sciences, but in reality for the purpose of seeking alliances with foreign powers and of arranging political and commercial agreements which could not but conflict very seriously with established British interests, and which could only lead to the encouragement of intolerable intrigues on the part of the foreign agents in Mandalay. So long as the kingdom of Ava occupied an isolated position, its overt unfriendliness could be borne with extreme forbearance by the Government of India ; but when once the external policy of the Burmese Government began to exhibit symptoms of desiring to prosecute designs which, if permitted with impunity, would result in the establishment of preponderating foreign influence at the Court of Ava and throughout the upper valley of the Irrawaddy, it became impossible for the British Cabinet any longer to view the situation without anxiety.

BURMA UNDER BRITISH RULE

While other European Powers held aloof and did not seek to mix themselves up with the affairs of Burma the absence of a British Minister in Mandalay, though inconvenient, was not attended with any very material disadvantage. But there were French agents, whose machinations and intrigues chiefly required to be guarded against. Already the stormy petrels of French diplomacy were in Mandalay inaugurating the policy of "pinpricks" against Britain, which was in turn followed in Upper Burma, then on the Niger, and again at Fashoda.

The Embassy thus deputed to Europe for about a year to visit the principal countries and cities on the Continent, remained there till the end of April, 1885, by which time it had concluded treaties with France, Germany, and Italy. The Ambassador was an *Atwinwun*, or Minister of the Secret Department of the Court, who knew no language other than Burmese; but the other members of the Embassy consisted of a *Wundauk*, or Assistant Minister, and a *Sayédawgyi*, or Clerk of the Great State Council, both of whom had been educated in Europe under the orders of King Mindôn, and were conversant with English and French. They had also been among the members of the Embassy which visited Simla in 1882. It was further accompanied by a French gentleman named M. de Trévelec.

It will be recollected (see p. 38 in previous chapter) that a treaty had been made by Burma with France on 24th January, 1873, which had never been ratified, owing to the French Agent sent to Burma for this purpose taking upon himself the responsibility of entering into a fresh treaty, in 1874, of so objectionable a nature that promises were given by France to the British Government that the latter would not be ratified. On the arrival of the Burmese Embassy at Paris, in 1883, they desired to renew negotiations regarding the unratified commercial Treaty of 1873, and gave out that they intended staying only about a month. Political subjects were not yet, so far as was known, under discussion, although excuses for broaching them lay close to hand. In April, 1883, the Myingun Prince—who, after rebelling in 1866, killing his uncle, the selected heir apparent to the throne, and nearly succeeding in assassinating his father, King Mindôn, had fled to Lower Burma, and had since then been a pensioner of the Government of India—escaped from Benares (in Lower Bengal), where he was living under surveillance, and sought an asylum in the French settlement of Chandernagore. Here he remained for a couple of months, declining all the overtures made to induce him to return to British protection, and hoping to utilize French territory as a base for operations against the Government of Upper Burma. In the absence of the Nyaungyan Prince, who was still living under the protection of the British, he was convinced that if once he could effect a landing in Upper Burma his endeavours to overthrow Thibaw and seat himself on the throne would secure many adherents. In June, 1884, he contrived to elude the vigilance of the police ordered to secure him if he should leave the French settlement, and to make his way on a French steamer to Colombo. He was promptly returned in the same ship to Pondicherry, where he was detained under the supervision of the Governor-General of the French Settlements in India.

But the Burmese Embassy stayed on month after month in Paris, apparently disregardful of the study of the industrial arts and sciences forming the professed primary object of their mission. In the diplomatic conversations held during the summer and autumn of 1883 between Lord Lyons, the British Ambassador, and MM. Challemel Lacour and Jules Ferry, the French Ministers for Foreign Affairs, no opportunities were lost of impressing upon the French Government the objections entertained by the British Cabinet to the conclusion of any agreement with King Thibaw containing stipulations beyond those of a purely commercial nature ; and it was understood that the British authorities desired that facilities should not be given to the Burmese for the purchase of arms. It was also particularly pointed out that in consequence of its geographical position with regard to British India, and of its political relations therewith, Upper Burma occupied a peculiar position, giving the British Government a special interest in all that concerned the kingdom of Ava. To France the affairs of that country could only be of secondary interest, whereas to Britain they were of the utmost concern, and, indeed, of vital importance.

As the year 1883 was nearing its close, Lord Lyons had again to make particular mention of the subject of the Burmese Mission in Paris. It was pointed out that they had presented no credentials to the President of the Republic, or that at any rate no intimation of their having had a formal audience had been notified in the *Journal Officiel*, and that they had not, as was customary, called upon the British Ambassador or the other members of the diplomatic body, although they were admittedly in direct communication with the Commercial Division of the French Foreign Office, and were believed to be negotiating a treaty of some kind. M. Jules Ferry replied that the Mission had submitted various proposals regarding commercial matters, but that no progress had been made, as the Envoy had apparently not sufficient powers to treat seriously, and that consequently, in the meantime, no arrangements at all with Burma would be concluded at Paris.

This was, however, mere diplomatic fencing and equivocation. In April, 1884, the assurance was given by M. Ferry that any treaties or conventions resulting from the negotiations would be of an entirely commercial or consular character, and that no facilities would be given to the Burmese for obtaining arms. The Burmese Ambassador was particularly anxious to obtain a clause authorizing the free passage of arms into Upper Burma; but the French Government were absolutely determined not to agree thereto, as they were by no means disposed to facilitate the introduction of arms into Tonquin. In May, 1884, M. Ferry was again informed that the British Government would naturally entertain the most serious objections to any special alliance or political understanding between Upper Burma and any other foreign Power. The notice of the Foreign Minister (Lord Granville) was at the same time brought to the fact that the Franco-Burmese Treaty of 1873, which it was now for the first time contemplated to bring into operation, provided for a reciprocal appointment of diplomatic agents of the two Governments. Endeavours were consequently made to obtain from the French Government a definite promise that the functions of any such agents who might be appointed would be only of a commercial and not in any sense of a political character. Such a promise would only have been in harmony with the friendly assurances previously given by M. Ferry.

In the course of an interview in July, 1884, during which Lord Lyons handed to M. Ferry a paper *pro memoriâ*, embodying the position taken up by the British Government, the French Foreign Minister observed that it was very difficult to draw any distinct line between commercial and political functions. He thought it likely a French Consul-General, or some agent of that kind, would be stationed in Mandalay ; but whatever might be his title, he must of course in practice have charge of French interests in general. Reference was also made to France and Burma becoming neighbours towards Tonquin. On Lord Lyons pointing out that the kingdom of Ava could not be a neighbour to France in any sense at all resembling that in which it was a neighbour to British India, M. Ferry then asked if any special treaties between Britain and Upper Burma precluded the latter from entering into independent political relations with other Powers. The obvious reply was at once made that, as British interests preponderated so vastly in Upper Burma, the British Cabinet relied on all friendly Powers abstaining from seeking any political alliance with Upper Burma. About a week after the note *pro memoriâ* had been handed in, Lord Lyons reminded M. Ferry of the assurances desired by the British Government, and was informed that the projected Treaty contained a stipulation that each party was free to accredit diplomatic and consular officers to the other. The present intention of the French Government was to station only a Consul at Mandalay ; but the title given to such agent, would, after all, be a matter of little consequence as, whatever title he bore, he would have to deal with general questions between the two countries; and it was impossible to draw an exact line between political and commercial functions. For example, there might be question of *voisinage* regarding territories on the left bank of the Mekong river, over which the King of Ava claimed suzerain rights without exercising practical authority.

It was admitted by M. Ferry that the Burmese desired a political alliance with France and asked particularly for facilities for procuring arms, but he declared that the French Government had no intention of forming with Upper Burma any alliance whatever of a special character ; and a distinct assurance was given to this effect.

Trouble had meanwhile been brewing on the British boundary between Manipur and Upper Burma. In consequence of certain disturbances which had occurred on this frontier, and of doubts regarding jurisdiction which had arisen through the omission to demarcate precisely the frontier line between Manipur and Upper Burma as described in the Kubo Valley Agreement of 1834, the Government of India, early in 1881, determined to depute a Commission to mark out the frontier boundary. When informed of this intention and invited to depute representatives to be present at the demarcation, the Court of Ava intimated their opinion that fresh demarcation of the boundary determined in 1834 was unnecessary. The reasons rendering necessary the precise demarcation of the frontier line were explained, and the Ava Government were again invited to co-operate. Failing this, they were asked to instruct the local officers to give reasonable assistance to the demarcating party, which would reach Sumjok, near the frontier, about 20th November, 1881. In October, the Ava Government reiterated their opinion that demarcation was unnecessary, and intimated that they would neither agree to nor abide by any demarcation which the British Government might persist in making. In November, the Foreign Minister of Ava was informed that the proposed demarcation would be carried out and that the British Government would expect the boundary line thus laid down to be respected by the chiefs and the people on both sides, to which communication he replied by intimating that he adhered to what he had already said in his letter of October.

The demarcation of the actual frontier line was carried out by the British Commission under Colonel Johnstone, no representative af the Court of Ava being present. As it was ascertained that certain villages hitherto supposed to be in Burmese territory were actually on the Manipur side, the local Burmese authorities were requested to withdraw an armed post stationed at one of these villages. The work of the Commission was approved by the Government of India and the British Government.

In February, 1882, the Foreign Minister of Ava intimated to the Governor of India that the local Burmese authorities had been directed to destroy the boundary marks and to station Burmese officials on the spot for the protection of Burmese subjects. In reply hereto the Government of India expressed a hope that the intention of demolishing the boundary marks would not be carried out, as the consequences might be very serious; and the suggestion was made that the matter might be left for discussion with the Envoy, then on the point of visiting Simla. While at Simla, the Burmese Ambassador was in August furnished with maps and records of the boundary, and was informed that the Government of India intended to maintain the boundary and to prevent interference with the boundary marks or encroachment beyond the frontier line.

During 1883 it was asserted by the Court of Ava that the Kongkal (Kaungkan) British outpost had been pushed into Burmese territory, and that men sent to examine the boundary line had not been permitted to reach the frontier. Both of these statements were incorrect. The Ava Government were informed that there was no objection to an examination of the frontier line being made, provided the boundary was not crossed or disturbed ; and it was asked that, if such a party were to be sent, intimation thereof might be previously given.

About a year after this, in May, 1884, another letter was received from the Foreign Minister of Ava expressing astonishment at the boundary line demarcated by Colonel Johnstone being referred to as binding between the two Governments. Objections were raised to it, and it was again threatened that the boundary marks and the Kongkal outpost would be destroyed if the British Government omitted or delayed to comply with the request for their removal. The obvious reply to this threat was a solemn warning to the Ava Government to reconsider their decision ; otherwise, if any such demolition or encroachment took place under their orders, the consequences might be very serious. This was almost an exact repetition of the warning given to them early in 1882.

It was not anticipated by the Government of India that the Burmese Government would act in defiance of this warning and attempt to carry their threats into execution ; but as a precautionary measure the Chief Commissioner of Assam was authorized to direct the Maharaja of Manipur to resist the destruction or removal of the boundary marks, and for this purpose a detachment of native infantry was to be sent to support him, if necessary. That was the last of this direct insult to the Government of India, whose prompt and decisive action was approved by the British Government.

During January, 1885, after the lapse of about six months since the last exchange of opinions, Lord Lyons had again to bring the subject of the negotiations of the Burmese Embassy into diplomatic conversation with M. Jules Ferry, the French Minister for Foreign Affairs, and to ask what was the state of his relations with the so-called Burmese Ambassadors. On being vaguely informed that the negotiation " *n'avait pas encore abouti,*" the British representative had again to urge the views expressed in the *pro memoriâ* of the previous July, when he was met by the statement that, as France was now also a neighbour of Upper Burma, it might be necessary to make treaty arrangements with regard to the frontier. The position thus taken up by France was most decidedly unfriendly ; and it was pointed out that, while the Indian Government had full means of bringing the Burmese to a sense of their obligations and their proper position, it would be very painful and very inconvenient that a question of resorting to those means should be raised by a treaty between Burma and France. A few days later M. Jules Ferry informed Lord Lyons that the Treaty which had been for over eighteen months in negotiation at Paris, between the French Government and the Burmese Embassy had at length been signed on 15th January, 1885, but that this

Treaty did not contain any political or military stipulations. It was merely, he said, one of the common treaties stipulating for rights of residence, intercourse, commerce, most-favoured-nation treatment, and so forth. It was added that a French Consul would now be sent to Mandalay, but that the question of obtaining consular jurisdiction over Frenchmen in Ava was still unsettled.

The duplicity and the covert hostility of France were, however, afterwards apparent in a letter, also dated 15th January, 1885, which came from Mandalay into the hands of the Chief Commissioner of British Burma towards the end of July, 1885. It was from the French Prime Minister to the Burmese Minister for Foreign Affairs and contained the following passage :[1] "*With respect to transport through the province of Tonquin to Burma, of arms of various kinds, ammunition and military stores generally, amicable arrangements will be come to with the Burmese Government for the passage of the same when peace and order prevail in Tonquin, and the officers stationed there are satisfied that it is proper, and that there is no danger.*" This episode cannot be explained away ; it showed deliberate perfidy, and entire disregard of national honour and good faith by France towards Great Britain.

There is no necessity for considering this Franco-Burmese Treaty in detail. It is sufficient to remark that, diplomatic *pourparlers* in Europe and acts in Burma being duly considered in their mutual relations, unmistakable indications were not wanting that King Thibaw's Government were bent upon welcoming to the upper valley of the Irrawaddy river foreign influence in such manner as, if allowed to become established and dominant, could not fail at some future time to trouble the political tranquillity of British Burma, and to engender complications extending beyond the British frontier. The law of the Senate and the Chamber of Deputies authorizing the President of the French Republic to ratify the Franco-Burmese Convention of 15th January, 1885, was not passed till the 24th November, 1885. It was published in the *Journal Officiel* of 26th November,

[1] *Vide* p. 170 of the Parliamentary Blue-Book, on *Correspondence relating to Burmah* [C—4614], 1886.

the very day on which the Burmese Ministers were begging an armistice from the British General off Ava. It may, however, be further remarked that this Franco-Burmese Treaty and the somewhat unfriendly attitude displayed during its negotiation by the French Government rendered absolutely impossible, on the conclusion of the third Burmese war, any question of deposing King Thibaw in favour of the Nyaungyan Prince or of enthroning any other scion of the royal house of Alaung Payá This first deep "pinprick" by France, and the intrigues of M. Haas, who reached Mandalay in May, 1885, as Consul of France, though not the actual *casus belli*, may therefore be looked upon as the direct and chief cause of the annexation of Upper Burma to the British Indian Empire, and of the extinction of the kingdom of Ava. An international treaty existing between France and Ava would have been binding on a King Nyaungyan ; but its operation ceased, *ipso facto*, when Upper Burma became part of the British Empire. Annexation, under these circumstances, was the only way of completely removing possible causes of friction between France and Britain in this particular matter.

Having effected their object with France after a year and a half's residence in Paris, the Burmese Embassy had now at length leisure to think of the courtesy of calling upon the British Ambassador in Paris. They were received on 4th February, when they intimated their intention of proceeding shortly to Rome, and then returning to Burma. Thoroughly aware of their previous extreme discourtesy in not having observed diplomatic etiquette, they first of all asked the Italian Ambassador at Paris, General Menabrea, to ascertain if Lord Lyons would be willing to receive their visit.

At Rome the Embassy delayed longer than they appeared to have anticipated, their stay there being utilized in endeavours to negotiate a convention with Italy on similar terms to the new Franco-Burmese Treaty. A treaty already existed between Burma and Italy, but it had been loosely drawn up by a naval officer, and did not contain the usual most-favoured-nation clause. The Italian Government declined to enter into negotiations till they had been assured that satisfaction had been given to the claims of two Italian subjects employed by the Ava Government, and whose salaries had remained unpaid for the last two years. The Burmese Embassy was hurriedly recalled in April, without any convention with Italy being agreed to ; but the Italian Government fully acknowledged the impossibility of the British allowing the transit of arms through British Burma, which was forbidden by treaty. The only result of the Envoy's stay in Rome was the conclusion of a treaty with the German Government, negotiated by Baron von Kendell, and signed on the 14th May. It simply secured for Germany the treatment of the most favoured nation, and entered into no details. There was nothing in it which could clash with the precautionary measures taken against the importation of arms through British Burma.

For all the three countries chiefly concerned there were storm-clouds above the political horizon in 1884 and 1885. For Britain, there had been very strained relations with Russia over the Panjdeh incident, and the crisis of 1885 was the turning-point. As the result of the Afghan Boundary Commission, a line was drawn beyond which Russian aggression would inevitably form a *casus belli*, whatever might be the political complexion of the British Cabinet in power. On 26th January, 1885, Khartoum fell, and General Gordon was killed ; on 24th June the Gladstonian Cabinet was replaced by one formed by Lord Salisbury. France, still with her hands sufficiently full in Tonquin, had undertaken a war with China which was terminated in April, 1885, about a week after the fall of the Ferry Cabinet. But it was over the kingdom of Ava that the storm-clouds lowered darkest.

King Thibaw's misrule had become so great and dacoity so prevalent by the end of 1883, that large numbers of Upper Burmese crossed the frontier to obtain the advantages of British protection. Early in 1884 it was estimated that, within a few months, about a quarter of a million people had thus flocked into Lower Burma, while the stream of emigration was only checked by detaining, as hostages, the wives and children of men who went down into British territory for temporary employment. The kingdom of Ava had at this time sunk to a condition of anarchy, and King Thibaw did not dare venture beyond the inner enclosure of his palace, where he was, to all practical intents, a prisoner. The greater part of the feudatory Shan States, forming nearly the half of the eastern portion of the kingdom, had been for about three years in open rebellion. In March, 1884, a serious revolt had also taken place in the northern districts peopled by the Kachin hill tribes, which carried fire and sword half way down to Mandalay. This rising subsided during the rainy months, but was expected to make head again during the open season commencing with November. In addition to this, rumours were current in Mandalay that the Myingun Prince had escaped from French surveillance in Pondicherry, and made his way to Bangkok, the capital of Siam, whence he intended to accomplish Thibaw's downfall, with the assistance of the rebellious Sawbwa of the Shan States. It was even suspected that the scheme originated with some of the Ministers, who were disgusted with the existing state of affairs. The jails in and near the palace were at this time filled with dacoits as well as political prisoners. Headed by the infamous Taingda Mingyi, certain of the Ministers went and told the King they believed some of the bad characters in the jail were conspiring against him, and they advised him to execute them, in order to prevent their escaping and joining the cause of the Myingun Prince. Some of the prisoners were instigated to make an attempt to escape, and the jailer was authorized to liberate certain of them. As soon as this order was carried out, on 22nd September, 1884, the jail-guard was called upon to quell the outbreak, the Taingda Mingyi and other Ministers and officials appeared at the head of troops from the palace, and the work of indiscriminate massacre began. Orders were given by the Taingda to set fire to the jail, and a continuous fire of musketry was kept up from the house of his son-in-law, the Governor of the South Gate, on the prisoners as they flocked out of the prison to escape from the flames. Those who managed to get outside the jail were pursued and slaughtered in the streets of the city, the gates being closed to prevent their escape beyond the city walls. The slaughter was not merely confined to the prison within the inner palace, to which fire was set, but was likewise extended to the other two prisons situated without the inner enclosure. Thibaw, alarmed and excited, directed that all political prisoners were to be killed, and that all who rebelled against his authority were to be immediately executed; while orders were given to the rural Governors that all the prisoners confined in the district jails should be sent to Mandalay.

The number of men, women and children thus brutally massacred on the 22nd and following days is estimated to have been between 200 and 300 in all. On the day after the chief massacre, the corpses were carted out of the city, and were exposed for some days in the burial ground to the west. Here they remained, mutilated, putrefying, and uncovered with earth, to show how terrible a thing it was to incur the royal displeasure. Hands and legs were hacked off to loosen the prison irons, before the putrefying bodies were thrown, in heaps of four or five together, into shallow graves and given an insufficient covering of about a foot of earth. While these atrocities were being perpetrated, and whilst pigs and pariah dogs unearthed the corpses and battened on the loathsome feast thus plentifully provided for them by the inhumanity of the King, his consort, and his Ministers, high festival was being held within the palace. Theatrical performances were given continuously night after night; boats, containing musicians, were moored along the banks of the river; the King's steamers plied between Mandalay and Sagaing, taking passengers free of charge; and everything was done to distract the attention of the people from the awful horrors that were being perpetrated round about them.

There is good reason for supposing that this wholesale massacre was instigated by the Taingda Mingyi and a few of the other Ministers, in order to save themselves from the consequences that might ensue if some of their followers, then in jail, should obtain their freedom by the disclosure of facts implicating these high officials in the dacoities and intrigues which they had long been carrying on. The ringleader of those who were instigated to attempt their escape, and who were, therefore, the first to be shot down, was a dacoit *Bo*, or chief, named Yan Min, an infamous robber, whose hands had often been stained with the blood of murdered victims. When captured some time previously, he had been liberated in order to go and fight against the rebellious Shan chiefs ; but, instead of doing this, he again began plundering, and continued pillaging until his recapture was effected.

A public meeting was held in Rangoon on the 11th October, when feelings of indignation were expressed, and resolutions passed memorializing the Government of India to interfere immediately in Upper Burma, and either annex the kingdom of Ava or constitute it a protected State under some other ruler than Thibaw. As grounds for this removal were urged the misery and distress caused by King Thibaw's misgovernment and the mutual interdependence of Upper and Lower Burma as regarded tranquillity and property. But trade returns showed that, notwithstanding King Thibaw's misgovernment, the value of the total trade between British Burma and Ava for the four years after Thibaw's accession was, despite the previously mentioned fall in 1881–82, when his monopolies were in force, considerably greater than during the last four years of Mindôn's reign, the average annual values being respectively £3,224,814 and £3,061,174.

In October, 1884, the Rangoon Chamber of Commerce had also memorialized to the same effect as the public meeting, urging either annexation or a change of king, the former for choice ; and undoubtedly trade had for the moment become paralysed. At the time of the public meeting being held handbills in Burmese were posted and distributed throughout Rangoon, describing King Thibaw as an inveterate drunkard and a monster of cruelty, and declaring it was necessary to call upon the British Government to annex Ava. Native merchants and traders fell into a state of panic, and trade naturally became stagnant until it was known definitely what line of policy the Government of India intended to pursue. But it was obviously not in accordance with modern ideas of international relations to interfere with the internal government of a neighbouring country, or to annex that country merely because commerce therewith was not increasing so rapidly as British Chambers of Commerce might wish.

To a certain extent the British Government were undoubtedly responsible for the existing state of affairs. Had it not been for the preventive measures taken by them, Thibaw would have before this time been deposed in favour of either the Ngaungyan or the Myingun Prince. But King Thibaw was an ally of the British. Though he had not proved a friendly ally, yet he kept to the Treaty existing between the two nations. The character and antecedents of his Government were such that it was not possible for the British Government to offer any assistance which might seat him more firmly on his unstable throne; but, at the same time, neither the atrocities which had marked his reign, both shortly after his accession and also quite recently, nor the internal condition of anarchy and misgovernment within his realm, seemed to justify the armed intervention of the British Government with a view of either annexing the kingdom of Ava or of reducing it to the level of a feudatory State, nominally governed by the Nyaungyan or the Myingun Prince.

While these matters were still receiving the consideration of the Governor of India, the town of Bhamo, situated about 200 miles north of Mandalay and the centre of trade with Western China, was captured and sacked by Chinese marauders on 8th December, 1884. Fortunately there was no reason to believe that this seizure was instigated by the Chinese Government, as this would have introduced a still further complication into the already existing tangle of affairs. Under any circumstances, however, it meant the strangulation of the trade between Rangoon and Bhamo until the country around the latter town was once more in a settled state. Between Mandalay and the frontier the country was overrun with numerous and powerful bands of dacoits. No troops could be sent against them, as all the rabble soldiery was required for the operations towards Bhamo. The Governor of Magwe was murdered by one gang, while the Governor of Salémyo was attacked in open court by another, and narrowly escaped with his life. To avoid attacks and international questions the commanders of the British mail steamers were desired by rural Governors to anchor their vessels in the river under steam at night, in place of following the usual course of mooring alongside the bank.

Of all these various matters the Government of India had full cognizance. They were also aware of the sensible alteration which the conclusion of the Franco-Burmese Treaty of 15th January, 1885, made in the political situation, and they could not but be apprehensive that the presence of M. Haas as Consul of France at Mandalay was likely to increase their difficulties in dealing with the Court of Ava. Hence they were of opinion that something should be done to restore British influence at Mandalay.

The situation was surrounded with difficulties, the satisfactory solution of which was far from easy. It was not considered desirable to insist upon the reception of a British agent at Mandalay. After the withdrawal of Mr. St. Barbe in 1879, the Burmese Government were informed that any overtures for revision of existing relations, or for the return of a political officer, must proceed from them. And if, despite the altered circumstances, negotiations with either or both of these objects had been opened by the Government of India, this would have amounted to a cancellation of their intimation of 1879, and might easily have been misconstrued in Mandalay as a sign of timidity or even of actual weakness on the part of the Government of India. It could hardly be anticipated that a British agent would be suitably received and properly treated save under pressure of an authoritative demand supported by a display of armed force, for action of which nature the season was inopportune. Again, if any secret political alliance, involving ulterior designs inconsistent with British interests, had been concluded between France and Ava, the reception and courteous treatment of a British agent, while not necessarily re-establishing British influence, would have the effect of embarrassing the British position if more direct measures of interference became unavoidable. Under these circumstances the Government of India were unable to recommend to the British Cabinet any specific course of action. They could only watch the affairs of Ava with special care and anxiety, in the hope that before long some satisfactory solution of the difficulty might present itself. And such did present itself most opportunely and satisfactorily within less than six months from the time when this resolution of the Government of India was taken in March, 1885. So desirous were the Government of India to avoid irritating the susceptibilities of King Thibaw and his Ministers that they did not even send any letter of remonstrance regarding the September massacres as was proposed by Mr. (afterwards Sir Charles) Bernard, the Chief Commissioner of Burma. There was no proof that British subjects were sufferers in the course of the barbarities ; and it was thought doubtful that a letter of protest would have any useful result, even if it pointed out that, by keeping away from Burma other claimants to the throne of Ava, the Government of India were assisting in maintaining Thibaw in undisturbed possession of the crown.

The declaration of this policy of non-interference for the present created much discontent in commercial circles, and the Rangoon Chamber of Commerce addressed a circular letter to the various Chambers of Commerce in Great Britain, practically desiring them to bring pressure to bear on the British Cabinet. British Burma's geographical position, its ethnological conditions, its natural wealth, and the undeniable fact that public works and internal development were starved owing to more than one-third of the revenue raised in Burma being appropriated by India, were all used as arguments for cutting British Burma adrift from the Indian Empire and constituting it a Crown colony. Their appeal closed with the words :—

"Were British Burma a colony independent of India, not only

would much more have been done by this time to develop its own resources, but a firmer policy in connexion with the petty kings beyond British territory would have done much to extend British trade through a large part of Indo-China, and have made Rangoon one of the largest trade centres in the world."

This agitation for the constitution of British Burma as a Crown colony would undoubtedly have been pushed with vigour but for the favourable trend affairs took later on in the year 1885.

The British Government, while concurring in the opinion that the state of affairs in Ava did not justify armed intervention, considered that, both for commercial and political reasons, diplomatic representations should be resumed at Mandalay. Under the Yandabú Treaty of 1826, the Court of Ava were bound to receive a British Resident with an armed escort of fifty men ; and they were not cognizant of any communication having been made in 1879 which need act as a bar to the adoption of this measure whenever convenient. But the time and the manner of resuming direct representation were left to the discretion of the Government of India.

The apprehensions entertained as to the activity of the French Consul at Mandalay in obtaining *"concessions"* of various sorts, and in generally creating a commercial and political position for France quite incompatible with the previously existing predominating British interests, were almost immediately verified. Before the arrival of M. Haas, the Consul of France appointed to Mandalay in charge of French interests at the Court of Ava, a French engineer, M. Bonvillein, was reported to be negotiating for a lease of the whole of the ruby mines at Mogôk and Kyatpyin for fifteen years at an annual rental of three lacs of rupees (£20,000 a year). But the endeavours of Lord Lyons to obtain authentic information regarding this reported concession were unsuccessful.

M. Haas, who reached Mandalay in May, 1885, had not been there a couple of months before abundant evidence was forthcoming of the strong position which he and other French agents were endeavouring to establish for themselves with a view to acquiring a predominant influence in Ava, which might be utilized at some future time in joining hands with the French possessions on the upper reaches of the Red River. His first efforts were towards the establishment of a French bank, having a capital of twenty-five million francs, the running of a French flotilla on the Irrawaddy, the working of the ruby mines, and the opening out of a trade route from Mandalay through the Shan States to Upper Tonquin. His main idea was to grant loans to the King and in return therefor to obtain industrial concessions, on the ground that, even if Britain should ultimately be driven to annex the country, actual concessions to French subjects would be respected. In pursuance of this policy he urged upon the Court of Ava the necessity of avoiding any collision with the British Government; and he also advised them to ask for a Resident, as otherwise they ran great risk of having one forced upon them on terms they would not like. This temporizing was declined in favour of a continuation of the policy of procrastination, for the more wilful and ignorant among the King's advisers believed that if the tension with Russia had led to actual war the British would have lost India, and the kingdom of Ava would once more have extended to the sea-coast skirting the Bay of Bengal. It was the intention of the Burmese Government that, if the British had at this time their hands full of troubles, the opportunity would have been taken to pick a quarrel with them. M. Haas pointed out the folly of such a course before the Court of Ava had strengthened their position by forming alliances with other European nations. He pressed the Ministers to profit by the present attitude of the Government of India towards Ava in forming treaties with France, Italy, and Germany, and to get each of these countries to proclaim Ava as neutral territory. In pursuance of this astute advice the Pangyet Wundauk, one of the Ministers of the State Council who spoke French fluently, was accordingly despatched once more to Europe during the second half of July, 1885.

Finding the Ministers reluctant to follow his views, M. Haas, early in July, endeavoured to work upon the King through the *Tháthanábaing*, or Buddhist Archbishop, who had frequent personal interviews with Thibaw for enumerating the advantages to be derived from a close and intimate alliance with France. M. Haas offered to work with the Burmese Ministers in organizing the finances and the general administration of the country, promised the maintenance of the integrity of Ava, and gave assurances that when Tonquin became tranquil the Burmese would have free passage for anything they required.

So far as concerned preliminary contracts for concessions of a valuable nature, M. Haas' machinations were successful. By the middle of July terms of contracts for the construction of a French railway in Upper Burma, and for the establishment of a bank in Ava, had been arranged, and the preliminary contracts already signed and completed in Mandalay, and before the end of the month they were being taken by the Pangyet Wundauk, or "chief of the glassboilers," then accredited as Ambassador Plenipotentiary to reside permanently in Paris, for formal completion by the French Government. The first contract related to the construction of a railway from Mandalay to the British frontier of Toungoo—to the chief town in which district a line had just then been opened from Rangoon—at the joint expense of the French Government and of a company to be formed for the purpose. The capital was to be about £2,500,000, and the line was to be completed within seven years. The concession was to last for seventy years, when the line was to become the property of the Burmese Government. Interest on the capital outlay was meanwhile to be at the rate of $7\frac{1}{2}$ per cent., and its payment was to be secured by the hypothecation of the river customs and the earth-oil dues of the kingdom. The other contract was for the establishment, by the French Government and a company, of a Bank of Burma with a capital of rupees 25,000,000 (or £1,666,666). Loans were to be made to the King at the rate of 12 per cent., and other loans at the rate of 18 per cent. The bank was to be administered by a syndicate of French and Burmese officials. It was to issue notes, and to have the management of the ruby mines and the monopoly of *Letpet* or "pickled tea."

FRENCH MACHINATIONS IN AVA

If finally ratified and carried out, these agreements would have given the French Government, or a syndicate on which the French Government would have been strongly represented, practically the full control over the principal sources of revenue in Ava, and over the only route open for traffic from British ports to Western China. The consequences would have been disastrous to British trade, and to the interests of British Burma. If once firmly established in Ava, the French would, no doubt, have tried to induce other European nations to neutralize Ava and have the Mandalay river declared, like the Danube, open to vessels of all nationalities. As the proposed arrangements were still in an inchoate state, there was yet time to take steps either at Paris or Mandalay to prevent their conclusion, and the startling discovery of the letter of 15th January, 1885, from M. Jules Ferry to the Prime Minister of Ava, already referred to (page 63), thoroughly opened the eyes of the Government of India and the British Cabinet to the unfriendliness of France and the hostility of Ava. The Government of India unanimously recommended that the reception and proper treatment of a British Resident at Mandalay, to whose advice in all matters of foreign policy the Court of Ava should submit, ought to be insisted on; and that, if those terms were refused, measures of coercion should be adopted.

In an interview at the Foreign Office in London on 7th August, Lord Salisbury informed M. Waddington, the French Ambassador, of the information he had received regarding a proposed concession to French capitalists, which would include the control over the Post Office, railways, steam navigation, and various branches of revenue; and he pointed out that, if such an undertaking were attempted to be carried to any practical issue, the necessary consequence would be that the British Government would have to intervene and materially restrict the liberty and power of the King of Burma. M. Waddington replied that he had no knowledge of the alleged concession, but promised to make inquiries and communicate again on the subject. As no such communication was forthcoming, Lord Salisbury on 9th September desired Sir J. Walsham, *Chargé d'Affaires* at Paris, to bring to the notice of M. de Freycinet, the receipt of reports from authentic sources clearly indicating that the French consul at Mandalay was pursuing a policy which British interests could not permit, and that the King of Burma would not be allowed to carry out any commercial projects which could issue in the establishment of any preponderating influence in Ava other than that of the Indian Government. Before the end of September M. Waddington was authorized to inform Lord Salisbury that the French Government knew absolutely nothing about any such agreements, and that they had given no kind of authority for making them. If made at all, they must have been made at the instance of some speculative company. Early in October M. Haas was " *mis en disponibilité pour raison de santé*," and his machinations and intrigues in Mandalay were at an end. M. Haas is now, or was until quite recently, Consul of France at Chunking in Szechuan, in the heart of the Yangtse valley—*absit omen.*

While these diplomatic representations were being conducted an occurrence took place, most opportunely, in August, 1885, which demanded even more prompt and decided action, while at the same time it had the unquestionable advantage of fixing the quarrel with the King of Ava on an issue with which the French Government could not under any circumstances possibly admit themselves to be mixed up. Hence their keen national susceptibilities could not in any way be touched by the action now forced upon, and about to be taken by, the British Cabinet.

For many years back the Ningyan teak forests covering the low hills north of our frontier above Toungoo, and drained by the Sittang river and its tributaries, had been worked by the Bombay-Burma Trading Corporation, Limited, a large Bombay joint-stock concern, whose chief offices and mills were in Rangoon, although direct and ultimate control lay with the firm of Messrs. Wallace Brothers, of Austin Friars, London. In April, 1885, representations were made by the Corporation to the Chief Commissioner of Burma that their working of

THE *CASUS BELLI*

the forests was being seriously impeded by action which was being taken on a charge, alleged to have been false, of having bribed the Governor of Ningyan to connive at the King being deprived of the full amount of revenue due on the timber extracted. In reply to a communication addressed to him on the subject by the Chief Commisioner, the Foreign Minister stated that the Corporation's foresters had extracted 80,000 logs, while only 32,000 had been paid for. Facilities were given for the examination of the Toungoo Forest Office records showing the number of teak logs imported from Upper Burma, and the Corporation were prepared to produce the acquittances in full signed by their foresters. It was likewise pointed out that the apparent shortage in actual revenue paid might be due to the fact of the working of the forests having taken place under three separate contracts. In 1880 the Corporation contracted to pay the King at fixed rates per log for all full-sized logs extracted; under another contract, of 1882, they paid a lump sum of one lac of rupees (£6,666) for all the undersized and inferior logs rejected under the contract of 1880; and in a third contract, of 1883, they agreed to pay from October, 1884, a lump sum annually of 3½ lacs (£23,333) for all full-sized logs and of one lac (£6,666) for undersized and inferior logs. The records of the Forest Department at Toungoo did not then make any attempt to classify the logs as to size and quality; and there was nothing to show that any given log came under the category falling under the contract of 1880, or of 1882, or of 1883. No reply was received to this letter, but the *Hlutdaw*, or High Court of Ava, on 12th August, 1885, delivered judgment that the Corporation had defrauded the King of revenue amounting to nearly 11 lacs of rupees (£73,333) and consequently fined them the double of that amount, while they further decreed the payment to foresters in the Corporation's employ of sums aggregating about five lacs of rupees (£33,333). In deciding thus the Ministers based their finding entirely upon the figures of the Toungoo Forest Office returns, ignoring the lump sum contracts of 1882 and 1883 and the records maintained by the Ningyan officials. The Cor-

poration were ordered to pay an amount of 23 lacs
(£153,333) in four equal monthly instalments, otherwise
their timber in the Ningyan forests would be seized to
the extent of the default.

The Corporation pleaded that under no construction
of their leases could such a sum as 11 lacs (£73,333) be
justly due from them, that they could not pay the enormous fine demanded, and that they feared their leases
and their property then in the forests would be taken
from them and transferred to others. It was also stated
on good authority that the French Consul had offered to
take the forests if the Corporation's lease were cancelled ;
and it is certain that M. Haas and M. Bonvillein were
intimately concerned with the proceedings of the Burmese Government.

These matters having been duly reported to the
Government of India and the British Cabinet, intimation
was, on 28th August, given to the Court of Ava that
the British Government insisted on British subjects in
the position of the Bombay-Burma Corporation receiving
a fair trial in place of being, perhaps unjustly, ruined by
the arbitrary imposition of an enormous fine, or by the
sudden cancellation of their leases. The suspension of
the realization of the decree of the *Hlutdaw* and of the
order as to cancellation of the Corporation's leases was
desired until the matter in dispute between the King's
forest officers and the Corporation could be fully investigated and adjusted ; and an offer was made to appoint
a judicial officer of experience to investigate the facts at
Ningyan and Toungoo, if the Court of Ava were willing
to abide by the decision of such an arbitrator.

It was not till the middle of October that a reply to
this communication was received from the Burmese
Government. They questioned the right of the Government of India to raise the subject, and very definitely
declined to agree to the proposed arbitration or to suspend action against the Corporation, whose rafts they
had begun to stop on 20th September, two days before
the first instalment of the heavy fine was demanded.
With the unanimous consent of his colleagues and the full
approval of Lord Salisbury's Cabinet, the Viceroy, Lord

BRITISH ULTIMATUM SENT

Dufferin, authorized the Chief Commissioner of Burma to despatch an ultimatum to King Thibaw, demanding the acceptance of certain definite proposals for the settlement of existing disputes and the establishment of satisfactory relations with Ava, and warning them that in the event of the proposals not being accepted the Government of India would take the matter into their own hands. The terms of this ultimatum, despatched on 22nd October, were the suitable reception of a Resident with free access to the King, the entire suspension of proceedings against the Bombay-Burma Corporation until the arrival of the Resident, and the acceptance of a permanent Resident with a proper guard for his protection. The Court of Ava were also warned that they would be expected in future to regulate their external affairs in accordance with the advice of the Government of India (as in the case of Afghanistan) and to grant proper facilities for the development of British trade with Western China through Bhamo. Simultaneously with the despatch of the ultimatum, troops were moved over from India to Burma in sufficient numbers to convince the Court of Ava that the British Government were in earnest, that any injury to British subjects or to their property would not be overlooked, and that undisguised hostilities to the British Empire would no longer be permitted. The ultimatum was despatched by a special steamer, the *Ashley Eden*, to Mandalay so as to reach there on or before the 30th October, and intimation was given that, if unmolested, she would remain there till 5th November, in order to bring back the King's reply. She was to leave Mandalay without fail on the morning of the 6th November; and, if she brought no satisfactory reply to Rangoon by the evening of the 10th, the British Government would proceed to take such further action as seemed fit.

King Thibaw and his Ministers little imagined that during 1878 a plan of campaign against Mandalay had been drawn up in the Military Department of the Government of India and had been carefully corrected and revised from time to time, that orders had already been issued to Major-General Prendergast commanding the extraordinary troops in Burma to carry out these military operations as soon as he received his orders to cross the frontier, or that a political officer had already, during October, been selected, and four young civil officers warned for service to accompany the army and arrange for pacifying the country through the native officials, under the orders of the military commandants. The Burmese Government were utterly unprepared for war, and never realized that the British Government would really proceed to extremities.

The reply to the ultimatum was duly received on the 9th November. It was tantamount to a refusal or evasion of the three terms. It declined to discuss or negotiate the case against the Corporation, and said that if the British Government wished to re-establish an agent, he would "*be permitted to come and go as in former times.*" As for external affairs, they intended to manage these for themselves, intimating boldly that "*friendly relations with France, Italy, and other States have been, are being, and will be maintained*"; while, with regard to the opening up of trade between Rangoon and Western China, commerce would "*be assisted in conformity with the customs of the country.*"

Simultaneously with this announcement, King Thibaw on 7th November issued a proclamation (see page 83) throughout his dominions, calling upon all his officials and subjects to expel the English, who threatened war and intended to destroy the religion and the national customs of the Burmese, and announcing his intention of taking the field in person if the British attacked his kingdom, of exterminating them, and of annexing their territory.

On 10th November the Viceroy telegraphed to the Secretary of State, proposing, with the approval of the British Government, to commence hostile operations at once. Next day the short reply was flashed back, "*Please instruct General Prendergast to advance on Mandalay at once*"; and the third Burmese war was begun. Had action been delayed, a situation most preju-dicial to the commercial and political interests of Britain would have been created in Upper Burma, and with which it might hereafter have been difficult to deal. As it was, the decree of the French Senate on 24th November, 1885, authorizing the ratification of the Franco-Burmese Convention of 15th January, 1885 (which might possibly have caused complications), was promulgated too late to save King Thibaw from downfall. The ancient kingdom of Ava was ultimately ruined, mainly through French machinations, and through Thibaw leaning on the broken reed of covert French political support. It was not until the extremest limits of forbearance had been exceeded that the declaration of war took place. Under the circumstances there was no other course left open. To have prolonged forbearance further, in the face of the many provocations received, would have soon brought about a crisis which would have had to be met under conditions more embarrassing to Britain, and more likely to curtail heavier sufferings upon the people of Upper Burma than they were now about to be called upon to endure. Major-General Prendergast was definitely instructed to remember that he was about to operate in a country inhabited by a people kindred to our own Burmese subjects in race, in religion, and in material interests, and that he was not attacking a hostile nation, but a perverse and impracticable Court. After the attitude of France, and the machinations of M. Haas, the French Consul, and other French subjects, nothing short of annexation had become possible : for the Nyaungyan Prince, the only member of the royal house of Alaung Payá whose abilities and character would have deserved serious consideration as to raising him to the status of the ruler of a protected State, was now dead.

Chapter IV

ON 21st October, 1885, the Government of India
ordered an expeditionary force to proceed to
Burma in readiness for active service in Ava, if necessary.
It was under the command of Major-General (afterwards
Sir Harry) Prendergast, V.C., and was concentrated at
Thayetmyo, the frontier military station on the Irra-
waddy river. On the 13th November the orders for its
advance on Mandalay were issued ; and on the 14th the
frontier was crossed, the line of advance being up the
Irrawaddy.

Early in November General Prendergast had been
made aware of the nature of the ultimatum despatched
to the Court of Ava, and had been warned to hold
himself in readiness to immediately carry out the plan of
operations prescribed by the Commander-in-Chief, Sir
Frederick Roberts, V.C. (now Earl Roberts, K.G.), in the
event of intimation being given that the reply from
Mandalay was unsatisfactory. From the moment of
entering Avan territory General Prendergast was invested with supreme political as well as military
authority, while Colonel (afterwards Sir Edward) Sladen
and some junior officers of the British Burma Commission were attached to the force as political officers
under his orders. Explicit instructions were given to
him that Mandalay was to be occupied and King Thibaw
dethroned, and that no offer of submission was to be
accepted which could affect the movement of the troops.
These facts were to be definitely made known to all the
Burmese authorities, and to the population, during the

progress towards the capital. In the event of annexation being decided on, Mr. (afterwards Sir Charles) Bernard would be directed to proceed to Mandalay and assume civil control ; but, in the meantime, General Prendergast was to garrison every important fort or town and leave there a civil officer who should, under the orders of the commandant of the troops, place himself in communication with the local Burmese officials, and through them pacify and administer the country, giving assurances that King Thibaw would not remain in power. As the objects of the expedition were the occupation of Mandalay and the dethronement of Thibaw, these results were to be gained bloodlessly, if possible, by the simple display of force. Any conflict with the population at large was to be avoided, and everthing was to be done to try and secure, without bloodshed, their acquiescence in the administrative and political changes that would be found necessary.

While these instructions were being forwarded from Calcutta to Rangoon, King Thibaw had uttered a feeble but vainglorious war-cry throughout the kingdom of Ava. Following immediately on his rejection of the British proposals on 7th November, 1885, he issued a bombastic proclamation to the following effect :—

" To the headmen of all towns and villages, heads of cavalry, chief umpires and referees, shield-bearers, heads of jails, heads of gold and silver revenues, mine workers, arbitrators, forest officials, and all the subjects and inhabitants of the royal territories :

" Those heretics, the English *Kala* (*i.e.*, non-mongolian barbarians), having most harshly made demands likely to impair and destroy our religion, violate our national customs, and degrade our race, are making a display and preparation as if about to wage war against our State. Reply has been sent to them in conformity with the usages of great nations, and in words which are just and regular. But if these heretic *Kala* should come and attempt to molest or disturb the State in any way, His Majesty the King, watchful that the interests of religion and of the State shall not suffer, will himself march forth with his generals, captains, and lieutenants, with large forces of infantry, cavalry, artillery, and elephants, and with the might of his army will by land and water efface these heretic *Kala*, and conquer and annex their territories. All the inhabitants of the royal kingdom of Ava are enjoined not to be alarmed or disturbed on account of the hostility of these heretic *Kala*, and they are not to avoid them by leaving the country. They are to continue to carry on their occupations as usual in a peaceful manner. The local officials are, each in his own town or village, to watch and see that there are no thefts, dacoities, or other State crimes. The royal troops now being sent forth will not be collected, as formerly, by forcibly pressing into service all who can be found : but the royal troops now banded into regiments in Mandalay will be sent forth to attack, destroy, and annex. The local officials are not to impress forcibly into service any one who may not wish to serve ; but to uphold the religion, the national honour, and the country's interests, will bring threefold religious merit—good of religion, good of the King, and good of the nation—and will result in leading along the path of the celestial regions to *Neikban* (Nirvana). Whoever joins and serves zealously will receive money and royal rewards, and will serve in the capacity for which he may be found fit. Loyal officials are to search for volunteers and others who may wish to serve, and are to send lists of them to the provincial governments."

General Prendergast was also, on the day on which the advance was ordered, provided with a Proclamation to be issued to all priests, officials, traders, agriculturists, and other inhabitants of the tracts he passed through ; but it was in a very different strain from Thibaw's manifesto. After briefly narrating the circumstances under which the Government of India had found themselves compelled to undertake the expedition, and their consequent intention to dethrone him, it concluded by saying :—

"It is the earnest desire of the Viceroy and Governor-General ot India that bloodshed should be avoided, and that the peaceful inhabitants of all classes should be encouraged to pursue their usual callings without fear of molestation. None will have anything to apprehend so long as you do not oppose the passage of the troops. . . . Your private rights, your religion, and national customs will be scrupulously respected, and the Government of India will recognize the services of all amongst you, whether officials or others, who show zeal in assisting the British authorities to preserve order."

The expeditionary force comprised a Naval Brigade, under Captain R. Woodward, R.N., formed of detachments from the ships of Admiral Sir Frederick Richards' squadron, then lying at Rangoon, three regiments of British Infantry, seven regiments of native Infantry, six companies of Sappers and Miners, one Field Battery and two Garrison Batteries of Royal Artillery, and one British and two native Mountain Batteries. Its total strength was 9,467 men, with 77 guns, of which 27 were quick-firing machine guns. Piloted by the river-steamer

OPERATIONS ON THE IRRAWADDY

I.M.S. *Irrawaddy*, the expeditionary force ascended in twenty-four steamers and twenty-three flats chartered from the Irrawaddy Flotilla Company. The land forces were divided into three brigades, respectively commanded by Brigadiers-General H. H. Foord, G. S. White, V.C., and F. B. Norman. The campaign commenced by the *Irrawaddy*, which crossed the frontier about noon on the 14th November, engaging and capturing a King's steamer, which was sent down to Thayetmyo in charge of the launch *Kathleen*, while the *Irrawaddy* brought down the two flats that she had been towing. One of these had been prepared for sinking in the river, and had rows of posts, each ten feet high by six inches square, let into the deck and sharpened into points which must inevitably have destroyed any shallow-bottomed river steamer that ran against them. When the steamer was shelled, and its deck cleared for action, the crew jumped overboard and fled, accompanied by Commotto, one of two Italian adventurers (Commotto and Molinari) who had become the hirelings of the King. Commotto had been allotted the task of blocking the river near the frontier, which he was on his way to accomplish, while Molinari was charged with strengthening the fortifications below Mandalay. From the papers left on the steamer by Commotto information was obtained as to the King's military preparations, which corroborated the news given by the commanders of the last two Irrawaddy Flotilla Company's steamers which had run the gauntlet of the forts in their latest trip down stream. On the 16th November the Burmese stockades erected at Nyaungbinmaw and Sinbaungwè, positions held respectively on the right and the left banks of the river, were carried without any serious fighting. On the following day the forts of Minhla on the right bank, and Gwegyaung Kamyo on the left bank were captured after some sharp fighting. The former was strengthened and garrisoned, while the latter was demolished. The ordinary garrison of Gwegyaung Kamyo was 700, but it had been reinforced by 1,000 men three days previously. They fled on the appearance at close quarters of the British infantry, who had marched

85

seven miles through the jungle to the rear of the fort. On the right bank three native regiments landed, and after breaking down two outer lines of defence stormed Minhla fort after three hours' fighting. The Burmese, well concealed, fired rapidly, and disputed every inch of the way to the redoubt; but, when once it was rushed, they fled from the fort and their rout was complete. The town of Minhla was burned down, being accidentally set fire to by the shells thrown at the redoubt. This was the only place where anything like stubborn resistance was offered to the British arms. Mr. Phayre, who had been Assistant Resident at Mandalay until October, 1879, was left behind as civil officer. The people and the priests appeared to willingly accept the new situation, though the high officials could not be expected to submit till they knew that Mandalay had fallen. At Magwe, on the 20th, Commotto and Molinari, the two Italians who had guaranteed to Thibaw that British troops would not be able to pass the frontier forts constructed and fortified by them, surrendered themselves as prisoners of war.

On 22nd November shots were exchanged with the batteries at Nyaungu, just above Pagán, but the works were soon abandoned by the Burmese and dismantled, the guns being spiked. The Burmese soldiers, who numbered 1,000, had been plundering and robbing all the villages in the vicinity. At Pagán another military post was established, with a civil officer to initiate the work of administration.

At Pakokko, which was passed on the 24th, about 1,000 soldiers from Mandalay had been stationed, but they ran away on the approach of the British. That same afternoon Myingyan, a large and important town near the mouth of the Chindwin river, was reached. A large Burmese force was reported to be holding the forts there. While the big guns were engaging the batteries on the river's bank, a body of about 2,000 men, dressed in red, white, and magenta coats, and with chiefs having golden umbrellas held over them, were seen on rising ground some three miles inland. These were the headquarters and the reserve of the Burmese army, but the force took no part in the fighting. Before operations could be resumed next morning the Burmese withdrew, and the twenty-one guns forming the two batteries were destroyed. On the previous evening the commander of the Burmese forces, the Hlethin Atwin Wun, who was considered to be the best of Thibaw's generals, telegraphed to the King that he had gained a great victory over the British; but the truth was soon known in the capital. This easy capture of Myingyan, where 6,000 picked troops are said to have been sent, practically decided the campaign; for it was afterwards ascertained that if the British had received any check here, the Burmese intended to hold out at Ava and Sagaing, and compel the expeditionary force to undertake siege operations. A garrison and a civil officer were left at Myingyan. Many Burmese, who had previously fled from the town while it was in the hands of Thibaw's troops, came in to welcome the British arrival. The head *Pôngyi* (or religious recluse) said the town had been an abode of misery whilst the soldiery was there, that two hundred ponies had been requisitioned for the King's cavalry, that robbery had been prevalent, that property had been stolen, and women had been dragged from their houses and ravished.

On the 26th November Yandabú, the extreme limit of the advance of the British troops during the first Burmese war in 1826, was passed, and on that afternoon, near the village of Nazu, the State barge, paddled by forty-four men, came flying a flag of truce at the bow and the King's ensign at the stern. Seated in the bows and wearing enormous Shan hats were the Kyaukmyaung Atwin Wun and the Wetmasút Wundauk, who came as Envoys bearing a memorandum from the Prime Minister. Coming on board without their shoes, they delivered this document to General Prendergast and Colonel Sladen. It was unsigned by the King, but bore the royal peacock seal. Beginning naïvely with the statement that the Burmese Government were under the impression that the former friendly conditions would still prevail, and that they could therefore not believe the British would make war against Upper Burma, it declared the King of Burma ready to grant all that was demanded in the ultimatum, desired the cessation of hostilities, and offered to enter into a treaty. Under the instructions upon which he was acting, General Prendergast could only reply that no armistice could be granted, but that if King Thibaw surrendered himself, his army, and his capital, and if the European residents in Mandalay were all found uninjured in life and property, the King's life would be spared and his family respected. A reply to this was demanded before 4 a.m. on the following morning. Meanwhile, the fleet continued to advance, and was anchored for the night off the village of Kyauktalôn, about seven miles below Ava.

As no answer was forthcoming, the fleet moved on at daylight; and orders, with plans attached, were issued for the attack on Ava. About half-past ten o'clock, when the proposed landing place was in view, the State barge was seen putting out with a flag of truce. The same Envoys this time brought a telegram from the King conceding unconditionally all the demands made on the previous day, ordering the Ministers conducting the military operations at Sagaing and Ava not on any account to fire on the British, and directing them to keep all the troops quiet.

At Ava fort some 8,000 troops, only about two-thirds of whom were armed with rifles or guns and the rest with spears, swords, and bills, were collected to oppose the advance of the British. General Prendergast insisted on this portion of the army laying down their arms, but the Commander of the forces, the Bohmu Kin Atwin Wun, who was senior in rank to either of the Envoys, refused to do so without a direct order from the King. Some delay occurred in finding and buoying an opening in the channel through the barrier, but by the time the British fleet had been placed by signal in the best positions in fighting order and the demand again pressed for the immediate surrender of the arms, the royal mandate had been telegraphed from Mandalay, eleven miles distant. Most unfortunately only some 550 of the rifles and muskets were then obtained; for, as soon as the

ARRIVAL AT MANDALAY

King's orders for the surrender became known, large numbers of the soldiers went off at once in all directions before British troops could be landed to ensure the disarmament of the whole force. The forts at Sagaing and Thambayádaing on the right bank of the river above Ava, likewise surrendered without a blow and were disarmed, though here again only about 400 muskets were collected. From Ava fort 28 guns were carried off as trophies ; while 32 were destroyed at Sagaing, and 14 at Thambayádaing in dismantling the forts and river bank batteries. With the exception of three transports left with the troops ordered to land and complete the disarmament of the forts and batteries, the fleet moved on to Mandalay, and arrived there at 10 o'clock on the morning of 28th November, 1885. Crowds of Burmese watched the arrival of the force from the banks, and appeared only too pleased to obey the royal mandate that had been issued prohibiting any opposition to the landing. Information was at once obtained that the King had been in the palace up to nine o'clock in the morning, and that the city was quiet.

At eleven o'clock the arrival of the British force was notified to the Prime Minister and intimation given that, in accordance with the terms of the previous day's communication received at Ava, the immediate surrender of the capital and the King was expected. He was further informed that, unless a reply was received by noon, the troops would land and be employed as circumstances might demand. As it was not until after midday that the Kinwun Mingyi's reply was received, to the effect that he would be on board the *Doowoon* to consult with General Prendergast and Colonel Sladen, the troops were landed at 1.30 p.m., all regiments being ordered to take their colours and bands.

The royal city of Mandalay is situated about three to four miles to the east of the Irrawaddy, with which there is connexion through the outer town along four main roads (still named A, B, C, and D roads) running due east from the river. The first brigade, under General Foord, marched by A road, and secured the southern and eastern gates of the city. The third brigade, under

General Norman, marched along C road, and secured
the western and northern city gates and the west and
north gates of the palace enclosure. The second brigade,
under General White, accompanied by Colonel Sladen,
proceeded by C road, entered the city by the south gate,
and secured the south and east gates of the palace enclosure. At the five main gates of the city, from which
bridges led over the broad moat surrounding the city
wall, the guards were disarmed and allowed to go to
their homes, being replaced by British and native soldiers.
As the troops marched through the western suburbs the
population thronged the roads, gazing in quiet amazement,
as if looking on at some ceremonial festival.

Knowing the road, Colonel Sladen, who had been
selected as political officer on the strength of his having
long since been British Resident in Mandalay, rode with
guides ahead of the troops in the hope of meeting the
Prime Minister. Hearing that the Kinwun Mingyi had
taken another route, Colonel Sladen merely sent a
mounted scout to tell him to come as quickly as possible
to the southern city gate. Without waiting for the
Prime Minister, Colonel Sladen entered the southern
city gate at 3 p.m., and proceeded, without interference
or obstruction, through the city to the eastern or main
entrance of the stockaded palace enclosure, accompanied
only by Mr. Nicholas, his clerk and interpreter, and
Commander Morgan, of one of the Irrawaddy Flotilla
Company's steamers, who was well acquainted with the
interior of the city and the palace. When they had
waited here for a few minutes, the Kinwun Mingyi was
descried coming in full haste on an elephant. After a
formal greeting, he asked Colonel Sladen to accompany
him alone into the palace enclosure, and not on any account to let the troops enter. Leaving a note for
General Prendergast, asking that the troops should not
be ordered to enter before again hearing from him,
Colonel Sladen entered the *Hlutdaw*, or Great Council
Chamber, and was shortly afterwards received by King
Thibaw in the Hall of Audience, as if at an ordinary
public reception. Queen Supayálat, who had been
watching the approach of the troops from a lofty wooden

outlook tower, at the south-east corner of the palace buildings, and the Queen-mother (Dowager Queen Sinpyumashin) were present, while the usual palace guards were in attendance. With very little preamble the King surrendered himself and his kingdom ; but he asked to be granted a day or two for preparation in place of being taken away suddenly, and he proposed meanwhile to leave the palace and go into a summer-house in the royal garden within the enclosure. In reply he was informed that General Prendergast was in supreme command to carry out the orders of the Government of India, but that he would not be interfered with in his palace that night, nor would the immediate palace precincts be interfered with ; and it was arranged that the King should now consider himself a prisoner, and surrender himself formally to General Prendergast on the following day. Thibaw having agreed to this, and the Ministers guaranteeing to deliver him safely next morning or pay the penalty with their lives, Colonel Sladen, about 5 p.m., returned to the eastern gate of the outer palace enclosure and communicated the news of the King's unconditional surrender to General Prendergast, and his intention to surrender himself personally and formally on the following day. The Hampshire Regiment, the 1st Madras Pioneers, and the Hazara Mountain Battery, which had all come provided with three days' provisions, cooking utensils, bakery, slaughterhouse establishment, and entrenching equipment, were left under the command of Brigadier-General White to guard the palace for the night, being ordered to enter and occupy the outer enclosure as far as the *Hlutdaw* and the royal Red Gate, or main entrance to the inner palace. The rest of the troops returned to the transports in the evening.

So far everything had gone well; but an inconceivably weak permission was now accorded, which led to an enormous amount of looting. At the instance of Colonel Sladen and the Ministers, who requested that palace women should be allowed exit and entrance through the western gate of the palace enclosure leading to the Queen's apartments, General Prendergast, against his first and better judgement, ordered that women were to be allowed to go in and out of the west gate of the palace. It was known that King Thibaw, in place of carrying out his bombast as to heading his army and effacing the British, had made arrangements for flight. Fifty elephants, with trusty friends, were waiting for him at Shwemaga, twelve miles north of Mandalay, to convey him to Shwebo (Môksóbo), the birthplace and the burialplace of Alaung Payá, the illustrious founder of the royal family, Môksóbo being the dynastic stronghold of their race. It was probably only the condition of Queen Supayálat, then approaching a confinement, that had hindered him from fleeing on the previous day. Aware of this, General Prendergast pointed out the danger which existed of the King passing out in the disguise of a woman, when one of the Ministers calmly proposed that the sentries should make personal examination of each individual passing in or out. In a weak moment, however, General Prendergast gave the required consent. The result was that, out of the 300 female attendants in the royal apartments, only seventeen remained faithful until the next morning, while crowds of common women from the city poured in and out all night through, looting from the royal apartments every valuable thing of small size they could lay hands on. How such a proposal from the Burmese Minister could have been supported by Colonel Sladen and sanctioned by General Prendergast it is impossible to understand. It was a blunder, and was subsequently admitted to have been one.

Almost entirely abandoned by their attendants,—for most of the guards of the previous evening had withdrawn, as well as most of the maids of honour,—and seeing the looting carried on. by the female scum of the city, the King and the Queens fell into a state of panic. Early on the 29th Colonel Sladen, having passed the night in the *Hlutdaw*, received a message from the Taingda Mingyi, who had remained with a strong guard inside the palace in charge of Thibaw. The Mingyi had himself come to say the King was in a state of panic, and fancied that soldiers would break into the palace and

kill him.   Proceeding into the palace, Colonel Sladen
found the King, Queens, and Queen-mother almost un-
attended, while women of low class were streaming in
through all the western portions of the palace.   Whilst
Colonel Sladen accompanied the Queens and their Queen-
mother to see what was going on in their private apartments, the King collected together a large quantity of
gold and jewelled vessels used on State occasions.   For
their protection Colonel Sladen went to the palace gate
and called an officer and twenty-five men of the Hampshire Regiment, who were dropped as sentries as each
of the several royal apartments was passed through.
Whilst this was taking place, King Thibaw, his two
Queens and their mother (Dowager-Queen Sinpyumashin) retired to a small summer-house at the edge of
the royal gardens.   A cordon of sentries was placed
round this little building, and the King remained a
prisoner here till his formal surrender in the course of
the afternoon.   Abandoned by all his Ministers, and deserted by most of the personal attendants and servants
of the palace, the King complained bitterly.

At a quarter-past ten o'clock on the morning of
29th November, 1885, Major-General Prendergast, attended by his personal escort of an officer, ten mounted
infantry and four orderlies, and accompanied by Brigadier-
General Norman commanding a brigade composed of the
Mounted Corps, the 9–1st (Cinque Ports) Royal Artillery,
the Royal Welsh Fusiliers and the 23rd Madras Infantry, proceeded to the eastern or royal gate on the
far side of the city, and marched through the latter to the
royal Red Gate or main entrance of the inner palace
enclosure, where he arrived at one o'clock.   The four
Mingyi, or principal Ministers of the Great State Council,
were sent for, and accompanied the General, his staff
and Colonel Sladen to an interview with the King.

Headed by the Taingda Mingyi, who, though not
the Prime Minister, had been placed in charge of the
King on the previous evening, the procession wended
its way through the south-east corner of the palace
buildings, past the Hall of Audience, by the Queen's
watch-tower and through passages in the palace towards

the little summer-house in the garden, near the south-western corner of the royal apartments.   Here the King was found seated with his two Queens (Supayálat and Supayágale) and the Dowager Queen Sinpyumashin, and gave himself up to General Prendergast.   The King was told he would have to leave at once and go on board a steamer.   He begged for delay, which could not be granted; and preparations were made for immediate departure.   As soon as these had been completed, the dethroned King walked with his two Queens and the Queen-mother, the latter heading the procession, through the palace buildings, down the stairs in front of the Hall of Audience, through the royal Red Gate, and past the *Hlutdaw* to the main road outside the palace enclosure. From the steps of the palace to the main gate of the outer stockade the cortège passed through double files of the Hampshire Regiment, and out on to the roadway. Here two Burmese carriages, or box-like two-wheeled carts, drawn by bullocks, had been provided for the King and his suite, while the remainder of his very scanty following, consisting of only a few female attendants, either walked or were carried in doolies.   This was the first occasion on which King Thibaw had ever been out-side of his palace since, more than seven years before, he had been declared heir apparent by the palace intrigue and *coup d'état* of his mother-in-law, Sinpyumashin.

At the main gate of the outer palace enclosure Brigadier-General Norman received the King and es-corted him to the river.   The procession consisted of the 23rd Madras Infantry, leading, the 9–1st (Cinque Ports) Royal Artillery, then the King and suite, while the Royal Welsh Fusiliers closed the rear.   A move was made at half-past three o'clock, eight white or royal umbrellas being held over the King and the Queens, in place of the nine to which he had been entitled whilst King of Ava.   This still exceeded by one, however, the number permissible to any of the reigning Sawbwa or feudatory Princes of the Shan States.   At first the number of Burmese onlookers was small, and no de-monstration was made.   As darkness came on and the river was approached, the crowds along the roadsides and at the corners of cross-roads became very large. Here and there the wailings of women were to be heard, and the crowd, in their anxiety to see the royal prisoners, showed slight signs of impatience. Nothing amounting to a demonstration was made, and there was no attempt at a rescue. At a quarter-past six o'clock the King and his retinue were safely placed on board the steamer *Thooreah* (" the Sun "), the river bank being lined with two companies of the Liverpool Regiment and the Naval Brigade. On receiving its royal freight the *Thooreah* put out into midstream, and left for Rangoon the following morning. The escort for the voyage consisted of two companies of the Liverpool Regiment under Colonel Le Mesurier. The Kinwun Mingyi, the Prime Minister, other two Ministers of State, and three Privy Councillors, were deported to Rangoon along with the King; but not one of them all was willing to accompany his royal master into exile. Without again putting foot on the soil of Burma, Thibaw was transferred, with his two Queens, to an ocean steamer at Rangoon on 10th December, and taken *viâ* Madras to Ratnagiri fort on the Bombay coast, where he still remains a prisoner of State. The Dowager Queen was sent to Tavoy, in Lower Burma.

On the evening of 29th November the city and the suburbs were much disturbed. The city, that is to say, the portion of Mandalay lying within the moat and walls, consisted of about eighteen to twenty thousand houses, containing a population estimated at from ninety to a hundred thousand souls; while about as many were to be found in the suburbs, situated chiefly between the city and the river on the west. Towards sundown Brigadier-General Foord marched in command of the 21st and 25th Madras Infantry from the transports to the city for the purpose of holding the five gates facing the bridges over the moat. Four companies were placed on each of the four sides of the city walls, the guard-houses were occupied, and strong patrols were constantly sent out during the night through the city and suburbs. Frequent shots were heard in all directions, but there was nothing like any general rising. On entering the south gate of the city, about 9 p.m., the 21st Madras Infantry were fired on, and returned the fire with section volleys. The French and Italian consulates and the neighbouring residences of Europeans, near the south-west of the city, were protected by a company of native troops. Besides the above precautions, the 12th Madras Infantry, under Colonel Rowlandson, posted guards and patrolled all night between B and C roads for the protection of the suburbs. That night a celebrated diamond was stolen by the ex-King's troops from the forehead of the great image of Gaudama in the *Atumashi*, or " Incomparable " Pagoda, situated to the north-east of the city at some distance beyond the British picquets : while another large diamond and a valuable golden bejewelled necklace were also stolen from the *Payágyi*, the " Great " or Arakan Pagoda, between two and three miles south-west of the city.

Next day, on 30th November, additional precautions were taken for preserving order. The city and the suburbs were patrolled day and night, and all men found carrying arms were taken and delivered to the Provost Marshal, whose quarters were at the southern city gate. Orders were issued for observance in the case of incendiary fires, and a committee was appointed to take over and secure all property found in the palace. That night the news of the almost bloodless victory was known in London, and the Viceroy, Lord Dufferin, received the congratulations of Her Majesty and Her Majesty's Government for the success with which the immediate objects of the military expedition had been attained.

On 1st December a proclamation was issued notifying King Thibaw's surrender, dethronement, and deportation, and intimating that, until the will of Her Majesty the Queen-Empress was known, the civil and military administration of the country was vested in General Prendergast, who desired to carry on the Government with the aid of such of the Ministers, Governors, and other officers of State at present in office as agreed to remain and perform loyal service to the British Government. This provisional *Hlutdaw*, or Council of State, included two *Mingyi* or Ministers of State, four *Atwin-*

wun or Privy Councillors, and seven *Wundauk* or Under Secretaries. Special notification was made that the *Pôngyi* or religious body would be protected, and allowed to carry on their religious duties unhindered, and that all religious buildings and their precincts would be preserved, while Buddhism would remain the national religion, and would be respected. Provided they remained quiet and peaceable, all were to remain unmolested ; and all were to be permitted to engage in their national sports and to follow the customs of the country. The Governors of districts (*Wundauk, Wun*), judges (*Nakán*), town magistrates (*Myoôk*), village headmen (*Thugyi*), and the officers (*Bo, Sitkè*), performing miscellaneous military-police duties, were provisionally and temporarily retained on condition that they should faithfully discharge their duties under the orders of the British civil officers, and should do their utmost to suppress crime, allay public anxiety, and pacify the towns and villages under their charge. Dacoits, robbers, and vagrants were to be arrested and sent to the British civil officer. The administration of the country being thus temporarily vested in the *Hlutdaw* or State Council of Burmese Ministers and officials, under the presidency of Colonel Sladen and under the orders and control of General Prendergast, their first act was to proclaim a general disarmament of the civil population. None except members of the Council and its staff were allowed to possess other arms than the common *Da* or bill, in ordinary use for all domestic, agricultural, and forest purposes, unless they received special passes. The inhabitants of Mandalay and its suburbs were called upon to deliver up at once, at any one of the twelve gates of the city, or of the four gates of the palace enclosure, or at one or other of the several criminal courts or guard-houses, any muskets, swords, spears, and the like in their possession. Any one found disobeying this order and retaining arms in his possession was to be seized, and would be liable to be shot. Many arms were given up ; but nothing like all of them. Encampments of British troops were formed round the city, and guards were placed around the gun and powder factories and the royal workshops. In the gun and rifle factories much valuable machinery of Swiss manufacture was found, and ten submarine mines in course of construction. The night passed quietly in the city, and tranquillity appeared to be established. A number of robbers were caught red-handed and made over to the Provost-Marshal, some being shot and others flogged.

Being interviewed by Colonel Sladen on 3rd December, the *Tháthanábaing* or Buddhist Archbishop promised to assist the British authority, and sent out proclamations to all the *Pôngyi* or heads of monasteries throughout the country enjoining them to support all notifications coming from the *Hlutdaw* under General Prendergast's orders.

On 7th December five Princes and two Princesses, children of the Mindat Prince—who, being the heir apparent nominated to succeed his brother King Mindôn on the throne, was assassinated when the Myingun Prince attempted to kill his father also and seize the throne in 1866—were, at their own request and that of the *Hlutdaw*, deported to Rangoon, after being relieved from their imprisonment endured throughout the whole of Thibaw's reign. On the 8th the royal albino elephant, figuring in all royal proclamations as a true *Saddán* or white elephant of miraculous powers, died in the palace of colic, and was dragged by parties of the Hampshire Regiment, the Hazara Mountain Battery, and transport coolies out of the palace and through the city to the royal burial-ground north of C road, where a grave had been prepared for it by the Burmese. The actual and very real importance of this death, and of the ignominious treatment of the carcase, can only be appreciated when the childish superstition of the Burmese, individually and nationally, is understood.

On 10th December the headquarters of the Burma field force were established in the palace, and on the 15th Mr. Bernard, Chief Commissioner of British Burma, arrived with a small staff from Rangoon in order to concert administrative measures till the final policy of the British Government could be declared. Throughout the whole of this month armed parties were scouring the country round about Mandalay in search of Thibaw's disbanded soldiery and of men in possession of arms ; movable columns were operating against the bands of dacoits, often large in number, formed of the runaway royal troops, while the garrisons left at Minhla, Pagán, Myingyan, Ava, and Sagaing were all busily engaged in operating against the dacoits infesting every district, and in endeavouring to assist the civil officers left at the three first-named places in introducing something like decent administration.

The military situation remained unchanged. There was no comprehensively organized armed resistance to authority ; but bands of dacoits overran the country in all directions, and every possible opportunity was taken to harass them and to destroy or capture them. The telegraph line to the frontier was constantly being interrupted, and the wires cut again as soon as repaired. No communication had yet been established with Bhamo, as British authority was only recognized as far as gunboats had gone up the river, that is, for fifty miles north of Mandalay. Accordingly, on 19th December, General Prendergast went with a strong force up the river to Bhamo, a detachment from which occupied Shwebo. The Governor of Shwebo sent in his second and third sons in token of submission, and also a pretender to the throne whom he had captured. Various other local authorities gave in their adherence ; but the Sawbwa of Wuntho, an influential Shan chief, refused to recognize the British authority, and had to be dealt with later on. The notorious Taingda Mingyi, who was responsible for much of the misgovernment during Thibaw's reign, and was known to be very hostile to the British, was also transferred temporarily to India. He died in Rangoon on 31st May, 1896.

On 19th December an expedition was also sent up the Chindwin river, whence news had been received of the murder of three of the Bombay-Burma Corporation's European employés, in order to join hands with another column marching down from Manipur. On General Prendergast's arrival at Bhamo on 28th December he found the town almost deserted ; but the people, on being reassured, soon returned to their houses. The country along the river banks was quiet, and the people generally expressed pleasure at the advent of the British. The Governor of Bhamo made a ready submission, and requested that his troops should be disarmed and disbanded. Although an important emporium of trade with Yunnan, Bhamo was only a small town of about 5,000 inhabitants—a motley mixture of Burmese, Chinese, Shan and Kachin. Situated on the left bank of the Irrawaddy, just below where this receives the Taiping river from the east, its northern, eastern and southern sides were protected by a stockade of teak posts about fourteen or fifteen feet in height. No Chinese troops were found in the vicinity, and there was no reason to anticipate unfriendly operations on the part of the Chinese. Only the usual small garrison was stationed at Momein, beyond the frontier. After being a week at Bhamo General Prendergast returned to Mandalay, leaving Brigadier-General Norman behind in charge of a strong force, and also a civil officer to organize administration, with the support of the military.

The lawlessness and disorder prevailing in Upper Burma had meanwhile communicated itself partially to Lower Burma. In the Shwegyin district the Mayán Chaung *Pôngyi*, a Shan priest, preferring to act under orders from Thibaw, raised a following of about 500 men. Troops from Rangoon and Toungoo managed to scatter this little army, but it was long before the smaller bands thus formed were completely suppressed and the priest captured. On Christmas day Colonel Street, Commissioner of Pegu, with a small body of sepoys and police, had a pitched battle with a body of about 150 men marching on Pegu from the south with flags and golden umbrellas. Twenty of them were left dead on the field. But for this timely check the flame of insurrection would have spread like wildfire throughout the whole of Lower Burma. As it was, the early months of 1886 brought with them, in sympathy with the excited condition of Upper Burma, a vast increase beyond the usual tales of dacoities committed throughout the southern districts.

On 1st January, 1886, a proclamation was issued by

ANNEXATION OF UPPER BURMA

Lord Dufferin that the territories formerly governed by King Thibaw had become part of the British dominions, and would, during Her Majesty's pleasure, be administered by such officers as the Viceroy might from time to time appoint.[1] The immediate objects of General Prendergast's expedition had thus been accomplished thoroughly and completely, and almost bloodlessly. Even up to the 23rd of February, 1886, the number of those who died on the field, or from their wounds, amounted to only four British officers, seven British privates, and ten native soldiers. But it was well known that this was merely the preliminary towards the serious work of pacification which had now to be faced and carried through.

Though nothing like so large in area or in population, and though much more accessible, the work of pacifying the province of Pegu, conquered in 1852–53, continued for about eight years before the newly acquired territory entered fairly on the path of peace and contentment. Though carried out with the strong support of a very large military force of local levies, and of gunboats which could operate throughout the network of tidal streams forming the delta of the Irrawaddy, and with a vigour which exposed Sir Arthur Phayre to charges of excessive measures brought against him in Parliament, yet at the end of the first year of the occupation large districts were still in the hands of insurgents and robber bands. At the end of the second year great armed bands were still at large, and vast tracts remained into which British influence had not yet extended. During the third and the following years parts of the new territory were still much disturbed, and it was not until 1861 that the pacification could be considered effected. But for the Indian

---

[1] This proclamation, dated 1st January, 1886, is probably unique in its terseness among historical documents referring to the annexation of large territories. It was as follows :—

"By Command of the Queen-Empress it is hereby notified that the territories governed by King Theebaw will no longer be under his rule, but have become part of Her Majesty's dominions, and will during Her Majesty's pleasure be administered by such officers as the Viceroy and Governor-General of India may from time to time appoint.

"(Signed) DUFFERIN."

Mutiny, in 1857, the work of pacification would no doubt have been much more rapidly effected.

The new territory that was now, on 1st January, 1886, incorporated into the British dominions had an area of about 120,000 miles, and a population estimated at about three and a half millions. A considerable portion of this vast expanse was inpenetrable jungle of tree-forest or scrub, and even in the least sparsely populated districts there were no proper roads or bridges. During the rainy season the difficulties of communication were much increased by the sudden rise of the rivers, and of the numerous streams intersecting the country in all directions. Large tracts of country often remained under water for weeks at a time. Though not a warlike race, the Burmese had a traditional and hereditary love of desultory fighting, raiding, gang robbery, and the like; and their inordinate national vanity preserved vivid recollections of the time when they were a conquering race, driving the Shan, Kachin, and Assamese into the hills. Villages had long-standing feuds with other villages, and the gangs of robbers mixed up in these were recruited from time to time by the young bloods from the villages concerned. After a time such young men went back to their usual occupations; but those who liked the hard, lawless life under a dacoit *Bo* could easily take to it permanently as partisans of one or other of the professional bandits who were usually in open revolt against the sovereign. This had been the case under all the Burmese kings, and King Thibaw had proved himself to be below the average of Burmese sovereigns in administrative capacity. One of the most notorious and formidable of these bandit chiefs, Bo Shwe, had for about twelve or thirteen years back been defying with impunity the authorities of Mandalay and levying blackmail from the southern districts.

These various difficulties arising from the nature of the country, the character of the people, and the existing political organization, were rather increased than lessened by the suddenness of Thibaw's overthrow. When the plan of campaign, matured years before in Simla, had been almost bloodlessly carried through in a fortnight, it was found that the raw and undisciplined levies hastily called out to oppose our advance had dissolved and spread themselves over the country in small lawless bands. The very ease with which Mandalay was taken and the King was deposed tended greatly to retard the work of permanent pacification. Had there been anything like a national army, its overthrow might have cost much bloodshed at the outset ; but, once its opposition had been overcome, this would have swept away the main difficulties and left a free stage for the introduction of a better organized system of administration, so that troops, treasure, and time would have been saved in the long run.

Aware of these peculiar difficulties, conscious of the state of anarchy which existed under Thibaw's rule, and knowing the experiences in Pegu a generation before, the Government of India quite understood the gravity of the situation as well as the magnitude of the task before them in undertaking the pacification of the new territories. It was felt that the necessary measures towards this end could only be satisfactorily concerted on the spot in communication with those having local knowledge and experience; hence the Viceroy and the Commander-in-Chief (Sir Frederick Roberts, V.C.) took the earliest opportunity of proceeding to Burma in order to draw up schemes for the future administration of the country and for the further military operations still requisite before a stable form of Government could be established.

Until future measures could thus be decided on British civil officers, supported by troops, were in command of each of the five districts, Mandalay, Myingyan, Pagán, Minhla, and Ningyan, and were working through the Burmese District Governors and headmen. The civil and ordinary criminal jurisdiction was in the hands of these civil officers, except where troops were stationed or operating, when, the country being still under military occupation, the Provost-Marshal's officers exercised some jurisdiction. Outside of these five districts the rest of the country was nominally governed by the *Hlutdaw* or State Council, presided over by Colonel Sladen ; but for various reasons the orders and influence of this *Hlut* carried little weight into the interior of these central and northern districts. In some places the ordinary local officials succeeded in enforcing partial order, but the country at large was in a state of anarchy and disorganization. At Ava, Sagaing, Shwebo, Tagaung, Myadaung, and Bhamo, on the Irrawaddy, and at some points on the Chindwin river, military detachments were stationed with civil officers in attendance, so that the whole of the districts which had been actually ruled by Thibaw were held in military occupation.

Though Upper Burma was now annexed to the British dominions, it had not yet been incorporated with British India; hence Indian codes did not apply. The civil officers were instructed, however, to proceed in criminal cases on the lines of the Indian codes, except that dacoity or gang robbery might be punishable with death, that flogging was to be administered in place of imprisonment on petty offenders physically fit for receiving such punishment, and that no appeal lay from criminal sentences. Rebels in arms captured on the field were liable to be shot, but the death penalty was not to be enforced by civil officers otherwise than after trial.

Chapter V

THE PACIFICATION OF UPPER BURMA (1886 to 1890)

WHEN Lord Dufferin and Sir Frederick Roberts were in Mandalay, from 12th to 19th February, 1886, the importance of the matters requiring consideration was only equalled by the difficulties connected with them. During the seven years of Thibaw's weak and incompetent rule dacoity had been permitted to overspread the country; while the melting away of the Burmese army on the British approach both strengthened the dacoit gangs already in existence, and formed the nuclei of fresh gangs of armed men in many cases engaging in organized opposition to the new Government. The main problems the Viceroy had to consider first of all were whether the new dominions should form a protected State under the Indian Government, or be annexed outright and brought directly under the British administration, and how good government could most effectively and cheaply be introduced; while the Commander-in-Chief had to formulate the plan of military operations, still necessary under any circumstances, and on a largely increased scale, for the pacification of the country in the event of annexation outright being decided on.

Lord Dufferin's personal desire was that Upper Burma should be converted into a protected or "buffer" State like Afghanistan, the ruling Prince being left perfectly independent in matters of internal administration, while the Government of India would have exercised the right of supervising all external relations. But, on closer consideration after hearing the opinions of the civil and military authorities in Burma, he found the country so disorganized, the State Council and Ministry so discredited and lacking in influence, and the chance of finding suitable candidates for the throne among the Princes of the royal line so slight as to admit of no possible rational alternative to direct administration of the country by the Government of India. No Prince who might be placed on the throne would have been able, without great assistance from British troops, to maintain his authority with any prospect of success against the numerous rivals who would be sure to rise up against him. Within a short time of Thibaw's downfall there were five such Princes, besides other pretenders to the throne, wandering about the jungles with small parties of followers. To keep on the throne a puppet ruler would have landed the Government of India in responsibilities almost as great as actual administration, while the intrigues, procrastinations, and slights of a Burmese ruler would probably soon again have become insupportable. It would have been beyond reasonable hope to secure a stable form of Burmese Government, which would gradually establish and maintain tranquillity and fairly good administration, and which would at the same time effectually exclude from the upper valley of the Irrawaddy undesirable foreign influences likely to produce at some future date the gravest political consequences. The Nyaungyan Prince had recently died, and his younger brother, the Nyaungôk, still under British surveillance in Bengal, was disobedient to orders, unpopular in Burma, and otherwise unsatisfactory. The Myingun Prince who fled in 1866 to a British asylum after attempting his father's life and killing the heir apparent, his uncle, and then, about the time of Thibaw's accession in 1878, had escaped to Pondicherry, whence he tried to carry on intrigues, might perhaps, if put on the throne, have held his own by killing off his rivals ; but he would have been almost certain to have given trouble by falling into the hands of foreign adventurers and concessionaries. Hence Lord Dufferin decided to recommend the pure and simple incorporation of Upper Burma with the Indian Empire, and the British Government at once (16th February, 1886), acquiesced in the recommendation and authorized him to proceed with the direct administration of the country.

The attempt to restore order and to govern through the *Hlutdaw*, or Council of State, was proving a failure. Even the best of the Ministers, who had so ignominiously failed to manage the country efficiently under King Thibaw, had little influence, and could not be relied on to use that little, under the new circumstances in which they were called upon to act. It was therefore determined to abolish the *Hlutdaw*, and to make use of only a selected few of the Ministers merely as a consultative body to be associated with the Chief Commissioner, in order that reference might be made to them, as occasion might arise, on points connected with the late administration. This was rather a matter of policy, to attach the more influential members of the late Ministry to the new Government, and to show consideration to the more deserving of the ex-King's servants, than an actual need for administrative assistance. Two of the members of the State Council, the Kinwun Mingyi, or Prime Minister, and the Taunggwin Mingyi, two of the Privy Councillors, the Pin Atwinwun, and the Shwedaik Atwinwun, and one Assistant Minister, the Tabayin Wundauk, were thus retained on salaries varying from rupees 500 to 1,000 per mensem (£400 to £800 a year); while small pensions were bestowed on some of the other ex-Ministers.

It was first of all found necessary to substitute for the existing arbitrary powers of the Viceroy an order in Council under anno 33 Vict. cap. 3, sec. 1, extending that section to the whole of Upper Burma except the Shan States. It thus became a scheduled district removed from the operation of the statute law applying to the rest of the Indian Empire. This enabled the local administration of Burma to frame simple Regulations with the approval of the Government of India, suitable to cope with the actual state of affairs. These Regulations differed from Acts in being issued by the Governor-General in Council, instead of being passed by the Legislative Council of the Government of India; but in their effect there was no practical difference between the two. Mr. Bernard, Chief Commissioner of British Burma, was placed in charge of the whole of Burma, which was consolidated into a Chief Commissionership in September, 1886; while Mr. Hodgkinson, one of the Commisioners, acted as his Assistant in charge of Lower Burma. Upper Burma was divided into fourteen districts, with British civil officers and Police Assistants in each. At first there were to be no divisional Commissioners or sessions Judges; and district officers were to work through indigenous local agencies, and according to local methods, in matters of revenue and civil justice. The village community system was thus retained as being thoroughly in accordance with the customs of the country and least likely to be irksome or to disturb the people, before the stability of the new administration was felt and appreciated by the population at large. Under this new system room was also found for the best of the old Burmese officials. Many of these, far truer patriots than the princely pretenders and the brigand chiefs who carried fire and sword into all parts of the newly conquered territories, in pursuit of no definite policy and no political aim, rendered valuable services to the cause of peace, and too often had to pay for their loyalty with their lives. The Shan States were to be treated as feudatory or tributary States, without attempting to bring them under any direct administrative control.

The Commander-in-Chief was at first inclined to recommend some reduction in the military force; but after mature consideration had been given to the subject, it was decided to send back one Madras regiment to India, and to move down two Ghurka regiments from Assam for work in the hilly districts.

The Upper and Lower Burma commands were united under General Prendergast, with headquarters at Rangoon, while the headquarters of two brigades were located at Mandalay (General White) and Bhamo (General Norman). As troops had been drawn from all the three Presidencies of India, the military administration of Burma was for the time being placed under the Commander-in-Chief. On 31st March General Prendergast vacated the command of the forces in Burma and

MILITARY DIFFICULTIES

the troops in Upper Burma were formed into a separate command under Brigadier-General White, who received the local rank of Major-General.

That a prolonged struggle was anticipated is clear from Sir Frederick Roberts' recommendation that free passages from India to England should be given to the wives and families of all military officers detained on field service in Burma, and that large rewards should be paid to all officers and soldiers, European or native, who learned sufficient Burmese to pass easy examinations in the language. Nor were the wives of civil officers permitted to reside with their husbands during the most troublous period.

Without attempting to dictate subordinate military arrangements from Calcutta and Simla, the Government of India urged the desirability of first thoroughly dominating the central area close to the main arteries of communication, and thence gradually extending administration and jurisdiction according to the means at disposal and the opportunities occurring. The despatch of spasmodic and disconnected expeditions into tracts which could not be at once permanently occupied and protected was deprecated. Such a method of procedure could only disquiet and compromise peaceable and well-disposed villages, because, if they showed themselves at all friendly to the military detachments visiting them, this only exposed them to subsequent ill-treatment and plunder at the hands of rebels and dacoits as soon as the British force had left. The difficulties and dangers to health unavoidable during the hot months of April and May were also humanely pointed out, and recommendations were made to move the troops about as little as possible during the hottest time of the year, and to locate them as healthily as possible during the approaching rainy season, even though this might for the moment retard the progress of operations.

In accordance with these instructions, British authority was first confined to the tracts bordering the Irrawaddy, to the country around Mandalay and Bhamo, and to the southern frontier districts of Minhla and Ningyan. Military posts were distributed in different localities, and small movable columns were organized, capable of marching in whatever direction circumstances required. When in Mandalay, Sir Frederick Roberts laid down a minimum strength for each post and column, and the judiciousness of these arrangements was proved by the fact of no post being forced. Although there was no regular well-organized enemy in the field, and therefore no particular objective requiring the concentration of large masses of troops, yet the country was generally overrun with armed bands. Five scions of the royal line were pushing their claims to the throne in different localities. The Myinzaing Prince, a son of Mindôn, held the Natteik pass into the Shan hills, and harried the plains lying to the south-east of Mandalay; while a pretender calling himself the Kyimyin Prince was troubling the districts to the south of that, as far as the Toungoo frontier. At Chaungwa, in the Ava district, the Chaungwa Princes, Yan Naing and Yan Baing, whose father was massacred in 1879 by Thibaw, were endeavouring to assert themselves; while Prince Maung Hmat Gyi, a son of the heir apparent killed in 1866, had a large following in the Shwebo and Yeú districts, north-east of Mandalay. Numerous dacoit leaders had become nominal supporters of these pretenders, plundering villages and levying blackmail in their names. Some of the dacoit *Bo* even went the length of themselves becoming pretenders to the throne. Bo Shwe, who had been harrying the Minbu and Minhla districts for the last twelve or thirteen years, boldly proclaimed himself King of Minbu, and appointed a Governor of the river. The most influential of the other dacoit *Bo* at this time were Nga Hlau, who had for years harried the districts between the Irrawaddy and the Mu river, north-west of Mandalay, the Thondatin Thugyi, Maung Min Po, in the Pindali district, U Paung in Meiktila, and Budda Yáza in Ningyan. The Myinzaing Prince even offered a reward of 2,000 rupees for the head of Sir Charles Bernard, the Chief Commissioner, and threatened to burn the palace in Mandalay, which was being used for the public offices and the residences of the civil and military headquarters' staffs.

MILITARY POSTS ESTABLISHED

Incendiarism had become rife. Early in April several fires occurred in the more crowded suburbs of Mandalay city, and other fires broke out in the city itself about the middle of the month, at which date the Burmese New Year happened to fall in 1886. About 800 houses within the city, and between 2,000 and 2,500 in the suburbs were thus destroyed, chiefly by some thirty to forty adherents of the Myingun Prince, who made an organized outbreak and rushed one of the town police stations. The citizens appeared to be demoralized for the moment, the shops and bazaars were closed, and business generally was at a standstill. From April onwards large bodies of armed men harassed the whole of the districts around the capital and all the principal towns, and before the close of the rainy season it had become very apparent that it was necessary to considerably strengthen the troops in Burma. Hardly a day passed without a skirmish taking place in some part of the country ; and the guerilla system of warfare adopted by them gave great advantages to the rebels and dacoits.

General White soon found, from the experiences around Mandalay, that mere visits from flying columns to different parts of the country were quite insufficient to maintain British supremacy, and that for the pacification of the country and the suppression of dacoity or other armed resistance, it was necessary to closely occupy the country by establishing strong military posts in each of the various districts of sufficient strength to maintain order in their immediate neighbourhood, and to afford contingents for flying columns to skirmish against rebel bands. It was only when they saw the troops, and felt they could rely on their protection, that villagers could be expected to give information or assistance against the rebel bands and dacoit gangs. It was only thus that military ascendancy and prestige could be secured, the main lines of communication by land and water protected, civil authority and administration established, and the population encouraged to render assistance. In addition to posts along the Irrawaddy, others were established along the route from Mandalay to Toungoo, and from Toungoo across the hills to Thayetmyo ; and the central part of Upper Burma was thus enclosed in a roughly triangular series of strongholds forming bases from which the further military operations were undertaken. Near the eastern base line the construction of a railway was being pushed on from Toungoo to Mandalay, and with great success and rapidity under circumstances of unusual difficulty and danger.

The expenditure on public works was intended to be limited at first to barracks, obligatory military roads, and telegraph repairs and construction ; but the great importance of continuing the Rangoon-Toungoo railway line to Mandalay was recognized and urged both on political and military grounds. The Secretary of State suggested that, in the meantime, it might be more advantageous to make good roads, passable at all seasons, between the various principal civil and military stations. The arguments placed before the Government of India by Sir Charles Bernard, Chief Commissioner of Burma, were, however, so convincing that sanction was given to commence construction in the autumn of 1886. It was successfully urged by him that a trunk road would be costly and unremunerative, that the expense of moving troops and supplies would be five times as great by road as by rail, while the time occupied would be ten times as long, and that, in short, the railway would be far more effectual in pacifying the country, in promoting trade, and in strengthening the position whether viewed from a military, a political, or an administrative standpoint.

The position in Lower Burma had meanwhile become such as caused much uneasiness. Partly through the emissaries of the royal Princes pretending to the throne, and partly in sympathy with the lawless feeling prevalent within the newly annexed territories, dacoity sprang up to an alarming degree throughout the older province. Troops had therefore also to be poured into Lower Burma, while the garrison in Upper Burma was being strengthened. In the summer of 1886 there were 17,022 troops in Upper Burma, distributed in forty-three posts, and 7,162 in Lower Burma, occupying no less than

DIFFICULTIES TO BE OVERCOME

forty-seven posts on the Sittang river, and the Irrawaddy with its delta. Everything resembling patriotic sentiment in the Burmese had become united with the inherent strain of brutality and lawlessness running through the national character; and this combination of innate forces found its expression in the bands of armed men infesting the jungles all over the new province. It was certainly not patriotism pure and simple, while it was equally certainly not merely dacoity in the true meaning of that word; but it was armed resistance to British administration, and as such it had to be put down with a heavy hand. Lurking in jungle recesses almost impenetrable for regular troops, these armed bands were seldom to be met in the open field, though bold and sudden in ambushes and surprise attacks on military and police posts. As a matter of course they were entirely dependent on villagers for food and other contributions, their demands for which they enforced with such barbarities as burning and devastating villages, slaughtering headmen, crucifying or otherwise executing men suspected of giving information to the British, and inflicting disgusting tortures on other men and women.

The enormous difficulties of contending against widespread revolt, rebellion, and crime of this sort can easily be imagined. It was necessary to attack the root of the evil by constantly harassing the armed bands so as to keep them in a continuous state of apprehension and of alarm, isolate them, cut them off from villages in which they had friends or relatives, and deprive them of their secret supporters. Experience showed that strong bodies of insurgents, numbering sometimes from 2,000 to 4,000 men, could be assembled rapidly and secretly in neighbourhoods not protected by military posts. Pillaging and burning wherever they went, these bands of freebooters reserved the refinements of their cruelties for those who had given assistance or information against them. Unless in the immediate vicinity of British troops, the villagers were forced through terror into compromise with the dacoits.

It had been at once recognized, however, that troops alone could not suffice for the work of pacification, but that the special difficulties in Burma would be overcome rather by the vigorous administration of civil government and by the creation of an efficient police than by the employment of military detachments scattered over the face of the country. Reinforcements of troops were at any time obtainable from India, but the available reserve of efficient police was much more limited. As the Burmese character is averse to discipline, and as the old Burmese police were incapable of coping with the dacoits and rebel bands, no time was lost in issuing orders for enlisting, training, and sending over to Burma a large body of police recruited from the warlike races of the Punjab and the North-Western Provinces of India. In addition to 2,000 volunteers from the Indian police, and to the ordinary native police force of Lower Burma, 6,530 trained recruits were sent to Upper and Lower Burma during the rainy season of 1886; so that, with the 24,184 troops already in Burma, the total of troops and military police for service throughout the whole province rose to 32,720.

The Irrawaddy Flotilla Company, which had rendered such brilliant assistance in the advance on Mandalay, did even more for the country after the annexation than before. They put on express steamers, without cargo-flats, to run once a week between Rangoon and Mandalay. They improved communication between Mandalay and Bhamo by running regular weekly steamers. They also instituted short services between Mandalay and important points up and down the river, and began to ply regularly on the Chindwin river. For these new lines the Company received no subsidy, though they obtained a large amount of Government work. Every steamer contained a small guard of troops or disciplined police for protection. A large flotilla of Government steamers had to be placed on the rivers to facilitate the movements of troops, to prevent the crossing of armed bands of rebels or dacoits, to keep down river piracy, and to patrol the rivers; but the assistance received from the commercial flotilla was indispensable.

For the civil administration of the district controlled by the military posts a code of provisional instructions was issued in March, 1886. This was drawn up in harmony with the spirit of the Indian codes, but at the same time gave due consideration to established Burmese habits and methods of procedure. On the whole these instructions worked well and smoothly, proving a great advance over the arbitrary method obtaining immediately after the annexation. The establishment of this form of just and simple administration, the gradual disarmament of the people, the opening up of communications, and the encouragement of trade were relied on, combined with the abundant evidences of armed strength, as being the shortest and the best way of attaining the eventual cessation of military operations and the pacification and settlement of Upper Burma. These measures involved a large expenditure on the newly-acquired territory, but it was borne in mind that the rich province of Pegu did not pay its expenses for the first eight or ten years after annexation. In August, 1886, a disaster occurred which tested the state of order to which the town of Mandalay had then been reduced under firm and judicious government. The earthwork embankment protecting the western suburbs burst from the pressure of a flood higher than had been known for sixty years past. Much destruction of property occurred, and some loss of life resulted. Food was at once provided for the absolutely destitute, and a regular system of relief distribution was organized. But the night on which the inundation occurred passed without the slightest disturbance.

The troops under General White in Upper Burma during the summer of 1886 were divided into three brigades, having headquarters at Mandalay, Bhamo, and Ningyan (now called Pyinmaná), near the Toungoo frontier. The garrison was, however, further augmented by three regiments of native cavalry, while nearly all the corps and batteries sent in October, 1885, were relieved in the autumn of 1886, and the command of future operations was given to Lieutenant-General Sir Herbert Macpherson, V.C., Commander-in-Chief of the Madras army, whose headquarters were to remain at Mandalay till the conclusion of the military operations. The truth of the matter is that the resistance encountered had proved far more widespread, and was likely to be much more continuous and obstinate, than was originally anticipated, even although enormous difficulties had been estimated and prepared for. Wherever rebels mustered strong, if the local posts were not sufficient to operate against them, the necessity had hitherto been met by sending troops from whatever reserve could best spare them ; and this, of course, led to much unsymmetrical distribution. On the arrival of the reinforcements of three battalions, flying columns were formed on a larger scale to supplement the system of posts and form a stronger reserve in every district. To render these columns as mobile and swift as possible, a corps of mounted infantry was formed. Each district headquarters had a mounted company composed of twenty-five British and fifty native infantry, which could be attached to the flying columns. The special reinforcements of cavalry were asked for, as this had proved a very effective branch of the force. The rebel *Bo* were always well mounted, and were usually the first to fly on the approach of British troops, while mere mounted infantry proved unable to overtake and capture them. But in a country where only ponies are bred, the cavalry horses seemed monsters to the superstitious people, while the long reach and the short shrift of the lance paralysed with fear the rebels in arms, as well as the general population.

The opposition to the British administration which was being felt during the second half of 1886 was as nearly a national uprising as was possible among the Burmese. Of a population numbering about three millions, exclusive of the Shan States, more than seven-eighths were agriculturists, while rather more than half of the urban population was congregated in the city of Mandalay and its suburbs. Throughout the whole of the villages and hamlets on the plains held under military occupation there was probably hardly a household whence some male member had not issued to join one or other of the rebel gangs, which were being hunted down with all possible vigour. The bonds of relationship thus existing between rebels and villagers, and the fear of acts of revenge if information were given against dacoit leaders, raised up a sort of passive resistance on the part of the general population, which rendered it harder to effect the seizure of the leaders of rebellion and increased the difficulties of military operations in a country of itself offering physical obstacles of unusual difficulty.

The reliefs and reinforcements for the Burma field force were carried out towards the end of the summer rains in 1886, and Sir Herbert Macpherson assumed the supreme command early in September. But before the cold weather operations for 1886–87 could well be said to have commenced, he died of malarious fever, near Prome, on 2nd October, 1886. In view of the large number of troops in Burma, the extended operations about to be undertaken, and the extreme gravity which the situation had now undisguisably assumed—for during the rainy season, when whole districts were rendered impassable by swollen streams, and the troops and officers suffered from ill-health, the rebels had made head against the British power—the Commander-in-Chief, Sir Frederick Roberts, was directed to transfer his head-quarters temporarily to Burma and assume command of the whole of the troops in the province. He arrived in Mandalay on 17th November, and remained there till 12th February, 1887.

The forces then amounted to about 32,000 troops and 8,500 military police, exclusive of the urban and rural native Burmese police, whose organization and discipline were being gradually improved. The Commander-in-Chief was assisted by two majors-general in command of divisions, and six brigadiers-general in command of brigades. To facilitate the free movement of troops jungle clearings, each of 100 feet in width, were made from post to post, and in other convenient places.

While measures were thus being concerted for putting down rebellion and dacoity with a strong hand, the necessity of directly and indirectly conciliating the people at large was not overlooked ; hence punitive measures, such as the burning of villages, harbouring or assisting rebels, were prohibited ; an amnesty was offered to all who should voluntarily submit within a certain time ; all imports and duties impeding the free course of trade were abolished ; the village system was adhered to, and the indigenous methods of administration were retained so far as possible ; demands for the collection of revenue were not pressed severely ; and various means were taken to try and bring home to the people the fact that there was no intention of undermining or interfering with the Buddhist religion. Endeavours were also made to develop the rich natural resources of the country. Agricultural interests, besides having for years back been hampered by dacoity, had suffered throughout the whole of the dry central zone from the state of disrepair into which irrigation works, dating from centuries back, had been allowed to fall. The ruby mines, jade mining, coal fields, oil wells, teak forests, and gold fields, were all valuable natural resources, whose exploitation would become of great importance so soon as the country began to be somewhat more settled.

As a means of pacification and of advance towards these desirable ends, the important step was taken of disarming the country. Begun in the Mandalay district, it was gradually, but without undue delay, extended throughout the whole of the fourteen districts of Upper Burma. All guns were called in from towns and villages, and were only partially distributed under proper safeguards. After being marked with distinctive marks and numbers, guns were only restored to licensees consisting of respectable men living in well-behaved villages and towns where there were at least five to ten armed licensees. Villages with well-kept *chevaux-de-frise*, bamboo stockades, and proper watch and ward kept at the small *Kin* or "guard-houses" placed near the gates, were safer with ten or more guns in the hands of licensees than they were before ; whereas hamlets with only two or three guns would, under any circumstances, have been unable to offer strong resistance to dacoit attacks, because experience showed that such small villages never attempted to defend themselves. As soon as the mass of the people living in the towns and villages on the plains were deprived of their arms, it became no longer possible for rebels and dacoits to replace guns lost in action or given up on acceptance of amnesty. Insistence was at the same time made that villages whose position exposed them to attack should surround themselves with substantial stockades, and that a proper watch should be maintained there day and night. Wherever this proved ineffectual, and in outlying tracts where military posts could not be established, small hamlets were grouped together to form a more easily defensible village, and villages were moved to more suitable sites. Inconvenience and a certain amount of hardship was inseparable from the latter measure ; but, as the houses in Burmese villages are only constructed of posts, bamboos, and thatch grass, easily obtainable from the neighouring jungles, the inevitable hardships were reduced to a minimum. Even in the royal city of Mandalay the houses were mostly of the same flimsy and uncostly description, and were worth only about fifty rupees ($£3\frac{1}{3}$) apiece, although some were, of course, much more valuable. The six thousand houses located between the palace and the city walls were also subsequently cleared out on payment of compensation reckoned according to the number of the posts supporting each house, and the householders thus ejected on payment of compensation for disturbance were granted building sites in the new extramural town of Mandalay, while the old *Shwemyodaw*, or "royal golden city," was retained exclusively for the civil and military servants of Government, and transformed into Fort Dufferin.

With a credulous and superstitious race like the Burmese, even trivial things often assume dimensions of enormous magnitude. In 1887 one of the seven-roofed *Pyathat* or ornamental buildings on the north wall of the city was utilized as the central portion of a Government House for the Chief Commissioner. This was a mistake. If it had any ornamental spire at all, Government House should have had *nine* graduated roofs to indicate clearly that it was the abode of the ruler of the province. Even the palaces of the Shan chiefs are allowed to have a seven-roofed *Pyathat*, and to put fewer than the nine representing supreme sovereignty, while the *Myenan* or imperial palace, "the Centre of the Universe," still stood among the palace buildings, showed great want of knowledge concerning Burmese sumptuary laws, ceremonial etiquette, and national ideas. It is not conceivable that there could have been any deliberate intention in thus giving a certain amount of hope to aspirants for the throne, or to rebel *Bo* and leaders of large dacoit bands. But the work of pacification in the immediate vicinity of Mandalay would probably have been accomplished more easily and speedily if the British Government had built for their representative a nine-roofed house, whose spire towered aloft higher than the pinnacle of the *Pyathat* above the lion throne in Thibaw's great Hall of Audience. The fact that this symbol of authority still remained is said to have been one of the causes leading to the great incendiary fires which later on broke out in and around Mandalay during April, 1892.

For the apprehension of noted rebel leaders and dacoit *Bo* large rewards were offered, and dissension was sown among their followers by liberal offers of pardon to the less prominent members of the various bands, as well as to the rank and file consisting of young or ignorant men, more misguided than criminal. In dealing with these rebels and dacoits there was neither extreme severity on the one hand, nor mawkish sentimentality on the other. Measures of repression and punishment were necessary to crush the armed resistance, and no one in authority shrank from the responsibility of inflicting them as the only way of ultimately bringing peace and prosperity to the disturbed and harassed country. The gangs were hunted down continuously, and every effort was made to capture the leaders. When captured or brought in as a prisoner by villagers wishing to be rid of his oppression, a dacoit *Bo* had a fair trial, and was hanged if convicted; but promises of pardon on voluntary surrender were performed with a scrupulousness which sometimes thwarted justice in favour of mercy. Proclamation was also made that, while in the meantime no clemency could be shown to those who were confined as prisoners in jails, the question of liberating them or reducing their sentences would be duly considered so soon as the state of the country permitted Government to take this step.

THE SHAN CHIEFS

The attitude of the Shan *Sawbwa* or chiefs on the hills to the east of the Irrawaddy was, fortunately for the work of pacification, such as gave reason to hope that the allegiance of these rulers would not be difficult to obtain. The problem with these, and with the other far less civilized hill tribes—the Kachin and Chin—on the north and west, was quite different from that among the Burmese on the plains, as they were all well-defined groups of men living under the rule of tribal chiefs whose authority was generally sufficient to preserve order amongst them. It was not a case of dealing with disintegrated masses like the rebel bands and dacoit gangs, but with large organized tribal units, each under the moral and administrative control of an individual ruler. At first there were some difficulties, but ultimately the Shan chiefs willingly accepted the British supremacy and agreed to preserve order among their people so long as their rights and dignity of chieftainship were recognized and troops were not quartered upon them. In return for this they agreed to restrain their people from internecine warfare and from raiding down into the territories under military occupation.

They were at once placed in a more advantageous commercial position than under Burmese rule, for the restrictions and imposts on *Letpet* or " pickled tea " were removed, and this most valuable of the hill products could be taken down to the plains. Under Burmese Government about $7\frac{1}{2}$ lacs of rupees of revenue ($£50,000$) had annually been realized in connexion with the monopoly affecting the importation and sale of tea. Owing to the disturbed state of the country no tribute was levied in 1886–87, and thereafter the demand made was only about half the amount fixed under Burmese rule, $4\frac{1}{2}$ lacs ($£30,000$).

The first of the great Shan chiefs to render allegiance to the British was Kun Saing, Sawbwa of Thibaw, one of the principal Northern Shan States lying due east of Mandalay. On 27th January, 1887, he came in person to Mandalay, and was formally received at the eastern gate of the city by Sir Charles Bernard. This was not the first time he had had an interview with a Chief Commissioner; but the circumstances were different. In 1884 the Thibaw Sawbwa fled from his State through fear of King Thibaw, and sought refuge in Lower Burma. He went to Rangoon to worship at the great Shwe Dagôn Pagoda. While residing there in one of the suburbs he executed two of his followers, who had been guilty of some act of commission or omission. Tried for murder by the Recorder of Rangoon, he was condemned to death ; but the capital sentence was commuted to imprisonment for two years, on account of his having had as Chief the power of life and death in his own State. In Rangoon jail he was treated like other convicts. His head was shaved ; he had to wear the coarse canvas prison garb stamped with the black broad-arrow, and he had to do his daily task of hard labour in husking rice with a grinding-mill worked by hand. It was while so engaged that Mr. (afterwards Sir Charles) Crosthwaite, then Acting Chief Commissioner, saw him on a prison inspection, and used the Government prerogative in granting him a free pardon. On King Thibaw's downfall Kun Saing recovered his State, held aloof from the combinations and dissensions of the other States, and took an early opportunity of intimating allegiance to the British Government. As a reward for this, the tribute payable by his State was remitted for ten years, and the three petty States of Mainglôn, Thônzè, and Maingtôn were made subordinate to the Thibaw State.

It is not impossible that his experiences in the Rangoon jail in 1884 had some direct connexion with Kun Saing's policy towards the British in 1886 ; but the Thibaw Sawbwa has since kept his allegiance well, and his lead was speedily followed by the majority of the Shan chiefs, who had been in open rebellion during the last three years of King Thibaw's reign. A digression may here, perhaps, be permitted to mention that in 1890 he sent his two sons to England for the completion of their education, that he himself came to see the country in 1893, and that he was nominated a member of the Legislative Council of Burma on its formation in 1897. And once again he returned to England, in the summer of 1898, to present a rare gem to Her Majesty at Windsor.

THE THIBAW SAWBWA

Between confinement with hard labour in Rangoon jail and a formal reception by the Chief Commissioner of Burma at the principal gate of Mandalay city, or an audience of the Queen-Empress at Windsor Castle, there are vast differences. It surely speaks well for the British administration of Burma that such things should have been possible ; and it speaks better still for Kun Saing, Sawbwa of Thibaw, that they actually took place. When, in May, 1898, he showed me over his *Haw* or palace, and did me the unusual honour of conducting me into the private apartments, and introducing me to his queens and princesses, then led me to his private chapel and the look-out tower, I could not help, during my conversation with him, thinking that I had been privileged to make the acquaintance of a singularly magnanimous as well as a very intelligent and far-seeing chieftain.

The wild, uncivilized tribes inhabiting the densely-wooded hills flanking and separating the valleys of the Irrawaddy and its tributaries were left to be dealt with later on, by means of punitive expeditions, and by the establishment of military forts in their midst, when once the plains had been brought into a more settled condition. Before Sir Frederick Roberts reached Mandalay the short cool season with which the northern portion of Burma is favoured had already begun, while the arrangements for work had been practically elaborated by General White and Sir Herbert Macpherson, and had been approved by himself as Commander-in-Chief : but he lost no time in issuing on 20th November general instructions to his brigadiers, and to officers in command of flying columns, for the conduct of operations throughout the coming season. Columns sent out in pursuit of rebel gangs were to be provisioned for ten days at least, depôts being laid down at convenient centres to supplement the supplies obtainable locally from villages. When two or more columns were acting in concert, communications were to be kept up as constantly as possible by means of signalling, scouts and patrols. Liberal rewards were to be given to guides and those furnishing useful imformation involving risk to themselves. As the success of operations and the health of the troops depended so much on the proper maintenance of commissariat arrangements and transport, the careful treatment of pack animals was enjoined on all officers. They were likewise exhorted to see that the troops did not injure the property of the people, or wound their susceptibilities, as it was of importance to cultivate friendly relations with them and gain their confidence, whilst putting before them evidences of military power. Chief men of districts were to be treated with consideration and distinction, and pains were to be taken to eradicate the fear that the British intended to overthrow the Buddhist religion and all the customs and privileges dear to the people. In operations against positions held by rebels in arms against British rule, efforts were to be made to surround their positions so as to inflict the heaviest loss possible ; for a severe lesson promptly administered, even at the cost of some casualties on the British side, was held to be the shortest and best way of crushing organized armed resistance. Villages and jungle retreats were therefore to be surrounded with cavalry, and carefully beaten through by infantry. As Princes, pretenders, and dacoit *Bo* would generally be found heading the columns of fugitives, part of the cavalry was to pursue them without wasting time over the rank and file, many of whom were villagers forced, *nolens volens*, into the gangs. Columns of occupation employed in the pacification of tracts from which rebels and dacoit bands had been dispersed were to make short marches and halt at all towns and large villages, so as to give civil officers opportunities of becoming acquainted with the districts, and military officers time for making reconnaissances and sketch maps. When civil officers accompanied columns, all prisoners were handed over to them for disposal, otherwise the officer in command had *ex officio* magisterial powers to inflict up to two years' imprisonment or thirty lashes : if heavier punishment were considered necessary, the cases were reserved till they could be disposed of by a civil officer. In view of the malarious and unhealthy nature of the climate to which they were unavoidably exposed during operations of this sort, and of the extremely arduous fatigue which they were constantly being called upon to incur, every reasonable effort was made, both in camp and on the march, to minimize the risks to which the troops were exposed from those scourges of the tropical jungles, malarial fever and dysentery.[1] The number of officers and men who succumbed to these climatic diseases and to their sequelæ was far in excess of that mown down in the hundreds of skirmishes which took place before Upper Burma was pacified. The little brick-walled cemeteries near Pagán, Hlaingdet, and other similar but now disused military posts, are filled with the grave-mounds of British soldiers, who thus laid down their lives to help pacify the new province. The tooth of time has already gnawed keenly into the little teakwood crosses upon which were inscribed the names and regiments of the rank and file ; and in a very few years all will be nameless graves save the spots where officers rest beneath more enduring memorials of marble, granite, or sandstone.

There was never a campaign in which so much initiative was left to the junior officers, and the captains and subalterns nobly upheld the best traditions of the British army as a fighting body. The improved education now given to military cadets at Sandhurst and Woolwich made itself very apparent in a practical way throughout the campaign of pacification, lasting for five years after the annexation. The country had never been surveyed, and there were no maps : hence officers were required to send in sketch maps, drawn to a fixed scale. These were pieced together in Mandalay, and made into a very serviceable map, from which operations and even com-

[1] The casualties between 17th November, 1885, and 31st October, 1886, were :

	Killed or died of wounds.	Died from disease.	Invalided.
Officers . . .	11	11	76
Men	80	919	1956
Total .	91	930	2032

bined movements from different bases could be directed at the headquarters of the Burma field force.

These operations were pushed on so vigorously during the cold season, that by March, 1887, when Sir Charles Bernard, whose health had suffered severely from the strain of the previous fifteen months, handed over the chief commissionership to Mr. (now Sir Charles) Crosthwaite, the number of posts held in upper Burma by troops had risen to 141. By this time seventeen districts had been formed and grouped into three divisions, under Commissioners who confirmed all capital sentences, and revised and superintended the proceedings of district officers. The civil officers were everywhere dependent on military escorts, and could nowhere move about their districts freely ; but the tide of affairs was already beginning to turn. While, on the one hand, the officers commanding posts and parties of troops in the field were acquiring a knowledge of the people and of the country, the rebels and dacoits, on the other hand, were beginning to get tired and disheartened with the continuous hunting down and harassing. The constant pursuit of the cavalry and mounted infantry was beginning to tell on both the leaders and their followers ; and the tactics pursued tended to cut them adrift from their bases of supply and their sources of information as to the movements of British troops.

Despite the progress, however, affairs were still very bad. The Mandalay district was to a great extent in the hands of three or four *Bo*, who headed large gangs and acted in concert so far as to recognize and respect the limits of each leader's territorial jurisdiction for the levy of blackmail on villages located therein. These *Bo* professed to act on behalf of the Myingun Prince, still a refugee at Pondicherry, and were kept together and instructed how to act in combination by a relative of his who styled himself the *Bayingan* or Viceroy. Sagaing was terrorized by dacoits that habitually murdered village headmen who refused obedience or neglected to pay blackmail. Nga Hlau still overran the Shwebo and Yeú districts. The Ruby Mines district remained quiet after an expedition under General Stewart took possession of Mogôk, its chief town ; but in the country to the north

of that a young Shan named Kan Hlaing had assumed a
position of open enmity to the British, because of their
declining to assist him in establishing himself as Sawbwa
of the Shan States of Mohlaing and Momeik. The upper
portion of the Chindwin valley was fairly quiet. The
Sawbwa of Thaungthut had made his submission, while
the Sawbwa of Kale was not in open hostility, though he
had not yet declared his allegiance. The latter arrested
and handed over a pretender calling himself Buddha
Yáza, who was promptly tried and executed. In the
lower Chindwin there continued to be much disturbance
in the Pagyi country, a wild tract to a great extent
covered with inaccessible and unhealthy forests. The
Pagán district was overrun with dacoits, who found refuge
in the tangle of scrub jungles and ravines clothing the
spurs extending into the adjacent plains from the remarkable hill of Pópa, lying to the north-east of Pagán and
about forty miles back from the Irrawaddy river. About
4,500 feet in height and conical in shape, Popa towers
upwards from the skyline, a solitary mountain peak surrounded by a vast extent of plain, in marked resemblance
to the sacred Fujisan of Japan. The scrub-covered
spurs and ravines, which hid a good deal of cultivated
land in the hollows, had ever been a favourite resort of
dacoit gangs. The villagers were mostly cattle rievers,
who stored their beasts in large pens or enclosures in the
jungle lest they might stray back to their lawful owners.
Further to the south, between Taungdwingyi and the
old frontier, Bo Min Yaung was ravaging the country
with a large following, accompanied by ponies and elephants.

In the south-eastern tracts drained by the Sittang
river four *Bo*, Maung Hmôn, Maung Gyi, Maung Lat,
and Buddha Yáza still had their hunting grounds. Time
after time they collected their men, but dispersed again
into the hill jungles when hard pressed by troops, who
left them no rest by day or night, and who prevented
them from disturbing the country south of the old frontier.

On the right bank of the Irrawaddy, below the confluence of the Chindwin, the country was not really under
administration. A pretender, calling himself the Shwe-

gyobyu Prince, had a large following, while the wild Yaw tracts to the west of that were overrun by dacoits. The northern part of the Minbu district was held by Ôktamá, while Bo Shwe swayed the southern portion towards Minhla and Thayetmyo. Both of these leaders had a strong organization and pillaged the country under a more methodic system than any of the other dacoit *Bo*. In the intervals between raids and forays into the open country near the Irrawaddy, they withdrew into the water-logged and densely forested tracts, reeking with noxious exhalations, skirting the base of the Arakan Yoma, the range of hills forming the western watershed of the Irrawaddy and its tributaries. Here they remained comparatively safe, finding a double protection in the thick jungles traversed only by small footpaths, and in the malarious climate deadly to those who had not been hereditarily acclimatized to it. But Bo Shwe's influence was now already on the wane. He had long been hunted vigorously by mounted infantry and Gurkhas, and had more than once barely escaped with his life.

In the Upper Irrawaddy valley, the Katha district was rendered fairly quiet except where the State of Wuntho marched with it on the south-west. The Sawbwa of this Shan State, comprising the hills between the Irrawaddy and the Chindwin, refused to come in or acknowledge allegiance to the British, and endeavoured to seize the town of Mogaung on the north, which was held by a Burmese town magistrate, acting nominally for the British Government, but in reality " eating the town " as in the old days. Between Mogaung and Bhamo the country was undisturbed.

Such was the condition of the Irrawaddy plain, the Chindwin valley, and the Sittang drainage, the three great riverine tracts forming the central portion of Upper Burma, in March, 1887, after Sir Frederick Roberts had, on 12th February, returned from Burma to India, leaving the Upper Burma field force under the command of Major-General Sir George White. On 1st April, 1887, this force consisted of 20,791 troops, divided into four brigades (Mandalay, Shwebo, Meiktila, and Myingyan), and three smaller separate commands (Bhamo, Ruby

Mines, and Chindwin). The garrison in Lower Burma was again formed into a separate force under Major-General B. L. Gordon, and consisted of 2,106 Europeans and 4,088 native troops.

During the following year satisfactory progress was made in the work of pacification. Order was almost completely restored in Lower Burma, while in Upper Burma a large Military Police force of 13,244 officers and men had been organized, and the work of maintaining order, previously performed by troops, was now efficiently carried out by these police, acting under the immediate control of the civil officers. On 1st April, 1888, the purely military force was reduced to 16,602, and ceased to be on the footing of a field force, while the number of brigades was reduced to three. But the total effective strength of troops and Military Police throughout Burma rose from 31,830 to 34,712 ; for while the purely military garrison of Upper Burma was reduced by over 4,000 men, the Military Police under civil administration rose by 8,400.

The organization of the Military Police and the establishment of Military Police posts, in place of posts held by troops, contributed greatly towards success. So soon as the pacification of any district was sufficiently advanced, the military posts were withdrawn and Military Police posts established. In time each district had its own battalion, recruited from the warlike races of Northern India, and officered by a commandant and an assistant commandant appointed from Indian regiments. These Military Police battalions were organized like native regiments in all except the scale of commissioned officers. Their duties were almost purely military. They supplemented the work of the regular troops by occupying posts and maintaining patrols when once the first step towards pacification, the breaking up and dispersal of rebel and dacoit gangs, had been achieved. Subsequently, when the work of pacification was completed, several of these battalions were bodily transferred to the Indian army. At first the minimum strength of any Military Police post was fixed at twenty-five men; but this was raised to forty in order that, when patrols of ten men or more were sent out, the force remaining behind would always be strong enough to hold the post against attacks, for experience showed that when troops were withdrawn there was a tendency towards recrudescence of dacoity.

The district magistrate had control over both the Civil and the Military Police in his district, and was responsible for saying what posts should be occupied, and what the strength of each should be. The general principle laid down for the guidance of civil officers in allocating the force was that the most important and central posts should be occupied by fairly large bodies of Military Police, to each of which should be added a small number of Burmese constables for the purpose of receiving reports, investigating cases, and collecting information. Stress was laid on maintaining constant systematic patrols, and on training the men in musketry practice. Between these protective Military Police posts intermediate posts were held by Civil Police, consisting of Burmese recruited locally. To enable long marches and prompt pursuits to be made, thus the better to supply the place of the regular troops whose work they had taken over, from eleven to twenty per cent. of the men in each Military Police battalion were mounted on small, hardy Burmese ponies.

The hands of the district magistrates were much strengthened, and the work of pacification greatly assisted, by the passing of the Upper Burma Village Regulation (XIV. of 1887). Designed to arrest that disintegration of village communities, and to prevent that undue centralization of authority which had resulted in Lower Burma from abandoning the previous customs so well suited to the Burmese character, the regulation gave considerable power to local headmen, and enforced joint responsibility on villagers in matters of police. Under the village system of administration, local headmen had been the foundation of the civil government, controlling the villages, collecting revenue, deciding disputes and dealing with petty crime. In Lower Burma, after the second Burmese war, this excellent system had been allowed to fall to pieces and it was likely to soon crumble away in Upper Burma also, unless specially protected. The Village Regulation secured, as nearly as possible, to headmen the position and the powers formerly possessed by them in Burmese times, and it enforced with much strictness the joint responsibility of the village in criminal matters. A great many petty criminal cases could, under it, be disposed of by the village headmen, who were also responsible for taking immediate action in, and for reporting to the nearest police post, any case of serious crime. Under its authority provisions were made for the better defence of villages, and for deporting temporarily to other parts of the country men known to be in league with rebels or dacoits, or the friends and relatives of those declared to be outlaws. This latter measure contributed very specially towards the establishment of order.

Before the end of the official year 1887–88, the Mandalay district was freed from all large or formidable gangs of rebels or dacoits, and most of those in the Shwebo district had been broken up and their leaders either killed or captured. In Sagaing the notorious Hla U had been killed by his followers, who broke up into small bands and terrorized the forest tracts; hence special measures had to be adopted against these. In Ava Bo Tôk and Shwe Yan were killed, and the district reduced to quietude. Of two pretender Princes in the Yeú district one died of fever and the other was executed as a rebel. The gangs troubling Kyauksè were pursued into the Shan hills and dispersed, but subsequently rallied again under a pretender calling himself the Setkya Prince, who soon took refuge again in the hills. In the Chindwin valley the rising of the so-called Shwegyobya Prince, who had been a vaccinator in Lower Burma, was quelled by most of the leaders being either killed in action or else taken, tried, and executed, while the pretender himself fled into the Chin hills. Serious Chin raids from the hills also took place, which had to be dealt with later on. Much was done to pacify Myingyan and Meiktila, but gangs headed by Bo Cho and Ya Nyun still remained unsuppressed, though their influence was on the wane. In Pagán the two chief leaders infesting the Pópa hill were accounted for, Tha Do being killed and Ya Kut tried and executed ; while the Yaw country to the west was settled and placed on a satisfactory footing. To the south of this Ôktamá still defied all endeavours to crush his power. He and his chief lieutenants were proclaimed outlaws beyond the hope of pardon, but an amnesty was offered to all minor followers, and over 1,200 of his men surrendered with their arms on these terms. From Minhla Bo Shwe was pursued in Lower Burma and killed by the mounted infantry after a Robin Hood career extending over about fifteen years. In Magwe Bo Min Yaung was killed and Tôk Gyi captured, while other gangs were dispersed. North of Mandalay, the Ruby Mines, Myadaung, and Bhamo districts were fairly free from organized rebellion, and the Wuntho Sawbwa had made his submission, though he sullenly refused to come in personally or to receive British officers in a befitting manner. A military column visited Mogaung and the jade mines, and established settled administration there.

The results of the work achieved in Upper Burma by the end of the first fifteen months of its administration as a British province had, in fact, quite surpassed expectation. Organized rebellion had been crushed in all except two or three of the seventeen districts, although the more sporadic occurrence of dacoity could only be expected to cease, and even then by no means entirely, when once public security and tranquillity had become more thoroughly established. In every district the people were becoming more accustomed and reconciled to British rule, and more willing to assist in the maintenance of order. One of the best signs of this was that on various occasions villagers, tired of the oppression of dacoits, resisted and killed them.

Several Acts of the Legislature were extended to Upper Burma under the Scheduled Districts Act, and a new Military Police Act was passed and applied to the whole province. Among the special regulations enacted for Upper Burma, the most important of all was the Village Regulation, but others provided also for the registration of documents affecting immovable property, the establishment of municipalities, the administration and control of the forests, the collection and realization of arrears of revenue, the limitation of suits, the declaration of the law concerning stamps, and the control of mining and trading in rubies and other precious stones. In May, 1887, the Chief Commissioner had resumed control of both Upper and Lower Burma, and by the end of the year the Secretariat establishments for both parts of the province were combined at the headquarters of Government in Rangoon.

The work of establishing authority firmly throughout all the plains and central lands forming the valleys of the Upper Irrawaddy, Chindwin, and Sittang rivers had already been so far accomplished as to enable steps to be taken towards dealing with the wild Kachin and Chin tribes, who inhabited the hills on the north and west and were continually raiding down into the valleys.

Things had meanwhile been progressing very favourably in the great Shan States extending eastwards across the Salween and the Mekong or Cambodia rivers, and marching with China and Siam. The first steps for the settlement of these States were taken early in January, 1887, when a mixed force of European and native troops, under Colonel (now Sir Edward) Stedman, accompanied by two civil officers, was despatched to Nyaungywé for the relief of the Sawbwa there, who had taken an early opportunity of intimating his allegiance to the British Government. Like the Thibaw Sawbwa, he gained greatly by taking this step ; for he was confirmed as chief, although he was then in unjust possession of the State. At the time of the occupation of Mandalay the ruling Sawbwa, Saw Maung, was at the capital, whence he at once returned to his State lying at the south-west corner of the Shan tracts. Here he was attacked by the supporters of the Limbin Prince and driven out, while his half-brother, Saw Chit Su, was appointed Sawbwa. The latter was attacked and expelled by another brother named Saw Ôn, who usurped the State, declined to join the Limbin Prince's confederacy, tendered his allegiance to the British, and implored them to assist his loyal efforts to maintain himself as their tributary. In this he was successful ; but in July, 1897, Saw Maung had the subsequent satisfaction of performing Saw Ôn's obsequies at Taunggyi, and of having the Sawbwaship bestowed on him once again by the British Government. In October, 1885, the Limbin Prince (a son of the heir apparent assassinated by the Myingun Prince in 1866), who had lived under British protection during Thibaw's reign, escaped from Moulmein and placed himself at the head of a confederacy organized by exiled chiefs in the Kengtung State for the overthrow of King Thibaw or the establishment of an independent Shan kingdom. By the time the Limbin Prince arrived and placed himself at the head of the rebellion, the Burmese troops had been withdrawn and the Kingdom of Ava had fallen, so that only the alternative remained to attempt to establish a Shan kingdom. The important States of Monè, Yatsauk, Maingpun, and Mawkmè, and about a score of minor States had joined the movement, while others held aloof, probably from motives of personal enmity to one or other of the allied chiefs, for, though many of the rulers of these States were allied by ties of consanguinity or by marriage, there were long-standing feuds always liable to break out into internecine warfare at every opportunity which seemed favourable. The most important States which refused to take part in the confederacy were the western States of Thibaw in the north, and of Nyaungywé in the south. Their prompt avowal of allegiance came opportunely for the British, and was richly rewarded.

Early in February, 1887, the British force relieved Nyaungywé, and a Superintendent was established with a sufficient garrison at Maingthauk, to which the name of Fort Stedman was given, on the north-eastern shore of the Inlè lake, a position suitable for the purpose of asserting the suzerainty of the British Government, of putting an end to the anarchy and internecine warfare which prevailed, and of maintaining order and encouraging progress in the various States. In May, 1887, the rebel confederacy was broken up, and the Limbin Prince was, on surrendering, at his own request sent to Calcutta as a pensioner.

During the rainy months of the summer of 1887

anarchy prevailed throughout all the Shan States except Thibaw; but, as soon as the state of the season permitted, two powerful columns were sent on tour throughout the country. These operations were successful in immediately obtaining the personal submission of all the principal Sawbwa, of confirming them in their positions as tributary chiefs, of settling their relations with the Government and with each other, of fixing the amount of tribute to be paid by each State, of placing the administration of the States on a satisfactory footing, and of getting the Sawbwa to agree to refer tribal disputes to the Superintendent in place of resorting to warfare. This peaceful settlement of the States on the great Shan plateau during the cold season of 1887–88 was obtained bloodlessly, and almost without a shot being fired. The only interchange of shots was when some men in the Taungbaing State attacked the rear guard of one of the columns.

During the year 1888–89 lawlessness was stamped out in Lower Burma, except in the north-western frontier district of Thayetmyo; while the progress of the pacification of the internal portions of Upper Burma continued to advance most satisfactorily along the same lines of action as in the previous year. While the suppression of dacoity was mainly left to the Military Police, the troops were utilized chiefly in pursuing and breaking up the few remaining bands of rebels still at large in two or three of the districts; and opportunity was also at length taken to send punitive expeditions into the hills to let the Chins and Kachins feel they had now very different masters to deal with than under the old effete Burmese administration, and to make them realize that raiding and lawlessness would have to cease. The Mandalay district remained free from organized crime, although a dacoit leader, Nga To, gave a good deal of trouble. From Kyauksè the Setkya Prince was driven into the Shan hills, captured, tried for rebellion and murder, and executed. Sagaing, Ava, and Shwebo were reduced to order, the most formidable of the robber gangs being broken up and their leaders either surrendered or else were killed or captured; but Yeú was still infested by Yan Gyi Aung and minor leaders, whose gangs found refuge in the dense forests of this thinly populated district. The Chindwin districts, being cleared of dacoits, were free from serious crime by the end of the year, and villagers who left their homesteads during the disturbed times were returning. In Myingyan and Meiktila Bo Cho and Ya Nyun were still at large, though many minor leaders were disposed of. In Pakôkku and the Yaw country various leaders sprang up; but the chief *Bo*, Tha Do, Saga, and Nga Kwe, were killed, and the whole of the district reduced to an undisturbed condition by the end of the year. In Minbu Ôktamá and his subordinates Oktayá, Byaing Gyi, and others, were still at large, but were being hunted down with such untiring energy that their power was rapidly waning. Yamèthin and Meiktila remained undisturbed throughout the year, and Pyinmaná (the old Ningyan district) was freed from organized crime; south and west of these districts Magwe was, however, more disturbed than any other part of the province. Seven large and numerous smaller dacoit gangs sprang up there during the rainy season of 1888, and two pretenders, calling themselves the Shwekyinyo Prince and Buddha Yáza, placed themselves in rebellion at the head of the gangs. Encouragement was given to this movement by the repulse of a party of military police in November. The troops in the district were reinforced, the provisions of the Village Regulation were worked vigorously, and amnesty was offered to all except some of the prominent leaders proclaimed as outlaws; but the end of the year found the Administration forced to admit that the state of Magwe was a reproach to it.

In the northern districts the settled portions of Bhamo continued quiet, but parts of Katha and the Ruby Mines district were infested with dacoits. The Wuntho Sawbwa paid the tribute demanded of him, but still declined to come in and make personal submission. The leasing of the Ruby Mines to an English company no doubt called forth a recrudescence of lawlessness by exciting the apprehensions and the ill-will of the resident miners who had previously enjoyed the practical monopoly of digging and washing for rubies. In Mogaung a rebellion was raised by Maung Po Saw, a former magistrate there, who succeeded in exciting the hostility of the Kachin tribes after the return of the military column which had visited the jade mines. The trade route was blocked, and in May, 1888, a determined attack was made on the stockaded town of Mogaung, where the rebels received severe handling from the Gurkha Military Police. As the Kachins siding with Po Saw refused to make formal submission and deliver up the rebels they were harbouring, punitive operations were undertaken against them under the direction of Sir George White, in the dry season of 1888–89, with complete success. Posts were established at important points, and the tribes, almost without exception, submitted and gave guarantees for future good conduct. In the south-eastern portion of Bhamo, lying between the Shweli river and the Chinese frontier, a good deal of trouble was also caused by the Pônkan Kachins, incited to disturbance by Saw Yan Hnaing, a grandson of King Mindôn, and Kan Hlaing, a dissatisfied claimant to the Shan States of Mohlaing and Möng Mit. Ever since the annexation these Pônkan Kachins had been a menace to the peace of the Bhamo district, but they were effectually reduced to reason by an expedition sent against them under Brigadier-General (now Sir George) Wolseley in the spring of 1889, on the return of the troops from Mogaung.

In the Shan States a military expedition had to be sent against Sawlapaw, the chief of Eastern Karenni, who made an unprovoked attack on the State of Mawkmè, expelling the Sawbwa, occupying the capital, and devastating the country. In May, 1888, he retired before the approach of a British force; but, on their withdrawal, leaving only a small garrison of native troops in the town of Mawkmè, the red Karens returned in July and again ravaged the country, burning villages, and plundering the people. The Karens were attacked by British troops and forced to retreat with heavy loss. After two insolent letters had been received from Sawlapaw and returned to him by the hands of his own messengers, an ultimatum was sent to him insisting, among other things, on his making personal submission to the Superintendent at Fort Stedman. Owing to non-compliance therewith, a strong column, under Brigadier-General H. Collett, C.B., marched against Karenni from Fort Stedman, while a second column, under Colonel J. J. Harvey, operated from the southern valley of the Salween. After encountering some resistance both columns reached Sawlôn, the capital, early in January; but Sawlapaw had fled before the arrival of the northern column. His nephew and heir apparent, Sawlawi, was inducted into the Sawbwaship of Eastern Karenni as a tributary state in subordinate alliance with the British Government. Apart from this expedition, the current of affairs ran smoothly throughout the southern Shan States. Durbars were held at Monè and Fort Stedman during May, 1889, and were attended by almost every chief of note. The northern Shan States were not quite so peaceful and settled, but nothing occurred which called for special military expeditions.

On the western frontier an important series of operations was undertaken against the Chins inhabiting the country bordering on the Yaw tracts, the Kalé State, and the Kúbo valley. The principal of these Chin tribes are the Siyin, Sagyilaing, and Kanhaw on the north, the Tashôn in the centre, and the Baungshè on the south. The central Tashôn tribe is the most powerful. The suspicions of these tribes were aroused by proposals to make a road across their hills from Burma into Bengal, and the feelings thus excited were acted upon by the Shwegyobyu pretender and the late chief of Kalé, who had been recently deposed by the British Government for active opposition. Incited by these two men, the Siyin and Sagyilaing raided into the Kúbo valley, and the Baungshè into the Yaw country; while, in May, 1888, the Tashôn swept down on Indin and kidnapped the newly-appointed Sawbwa of Kalé. Towards the end of the rainy season further raids occurred, and Kalémyo itself was attacked. A commencement was made with the Siyin and Sagyilaing, all of whose villages were destroyed after stubborn resistance in many cases. The Kanhaw were next operated against, nearly every village belonging to the tribe being taken and destroyed. In April, 1889, active operations were also commenced against the Tashôn, but had to be interrupted on the advent of the rains. The results of the punishment in course of infliction was, however, that nearly 200 kidnapped captives were restored to their homes, and that an exemplary lesson had been taught the three tribes dealt with.

During February, 1889, the extension of the Rangoon-Toungoo railway line to Mandalay was completed, and on 1st March it was opened to traffic of all descriptions. Sanctioned during September, 1886, the surveys were at once put in hand, and the construction of the various sections took from sixteen months to two years to complete. About 24,000 coolies, two-thirds of whom were Burmese, were employed on the work during the greater part of the time. The construction, at a cost of nearly two million pounds, of these 220 miles of railway, running through a country infested during most of the time with rebel bands and dacoit gangs, was a magnificent achievement; and, but for a severe epidemic of cholera, during which the works were almost entirely deserted over nearly a third of the line, it would have been open to traffic by the 1st January, 1889. Even before its formal opening, so soon as trolleys and construction trains could be run, it was found of great service in military and police operations, and both directly and indirectly its construction contributed in a marked degree towards the pacification and settlement of the country. During the open season of 1888-89 surveys were carried out to the west of the Irrawaddy from Sagaing northwards up the Mu Valley and through the Wuntho State into the Katha district, so that similar advantages might soon be secured to the northern districts in the direction of Mogaung.

No fresh regulations were passed for Upper Burma during the year, though several enactments were extended to it under the Scheduled Districts Act; but a Shan States Act provided for the administration of these States by the native chiefs subject to the control of the Local Government exercised through Superintendents at Fort

Stedman and Lashio. A Lower Burmese Village Act was also passed, extending to the older parts of the province provisions for the administration of the rural tracts similar to those preserved for Upper Burma by Regulation XIV. of 1887.

So satisfactory had been the progress of pacification and settlement that it was considered unnecessary to retain Upper Burma as a separate military command after 1st April, 1889. Sir George White therefore handed over his charge to General (now Sir Benjamin) Gordon in Rangoon, and the troops were once more brought under the Commander-in-Chief of Madras. The Burma command thus reorganized consisted of three districts in charge of Brigadiers-General at Rangoon, Mandalay, and Myingyan, and of six smaller commands at other important centres. During the year the troops in Upper Burma were reduced from 13,250 to 11,335; but this apparent reduction was again, as in 1887–88, more than over-balanced by the numbers of the Military Police being raised from 13,244 to 17,880. The total strength of troops and Military Police in Upper Burma thus rose from 26,494 in April, 1888, to 29,215 in April, 1889; while throughout the whole province it increased from 32,890 to 34,446 men. In October, 1888, the whole of the police forces of Lower and Upper Burma, which had hitherto been separately administered, were amalgamated under Brigadier-General Stedman as Inspector-General, assisted by two Deputy Inspectors-General, one for Civil, and one for Military Police.

By the end of the following year (1889–90) the troops throughout Burma still numbered 15,608, while the Military Police force aggregated 18,618, giving a total fighting strength of 34,226 men. But matters had meanwhile progressed so favorably that the six separate minor commands directly under the Major-General commanding were abolished, the troops being distributed among the three district commands under Brigadiers-General at Rangoon, Mandalay, and Myingyan, and the Chin expeditionary force under Brigadier-General (the late Sir William Penn) Symons. The energy with which rebels were run down and dacoit gangs dispersed effected a marked reduction in violent crime throughout almost every district. Lower Burma had regained its normal condition as before the last war. Mandalay was freed from a troublesome gang, headed by Nga To, and district officers no longer required escorts for their protection on tour. In Kyauksè a rebel band raised by Kyaw Zaw, one of the late Setkya pretender's adherents, was dispersed. Pakôkku, Yamèthin, Meiktila, Pymmaná, and Sagaing remained undisturbed throughout the year; while the Upper and Lower Chindwin districts, Katha, the Ruby Mines, Shwebo, and Yeú were reduced to order. In this last district the two remaining leaders of note, Yan Gyi Aung and Nga Aga, were induced to surrender through the intermediation of the Gaing Ôk or Buddhist bishop of the district. The Sawbwa of Wuntho at length made his personal submission at Katha, and sent his wife and his sons to visit the Commissioner at Mandalay.

In Minbu Ôktamá was captured in June, 1889, while most of his lieutenants and other independent dacoit leaders either surrendered themselves or else were killed or captured, and organized dacoity was practically suppressed. For the reduction of the lawlessness and disorganization of the turbulent Magwe district special operations were undertaken with so marked success that during the third quarter of the year only one violent crime, a petty robbery, was reported.

As district after district became pacified and settled the gradual replacement of military posts by Military Police posts in the interior of Upper Burma was effected. At the beginning of 1887 there were 142 posts held by troops and 56 by Military Police; by the following year the numbers had changed to 84 and 175 respectively; and early in 1889 only 41 were held by troops and 192 by Military Police. By the summer of 1889 organized resistance to the British Government had collapsed so thoroughly throughout Upper Burma that it was found possible to reduce the number of Military Police posts and to maintain smaller garrisons at those still kept up. In all the more settled districts arrangements were therefore made to concentrate, as a strong and highly trained reserve, about half the strength of each battalion at the headquarters of each civil district; but this scheme of course did not apply to districts like Bhamo, where the Military Police had to protect extensive tracts against the raids of wild hill tribes, or Katha, where disorder on the borders of the Wuntho State still rendered such a scheme impracticable. Changes were also made in the organization of the Military Police by the amalgamation of two or more battalions with the object of reducing the strength and the cost of the large total force.

After General Wolseley's expedition in April 1889 the Pônkan Kachins to the south-east of Bhamo gave no further trouble, while that part of the district was also relieved by the capture of the pretender, calling himself Buddha Yáza. Kan Hlaing, the Mohlaing-Momeik claimant, and Saw Yan Hnaing, King Mindôn's grandson, were harboured by the Lwèsaing-Tônhôn Kachins, and continued to cause trouble in the Sinkan township, and on the borders of the Möng Mit State. Columns were therefore sent against them in December, 1889, from Bhamo and Möng Mit, which destroyed the village of Lwèsaing, received the submission of all the villages in the Lwèsaing-Tônhôn tract, levied fines on all villages which had harboured or assisted the pretenders, and brought in some of the headmen as prisoners. The result of the expedition was the complete submission of the Kachin tribes in the Upper Sinkan valley, who were taught a severe lesson; but Saw Yan Hnaing and Kan Hlaing, though expelled from their retreats, evaded capture and managed to effect their escape into Chinese territory.

To the west of the Chindwin river the operations of the previous season against the Chin tribes, which had been interrupted by the rains, were also in December, 1889, recommenced under Brigadier-General Symons. The objects of the expedition were attained without any serious resistance. The powerful Tashôn tribes and the Baungshè tendered their submission, gave up captives they had kidnapped, paid the fines levied on them, and promised compliance with the demands of Government. The ex-Sawbwa of Kalé surrendered himself from his retreat among them, and was permitted to resume the pension previously allowed to him after his deposition. For dealing with the Chins, military posts with political officers were established at Fort White among the northern tribes, and at Háka for the southern tribes.

The Shan States remained peaceful and undisturbed, except for a petty abortive insurrection in North Theinni, which was promptly stopped, on Kun Yi, the pretender, being killed in action. The whole of these States were now entirely garrisoned by Military Police. In the southern and eastern Shan States the chief events of the year were the submission of the Sawbwa of Kengtung, the most important of the Shan States lying to the east of the Salween river, to the Superintendent, and the work carried out by the Anglo-Siamese Commission under Mr. Ney Elias, C.I.E., appointed by the Government of India for the settlement of various territorial questions on the south-eastern frontier of the Shan States and Karenni. At the time of the expedition against Eastern Karenni in 1888–89, Siamese troops occupied tracts east of the Salween, which had long been inhabited by settlers from Eastern Karenni. This territory was claimed as part of the Siamese province of Chiengmai (Zimmè); new claims were also advanced to the trans-Salween tracts of Maingmaw and Mèsakôn, appanages of the State of Mawkmè; and old claims, previously asserted, were maintained in respect of four small States which had been made over to the Maingpan Sawbwa late in 1888. The points in dispute were to have been investigated by a joint commission, but finally the Siamese Government declined to join in the enquiry, which had accordingly to be carried out *ex parte*. The two appanages were restored to Mawkmè, and the four small States made over to the Sawbwa of Maingpan and Maingtun, while a report on the more important territorial question was submitted for the orders of the Government of India. It was not until 1892 that Sawlawi, chief of Eastern Karenni, was, with the concurrence of Siam, reinstated in his trans-Salween possessions.

In March, 1890, Sir Charles Crosthwaite, Chief Commissioner of Burma, visited the Shan States for the first time and held a durbar at Fort Stedman, which was attended by nearly all the cis-Salween chiefs and the notables of the eastern and southern States.

The only fresh legislation relating to Upper Burma was the Land and Revenue Regulation, 1889, declaring the law regarding rights of land, providing for the assessment and collection of revenue, and formulating a complete system of revenue law, based as far as possible on the ascertained customs of the country.

By the end of 1890 the work of pacification throughout Upper Burma was complete, and there were fewer violent crimes there than in Lower Burma during the year 1890–91. Reductions in the strength of the garrison could, however, not yet be ventured on, as much still remained to be done in the frontier tracts. Three battalions of military police, numbering over 3,000 men, were converted from frontier levies into battalions of the native army, and further conversions, affecting other 3,000, were under consideration and soon to be sanctioned. Major-General Gordon made over charge of the Burma command on 31st May, 1890, to Brigadier-General Wolseley, who was relieved on 26th October by Major-General R. C. Stewart, C.B. The troops amounted to 18,763, while the Military Police numbered 16,506, representing a total effective strength of 35,269 men.

During the first year after the annexation the crushing of organized rebellion and of armed resistance occupied the attention of Government so fully that it was not possible to introduce regular methods and systematic administration, but in the succeeding four years every district in Upper Burma was gradually reduced to order, and organized crime had entirely disappeared from any part of the whole province. The only remaining elements of disturbance were the wild tribes inhabiting the forest-clad hills of the northern frontier districts. Before the end of 1890 no pretender, no rebel, or no dacoit *Bo* having any considerable following was to be found throughout what had formerly been the kingdom of Ava. All such leaders who had not surrendered or died, or else had not been killed or captured, were in hiding and deserted by their former adherents. Except among the

SYSTEM OF ADMINISTRATION

Chin and the Kachin hill-tribes, district officers could move about freely without escorts. In every case in which organized rebellion or dacoity was suppressed, terms were offered to all except the principal leaders and men personally concerned in atrocious crimes; and in almost every district in Upper Burma large numbers of released or surrendered dacoits were living under surveillance, but otherwise unmolested, and engaging in peaceful pursuits. The powerful and efficient body of Military Police was in course of transformation into battalions of the regular native army; civil police had been organized in every district, and real progress was being made in the prevention and detection of crime; and the district administration had been gradually assimilated to that obtaining in the older portion of the province. But no encouragement was given to the natural tendency of officers to attempt to arrange district work after the pattern to which they had been accustomed in Lower Burma. While purifying corrupt methods and removing barbarous enormities, the maintenance of the spirit of the Burmese administration was desired; the customs and prejudices of the new subjects were interfered with as little as possible; and particular care was taken not to attempt to force upon them a brand-new system of administration, inconsistent with their national genius or habits. Special attention was given to the maintenance of the village community system, which was at the earliest possible opportunity placed on a secure legal basis. In training the necessary subordinate staff to provide for the administration of justice and the collection of revenue, full use was made of loyal Burmese officers, many of whom rendered conspicuous service. Government public offices had been erected at the headquarters of districts, and suitable jails were constructed; while the judicial administration was under the control of an experienced officer. In the larger towns a simple system of municipal government was introduced, but no attempt was made to extend the principle of self-government beyond the limits which the circumstances of the newly-acquired province rendered necessary. The educational needs of the country were examined, and steps were being gradually taken to strengthen and improve, while abstaining from needless interference with, the simple elementary tuition in reading, writing, and arithmetic at monasteries by the gradual introduction of a sound and practical scheme of public instruction. Dispensaries were open at the headquarters of every district, and during 1890 medical relief was afforded to nearly 100,000 patients, representing more than one-thirty-fifth of the total population. The revenue system had been examined and put on a satisfactory footing, with the result that it had increased to about 113 lacs of rupees (£753,333) during 1890, or some 8 lacs (£53,333) more than the largest revenue which had ever found its way in any year into the royal treasury at Mandalay; and this increase was effected without imposing any fresh taxation or burden on the people, although during the same time some obnoxious and oppressive imposts had been abolished. In the dry central zone—where denudation of the original forests in times past now very seriously affects the rainfall, the humidity of the air, and the water-storage capacity of the soil, where agriculture is consequently precarious, and where scarcity often amounting almost to famine is liable to occur to a greater or less extent every few years—the irrigation works of former days, which had long since been allowed to fall into disrepair, were examined with a view to the repair of the old works and the construction of a new irrigation system. The forests, containing the richest supplies of teak timber in the world, which had been worked in a most wasteful manner during the King's time, had already been brought under systematic management by the Forest Department, and considerable progress was being made in their examination and survey, and in the selection of the better portions for the formation of permanent State Reserves.

The material welfare of the people and the development of the natural resources of the country had meanwhile not been neglected. Next to the establishment of peace, the most urgent need was the improvement of means of communication. There was a large expenditure on public works. The extension of the railway from Toungoo to Mandalay provided the best possible means of communication through a land-locked part of the province, enabled food supplies to be easily poured into the dry central zone liable to suffer from scarcity, and gave the population there the means of going away and settling in other districts where agriculture was less precarious. So peaceful were the tracts between Mandalay and the old frontier that passenger trains were now running through from Rangoon by night as well as by day. To the west of the Irrawaddy the construction of a line, begun in 1889–90, was being rapidly extended northwards through fertile tracts rich in natural resources. The open season of 1889–90 also saw the commencement of reconnaissance surveys for a railway running eastwards from Mandalay across the Shan plateau, through Thibaw and Lashio, onwards towards the Kunlôn ferry on the Salween, whence important trade routes branched northwards, eastwards, and southwards into Yunnan and the eastern and the Siamese Shan States. Well-aligned cart roads were opened out from Meiktila to Fort Stedman, the capital of the southern Shan States, and from Mandalay to Thibaw on the way to Lashio, the headquarters of the northern Shan States; while Mogôk, the centre of the ruby mining industry, was similarly brought in touch with Thabeitkyin on the Irrawaddy river. Telegraphic communication had existed from Mandalay to Rangoon in the Burmese time, but the line had to be reconstructed and maintained in spite of continual interruptions occasioned by dacoits, who cut up the wire to use as slugs. Now a network of lines connected the heart of the Chin hills on the west, the centre of the Shan States on the east, and Bhamo and Mogaung on the north, with the lines converging on Rangoon and extending everywhere throughout the older part of the province. By the end of 1890 there were nearly 4,000 miles of telegraph lines and some fifty offices open in Upper Burma, and over 700,000 messages were conveyed across them during that year. The work done by the Telegraph Department contributed greatly to the progress of the civil and military administration.

In the settlement of frontier affairs equally good progress had also been made. Before the annexation, and for about a year after it, the Shan States were in a chaotic state of anarchy; but now all the chiefs who owed allegiance to the King of Ava had tendered their submission and become peaceful subjects of the British Government, whose influence had been extended across the Salween river so as to bring Kengtung, the most important of the trans-Salween States, into subordinate alliance. Internecine warfare had been stopped, and the paths of peace were open leading towards a prosperity hitherto unknown. Eastern Karenni had been brought under British protection, and satisfactory arrangements made for its administration. On the northern and north-western fringes of the province the Kachin tribes had learned by drastic lessons that raiding and acts of violence were no longer to be permitted; while the more important of the Chin tribes on the western border had by similar punitive treatment been brought to tender their submission, and arrangements were being made for the permanent occupation of their country, for the enforcement of administrative authority, and for opening it up by means of good lines of communication.

These admirable results were attained within five years of the annexation of Upper Burma, or in about half the time that had been required for the pacification of Lower Burma after the second Burmese war. When Sir Charles Crosthwaite handed over the Chief Commissionership of Burma to his successor, Sir Alexander Mackenzie, on 10th December, 1890, after nearly four years of the heaviest responsibility that had fallen upon any of the Indian administrators of that time, the foundations of future prosperity and happiness were securely laid for a people who had borne, with admirable patience, contentment, and passive fortitude the misfortunes brought upon them by the misgovernment of their King and his Court, and by the crimes and barbarities of their own fellow-countrymen. Since the days of the Indian Mutiny, in 1857–59, neither civilians nor soldiery had had such calls made upon their strength, energy, endurance, and devotion to duty as during these five anxious and eventful years of the pacification and settlement of Upper

COST OF ANNEXING AVA

Burma; and these calls were responded to in a manner befitting the heirs of the noble heritage to which Englishmen are born, and worthy of the best and noblest traditions of the Civil and Military Services in India.

What the third Burmese war and the pacification of Upper Burma actually cost in money, incurred on purely military expenditure, may partly be seen from the table given below. Apart from the special expenditure, the normal military charges incurred by Burma have been raised from a little over £190,000 for Lower Burma during the year 1884–85 to somewhat over £600,000 a year now for the whole province. But the territory to be protected has been increased by nearly 150 per cent., and the frontiers have been advanced so as now to march with those of Siam, French Indo-China, and China beyond the new territories acquired to the north-east. Regarded from a financial point of view, the conquest was abnormally cheap at the price. The garrison on 31st March, 1900, consisted of only 10,324 troops (2,811 European and 7,513 Native), but this was about 2,000 below the normal strength of the previous year.

The war, and the five years occupied in the work of pacification.		The period of transition to settled administration.		The normal garrison of Burma.	
Year.	£	Year.	£	Year.	£
1885–86	635,600	1891–92	864,667 [2]	1894–95	648,000
1886–87	1,230,000	1892–93	777,334	1895–96	636,667
1887–88 [1]	(not obtainable)	1893–94	682,000	1896–97	620,667
1888–89	657,334			1897–98	610,000
1889–90	653,334			1898–99 [3]	(not ob-
1890–91	749,334 [2]			1899–1900	tainable)

[1] The figures for 1887–88 are still regarded as confidential.

[2] The decrease in 1887 to 1890 was due to the formation of the Military Police, maintained from civil expenditure; and the increase beginning again in 1891 is due to the conversion of several battalions of Military Police into regular troops as Burma regiments.

[3] "It is not possible to furnish the figures . . . showing separately the military expenditure incurred in Burma . . . the military expenditure is classified only under the heads of the four commands, viz.: Punjab, Bengal, Madras, and Bombay" (India Office, f. 1022, dated 5 March, 1901).

149

Chapter VI

CIVIL AND MILITARY ADMINISTRATION UNDER BURMESE RULE

"*THE Burmese Sovereign of the Rising Sun who rules over the country of Thunáparánta and the country of Támbadípá, with all the other great dominions and countries, and all the Umbrella-bearing Chiefs of the East, whose Glory is exceeding great and excellent, the Master of the King Elephant, Saddán, the Lord of many White Elephants, the Lord of Life, the eminently just Ruler*"—so ran the descriptive legend heading all royal letters—was a despotic ruler. The King's power was absolute : but the administration of the kingdom of Ava, extending to about 120,000 square miles, scantily populated with some three and a half millions of inhabitants, was carried on by means of Ministers whose number, rank, and functions were defined by constitutional precedent. The details relating to their appointment and duties were embodied in a book called the *Lawka Pyuha* or *Inyôn Saôk*, which likewise described with minute detail the ceremonies and etiquette of the court, and might be considered the official code of Sumptuary Laws.

Immediately after the close of the second Burmese war King Pagán was deposed by his brother, the Mindôn Prince, who, occupying the throne in 1853, ruled the kingdom with a considerable degree of enlightenment till his death in 1878. King Mindôn, or *Min Tayágyi*, "the great lawgiver," had strong commercial instincts, which were allied to a desire to bring his country more in a line with the position of the civilized nations of the West. He was, for a ruler of Ava, a humane man. In place of putting the Pagán Min to death, according to ancient custom with regard to rivals in Burma, as in most eastern countries, the deposed monarch's life was spared. He lived in his own house; he survived his successor on the throne; and he finally died a natural death in his bed. King Mindòn was an enlightened ruler. Though he professed no love for the British, he recognized their power and kept on friendly terms with them. So far as was compatible with the maintenance of his own autocratic power, he was anxious to introduce Western ideas and civilization into his kingdom. He deputed envoys to Europe in order to study the industrial arts, and sent young men of good families to England, France, and Italy to learn the languages and customs of those countries. Though his zeal was not always tempered by discretion, he did much to improve the revenues and promote the prosperity of his country.

The wisest of all the Burmese monarchs, Mindòn kept the reins of government firmly in his own hands throughout the whole of the quarter of a century of his rule. Though he held sway over much less territory than his forefathers had done, yet he was deeply anxious to maintain untarnished their full regal splendour.

At the Court of Ava there were two classes of Burmese Ministers. The authority and the responsibility of one class were restricted to the palace, somewhat in the manner of officers of the Royal Household, whilst within the other class were included all the important administrative offices of the State. During the latter days of the kingdom of Ava, however, these original distinctions had become materially obliterated for all practical purposes, though the two classes of officials were still maintained in separate categories so far as mere nomenclature was concerned.

The first class comprised the officials of the *Byèdaik* (literally "bachelors' quarters"), the Privy Council or Secret Department of the Burmese Court, whose public offices were located in a part of the northern side of the palace which had formerly been allotted to the King's young men, and to which the King used sometimes to go in order to see the royal elephants at exercise. The second category formed the *Hlutdaw* or Great Council of State, whose functions combined those of a Legislative Chamber, a Ministerial Cabinet, and a Supreme Court of Civil and Criminal Justice. The State Council Chamber—for both the Council and the Council Hall were included in the word "*Hlutdaw*," meaning literally "the place of release," or "*place du congé d'élire*"—was situated in the outer court or esplanade between the *Tagáni*, the "Red Gate," or royal entrance to the inner portions of the palace on the eastern side, and the outer gate of the palace enclosure. The offices of the various Ministers of the *Hlut* were enclosed near at hand within the same space.

The King was the nominal head of the *Hlutdaw*, but on all ordinary occasions its meetings were presided over by whomsoever happened for the time to be the most influential of the four *Mingyi* ("great rulers") or *Wungyi* ("those bearing the great burden"). These were the highest officials in the kingdom, occupying posts somewhat similar to those filled by our Cabinet Ministers or principal Secretaries of State. The offices were not hereditary, being merely conferred from time to time by the King. Each of these four chief Ministers had his own portfolio or department, though at the same time there was no hard and fast line drawn as to the distribution of the work coming before the council for disposal. Each *Mingyi* might have all sorts of administrative work to investigate and dispose of, and each had his own separate departmental seal to affix to orders and palm-leaf correspondence. The business demanding his attention might range from questions relating to agriculture, forestry, finance or politics, up to the decision of civil or criminal law cases, and might at times involve military duty even to the utmost extent of personally taking the field in charge of an army.

Lower in rank than the four *Mingyi* came two other high officials charged with the performance of very miscellaneous duties, as is almost implied in their designations, the *Myinzugyi Wun*, or "governor of the chief cavalry regiment," and the *Athiwun*, or "governor of those who are not in the royal service."

A grade lower still came the four *Wundauk*, the

Under Secretaries of State, or "sharers of the burden" of the *Mingyi*, each of whom had one or more departments of official business allotted to his care, here also without any rigid lines being prescribed as to the distribution of work. This title of Assistant was also often bestowed *honoris causâ* on provincial officials such as Governors of Townships, much in the same way as appointments are made in Britain to the Privy Council. This mark of royal favour neither involved or authorized attendance at the *Hlut* or Council of State.

All of these ten highest officials— four *Mingyi*, two *Wun*, and four *Wundauk* — in addition to possessing various other grandiloquent titles, were usually known by some territorial appellation having reference either to a province or to a large district or town made over to their special administration. The whole kingdom was subdivided into districts called *Myo* or "townships," which were handed over to these and to less exalted officials for administrative purposes. Each such official, no matter what his higher title might be, was called a *Myosâ*, or "eater of a township"—a term which very graphically hits off the manner in which the bad ones among them squeezed the district of all the revenue it was possible to lay hands on from a submissive, peaceful and helpless peasantry. The great officers of the *Hlutdaw*, resident close to the main gate on the eastern side of the palace in Mandalay, could, of course, only perform their duties as Governors of districts by means of deputies, who remitted to them enough to pay the royal revenue demand and to maintain themselves and their establishments. All the Governors of these townships had to pay in fixed annual contributions to the *Shwedaik* or Royal Treasury, but whatever they could raise beyond this, by taxation or otherwise, they retained for themselves. It was in this manner that they were able to "eat a township." Each *Myosâ* or "eater of a township," was in reality a local magnate paying tribute either to his overlord the *Mingyi*, or to their suzerain the King of Ava; and within his own district he had enormous power and influence. The vast distances of many of the towns from Mandalay, the capital, the entire want of good roads, or of any other means of communication except along the great water highway, the Irrawaddy river, and the difficulties of travelling by jungle tracks for the greater part of each year, all helped to strengthen the semi-independence of their position. They were uncontrolled by telegraph lines or daily postal service, and no public press existed to indicate any opinions held by those under their rule. Instructions from the central authority were often treated with indifference, and orders from Mandalay did not necessarily carry the same weight as attaches to similar missives in more civilized countries. Even the execution of royal orders could sometimes only be relied on as far as they could be carried out by armed force.

Until the kingdom of Burma began to be shorn of its coast provinces by wars with the British, each of the principal provinces of Rangoon, Tenasserim, Martaban, and Arakan was ruled by a *Wun* or Governor, who was in reality a Viceroy appointed by the King with full civil, judicial, fiscal, and military powers. So long as he remitted the full amount of revenue to which his province was assessed he was responsible only to the central Government. A Provincial Council, consisting of *Myo Sayé* or "town-writers," *Nakándaw* or "receivers of royal orders," and *Sitkè* or "chiefs of war," met daily in the courthouse and made reports to the Governor. The other chief officials at the seats of provincial government were the *Taunghmu* or "jailer," the *Ayátgaung* or "heads of quarters" of the town, and the *Tagáhmu* or "warden of the gates." The governorship was divided into townships, each in charge of a township officer who was called *Myo Ók* or "ruler of the town," if he were only appointed to the office from time to time, but was known as *Myo Thugyi*, or "mayor of the town," if he held office by hereditary right. The Viceroy of Pegu had more extensive powers than any of the other Governors, but he could not interfere in any way with their authority in their own jurisdiction. In addition to the usual staff he had the special assistance of an *Akunwun* or "revenue officer," an *Akaukwun* or "collector of customs," and a *Yéwun* or "conservator of the port," whose jurisdiction extended for a considerable distance inland on the river Irrawaddy and in the country situated within the immediate vicinity of its banks. Besides the fixed revenue demand levied direct from householders, there were many imposts of various sorts, including taxes on ploughs, on palm trees, and on brokerage, transit dues, dues on sale of cattle, on produce, and on fisheries, fees on lawsuits and criminal fines, and special remittances annually as presents for the King. The local officials received no regular salary, but were paid by a portion of these fees and dues, so that their interests lay in raising them as high as they could or dared. They had just to feather their nests as they best could. Whenever men were called out to perform any particular duty, or to protect the frontier, they had to be supported by the tract in question ; and, finally, special royal demands had to be met from time to time. Of these the most excessive was probably that of thirty-three and one-third ticals of silver per household levied by King Bodaw Payá in 1798, which took two years to collect, and brought in sixty lacs of rupees (£600,000) to the royal treasury.

When walking abroad, a red umbrella was borne above an official, while his residence was marked by having a cross-bar over the gate and the privilege of having it painted red.

As the amounts fixed as tribute were comparatively light it did not necessarily follow that the *Myosá* ground down and oppressed the people in his township ; but, of course, the various districts ruled over by the deputies of the high officials of the *Hlut* had practically to satisfy the demands of two "town-eaters." To be known as possessed of much ready money was to become exposed to the danger of being squeezed. This apprehension, no doubt, acting in addition to the religious feeling of the Buddhist and the desire to acquire benefits in the next state of existence, impelled many, who might otherwise have accumulated wealth, to be lavish in works of " religious merit," such as building monasteries, pagodas, shrines, bridges, etc., and to spend surplus cash in feasting priests or entertaining the country-side with public theatrical performances. In a state of society such as

existed in Upper Burma under Burmese rule, the reputation of having money must, in a district governed by
a grasping, rapacious, or unconscientious official, have
always carried with it a sense of insecurity and even of
personal danger. The very obvious disadvantages of
such a system became fully apparent to King Mindôn,
who abolished it and decreed that officials of all classes,
both civil and military, should be paid by fixed salaries,
while the plan of levying definite and regular taxes was
at the same time introduced. This was, however, only a
theoretical reorganization. The salaries were never paid
punctually, and often not at all ; hence the innovations
were of little practical effect. But, in any case, the title
of *Myosá* was retained by the district Governors as long
as the kingdom of Ava existed.

In the *Hlutdaw* the authority of the four *Mingyi*
or *Wungyi* was paramount, though it was partially
shared by the *Wundauk* or Assistants. The King was
nominally the President of the Council, or in his absence
the heir apparent or other member of the royal family:
but, practically, the Prime Minister for the time being
presided. The latter bore the title *Kinwun Mingyi*,
or "governor of the guard-houses." Under the term
Kin were comprised not only all octroi stations round the
capital and the chief towns and the "guard-houses" of all
descriptions, but also the places at which customs dues
were levied, and the military posts commanding all the
several trade routes crossing the administrative frontier.
Hence the honorary title borne by the Prime Minister
combined the idea of "Warden of the Marches" with
"Minister of Customs and Revenues." His departmental
seal was a "scorpion" (*Kin*).

All important business was submitted to the *Mingyi*
first of all, a large number of subordinates relieving them,
however, from the tediousness of troublesome details.
It might even happen, and as a matter of fact such occasions were not infrequent, that for the time being a *Wundauk* enjoyed the royal confidence in larger measure than
any of the *Mingyi*; and in such case his influence with
the latter, his direct official superiors, was always very
great. These eight Secretaries and Assistant Secretaries

of State, together with the eight *Atwinwun*, the Privy Counsellors of the *Byèdaik* or "Ministers of the Interior," who will be more especially referred to shortly, formed the Ministry of the kingdom of Ava.

The chief officials in the departmental secretariats of the *Hlutdaw* were the four *Nakándaw*, the "royal listeners" or "receivers of royal orders," who were charged with the duty of conveying communications to and from the King and the Council of State. As insignia of their high office they bore large notebooks with gilt covers within which the written orders or counsels were inscribed.

Next to these in rank came the *Sayédawgyi* or "great chief clerks." Of these there were originally four, but in course of time the number was increased to about twenty. They performed multifarious duties, and were really officers of considerable importance. They practically did the bulk of the executive work and of the general business; and as all the details were arranged by them, little or no business of any sort could be gone through in the *Hlutdaw* without their assistance. In addition to this, they held all preliminary investigations concerning any judicial matters of importance, and gave judgment in minor civil or criminal suits, subject to the approval and confirmation of the *Mingyi*.

The four *Ameindawyé* or "writers of the great orders" ranked next in dignity and position. Their duty was to prepare and issue the orders of Government after all the necessary preliminary steps had been duly taken. The handwriting of these Clerks of the Great Council was very beautiful, and their inscriptions of royal orders were really works of art—an art that is now likely to become entirely lost.

After these came the *Athônsayé* (lit. "writers of use") or Clerks of Works, to whom were entrusted the construction and the repairs of all public buildings. Below these, again, came two classes of correspondence clerks, the *Ahmádawyé* or "recorders of orders," who drafted the orders and letters to be issued by the Council of State, and the *Awéyauk* (lit. "distant arrivals"), who received and read letters coming from a distance before

submitting them to the Ministers.   Letters for the King
were received by two special ceremonial officers called
Thandawgán, one of whose particular functions was to
open the letters of apology received from all such
feudatory Chiefs, Ministers, and other high officials as
could not, or would not, personally attend and do
homage to the King at each of the *Kadáw Pwè* or "beg
pardon festivals" which formed the royal levées held
three times a year in the palace at Mandalay.   These
constituted the chief ceremonial gatherings of the year,
when tributary Princes from the Shan States, Ministers,
members of the royal family, and all court officials
appeared in the gorgeous apparel prescribed for their
rank or office, and when tribute and presents were submitted to the King in the great open Hall of Audience
surmounted by the lofty, glittering, and graceful nine-
tiered spire of the *Myénan*, held to be "the centre of
the universe," whose apex towers above the spot upon
which stands the Lion throne, the chief of the eight
thrones erected at various places within the palace
buildings.

Still lower down in the scale of officials connected
with the Council of State were three classes of ceremonial officers.   The highest of these were the *Let-
saungsayé* or "clerks of the presents," who read out
the lists of the offerings made to the King at the royal
levées.   Next came the *Yônzaw* or "masters of ceremonies," who had charge of all the arrangements connected with durbars and audiences of the King.   They
furnished the necessary intimation to the officers whose
attendance might either be specially commanded or was
required in the usual rotation, communicated to them
the nature of the business to be transacted, informed
them as to what particular kind of dress they were to
appear in, and gave any other requisite instructions.
The last or lowest class consisted of the *Thissádawyé*
or "recorders of great oaths," who administered the
oath of fealty to all who were about to enter the royal
service.   Such enlistment took place under a prescribed
ceremonial.   After the oath had been written down on
paper, it was repeated verbally in front of an image of

Gaudama by the candidate for employment. The paper was then burned, and the ashes were put into a cup of water. After this had been stirred with a small stick containing models, all tied up together, of the five weapons of warfare used by the Burmese—bow, spear, sword, musket, and cannon—the solution was finally drunk by the person taking the *Thissá* or " oath."

The highest officers of the *Byèdaik*, the Privy Council or Secret Department of the Court, were the eight *Atwinwun* or " Ministers of the Interior." Their chief duties were to communicate the business of the *Hlutdaw* to the King; but they were likewise charged with the transaction of general affairs relating to the interior of the palace. So far as precedence was concerned, they ranked below the four *Mingyi*, but somewhat in advance of the four *Wundauk* or Assistant Secretaries of State, though the relative positions of these two different classes of officers depended to a very considerable extent on the amount of favour bestowed on the given individuals by the King.

These eight *Atwinwun* of the *Byèdaik* slept in turn within the palace, two at a time, along with an equal number of the high officials of the *Hlutdaw*. Thus there were always four Ministers at the palace in attendance on the King. The *Atwinwun* went to office in the *Byèdaik* at seven o'clock in the morning, and were relieved at three o'clock on the following day. About nine o'clock in the morning a *Mingyi* and a *Wundauk* came in from the *Hlutdaw*, and for about half an hour or so discussed with the two *Atwinwun* any business under consideration before accompanying them to the royal presence. Such ministerial levée was held by the King every morning. Each afternoon another informal audience was given by the King, which was termed the *Boshu* because military officers (*Bo*) were then permitted to accompany the *Atwinwun* into the royal chamber. About eight o'clock every evening a third reception took place, when members of the *Hlutdaw* again presented themselves before the King in company with the *Atwinwun*. It was then, in the still of the evening, when, even in the longest days of June, the short tropical twilight had long since faded into the darkness of night and the fierce heat of the day had passed away, that the general affairs of the State were quietly discussed from various points of view and settled, whilst all business of a more purely formal or of any special character was disposed of during the daytime. On all sides of the palace there were small open lounges or *Samôk* surmounted by spires of several tiers of roofs, while the quaint and fantastic gardens and palm groves immediately to the south-west of the royal chambers afforded a cool and pleasant retreat in the evening where the breeze from the south could best be enjoyed. Here paths meandered along the edges of narrow artificial watercourses, crossed here and there by quaint rustic bridges, while steps led through grottoes and up and down curiously contorted and grotesque rocks made artificially with Portland cement. Even now, when this little royal garden is no longer kept up as it once was, it is the pleasantest spot in Mandalay during the long arid and hot season of the year.

Next in rank after the *Atwinwun* in the Secret Department of the Court came the *Thandawzin* or "heralds," who were at the same time charged with the performance of secretarial business. Their chief duty consisted in attendance at audiences for the purpose of noting the King's orders and forwarding them to the *Hlutdaw* or Great Council for inscription ; but they also discharged various ceremonial offices, such as carrying forth royal letters in state from the palace.

After these heralds came the *Simitunhmu* or "lamplighters" of the palace, who were at the same time responsible for performing the more important duties of keeping a list of all persons sleeping inside the palace and of intimating to those concerned when it might be their turn to have the privilege of remaining out all night beyond the palace enclosure. If any one whose name was not on these lamplighters' lists happened to be found within the stockade and the main gates of the palace after dark, grave suspicion always fell upon him or her, and punishment usually followed. To obtain entrance after dark was difficult, unless the individual

in question was entitled by position to exercise such a
privilege.   King Mindôn retained a number of spies,
called *Ataukdaw* or "royal assistants," to keep him
secretly informed of the illegal acts and general doings
of his Ministers and provincial Governors.   Finding
these spies unreliable, he looked about for others in
whom he could place more trust, and came to the conclusion that he would best be served by monks who had
cast off their yellow robes and re-entered the world of
men.   Enrolling one thousand men of this class (*Lu-
byandaw*, "the great returned"), he thought it might be
a good thing to issue medals to those of them who distinguished themselves by meritorious service.   These
medals, intended to be worn round the neck like a
locket, were to bear the effigy of a *Chinthé* or "lion" on
one side, and the inscription *Yazamatika*, "the King's
seal," on the other.   But the King died before any were
issued. What may probably be a unique specimen of this
medal I had the good fortune to pick up in Mandalay
bazaar, in 1891, for the price of one rupee.

The lowest grade among the officials of the *Byèdaik*
consisted of the *Teindeinyanhmu* or "caretakers" of
the palace furniture, draperies and other appointments,
whose functions were menial rather than administrative.

Apart from the *Hlutdaw* and the *Byèdaik*, the Great and
the Privy Councils of the State, were the officers of the
Shwedaik, the "gold house" or Treasury, within which
were also contained the State archives and records of
various kinds, such as the genealogies of all hereditary
officials and the lists of the royal artificers, whose offices
were likewise hereditary, the head of each family being
one of the permanent Treasury officials.   These latter
comprised the *Shwedaik Wun* or Chancellor of the
Exchequer, the *Shwedaik Só* or "Governor of the
Treasury," the *Shwedaik Kyat* or "Superintendent,"
the *Shwedaik Sayé* or "clerk of the Treasury," and the
Shwedaik Thawgaing or "keeper of the key of the
Treasury."

When King Mindôn swept away the wasteful and
oppressive system of allowing districts to be squeezed
by the "eaters of townships," and substituted for this

ancient custom the levy of regular taxes and the payment of fixed salaries to officials of all descriptions, the village community system was adopted as the basis of the revenue administration of the Kingdom. Teak timber, earth-oil, and precious stones of all kinds were included in the royal monopolies, and all the revenue from these rich stores was supposed to go direct into the privy purse. Under this reformed system the principal item of the State revenue was the *Tháthamédá*[1] or house tax, which was levied in the form of a house tax, but was in principle somewhat of the nature of an indirect income tax. It was not a Land Revenue demand in the true sense of this term. It was levied on all classes throughout the whole country, with the exception of the inhabitants of the royal city of Mandalay, who appear to have been exempt from direct taxation of any kind. The largest amount of revenue that ever reached King Thibaw's treasury in any one year was about 100 to 105 lacs of rupees (about £700,000); and of this total between 25 and 35 lacs (about £166,666 to £233,333) were the proceeds of customs, monopolies, and transit dues. Classified as to their remunerativeness, the sources of royal income were *Tháthamédá*, monopolies and imposts, rent of royal lands, irrigation taxes, and tribute from the Shan States.

In the assessment and collection of this *Tháthamédá* or house tax every district and town, except the capital, was classified according to its situation, wealth, and prosperity : and the total assessment for each such unit was based upon this classification, so as to range from about 6 to 10 rupees (9 to 15 shillings) per household. But in the vast majority of cases the maximum rate of 10 rupees was fixed, so that the total demand falling on a village of 50 houses would be 500 rupees (£33⅓).

---

[1] Originally the term *Tháthamédá* is said to have been *Thattamédá*, meaning revenue levied by royal authority once in *seven* years (from *Sattamá*, " seven "). Subsequently such special demand was made only once every *ten* years (*Dathamá*, " ten "). Ultimately it became an annual demand. It is not a *tithe* or tenth part, as might easily be imagined from the obvious similarity of the name with the Pali word for ten.

THE HOUSE TAX

The highest assessment was levied upon villages situated on rich stretches of fertile alluvial lands lying within easy reach of the rivers forming the vast silent highways along which all surplus produce was borne to market; for the Irrawaddy river and its tributaries, many of which are themselves worthy of being ranked as large rivers, formed the main arteries of trade and communication.

The average quality of the soil and the proximity or remoteness of given tracts from river communication were the chief considerations which mainly influenced the authorities in Mandalay in determining the incidence of taxation in a general way. But the assessment might vary from year to year, and it never became of the nature of any Settlement extending at fixed rates over lengthy periods. The basis for such a Settlement as was introduced under Akbar by Todar Mull in India had been laid by King Bodaw Payá in 1783 A.D. (1145 Burmese era), when the *Shwedaik* or Burmese Dooms-day Book was compiled, containing a complete record of the population and resources of the empire. But the genius of the Burmese rulers did not run on similar lines to that of the great Mohammedan conquerors of India.

A bad harvest through insufficient rainfall during the south-west monsoon in the summer months, or the destruction of a village by fire, or any other of the numerous causes which might affect the ability of the villages to satisfy the demand of the tax levied, was duly taken into account in assessing this *Tháthamédá*. In order to guide the revenue officials at Mandalay in such matters, fortnightly reports were submitted by the district officials regarding any local circumstances likely to affect the assessment.

This revenue demand was collected either by the local officers or else by specially appointed tax collectors called *Thugyi* or "headmen," the procedure varying sometimes from year to year, and in other cases according to the locality. Instructions under the royal authority were issued from the *Hlutdaw* to the officials concerned, the incidence of taxation per house being laid down for each local unit of assessment, and the exemptions to be granted being specified in detail.

Provided thus with the tax lists, the collector levied the prescribed contributions during the months of April and May, after the winter crops had been harvested and when inland communication from village to village was easiest. On arrival at each town or village he enumerated the houses. Multiplying this number by the rate fixed per house, he easily arrived at the total demand to be satisfied. On receipt of this revenue assessment the *Ywálugyi* or " village elders " met together in conclave, usually sitting *coram publico* on a wooden dais erected under the shade of some large and spreading tree in the middle of the village ; and here they arranged among themselves the amount to be contributed by each individual householder towards the entire satisfaction of the demands of the royal Treasury. This local readjustment of the incidence of taxation by the elders of the people rendered possible the distribution of the burden in a fairly equitable manner among those best able to bear it. Destitute persons and all such as were incapacitated from work through age, sickness, or accident were exempted from paying any share, whilst the heads of the village community sought to apportion the burden equitably among those most able to contribute towards the payment of the full sum demanded.

This was, of course, no difficult matter in villages where each man and woman had a most intimate acquaintance with the affairs of their fellow villagers. Objections would naturally sometimes be made to this informal sub-assessment; and, when these differences of opinion could not be amicably settled, the tax collector frequently acted as arbitrator to settle the disputes. Sometimes village assessors, called *Thamádi*, were appointed by the elders, in which case they were solemnly made to swear at the village pagoda that they would be just in determining the sum payable by each householder. Thus, so far as the Treasury was concerned, the *Tháthaméda* was assessed and levied as a house tax fixed mainly according to the remunerative-

THE HOUSE TAX

ness of the land or of trade; while in being raised by
the local headmen it was collected practically in the
form of an income tax.

This redistribution of the tax having been made by
the village elders, the total revenue demand from the
village was usually paid in cash at once, though sometimes a concession was given permitting payment in two
or more instalments. The money thus collected was
remitted to Mandalay and paid into the Treasury, where
the taxation lists and the accounts were checked and
audited. Peculation was, however, rife. The lists of
houses on which the assessments were based were
falsified to such an extent that about a fifth of the
average annual revenue from this source went into the
pockets of officials instead of into the royal Treasury.
The prevalence of dacoity during Thibaw's reign also
affected agricultural interests to such an extent that in
some localities the revenue from this source had
dwindled away to a mere fraction of what it had
formerly been.

This principle, well suited to the Burmese character
and a natural evolution of their former political system,
was wisely retained in force after the annexation of
Upper Burma in 1886, though the village community
system upon which *Tháthamédá* was based had been
abandoned in Lower Burma, after the annexation of
1852, in favour of a capitation tax and of a land tenure
more consistent with Western ideas. But even Governments profit by experience. To have endeavoured to
overthrow the *Tháthamédá* in favour of the capitation
tax and the land tax levied in Lower Burma would have
been raising up an even stronger opposition to the
imposition of British rule than that which cost, during
1886 to 1890, more than enough of good English blood,
of brave Indian troops, and of poor depreciated rupees.

The land-tenure system was not very precise or clear.
The cultivated tracts were either Crown lands, or else
lands held under various tenures of a feudal nature, or
private and hereditary lands. There were no great
landowners save the King. The Crown lands comprised the *Lèdaw* or "royal fields," the *Ayádaw* or

165

"government property," including islands, alluvial formations, and lands subject to periodical change through riverine action, and the *Lamaingmyé* or tracts cultivated by the royal predial slaves (*Lamaing*), large colonies of whom were located in the irrigated tracts near the Nanda and Aungbinlé lakes or water reservoirs lying to the north-east and south of Mandalay. Except as regards the tracts cultivated by the predial slaves, these Crown lands were let out to tenants at will, who had to pay a fixed proportion of the gross produce, the actual amount payable depending on the outturn harvested. The rent was fixed by custom and was ordinarily one-fourth of the gross produce. The tenant was liable to eviction at any moment. In some parts of the country evictions were common, while in other parts they were so rare that the tenants had practically a fixity of tenure.

The tenures of feudal nature were those obtaining with regard to all *Chámyé* or land bestowed by the King. It became the property of the recipient, but was heritable only if it were so set forth in the royal order. Such land was held either on condition of rendering public service or as an appanage to, or emolument of, a public office held by persons who actually or nominally rendered, or were liable to render, service to the King. Of tenures thus assigned for actual or nominal service there were a great variety and a surprising number; but only a few of the principal varieties need be noted as of interest. Some lands were assigned for life, or for several lives, or for a given period to members of the royal family (*Minmyé*); while the produce of other lands (*Wunsá*) was enjoyed by Governors of rural districts (*Wun*), or it was "eaten" by revenue collectors (*Thugyisá*), or by the soldiers of the King's cavalry (*Sisá*), or by foot soldiers, or by royal pages, boatmen, litter bearers, carriers of the betel box, and others employed in the royal service (*Ahmúdánsá*). In point of fact, all the royal grants were really nothing more than assignments, in actual practice revocable at will; for the sovereign could, and not infrequently did, arbitrarily degrade subjects and escheat their possessions.

The *Thugyisámyé*, or land bestowed by the King on

LAND TENURE

a revenue collector as an appanage of his office, may be considered more closely as a typical instance of the sort of feudal tenure obtaining in Upper Burma. If such land were mortgaged on account of having to provide money for the King, the *Thugyi's* successor in office was bound to redeem it. But if mortgaged for the *Thugyi's* own private debts, then his children were bound to redeem it either for one of themselves, if one of them should succeed his father in office, or else for the new incumbent. The sale of such land was illegal, and consequently void. These revenue collectors were usually appointed direct by the King, by whom alone they could be dismissed after they had once taken the oath of allegiance. They were included as a class among the 80,000 *Amát* or petty notables of the empire. Apart from the royal house of Alaung Payá there was no aristocracy whatever in the country. Nor was there any leading class. Owing to the monastic schools, all were of about the same low level of education ; owing to the fear of oppression, there were no rich men ; and owing to the sparseness of the population, there were no poor. Any man might rise to the highest offices under the Crown.

Private and hereditary lands were neither subject to any incidents of service nor to the payment of land revenue. Waste land or unreclaimed forest jungle could be cleared without asking permission (*Damáúgyá*). When thus brought under cultivation, it became the private property of the person who cleared and tilled it ; and it could descend to his heirs or be disposed of by him or them, by sale or otherwise. These, together with lands granted under the written orders of the King, comprised the *Bóbábaing* or hereditary lands " owned by the father and grandfather" of the person in possession. Along with these may also be classed the *Wuttagán* lands assigned to the maintenance of pagodas, monasteries, and other religious institutions. For tenants of such private lands there was neither fixity of tenure nor legal limits as to rent. When let out for cultivation, the produce was usually divided in equal shares between the owner and his tenant. When private land was sold, it was customary, at the time of making it over to the purchaser, to walk round the small ridges (*Kazínyo*) dividing the ricefields. The unit of measurement of agricultural land was the *Pè* of 1,200 square cubits, equal to 1·75 acres. In some parts it was roughly computed as the area covered by five baskets of paddy sown broadcast.

From what has been said above it will be seen that the village was practically the unit for revenue purposes ; and the general administration was also based on the village system. Each village had a *Thugyi* or "headman" elected by its inhabitants, who had specific duties to perform and certain responsibilities thrust upon him, and who was invested with substantial powers to enable him to discharge his functions efficiently, and to maintain his authority. He could call upon the villagers to assist him, and could, at his own instance, inflict punishment for disobedience to his lawful requisitions. He was frequently not only the tax collector, but also the village magistrate ; and sometimes, in addition thereto, he performed the functions of a judge. But the village was, as a whole, held responsible for the payment of the annual revenue demand, for its own general good order, and for its own defence against dacoits or gang-robbers. The whole village was held liable to fine if stolen cattle or other property were traced to its limits, if the perpetrators of serious crime committed within its borders remained undetected, or if it could offer no reasonable excuse for failing to resist an attack by dacoits.

The villages were surrounded by stockades consisting of *chevaux-de-frise* of bamboos with sharp ends pointing outwards, or formed of posts and thorny branches of the zibin (*Zizyphus jujuba*) and other prickly shrubs or small trees growing even in the dryest parts ; and exit therefrom could only be made at gates facing the cardinal points. In the smaller hamlets there were usually only two gates, but larger villages had four. In every case each gate was guarded by a *Kin* or "watch-house," in which two young men were always supposed to remain at night keeping watch and ward. They were nicknamed *Kinkwé* or "watch-dogs," as it was their duty to hail all passers by, like a dog barking at any one passing his kennel.

Under such a system, which united the village community both by common interest and local feeling, it was of course necessary to maintain a careful watch over the movements of strangers within the gate. Whoever entertained any stranger was bound to report to the *Thugyi* the arrival and departure of the guest. No one could squat in the village lands, or settle in the village, without the permission of the headman ; and he could petition the *Wun* or *Myosá* in charge of the rural district to order the removal of persons suspected to be of criminal tendencies. The village lands were demarcated, and in autumn, at the commencement of the dry season, rough tracks were cleared by every village up to the wooden posts fixed where the communal lands marched with those of the adjoining villages. This was a simple and tolerably effective means of communication, which cost nothing to the administration. When officials travelled, they were met at the village boundaries, and passed thus from village to village during the whole course of their progress.

The central authority controlling the Burmese system of village communities was weakened to a considerable extent during King Mindôn's reign by innovations introduced by him (see p. 156). And later on, during the seven years Thibaw occupied the throne (1878–1885), the rural Governors became less and less easy to control. It was only in the broad plains of the Irrawaddy and its main tributaries that orders could be enforced. In the hills to the north and north-east, which were inhabited by wild Kachin tribes, these nomads were very much left to themselves. They had a reputation for blood-thirstiness, from the fearlessness characteristic of most mountaineers. The plains fringing the outskirts of most of the Kachin country, near where the Mèza from the west and the Shweli from the east join the Irrawaddy river about 200 miles north of Mandalay, formed the Siberia of Upper Burma. Subsequently Mogaung, a wilder and more nearly inaccessible place much further to the north, became the penal settlement. These were all highly malarious and unhealthy localities, banishment to which was popularly considered as equivalent to a sentence of death. In the north-west the hill tracts were peopled by the equally wild Chins, who were likewise a terror to the Burmese. All these hill tribes throughout the northern portions of the country had for generations been accustomed to find profit and pastime in raiding villages on the plains, in pillaging travellers, and in levying blackmail from those within reach of their attacks.

Even in the more settled districts of the plains to which the central authority extended in its fullest sense, whole districts were overrun by bands of dacoits or gang-robbers, some of which were actually in league with and under the protection of high officials at the Court. The notorious Taingda Mingyi, one of the blackest of scoundrels, is known to have aggrandised his income by sharing the spoils with the robber bands, and to have protected them by giving timely information of any expedition intended to be sent against them. In 1885 he instigated the massacre of the leaders of the bands who were then in captivity in Mandalay, in order to obtain the security which comes of dead men telling no tales. These dacoit bands often included hundreds of men, and sometimes assumed the proportions of small armies.

Under the law of British India the term "dacoity" is defined as gang-robbery by five men or more, but the Burmese term *Damyá* simply means "many swords." The dacoits of Upper Burma were bandits or freebooters, who harassed more or less definite tracts of country, like the brigands of Greece and Italy. Dacoity was, in reality, a more or less organized guerilla system of attack and defence, which had been customary from time immemorial and had its origin in the village community system of administration. In the absence of the strong hand of a central government, it was the natural method by which force could be repelled by force, and public or private wrongs righted. The dacoit bands were recruited from among the young men of the vicinity, and no loss of social caste was entailed thereby. Each *Bo* or leader of a band was a sort of Robin Hood, at once feared and looked up to by the villages within his reach. Subsidized by them, he became their protector and defender against the raids and exactions of other *Bo.*

As the monarchy was not strictly hereditary, but hereditary only in the sense of being confined to the members of the family of Alaung Payá, which had been in possession of the throne for the few generations since 1755, each scion of the royal line considered himself justified in raising the banner of insurrection whenever he thought he had a fair chance of success. Generally he could plead, if excuse were required, that the successful rival on the throne had endeavoured to secure himself by putting all his near male relatives to death. No King of Burma had ever been able to suppress insurrections of this sort. Some sovereigns of unusual energy obtained temporary tranquillity by executing or imprisoning all formidable rivals and by employing leaders who were able to break up the larger bands of dacoits; but these peaceful periods were never of long duration, because the efforts to organize a regular army and an efficient police were always neutralized by the incapacity and procrastination of the officials, and by the inherent dislike of all kinds of discipline which is ingrained in the Burmese character.

The ease with which any Prince of the house of Alaung Payá was able to raise a following explained not only the jealousy with which the reigning monarch kept his near relatives shut up within the palace enclosure, but also the closely secluded position which he himself maintained. It was seldom that a royal progress could be undertaken to any distance, as there was always the fear either of an attack outside of the palace, or of finding the palace gate closed against him on his return. On one of the rare occasions on which King Mindôn went forth to enjoy an outing in a royal garden in the vicinity of Mandalay he was attacked by his own son, the Myingun Prince, and barely escaped with his life by the back door of the summer-house in which he was sleeping; while the King's brother, the Mindat Prince, had to pay with his life the penalty of having been appointed *Einshé Min* or heir apparent, and thereby nominated formally as his brother's successor on the throne.

BURMA UNDER BRITISH RULE

The appointment of an heir apparent and successor was one of the royal prerogatives. This want of strict hereditary succession to the throne was the main cause of much bloodshed, intrigue, and disorganization. The Myingun Prince's insurrection occurred in 1866. He escaped into British territory, and was for many years maintained as a prisoner at Benares, in Bengal, but ultimately escaped and lived under French protection at Pondicherry. King Mindôn seldom left his capital after 1866, and King Thibaw was probably never once outside of the palace enclosure during the whole of the seven years of his reign.

In administrative capacity King Thibaw proved a very degenerate son of Mindôn. In fact, he was below rather than above the average of Burmese sovereigns. Placed on the throne, while yet a boy, by means of a palace intrigue cleverly carried through by his prospective mother-in-law, he was weak and excitable, his conduct exhibiting the extremes of temerity and timidity. Many stories have been told of his fearful drunkenness and personal vices ; but they were partly false, and in any case were gross exaggerations. Under the control of Queen Supayálat, and influenced strongly by ignorant and unworthy favourites among his Ministers, he overthrew Mindôn's policy of keeping on good terms with the British, and he suffered laxity and corruption to canker the administration of the State : and for these things he was in due time heavily punished by dethronement, exile, and the downfall of the ancient kingdom of Ava.

During the closing years of the kingdom of Ava the authority of the central Government had become so disorganized that anarchy prevailed throughout the country, and officials of all classes did very much what seemed good in their own eyes. So long as the *Tháthamédá* revenue was regularly remitted to the due amount, the other details of administration were not very closely watched. There was a stand of between 10,000 and 15,000 serviceable fire-arms in the royal arsenal, and an army of about 13,000 infantry, 2,000 cavalry, and a few artillery was maintained in and around the capital, but these troops were next to useless. There was no real military organization. The Ministers of State, Privy Councillors, and Assistant Ministers were all generals of sorts who might be ordered to take the field in charge of an army; but the only actual military ranks were the *Bo*, or captain, and the *Sitkè*, or lieutenant, who performed duties partly of a military and partly of a police nature. The rabble forming the army was recruited as circumstances required, the soldiers being paid on a sliding scale according to the length of service agreed on. A military rank abolished by King Mindôn included the *Thwéthaukgyi* or "great blood drinkers," who were captains of fifty, and to each of whom seven families were assigned, together with lands for his maintenance.

The whole country was terrorized by the various dacoit *Bo*; all social and political bonds became loosened; villages and towns were burned; and, not infrequently, even the district Governors were murdered by dacoit bands. Bhamo, the emporium of trade with China in the north-east, was burnt by Chinese freebooters, and the Kachin tribes were in insurrection; while in the feudatory Shan States, extending from the range of hills near Mandalay eastwards to Yunnan, a league had been formed to throw off the Burmese yoke, and many of the Sawbwa or ruling Princes were in open rebellion. So bad did affairs ultimately become that King Thibaw actually ruled over little more than the royal city of Mandalay and its immediate vicinity, and the tracts commanded by the main channels of communication; and even within this limited area there was always a vast amount of maladministration. The case of the sack of Bhamo, on 8th December, 1884, was a typical instance of the way affairs were conducted in outlying parts of the kingdom. When the Kachin hill tribes revolted and attacked Bhamo, the Governor employed a number of Chinese to help in defending the town, and promised them a certain sum for their services. The Governor failing to keep his promise, these Chinese free-lances collected at a place called Matin and swooped down on Bhamo, first of all looting it, and then setting fire to it. The Chinese authorities had no hand in the matter. It was simply an act of Yunnanese marauders, out of personal revenge for being defrauded of the price agreed on for their defence of the town against Burmese subjects in revolt.

The Burmese Shan States extended over enormous tracts of country beyond the Salween and Mekong rivers till they marched with the Chinese province of Yunnan on the north-east, and with the Siamese Shan States on the east. They were mutually independent States, each ruled by its own Prince or Chief, whose title might be either *Sáwbwa, Myosá*, or *Ngwégunhmu*, according to the size of his State, and his power and influence. There were some sixty to seventy of these chieftains, some of whom were powerful and practically independent Princes, forming the remnants of the great Shan nation which centuries ago held the whole of Further India. The name *Shan* is a Chinese word meaning "mountain." Some fifteen of the smallest Shan States formed the *Myélat*, or "fallow tracts," bordering on the plains of Burma, which, though of great fertility, had become almost depopulated, owing to constant raiding and petty warfare. But all the different States had their constant feuds among themselves as well as with the Burmese on the plains; and during the last years of Burmese rule they were torn and decimated by internecine struggles. The Burmese Government asserted its supremacy over the whole of these Shan States, and the King of Burma appointed to each its chief. The States adjacent to the Irrawaddy valley were controlled from Mandalay, but in those lying far from the capital two *Sitkè* or Military Prefects, supported by garrisons of Burmese troops, were established at Monè and Mobyè for controlling the general administration of the States. Although professing to decide disputes between the mutually independent States, these *Sitkè* left to the chiefs the management of their domestic affairs. Since the time of King Mindôn, if not earlier, the western Shan States had regularly remitted to Mandalay tributes assessed, like the *Tháthamédá*, on the number of households; but the suzerainty over the eastern States beyond the Salween and the Mekong was of a shadowy nature, and the tribute exacted was rather of a nominal and purely formal kind than of any really substantial value.

The administration of the Shan States, as of other parts of the kingdom of Ava, fell into great disorder when Thibaw succeeded King Mindôn. The tribute payable by these amounted nominally to about £30,000 a year, only a small portion of which was latterly paid. But about £50,000 were collected by means of imposts and restrictions on the importation and sale of *Letpet* or "pickled tea," which formed the most valuable product brought down from the hills.

In 1884, six of the Sawbwa became embroiled with the Burmese Government, and had to seek refuge in the Kengtung State east of the Salween, whose powerful Chief, remote from Mandalay, enjoyed a large measure of independence, and was for personal reasons thoroughly disaffected towards the Court of Ava. In this asylum the exiled Sawbwa entered into a plot either to overthrow King Thibaw or to establish an independent sovereignty in the Shan States. The Prince selected to be their leader was the Limbin Prince, a son of the heir apparent who was killed in 1866, when the Myingun Prince attempted to kill both his father (Mindôn) and his uncle (Mindat) and usurp the throne. On Thibaw's accession the Limbin Prince escaped to Lower Burma, where he was employed as a *Myo Ôk* or magistrate in charge of a subdivision of a district. Removed from this appointment for incompetency, and for abusing his liberty by trying to organize rebellion in Upper Burma, he was living under nominal surveillance in Moulmein when he received the invitation from the exiled Sawbwa, and hurried away to accept it, in October, 1885, just before the outbreak of the third Burmese war. The end of this futile insurrection has, however, been elsewhere told (p. 134). It is mentioned again here merely to illustrate the condition of anarchy into which the kingdom of Ava had fallen under Thibaw's rule.

Chapter VII

LAW AND JUSTICE UNDER BURMESE RULE

UNDER their own King the Burmese were not litigious. Differences of opinion were for by far the most part settled amicably by the parties themselves, or else by one or more arbitrators (*Anúnyátá Kun*), jointly appointed, or by official arbitrators (*Kundaw*) appointed by the King, who formed a class enjoying considerable judicial reputation.[1] To those who were dissatisfied with the awards of such arbitrators, or for cases between parties not both resident in the same place, the court of the *Myowun*, or district Governor, was open; and if satisfaction was not obtainable there, suits might be filed in one of the five civil courts in Mandalay. The ultimate court of appeal was the *Hlutdaw*, to which also direct application might be made in more important cases. In this highest court the King usually appointed the heir apparent or one or two of the senior Princes of the blood royal to decide the cases in consultation with the four *Mingyi*. From the decision of the *Hlutdaw* there was ordinarily no appeal; but, in specially important cases concerning hereditary, territorial, and other claims, the parties to the suit were sometimes brought before the royal presence, after having petitioned through the *Hlutdaw* for such privilege, when the case was either re-heard or the *Mingyi* were invited to explain the reasons of their decision before the latter was either confirmed or reversed by the final judgment of the King.

---

[1] Among the alterations made in the judicial administration during King Thibaw's time the practice of appointing *Kun* to try cases was abolished, and civil courts were constituted of different grades as to powers, jurisdiction, value of suits, appeals, etc.

THE LAWS OF MANÚ

In the *Dammathât*, or Laws of Manú, an ancient civil and criminal code existed, which was followed to a certain extent; but, as there was no authoritative code of procedure, the arbitrators and judges acted very much on lines of their own. They administered justice rather by equity, according to their own lights and ideas, than by law : and this naturally often led to the civil suits being settled by a compromise. Nor was impartiality one of the ruling characteristics with which Burmese judges were usually credited. Oaths were not administered on ordinary occasions, because an oath was regarded with a deep-rooted, semi-religious dread as a kind of solemn ordeal; hence they were only resorted to when one of the parties to the suit agreed to be bound by the effect of his adversary's statement made on oath.

When the ordeal by oath was decided on, it was, like most solemn ceremonies in Burma, made the occasion of a festival. The litigants and their friends, all dressed in the gayest of garments and accompanied by a band of music, proceeded to a sacred edifice, where the statement upon oath was made in front of an image of Gaudama. Four forms of ordeal might be resorted to with regard to lawsuits. The other three comprised the ordeal by water, the ordeal by molten lead, and that by candle.

In the first of these the plaintiff and the defendant went into deep water : their heads were pushed under water with poles, and right lay with him who could remain longest under water. As this ordeal could be performed by deputy, it seems to have been one of the most unsatisfactory description, which could only be resorted to by a childishly superstitious race such as the Burmese undoubtedly are. The ordeal by molten lead consisted in plunging the forefinger of each party into molten lead after the finger had been so tied round with feathers that only the tip remained exposed. If one party came out of the ordeal with less injury to his finger than was sustained by his opponent, he won the suit : otherwise the inflamed and damaged fingers were pricked, and the glorious uncertainty of the law decided in favour of him from whose badly burned finger-tip the less amount of serum flowed. The ordeal by candle took place, like the ordeal by oath, in a sacred edifice and in front of an image of the Buddha. Two candles, equal in every respect, were lighted after the usual formula of pious invocation had been repeated, and the suit was lost by that party whose candle first burned out and became extinguished.

The *Myowun*, or Governors of districts, practically exercised full civil and criminal jurisdiction in all ordinary suits. As there was no authoritative penal code throughout the land, punishments were awarded according to the discretion of the judge; but his zeal, or whatever other more appropriate name may be given to the characteristic of his mind at the moment, often outran his discretion. The quality of mercy might or might not be strained, yet appeals were extremely rare in criminal cases. The real explanation of this is, however, that, if any successful appeal were made, the village to which the appellant belonged could be harassed and annoyed in so many ways which were open to no appeal that finally the mischief-maker would be turned neck and crop out of the village in order to promote peace and welfare once more. It was recognized that there was no use in fighting when one had only the very thin end of the stick. Monetary fines were usually inflicted, though cruel punishments were often adopted when the frequency of crime began to be specially noticeable. Whenever dacoity became so prevalent as to call for remonstrances from Mandalay, prisoners caught red-handed were usually crucified to serve as a terror-inspiring example. When undue or habitual severity on the part of a rural Governor was brought to the notice of higher authority at the capital, the ready explanation was given that the zeal of the *Myowun* had outrun his discretion, or, as the Burmese equivalent puts it, " his hand had reached further than he intended." Even at the capital, inhuman punishments were common for trivial offences. Thus, disobedience to a royal order might entail the slitting of the mouth and cheeks with a knife, after the jaws had been stretched wide open with a wooden instrument. To have ordered the death of any man or woman would have been an unpardonable sin in a Buddhist; hence the pronouncement of the death sentence by the King was in the formula, " Let his property be confiscated, and let him travel by the usual road." In Thibaw's time (1878–1885) it is said to have been more tersely summed up in a mere wish not to see the person again.

The chief civil and criminal Courts of First Instance in Mandalay were situated, like the *Hlutdaw*, at the Red or King's Gate on the eastern side of the palace, but beyond the stockade or external inclosure. The Civil Court decided important suits arising in Mandalay, and considered appeals from provincial and subordinate courts. But as, theoretically, no civil case was beyond the jurisdiction of the *Hlutdaw*, all appeals concerning landed property and hereditary offices were brought before the latter. All criminal appeals were also brought before the *Hlut*, whilst the Criminal Court merely disposed of cases which occurred at the capital.

The *Dammathát* or Laws of Manú, the great primary judicial code forming the Institutes of Law in both civil and criminal matters, consists of fourteen sections. It is a theoretical guide to the statute law, in which the precepts are very frequently illustrated by means of parables, according to ancient custom throughout all the East. Some of the sections are practically confined to one subject, and are more or less complete, as, for example, the third section, dealing with borrowing, lending, and debts ; the seventh, detailing the laws of slavery; the tenth, laying down the law of inheritance ; and the thirteenth, treating of betting ; but there is a general want of anything like codification or systematic collection of different subjects under groups in logical sequence. So far as any system in the arrangement can be traced the *Dammathát* begins by dealing with the boundaries of land, for " *Cursed is he that removeth his neighbour's landmark* " found a foremost place in the ancient laws of all eastern nations. It then goes on to deal with movable property, with laws relating to pledges, hiring, master and servant, taxes and contracts, with theft and assault, with the law of husband and wife, with laws relating to other men and women, with slaves and slavery, with rights in land, gifts, borrowing, lending, and hiring, with miscellaneous matters connected with persons and personal property, with inheritance, with divorce and the partition of property on separation, and with betting; finally it ends with miscellaneous matters chiefly regarding the *Upazá* or "precincts" of houses, monasteries, villages, towns, etc., and the law of trespass by huntsmen, fishermen, gatherers of honey, marriage parties, and funeral processions.

Some of the matters dealt with are very amusing. Thus, in the fourth section there are laws "*regarding one person kicking another,*" or "*when one person pulls another's hair,*" and "*when a degraded person points with the finger at a respectable one,*" as well as "*the law by which men are divided into three classes — excellent, middling, and depraved,—and each of these is also subdivided into three classes.*" Again, in the eighth section, laws are laid down regarding borrowing clothes and going to a funeral in them, or unthinkingly wearing them whilst washing the head in order to avert the evil influence of the stars. The section following this contains the laws when a father-in-law assaults his son-in-law, and *vice versâ*, also when the property of a visitor is lost whilst he is residing as guest in any house, or when the property of the house-owner is lost during the guest's stay; and the laws relating to the seven kinds of witches or wizards, and their trial by ordeal of water.

The perusal of these Laws of Manú is of considerable assistance in arriving at a true comprehension of the Burmese national character. They have a strictly religious basis. Though the laws take cognizance of murder and homicide, wilful and otherwise, and the killing of animals, yet they do not prescribe or sanction the infliction of capital punishment; and in this they differ considerably from the more ancient laws in other parts of the East, which demanded a life for a life, an eye for an eye, and a tooth for a tooth. Thus,—

The law relating to murder is that, from any man who has killed another with a sword, spear, bow and arrow, or any other instrument, it is proper to demand restitution in an increased number of men; it is not proper to put him to death. If a dog bite a man's foot, it is not proper for that man to bite the dog's foot; nor is it right to put any man to death because he has killed another. A king who does not put a murderer to death will be praised by the good spirits and all good men, and will be supported and assisted by them ; while all evil beings, who have no respect for the laws, will keep afar off. The country ruled over by such a king will be pleasant to dwell in, and the inhabitants thereof will be prosperous and happy.

No mention whatever is made of imprisonment, the punishments prescribed for offences invariably taking the form of compensations or fines, either in kind or else in silver or gold, commensurate with the amount of injury inflicted and with the manner or intention of inflicting it. Under certain circumstances slavery was a punishment for debt; and of the sixteen kinds of slaves four became so from this cause. Impartiality on the part of judges was exhorted as essential for the proper administration of justice, and for their guidance it was duly recorded that "*the unjust judge shall suffer punishment in hell with head downwards, while the just judge shall ascend to the land of spirits and attain Neikban*" (*Nirvana*). Truthful evidence, ranking equally in importance with impartiality in the judge, is enjoined under pain of immediate degradation, the "*law of evidence*" being tersely summed up thus :—

Oh, King! if any man, whether produced as a witness or not, who habitually prevaricates in place of speaking truthfully—who calls the elder the younger, and the younger the elder ; the greater the less, and the less the greater ; the good bad, and the bad good—when examined as a witness between two parties, does not tell the truth, and the case is decided in consequence of his false evidence : let this false witness be taken before the house of him who hath thereby suffered damage, and let him there beg for ten to fifteen days, with his face blackened with soot, with his body whitewashed with lime, naked, and holding in his hand a potsherd ; and then let him be turned out of the country, and called a degraded fellow, whose word cannot be believed.

The laws of husband and wife, of divorce and partition of property on separation, and the laws of inheritance, are given with very full detail, and are much more practical and concrete than the above theoretical treatment of perjury. Marriage consists in a man and a woman being given to each other by their parents, or being brought together by the intervention of a go-between, or by coming together by mutual consent ; but, in each case, living and eating together out of the same dish constitute the legal outward sign of marriage. The seven kinds of wives are enumerated and described both in the fifth and the twelfth sections of the *Dammathát*, the title of the latter section being *The Seven Kinds of Wives, the Three Ways of Contracting Marriage, and the Law of Divorce.* The descriptions of the seven kinds of wives afford so good an insight into certain phases of Burmese character and of domestic relations that they are worth quoting at length :—

1. *A Wife like a Mother is this :*—A mother takes care that no bugs, gnats, mosquitoes, or horseflies bite or sting her child. If he be in charge of any other person, she fears he will receive hurt or get improper food, that they do not love him, or that they love and hate him at the same time. If he cries, she thinks he is being beaten. If others give him the best of food, she thinks there may be poison in it, and wishes him to eat only what she herself selects. If he be asleep or doing nothing, she is happy and contented ; and no matter how he is dressed, she thinks him handsome. Lest anything befall him while asleep, she will not leave him till he wakes. If he walks out in the sun or rain, she is anxious lest he be sunstruck, or slip and fall. Though she may have neither rest nor food, she is happy if her child has ; and if she can hear his voice, even abuse and bad language sound pleasant, though kissing him she gently chides him, and bids him not repeat such bad words. When alone, so that others cannot hear, she makes known to him the proper time for going or for tarrying, for coming or for staying away, for remaining or not, for sleeping or for waking, for eating or for fasting, and various other matters. She repeatedly warns him against the five sins of taking life, stealing, committing adultery, lying, and drinking, and reminds him that only the three precious gems—the Buddha, the Law, and the Assembly—are worthy of reverence. She places him with a good teacher for instruction, and rejoices if he earn praise from his teacher and wishes to become a probationer for the religious life. But if he wish to live the life of a layman, her heart's desire is that he should only espouse a girl of good family, and that she should tend him till the end of her life. In childhood, when she holds him to her bosom, he pulls at her, scratches her face, bites her, tears her breasts, and pulls at her mouth, yet she is not annoyed.

A wife who thus loves her husband as a mother loves her child, who reflects that her husband has been given to her by her parents, or that her marriage was arranged by a go-between, or that she chose him of her own free will, will only eat when he eats and sleep when he sleeps. She will say to herself, " *My husband is a man; and manhood is a great gift, which can only be attained by a woman after much striving*" ; and she will think her husband comely in dress and well-behaved in eating.

THE SEVEN KINDS OF WIVES

When he goes to festivals or assemblies, she will so dress and bedeck him that he may outshine others, and will wish to know why he goes and when she may expect him back. She lays out his dress for him, and prepares his food. If he hanker after another woman, she does not publish this fact to every one, but conceals it, and only in the privacy of their chamber she discusses whether philandering in this way be right or not. A wife who thus considers the good of her husband and his affairs, and is filled with kindly sentiments towards him, is a wife like a mother; and such a wife is deserving of love.

2. *A Wife like a Sister is this :*—When a sister grows up, she is becomingly modest and timid. In her comings and goings, in her conversation, in dress and in adornment, from the soles of her feet up to the crown of her head, she is circumspect, being careful not to expose herself immodestly even before her brother. In laughing and talking with her brother she is bashful, and speaks with downcast countenance. A wife who thus tries at all times to appreciate the position of a husband, to behave with becoming modesty and reserve towards him, and to do all she can to make him happy and fill his heart with sweetness, is a wife like a sister.

3. *A Wife like a Friend is this:*—When one arrives on a visit to a good friend, after the interchange of greetings, he brings water to wash one's feet and hands and to refresh one's brow and face, and prepares a pillow, a bed, tobacco, betel, tea, sweets and sours good for eating. Then he offers pleasant greetings to the guest, addressing him with a joyful countenance. A wife who thus looks after her husband's wants, who feels kindly disposed towards him, and talks to him affectionately and in moderation, who, in his comings and goings, in his friendships, and in the great and the little affairs of life continually assists and works for him like a good friend, who looks cheerful when she sees her husband and talks pleasantly to him, who wishes to wash and dry his feet, to lay out his clothes and his food, to prepare his resting-place, to give him sweet foods and sour in due season, and to look after his comfort, is a wife like a good friend.

4. *A Wife like a Master is this:*—A master makes his slave give him his sandals and his fan, prepare his pillow and his couch, get ready water for bathing, accompany him on journeys, and bring him information as to what is going on. If the slave fails to do these things properly, the master does not chide him gently, but passionately exclaims in pride and haughtiness, "*Hey ! you ugly brute, you fool, you son of poverty-stricken parents plunged in debt and reduced to slavery !*" He pulls his servant's front hair, punches him with his elbow, beats him with whatever he happens to get hold of, and kicks him, unheeding that the poor fellow works for him without getting good food or clothing, and without being well cared for. A wife who thus haughtily addresses her husband, saying, "*Hey ! you ugly fellow, you dirty, low brute !*" who reviles his parents and other relations, who, in distributing clothing and food, keeps the best clothes for herself and leaves the rest for her husband, who, first of all, eats the tit-bits and gives him only the leavings, and who will not allow him to say a word although she herself speaks far more than she ought to, who sleeps on the best and most

BURMA UNDER BRITISH RULE

comfortable part of the bed, and makes her husband sleep on the lower part, and who does not consider the feelings of her husband but only thinks of herself, is a wife like a master.

5. *A Wife like an Enemy is this:*—An enemy's thought is to do violence whenever he sees the object of his enmity, or to contrive his death or ruination. If he cannot attain this, he feigns affection, and gives him poison, when pretending to give him good things to eat and drink. If this be discovered, he bribes others to destroy his enemy by means of spells or charms. If these cannot affect his person, he tries to ruin him by killing his buffaloes, cattle, horses and elephants, or by secretly getting others to set fire to his house, garden, granary, and property; and, while he speaks as if he loved him, he intends his death or ruination. The origin of such intention may have been the refusal of some animate or inanimate object that has been desired, which has occasioned anger and has changed the former friendy feeling into the deadly hate of an enemy. When a wife acts in something like the above manner, wishing to have another lover, and desiring to attain this object by compassing the death of her husband by means of poison or charms, reviles him and his parents, his grandparents and his other relatives, she is a wife like an enemy.

6. *A Wife like a Thief is this:*—A thief plots day and night how to get things that belong to others. Stealing secretly himself, he also gets others to steal for him. Changing marks, he misappropriates articles, substitutes bad for good, or steals in other of the twenty-five ways enumerated in the sacred precepts. A wife who thus acts without the knowledge of her husband, secreting things and giving them away without her husband's consent, is only fit to be called a wife like a thief: and she is a wife like a thief.

7. *A Wife like a Slave is this:*—She lays out her husband's clothing and sees to it being in proper order. Having considered what is best for her husband to eat and drink, she prepares his food nicely and places it before him like a slave serving her master in trembling and respect. When he arrives from a far journey, she receives her husband respectfully by kneeling down, sitting upon her feet, and folding her hands, and gives him water for washing his feet, for bathing, and for drinking. If he should happen to find fault about any household matter, she does not speak back, but is afraid of ruffling his temper still further by saying a single word in a cross manner. She does not venture to eat and drink while her husband is still eating and drinking, but waits till he has finished and then eats what is left. Such a wife is a wife like a slave.

Oh, wise judges! Of these seven kinds of wives, a wife like an enemy and a wife like a thief should, if their shortcomings are clearly proved, receive judgment as if they were enemies and thieves.

Of these seven kinds of wives, the wife like a mother, the wife like a sister, the wife like a friend, and the wife like a slave ought not to be put away by any man, but should be lived with for life. But the three

184

others, the wife like a master, the wife like an enemy, and the wife like a thief, may be put away even if they have borne ten children : they need not be lived with even for one day longer. Of these seven kinds of wives, the wife like a slave will not be disappointed should she pray to become a man in the next state of existence, for her desire shall be fulfilled, and she will attain Neikban (Nirvana) before any of the others.

Marriage was not a union irrevocably binding. Divorce was obtainable by mutual consent, or at the instance of either party ; and the partition of property on separation was provided for in about fifty laws taking cognizance of the reasons for separation and the social status of husband or wife.

The simplest form of divorce was the separation by mutual consent of a husband and wife, both born of parents who were freemen. In this case the husband and wife were each allowed to take their personal clothes and ornaments. Any property acquired by the husband alone, or by the wife alone, was to be divided into three portions, of which the person who had separately acquired it took two, while the third went to the other party ; but property acquired by joint endeavour, or where both had an equal share in the capital, was equally divided. If the clothes or personal ornaments of the one were much more valuable than those of the other, they were to be valued and the difference made good. With regard to children of the marriage, the father took the boys, unless they were too young to be taken from the mother, and the mother took the girls. If debts had been incurred during the period of cohabitation, they were to be borne equally. After separation and division of the property, each party had full right to form any new connexion in marriage.

When only the husband or the wife wished to separate, but the other party did not consent to a divorce, and no particular cause was specified for dissolution of the marriage, but merely the broad generalization of incompatibility from "*their destinies not being cast together*," all property, animate or inanimate, went to the non-consenting party ; while the party wishing for a divorce only retained his or her clothes and ornaments, and had to pay any expenses incurred in obtaining the separation.

When there was no property beyond clothes and household articles to dispose of, if the man wished to separate he could only take away with him one turban, one jacket, one loin-cloth, and one *Da* or bill ; while the wife, if suing for the divorce, in addition to her jacket, loin-cloth, and kerchief, could also remove the cloth woven and rolled up on her loom, the loom, the shuttles, and the other implements belonging to it.

When a divorce took place by mutual consent, each party had to pay an arbitration fee of fifteen rupees (£1) ; but otherwise this fee had only to be paid by the party seeking the dissolution of the marriage.

If a husband, having taken a lesser wife, abused and beat his first wife and oppressed her, they were to try to live again on good terms ; but if this conduct were repeated, the chief wife could, under the special circumstances, claim a divorce on the same terms as if both parties were consenting, even though the husband declared his unwillingness to separate.

Certain improprieties in conduct on the part of a wife, being regarded merely as gross breaches of wifely etiquette, did not form legal grounds for a divorce ; while she was further protected by law with specific reasons justifying her abusing her husband and imprecating evil on him—a license which many wives freely availed themselves of. The fivefold improprieties which a wife might thus exhibit without affording adequate grounds for a divorce included impropriety in dress, in eating, in relations with other men, in property, and in behaviour.

*Improprieties with regard to Dress are these :—*If any woman, whether well or sick, goes inappropriately dressed to a festival or even where there is no public entertainment, or inconsiderately goes to the house of the dead in other than the customary dress, or if, not having clothes of her own, she pays more than she ought to for clothes to bedeck herself with, or has many more clothes than she requires and overdresses herself day and night, or if she hides her dresses from her husband and only puts them on for the sake of being praised by others, or if she gets into debt by buying clothes and will even go the length of selling her children into slavery for the sake of dress, or would have herself better dressed than her husband, such a wife acts with impropriety in regard to dress.

*Improprieties with regard to Eating are these :—*If any wife eat before her husband has eaten, or eat frequently without his knowledge, or take

IMPROPRIETIES IN WIVES

the good things for herself, so that her husband only has the coarser food, or continually overeats to a dangerous extent, or who, being a woman, eats raw meat with the blood in it such as is fit only to be eaten by a man, or, contrary to custom, wants to eat at all sorts of times even in presence of others, she is a woman without shame or fear, and is guilty of impropriety in eating.   Men may eat of many dishes that may be succulent, sweet, astringent, bitter, sharp, or sour ; but if a woman wishes to eat ¸thus from many dishes, or heaps all sorts of food into one dish for herself, this is excess in eating.   Whether she eat openly before others or secretly, whether with her husband's knowledge or without it, the woman who eats thus commits an impropriety in eating. Or when several people are together at food, it is improper for a woman to be always dipping her fingers into the dishes, or to be continually rising up and then sitting down again, or standing and making faces : these are all forms of impropriety in eating.

Improprieties with regard to Men are these :—If any woman assumes a smiling countenance on seeing other men than her husband, if she take men by the hand and seem delighted, if she call any man to her to make friends with him or ask men passing by to stop and sit down, if she seek acquaintances only among men rather than among women, these are all improprieties with regard to men.

Improprieties with regard to Property are these :—If any woman place in the outer portion of the house things that ought to be in the inner room, or *vice versâ*, if, having but little to live on, she spend a good deal for the sake of display before others, if she give presents without her husband's knowledge, if she intentionally put in prominent places things that should be kept out of sight, or if she be continually showing off and talking to others about her own things, she is a woman guilty of improprieties as regards property.

Improprieties with regard to Behaviour are these :—A self-respecting woman should behave with decorous reserve on hearing the voice of any other man than her husband, or even without hearing any man's voice.   If she look out from the entrance of her house beyond the fence, if she be continually looking up and turning her eyes and her face in all directions, or if, when she goes out, she be constantly turning and looking at men whom she sees, or whose voices she hears, such a woman is guilty of impropriety in conduct.

Though a wife could not be divorced for any or all of these improprieties, the *Dammathât* laid down that the husband had a right to inflict personal chastisement on her.   If, after frequent chastisement, she still continued to be guilty of improprieties in conduct, a divorce was obtainable, each taking the separate property held at the time of marriage, and the husband taking also what had been acquired during the period of cohabitation.   It was further laid down that for drinking, want of order or neatness in household arrangements, scolding her husband or reviling him when absent, gadding about and talking in other people's houses, and lolling about the front of the house, similar chastisement should be inflicted for at least three times before the husband should be justified in seeking divorce from such a wife. If he failed to master her, and she continued her former habits, divorce was obtained on similar conditions to those above. For excessive pride about family, personal appearance, or property, or for running down her husband's family or friends, personal correction was also prescribed to be inflicted thrice before separation became justifiable. And the method of chastisement was duly prescribed :—

In chastising his wife the husband is not to beat her with his elbow or fists, or with a doubled rope or a thick stick, or kick her on the breasts, or tread on her neck, which is only treatment fit for a slave or an adulterous wife ; but he may whip her with a thin wand, or with the palm of his hand, on the loins, buttocks, or feet.

A wife had the right to abuse her husband and imprecate evil upon him for any one or other of eight specific causes. If they were very poor, and he could not contrive anything for their subsistence ; if he were sorely afflicted with disease, and unable to work ; if he were ignorant of, or cared nought for, the "three precious gems : the Buddha, the Law, and the Assembly"; if he were a fool, who did not know a good man from a bad ; if he were skilled in handiwork, or could talk well, but was lazy and would not exert himself to work ; if amorous to excess ; if he were apt to frequent loose places ; or if he were much given to betting and gambling, she could abuse him without being held guilty of anything justifying a divorce. If the husband were, however, subjected to such continuous nagging that married life became insupportable, then a divorce could be obtained as by mutual consent, the property being equally divided on separation. According to the *Dammakán*, or Sacred Law, it is wrong for a woman to abuse her husband for faults that she sees in him; but according to the *Dammathát*, or Judicial Law, there is no justification for a husband separating and taking all the property simply because his wife may be abusive.

A wife having long moustaches or whiskers, small feet

and large hands, who walks with irregular steps, and who has no well-developed breasts, may be divorced as a woman with whom it is improper for other people to sit on the same level, or to converse on religious subjects; because these personal defects are the result of bad deeds done in a former state of existence. This religious idea, indeed, underlies the Burmese legal aspect of divorce. The proper term for divorce, *Akaungkun*, literally means "*a cessation of the coalescence of the destinies of a married couple*," although, colloquially, the word *Kwa*, "to separate," is almost invariably used. A childless wife, or one who has borne several daughters but no son, could also be separated from; and for these and a great many other concrete cases the partition of property was duly regulated by law.

The extreme case of divorce was that in which, after husband and wife had lived together very happily, the wife committed adultery. In this case, if she had no property, her husband had the right to sell her.

As a matter of fact, divorce or separation, an event of somewhat common occurrence, is far more frequently claimed by wives than by husbands. Slippering of husbands is much more common than beating of wives; and violent, foul abuse of husbands is often heard issuing from the mouths of wives who have worked themselves up into a frenzied state of fury. It cannot be denied that the *Dammathát* does not hold anything like an even balance between husband and wife; but then, according to Burmese Buddhism, the wife occupies, and herself admits that she occupies, a very inferior position to a man upon "the ladder of existence" leading upwards to *Neikban* or annihilation. As a woman, however, she can play her part well, and thereby earn religious merit; for in these Laws of Manú it is recorded that—

Even a man is worthless if he have no good habits; while a woman may be excellent if her conduct be good. . . . If a wife *assist in completing her husband*, her conduct gives her the advantage of good deeds throughout future existences. Though she may not approve her husband's habits, yet, if she respectfully yield to his wishes, she is worthy of being called an excellent wife. She thereby frees herself from hell, and is brought upon the road leading straight towards the land of spirits.

BURMA UNDER BRITISH RULE

In addition to the *Dammathát*, or Statute Law, there is also a small collection of ancient precedents in law known as the *Pyatdôn* or "decisions" of Princess Thudammasári, somewhat in the nature of a very brief compendium of Common Law perpetuated in the form of narratives according to the ancient Eastern style.

As these fundamental Institutes of Law had from time to time undergone various modifications, a new compilation of the laws actually administered was undertaken during King Thibaw's reign by the Kinwun Mingyi, the Prime Minister, after consideration and comparison of all the available texts. This compilation, known as the *Attasankhepa Vannaná Dammathát*, was first printed in Burmese in 1882. Since then it has always been recognized as an authoritative statement of the Burmese Buddhist law; although under British administration it, of course, does not form the ultimate authority in legal cases.

In this latest edition of the *Dammathát* the original Institutes have been altered to suit the necessities of latter-day life, although the principles underlying the new version remain unchanged. The law of inheritance and partition is exceedingly complicated, and this alone requires no less than a hundred and thirty-five sections in its enunciation, while marriage and divorce have as many as one hundred and twenty-three sections allotted to them. These latter developments of Burmese law are exceedingly interesting both as complements to the extracts above given from the ancient *Manú Dammathát*, and also as exhibiting the evolution of legal ideas regarding the family tie and domestic union. They possess so many points of peculiar interest in these regards, and are at the same time so illustrative of national habits and ideas, that a comprehensive summary of the last thirty-five sections relating to divorce deserves to be given. It will accordingly be found as an appendix at the end of the present volume.

Of prison administration there was next to none. There were jails at the chief towns of districts; while at Mandalay there were three, namely, one inside the palace and two outside. It was not the custom for the Burmese Government to feed convicts. They were fed by their relations, and a certain number of those who had no friends willing or able to support them were allowed to go out and beg for food or to earn it by carrying water, collecting firewood, or doing other odd jobs. The jails were loathsome and insanitary, and the punishments inflicted were barbarous in the extreme. In criminal cases torture was often freely applied both to the accused and to the witnesses, while the sentences varied from fines and a few stripes with a cane up to imprisonment, slavery, and death. If condemned to slavery, the serf and his descendants became slaves, who were allotted to pagodas as sweepers of the precincts. The taint of slavery of this sort could not be cleansed away : even if a freeman took the daughter of a pagoda-slave to be his wife, their children were serfs.

Those condemned to imprisonment usually had to undergo great sufferings. For safe custody, their feet were tied to a long pole or bamboo ; and at night this was often raised by blocks so that only the shoulders and head rested on the ground, and the whole weight of the body was thrown on them. Or, if they wore fetters, a bamboo would be passed between the legs of several prisoners, and then raised in similar manner. The capital sentence was usually carried out by decapitation or disembowelment, but in the case of royal prisoners the head was drawn back and blows inflicted on the throat with a bamboo. In 1879 a sister of the Nyaung-yan Prince was thus executed, and as she was a strong young woman it took seven blows to kill her. Thrown into prison along with her mother on the Nyaungyan's escape to Lower Burma in 1878, they were for some time supported by alms sent from the British Residency; but, when rumours of a rising by the Nyaungyan Prince reached the palace, the go-between grew alarmed and fled, and the Princess and her mother were fed by the mother of Thibaw's Queens till the order was given for execution. Sometimes such victims were trodden to death by elephants, as happened in the case of the widow of King Bágyidaw, who was put to death by King Tharrawaddi in 1840. The disembowelment of heinous offenders usually took place on crucifixes, consisting of two or three upright posts with crossbars in the shape of a St. Andrew's cross, which were fixed at places of punishment. Sometimes, too, after decapitation the corpses were lashed to these crucifixes, and in either case the bodies hung there till the flesh had been torn off by vultures, and the bones fell to the ground. This punishment was often inflicted on dacoits. It is perhaps only fair to add that although the apparently inevitable massacres which took place when he deposed the Pagán Min in 1853 could not have been unknown to King Mindôn, yet throughout his reign but little blood was shed with his sanction or previous knowledge; when executions of criminals took place, the facts are said to have been carefully kept from him.

Judicial business was conducted with great solemnity and ceremonial within the *Hlutdaw*. When the Council was presided over by the heir apparent, or by any other member of the royal family acting as vice-president—for the King was the president *ex officio*—only the suitors or their advocates were permitted to appear, the cases being heard in chambers, as it were. The members of the Council always wore a uniform proper to the occasion. This consisted of a loose robe of muslin thrown over a tight-fitting white coat made of cotton, whilst a narrow fillet of rolled white muslin was bound round the head and tied with the ends pointing upwards. Both parties to the suit had to wear the dress considered suitable for such an occasion; but, previous to their being allowed to appear, they were robed in long loose white coats and then capped, the plaintiff's cap being green and the defendant's red. These distinctive articles of dress were usually worn by the advocates only. They were provided from the public purse and kept at the *Hlutdaw* in place of being, like a barrister's wig and gown, the private property of the individual advocate.

Whether one gained or lost, a lawsuit was always an expensive matter. Fees, presents, and bribes were unavoidable, not only in law matters but whenever officials of any high degree were approached on business. When presents were offered to the King, as, for example, when concessions were asked for regarding extracting teak timber, or mining earth-oil—and without such douceurs no petitioner had the slightest chance of success—a present of half the value was also made to the Minister, who urged, or was about to urge, the grant of the concession. The whole administration in all its branches was rotten with corruption and bribery, while the judicial system in particular was lax and corrupt to a degree.

The institution of a civil suit was made by presenting a written petition or plaint to the judge, who thereupon appointed his *Nakán*, or assistant (lit. " listener ") to report after holding preliminary enquiries among the parties to the suit and their witnesses. Together with this report the plaintiff and defendant submitted their pleadings, respectively setting forth in detail the causes of action and replying thereto with full statements of defence. A day having been fixed for hearing the case, advocates were chosen and the suit came on in due course. Guided by the investigations and report of the *Nakán* the issues of fact were fixed by the judge, who ordained that the plaintiff must prove certain issues, and that the defendant must, if he could, in like manner prove given points. After the examination of witnesses, judgment was pronounced. If the parties to the suit consented to accept the judge's decision, they ate pickled tea (*Letpet*) in token of being satisfied with the decision of the court, and the judgment thereby became binding and final. Whether before arbitrators, or in the courts of the district Governors, or in the civil courts at the capital, the eating of *Letpet* was the formal acceptance of the judgment by both parties; and refusal to eat it meant an appeal to the next higher court. The judgments of the *Hlutdaw* being final, however, there was no custom of eating *Letpet* upon their decisions being declared.

It not infrequently happened that when the non-consenting party proved contumacious and unreasonable in the eyes of the judge, such contempt of court led to his being cast into prison, a not very comfortable place under the best of circumstances in Upper Burma in those days, and he was kept there until his frame of mind became sufficiently mollified to induce him to eat tea and thus accept the verdict pronounced by the court. Like criminals, such persons were not maintained by the State, but had to depend on relatives and friends for their daily food.

It appears to have been a sort of fundamental axiom with the civil courts of Ava that, when suits were instituted, both parties probably had a certain amount of right on their side, but that both were at the same time more or less in fault. A happy compromise, therefore, usually seemed to the judge the best and most satisfactory way of terminating the differences of the suitors. Though devoid of anything like a legal basis, this guiding principle seems to have contained a good deal of sound common sense. But the character of the judges for impartiality was held rather at a discount, and the rich suitor with an open purse had a better chance of obtaining satisfaction than his poorer rival. At the eating of tea after the judgment the *Letpet* was almost sure to taste sweeter to the former than to the latter. Bitter, indeed, it must often have proved to the poor man unjustly sued for malicious motives, and mulcted in money, cattle, or land by the inequitable judgment bought with the wealth of his enemy.

For the trial of civil suits between European British subjects and Burmans a mixed court was held in the palace at Mandalay, where the British Resident, or the Assistant Resident, sat about once a week to try cases along with a Burmese judge. This custom of course lapsed when direct diplomatic relations were broken off by the withdrawal of the British representatives in October 1879.

Chapter VIII

EVEN before King Mindôn ascended the throne, early in 1853, he had two dreams which impressed him greatly. In the first of these he saw a large city lying at the foot of Mandalay hill, a few miles to the north-east of Amárapúra. In the second dream he was riding a white elephant which took him to the foot of Mandalay hill, where he dismounted. Here two women, calling themselves *Ba* and *Ma*, took hold of his right and his left hands and led him to the summit, where a man offered him a handful of scented grass, and told him that his elephants and horses would always thrive if fed with the grass that grew round about the hill.

When Mindôn became King, he had to follow the custom prescribed for the maintenance of a line of sucession having the pure blood royal. For this purpose one of the King's daughters, always known as the *Tabîndaing* Princess, remained unmarried in order to become the wife of the next monarch. In case of any accident befalling the *Tabîndaing* with regard to producing heirs, the second available Princess nearest of kin to the royal blood was also wedded to the new King. The former became the "chief" Queen (*Nanmadáw*), and the south palace (*Taungnya*) was assigned to her use; while the latter became the "middle" Queen (*Alènandaw*), in contradistinction to any and all inferior wives raised to queenly rank. Thus Mindôn received his step-sister and his cousin as royal consorts. This had now become nothing more than the survival of an ancient custom, since the throne did not descend by direct lineal succession, but was filled by any prince, usually a brother or a son, who had been nominated as heir apparent by the King. The only requisite qualification was that he should be a son of one of the four chief Queens of a King.

Now it happened that these two Princesses, who became Mindôn's chief Queens, had each been born on a Thursday, and had therefore, for reasons elsewhere explained (*vide* chapter xxi.), received names beginning with *Ba* and *Ma*. This apparent confirmation of part of his second dream made Mindôn ponder over the desirability of founding a new capital on the level plain stretching towards the south-west from the base of Mandalay hill.

Many religious recluses of saintly reputation, many men of light and leading, and the royal astrologers were made to assemble and consult on this matter; and they almost unanimously advised that a new capital should be founded. Only two men, a recluse and an astrologer, dissented from the consensus of opinion, and urged that, for all practical purposes, Amárapúra lay near the foot of Mandalay hill. But Mindôn was bent on having a new capital, so, in 1857, the foundations of that city were laid which became known to the English as Mandalay, although to the Burmese it was always, previous to the British annexation, *Shwemyôdaw*, "the Royal Golden City," or else *Yadanábôn*, "the Cluster of Gems." King Mindôn, though a very pious Buddhist and strongly averse to the shedding of blood, was, like the vast majority of Burmese, simply saturated with superstition. So in founding the new city he acted on the advice of his chief astrologer, and a pregnant woman was slain one night in order that she might become the guardian spirit of his palace. Throughout the whole of his reign offerings were openly made in the palace by the King to the spirit of the murdered woman, which was supposed to be incarnated in the body of a snake. This is a strange and strong proof of animistic worship on the part of one who was unquestionably a most religious Buddhist, and the most enlightened of all the monarchs of the Alaung Payá dynasty.

Small spirit-houses (*Natsin*), like dove-cots, are still to be seen on the tops of all the remaining buildings in the palace; and in the King's apartments there are holes in the roof which were made in order to allow the resident spirits to visit him whenever inclined.

At all the gates in the city walls, and at the four corners, male victims were also done to death—being buried alive, it is said, along with large jars of oil—according to the ceremony known as *Sadé*, for the purpose of providing guardian spirits to keep watch and ward over all the lines of approach to the city. Small, whitewashed, pagoda-like tumuli outside the gates and the corners of the outer walls still form the abodes of these guardian spirits of the city (*Myôzadé*).

As the city was founded in 2,400th year after the death of Gaudama, the city walls were made to measure in all 2,400 *Tá* (of 11·11 feet), each one of the four sides of the perfect square being thus a little over a mile and one-third in length. Including their battlements they are 28½ feet in height, are built of red brick, and are flanked with a broad earthen rampart. The walls face due north, east, south, and west.

On each side at regular distances of sixty *Tá*, they are (or originally were, for some have now succumbed to decay) surmounted by ornamental spires (*Tazáung, Pyathat*) richly painted with cinnabar and profusely gilded. Those over the four main gates have nine roofs, the number allowed to be erected only over the King's palace and above monasteries. Often, however, some difficulty is to be found in counting the whole of the nine roofs, even in cases where they all really exist, as two or even three partial false roofs are sometimes introduced to simplify construction. The two minor gates on each side of the city wall are topped by seven-roofed spires, the number allowed by the Burmese sumptuary laws to tributary chiefs like the Sawbwa of the Shan States; while all the other smaller *Tazáung* have only five roofs. Some of these have already fallen down through decay and neglect. Outside, the city was surrounded by a moat, which is fed by springs preventing the water from stagnating; for the three requisites of a Burmese city (*Myô*) were a bazaar, a fortress wall, and a moat.

Within these city walls, which enclose what is now known as Fort Dufferin, the capital was laid out in a series of squares and blocks, whose sides were parallel to the outer defences. In the centre were the grounds and the palace of the King, forming a square fortified enclosure, each side of which was somewhat over three furlongs in length, defended by an outer palisade of sharp-pointed teak-posts, about sixteen feet high, which was neither loop-holed nor provided with flank defences. About sixty feet behind this, separated by a clear space, came an inner brick wall, which has now been almost entirely removed, though portions may still be seen (1898) near the north-east corner. Another inner wall, now almost entirely destroyed, enclosed the private apartments of the royal family and the state rooms.

Around the palace, outside the stockade, were grouped the residences of all the great Ministers of State, with one exception. Each was in the centre of a block, the outer portions of which were crowded with the huts of their retainers and by persons keeping petty shops or stalls. The only building of this sort now remaining (1898) is that occupied by the ex-Kinwun Mingyi, to the south-east of the palace. No masonry buildings were allowed to be erected save within the palace grounds, so that the royal city was, for the most part, a rude collection of wooden houses and bamboo huts. The solitary exception above noted was the notorious Taingda Mingyi, a ferocious, bloodthirsty ruffian, who was directly responsible for some of the massacres during Thibaw's reign, and indirectly responsible for the third Burmese war and the extinction of the kingdom of Ava. He lived in a house, now totally destroyed, near the southern gate of the inner palace enclosure.

Outside the walls of the city, a straggling native town stretched southwards towards Amárapura and westwards to the Irrawaddy. Settlements here were encouraged by King Mindôn, not only because they naturally meant increase of trade and traffic, but also because the embankments rendered necessary for the protection of these suburbs prevented, as he thought, the possibility of the palace ever being shelled from hostile war-vessels that might lie at anchor in the river.

All the main roads, both in the city and the suburbs,

Plan of the Palace Buildings within the Royal City of Mandalay.

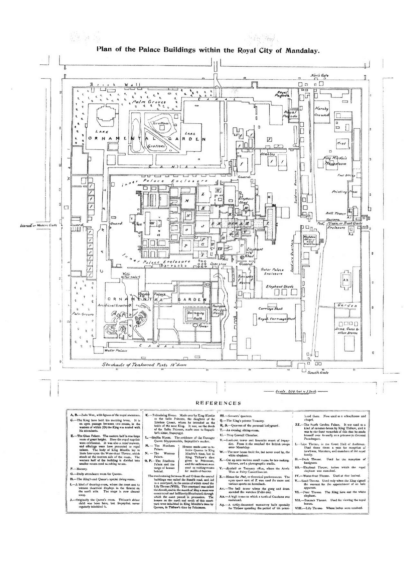

Scale 200 feet = 1 inch

REFERENCES

A, B.—Juda Won, with figures of the royal ancestors.

C.—The King here held his morning levee. It is an open passage between two rooms, in the wainscot of which (D) the King was seated with his attendants.

E.—The Glass Palace. The eastern half is one large room of great height. Here the royal regalities were celebrated. It was also a royal nursery, and offerings were here presented to royal infants. The body of King Mindön lay in State here upon the Water-float Throne, which stands at the western side of the room. The western half of the building is divided into smaller rooms used as robing-rooms.

F.—Nursery.

G.—Daily attendance room for Queens.

H.—The King's and Queen's special dining-room.

I.—A kind of dressing-room, where the court met to witness theatrical displays in the theatre on the south side. The stage is now cleared away.

J.—Originally the Queen's room. Thibaw's eldest child was born here, but Supaÿálat never regularly inhabited it.

K.—Fabricking House. Made over by King Mindön to the Salin Princess, the daughter of the Limbun Queen, whom he intended as the bride of the next King. It was, on the death of the Salin Princess, made over to Supaÿálat's sister, Supaÿágyi.

L.—Sinbin House. The residence of the Dowager Queen Sinpyumáshin, Supaÿálat's mother.

M.—The Northern Palace. House made over to inferior Queens in King Mindön's time, but in King Thibaw's time given to Princesses, and the entrance was used as waiting-rooms for maids-of-honour.

N.—The Western Palace.

O, P.—The Southern Palace and the range of houses behind.

The road running between M and O from the central buildings was called the Bazaár road, and led to a courtyard, in the centre of which stood the Lily Throne (VIII). This courtyard was called the Zanádi, and to the month of May a mart was constructed and brilliantly illuminated, through which the court passed in procession. The houses on the north and south of this courtyard were inhabited in King Mindön's time by Queens, in Thibaw's time by Princesses.

M1.—Servants' quarters.

Q.—The King's private Treasury.

R, S.—Quarters of the personal bodyguard.

T.—An evening sitting-room.

U.—Privy Council Chamber.

V.—Look-out tower and favourite resort of inspection. From it the watched the British troops enter Mandalay.

W.—The new house built for, but never used by, the white elephant.

X.—Cut up into various small rooms for tea-making kitchen, and a photographic studio.

Y.—Spatádi or Treasury office, where the Atwin Wun or Privy Councillors sat.

Z.—House for Pwé, or theatrical performances. The open space east of Z was used for more and various sports on horseback.

A1.—The hall tower where the gong and drum sounded the watches (Pahó-zin).

A2.—A high tower in which a torch of Cardamon was suspended.

A3.—A richly-decorated monastery built specially for Thibaw spending the period of his penance.

hood there. Now used as a schoolhouse and chapel.

ZZ.—The South Garden Palace. It was used as a kind of summer-house by King Thibaw, and it was to this hotel verandah of this that he made himself over formally as a prisoner to General Prendergast.

I.—Lion Throne, in the Great Hall of Audience. Used three times a year for reception of learbenes, Ministers, and members of the royal family.

II.—Duck Throne. Used for the reception of foreigners.

III.—Elephant Throne, before which the royal elephant was marshalled.

IV.—Water-fowl Throne. Used at the festival.

V.—Snail Throne. Used only when the King signed the warrant for the appointment of an heir apparent.

VI.—Deer Throne. The King here met the white elephant.

VII.—Peacock Throne. Used for viewing the royal horses.

VIII.—Lily Throne. Where ladies were received.

were well planted with avenues of trees. The latter were mostly tamarind, which thrives well in that dry climate.

In 1886, there were close upon 6,000 dwellings within the city walls, and about 24,000 forming the various suburbs, containing a total population of about 180,000 souls. Most of the houses were built merely of bamboos with mat walling, and their worth could not exceed about fifty rupees each (£3 6s. 8d.), even on a liberal estimate. The houses within the walls were cleared away on the British occupation, and the populace transferred to blocks well laid out to the south and west of the city, liberal compensation for disturbance being paid on a scale varying according to the number of posts in each building.

King Mindôn's new capital was occupied in 1860. His palace is a strange mixture of barbaric art and matter-of-fact utility. It is a maze of buildings of all sorts and sizes chiefly constructed of teak-wood, richly carved and thickly gilded, or else resplendent with looking-glass mosaic of showy, tawdry description, though crudely effective from a distance. All these profusely decorated wooden buildings are roofed with corrugated iron.

The principal entrance to the palace stockade was at the *Tagâni* or " Red Gate " on the eastern side. This was never opened except on great state occasions, and entrance could only be effected through a small door in the same, whereby one was forced, *nolens volens*, to bow the head in the direction of the palace as if making obeisance to the great central spire above the chief throne.

Immediately to the left of the Red Gate stands the tower enshrining the sacred tooth of Gaudama received long ago as a gift from the Emperor of China. In front of that is the *Hlutdaw* or Great Council Hall and High Court. At some distance to the south is the miniature monastery, a gem of looking-glass mosaic work, to which Prince Thibaw withdrew for a time in order to perform the term of monkhood or religious retreat obligatory on all male Burmese. To the north of the main gate is the bell-tower (*Pahôzin*), from which the time of the day and night was told every third hour by beat of drum-gong. A little further on stand the three pagoda-like tombs of

BURMA UNDER BRITISH RULE

King Mindôn and his two chief Queens, whose names
were indirectly the cause of the foundation of this last
capital of the kingdom of Ava.

Of the palace buildings within the innermost wall the
chief, occupying the most easterly position, is the *Myè
Nandaw* or Imperial Palace, best known to Europeans
as "the Centre of the Universe." This is a lofty nine-
roofed spire (*Pyathat*) with graduated roofs, ascending
above the Lion throne at the end of the Great Hall of
Audience (*Yôndaw*). The only other very lofty erection
among the palace buildings is the look-out tower to the
south of the Centre of the Universe, built by Thibaw's
Queen, Supayálat, where she used to enjoy the cool
breeze in the evening, and from which she witnessed the
entry of the British troops into the south gate of the city,
at the close of November, 1885. A little to the west
of this tower, and adjoining the garden, was the open
pavilion (*Mandat*), roofed only, but without any walls,
where theatrical performances took place.

The main buildings themselves were the various
palaces of the King and his Queens, and the private
apartments of the dowager-Queens and the maids of
honour. They are now used as Government offices.
The most artistic and the most interesting of all the
buildings is the western hall containing the Lily throne,
where ladies were received in audience. This now very
appropriately forms the ladies' room of the Upper
Burma Club. Here, on the further portion of the gilded
doorway to the north of the throne, are the four finger-
marks which have given rise to the story that they are
bloodstains from one of Supayálat's victims. That she
was jealous, cruel, and remorseless is a matter of fact;
but these red finger-prints have no connection with that.
They are merely the effect of some incautious person
coming from behind having opened the right-hand half of
the door before the gilding had become thoroughly set
and hardened, and ever since then the red grounding of
cinnabar has shown through wherever the gold came
partially away. However, this Burmese story of the
palace tragedy is quite as good in its way as Rizzio's
bloodstains in Holyrood, or as the stains made on the

wall in the Wartburg at Eisenach when Luther threw the inkpot at the devil's head. There were only too many real tragedies of blood in the palace, without inventing mere twaddle of that sort about any of them.

To the north and the south of the western portion of the palace, which formed the ladies' apartments, there were ornamental gardens with spring-fed ponds and canals. Here, amid palms and umbrageous evergreen trees, the royal family took the air in the evening, while gliding along the canals in the royal barge or wandering through the grottoes and labyrinths strangely and wonderfully made of Portland cement. Quaint in every respect as to its rocks, its trees, its tiny lakes and canals, and the rustic bridges crossing these, the royal gardens form a charming lounge at any time of the day, and at any period of the year. But, to appreciate them to the full, one must visit them in the evening in April or May, when the thermometer has all day long been registering above 100° in the shade.

Within the palace there were eight thrones of carved teak wood, richly gilded, while a ninth occupied the central position in the *Hlutdaw* or State Council Chamber. The Lion throne at the western end of the great Hall of Audience, above which towers the lofty spire of the Centre of the Universe, was the principal throne occupied on solemn ceremonial occasions ; while the seven others were each used for special purposes. Seated on the Duck throne, placed further westward in the interior of the royal apartments and behind the Lion throne, the King received foreigners in audience. Behind that again, nearer to the centre of the royal chambers, stood the Water Festival throne used at the beginning of each new year in April. From the Elephant throne, in the *Byèdaik*, the royal elephant was watched at exercise. The Snail throne, situated somewhat southwards from the Duck throne, was used only when the King signed a warrant for the appointment of an heir apparent who should succeed him on the throne. At the Deer throne, on the north side of the palace, the royal white elephant was met by the King on great occasions ; while directly opposite this, on the southern side of the palace buildings, stood the Peacock throne, from which the royal horses were inspected. The Lily throne, by far the most beautiful and most artistic of all, in front of which ladies were received, was situated at the western extremity of the palace. All of these thrones were elevated between four and five feet above the ground, so that their occupant should be raised well above the level of those receiving an audience and making obeisance on the floor below. In front of the Judgment throne in the *Hlutdaw* the floor was punctured with ✛ holes at fixed distances for the Ministers and other great officers of state, and for lesser notables sitting round the edge of the chamber. These small cross-holes were for passing up long pipe-stems to the lips of those seated on the floor, while the bowls were fed and lighted by attendants below ; for the building was raised seven or eight feet above the ground on piles. To have smoked cigars or the huge Burmese cheroots in the royal presence or before the throne would have been a breach of etiquette, but the concession made in the Great Council Chamber showed how necessary smoking was apparently considered.

The British Residency lay some distance to the west of the city, and the Resident was only permitted to enter the city walls by the western or " accursed " gate, through which corpses were conveyed, and the passage through which by any King meant the open avowal of abdication. The Residency was the property of the King. Apart from the British flag flown from the roof-top, there was nothing whatever to mark it with any of the importance which ought to have been attached to Her Majesty's representative at a foreign court. The compound or ground surrounding the house was roughly fenced in with bamboo matwork, supported by a framework of teakwood, but it formed no defence capable of resisting any persistent attack. The gates were guarded by Burmese soldiers, who were in reality rather a band of spies making daily reports to the palace than a guard of honour.

The whole of the Residency staff resided within this building, which also comprised the post office and the

THE WHITE ELEPHANT

mixed court wherein, according to treaty all cases involving British subjects were tried by a bench consisting of a British magistrate and a Burmese official.

Intercourse between the townspeople and the Residency was limited owing to the system of espionage in force; and access to the palace was difficult, even when matters of importance required personal discussion.

The services of the Residency Surgeon were sometimes, however, invited in serious cases, but usually only after the patient had advanced to an almost moribund condition, and had been given up by the Burmese medicine men. Practice of this sort was not hankered after. In most cases, the doctor arrived too late to be of any use; and practice did not always prove lucrative. For example, after curing one of the Ministers of a severe internal disease, a doctor who was Residency Surgeon for several years told me he was sent a gift of two cocoa-nuts and a bunch of plantains in return for his services. He had from time to time, however, opportunities of seeing strange sights within the inner precincts of the palace. Thus, on one occasion, during King Mindôn's time, about 1875, he saw the white elephant receiving its morning draught of human milk. About twenty women having been placed in a row, the elephant went behind each, put the tip of its trunk over the woman's shoulder, and sucked each breast dry of its milk. It was a disgusting sight, he said, to see the nervous state into which the women fell as the huge brute slowly made its way down the line. So nervous and excited did they become, that the milk even spouted from their breasts before these were touched by the big beast's trunk. But this feeding of the celestial *Saddán* elephant was an act of great religious merit, and there never was lack of mothers to earn this for the sake of their souls in the next incarnation.

A curious zoological fact with regard to a Burmese white elephant is that its skin need not necessarily be white. This may even be perfectly black; but there are other signs whereby the true nature of this pearl among brute animals may be known, despite any mere superficial shortcomings. Among these invariable signs one is the presence of a boss on the nape of the neck, just where this is joined on to the back of the skull.

All ceremonies connected with royalty and court etiquette were duly prescribed and were carefully attended to in every particular, except on the part of the King, who followed antecedent customs only in so far as suited his convenience. When a King was pleased to ascend to the land of spirits—so ran the phrase for his demise—the royal white umbrella was broken, and the great drum-gong on the bell-tower at the eastern gate of the palace enclosure was perforated. These two customs were omitted on Mindôn's death in 1878, as the parties intriguing to place Thibaw on the throne wished to complete all their arrangements before proclaiming the death of the late King.

A white umbrella, the sign of sovereignty, was only carried over the King and his chief Queen. The white umbrella (*Tipyu*) was, in fact, one of the five articles reckoned as regalia, the other four being the crown (*Makô*), the sceptre (*Thanlyet*), the sandal (*Chenin*), and the fly-flap (*Thámyi Yat*). On receiving these insignia a new King was blessed by the Brahmins, and water was poured out, this ceremony (*Abeiktheik*) being the equivalent of the ancient custom practised elsewhere of anointing with oil.

The use of golden umbrellas was permitted to the members of the royal family, the tributary chiefs, and the highest officials ; while officials of lower degree were allowed to have red umbrellas and large fans of a particular shape borne over them. When high officials or members of the royal family passed along the streets, the way was prepared for them by lictors (*Letyádaung*) armed with stout long rattans, which they took much pleasure in using on any one within their reach.

When any great personage went abroad, the whole of the roads along which he made his progress were fenced in trellis with " royal lattice-work " (*Yazahmat*) of bamboos or laths in front of all the houses, and the people were not permitted to approach from behind that. Indeed, it was considered much safer to retire altogether within their houses, and to peep only between the chinks of the bamboo-mat walls rather than allow themselves to be seen. It was not altogether safe for men, and often very unsafe for women if they happened to be young and good-looking, to fall under the eyes of great Princes or powerful Ministers.

The King himself, however, never went abroad of late years. Possession of the palace meant possession of the throne. If the King left the inner palace inclosure, he could never be quite sure that on his return he might not, in place of obtaining re-admission, have to flee through the western gate of the city in token of abdication. After the attempt on his life by two of his own sons, in 1866, King Mindôn seldom went abroad from his palace, and King Thibaw probably never ventured outside of the fortified inclosure during the whole of the seven years of his reign. Thus the prescribed annual festival of breaking ground with the plough in the royal fields to the east of the city—"the blessed ceremony of ploughing" (*Mingalátún*)—upon which the copiousness of the rains during the months of June to October was supposed to depend, fell into abeyance : and naturally, the people said, this led to the more frequent recurrence of years of insufficient rainfall, and of scarcity and grievous want among the people all throughout the dry zone. Thibaw never performed this ceremony, similar to that annually observed by the Emperor of China and by the Minister of Agriculture in Siam ; and this, the people said, was why drought became chronic and severe during his reign.

The ladies of the royal household and their apartments were in charge of eunuchs (*Meinmasó*), who were only to be found at the capital and nowhere else in the country. None of the inferior Queens were permitted to reside within the main palace buildings when the time of their accouchement was at hand, but were removed to special apartments (*Einneing*) reserved for this purpose. When they went abroad to visit religious shrines, or for any other purpose, their mode of progress was in richly carved box-like carriages mounted upon two cart wheels. As these were small and had no springs, and as the roads were bad, unmetalled and full of deep ruts, a drive to any pagoda in the suburbs was hardly a pleasure. Men of high degree or filling great offices of State usually rode on elephants.

Many of the royal ceremonies were peculiar, and all were directly or indirectly connected with the national religion. Two of these may perhaps be briefly mentioned as examples. Twice annually, at the great religious festivals of the new year in spring and of the termination of lent in autumn, the King's head was ceremoniously washed in water which used to be specially brought for this purpose to the capital from "the head wash island" (*Gaung-zé-Gyun*) between Martaban and Moulmein, near the mouth of the Salween river. This custom was continued till after the second Burmese war, when purified water from the Irrawaddy was used. It was then that the two greatest of the levées or receptions known as the *Kadáw* or "beg pardon" were held, when the court was *en fête* and all who were in any way connected with it, or had anything to hope from it, laid tribute or presents at the "golden feet" of the King. Every day the King wore a new silk waist-cloth (*Pasó*), and as each was discarded after being once used it was lacquered in red, richly ornamented with gold, and then cut into strips upon which the Pali text of the ordination service for monks (*Kammawá*) was written in Burmese characters with black varnish (*Thitsi*).

So long as Mindôn was able to hold the reins of government in his own hands matters within the royal city went on fairly well, although direct intercourse between the British Resident and the King had even then for about three years been interrupted on account of the "shoe question" elsewhere referred to (*vide* page 30).

There was, however, one ever-threatening cause of political disturbance connected with the succession to the throne. Early in his reign Mindôn appointed as heir apparent his brother, to whom he was much attached. As the King's sons grew up, they deeply resented this nomination of their uncle; so two of them, the Myingun and the Myingundaing Princes, rose in rebellion in 1866, and attempted to seize and dethrone their father while he was residing for a few days at a royal pleasure garden situated about a couple of miles to the south-east of the city. The King managed to escape, but the heir apparent was killed along with three of the King's sons and the Myadaung Mingyi, then Minister of War. The attempt thus proving futile, the rebel princes fled into British territory. For some years they were kept under supervision in Rangoon, till the Myingun Prince tried to escape, when they were both transferred for greater safety to Fort Chunar in Bengal.

After that, King Mindôn felt nervous about appointing an heir apparent, and his nervousness was not in any way dissipated by another of his sons, the Prince of Katha, heading an attempt to dethrone him in 1870. But although he must have known that his action was not what could be regarded as constitutional, Mindôn would not appoint his successor. He had no lack of sons, duly qualified by blood, to choose from. His family by chief Queens, inferior Queens, and mere concubines numbered about a hundred, and about thirty of these were sons. But the number of Princes who had any special chance of finding sufficient support upon which to base aspirations to the throne was practically limited to about half a dozen. These were the Thônze, Mekkayá, Myingun, Myingundaing, Nyaungyan, Nyaungôk, and Thibaw Princes. The two first-named, the eldest, were unsuitable from their cruel and overbearing disposition, while the next two had been outlaws and refugees under foreign protection since their dash for the throne in 1866. Hence the real issue as to succession lay between the Nyaungyan, the Nyaungôk, and the Thibaw Princes.

It had always been understood that, rightly or wrongly, there were some doubts as to the parentity of the last named. Mindôn had consequently often expressed his intention that this particular member of the royal family should not succeed him on the throne. Actuated either through personal fear, or else hoping to avert fratricidal bloodshed, he put off the nomination of an heir apparent till too late. By the middle of 1878 he was so ill as to be unable to exercise any real authority over affairs, and as early as August rumours of his decease had already begun to find their way into the various districts. The palace now became the scene of continuous intrigue by various parties, but definite action was taken early in September by the party then in power.

It is said that, while on his deathbed, Mindôn actually nominated the Nyaungyan Prince as heir apparent and successor. This seems to have been, in fact, by far the most suitable selection that could have been made. He was 'of pure royal blood, was very popular throughout the country, and was much esteemed and trusted by Mindôn both on account of his intellectual qualities and his humane disposition. But it was now too late. The chief Queen had three daughters, Supayágyi, Supayálat, and Supayágalé. The young Thibaw Prince, son of a Queen of Shan extraction, was known to be enamoured of one of these; so Queen Sinpyumashin, an ambitious and crafty woman, resolved to secure the throne for him, raise all her three daughters to the highest queenly rank, and be the guiding hand controlling the destiny of affairs through these, her puppets. The Taingda Mingyi, the most powerful of the Ministers, fell in with these plans; and even the Kinwun Mingyi, the Prime Minister, was won over to the plot. A forged order, purporting to come from the King, was sent to all the royal Princes and Princesses, who were therein summoned to appear before his Majesty to hear his nomination of a successor and his last words of formal farewell. As they came to the royal apartments they were one by one seized and placed in confinement. Thus, on the 12th September all the Princes of the royal blood had been secured save two, the Nyaungyan and Nyaungôk Princes, who, warned either by instinct or by some friendly hint, fled to the British Residency for protection. Opposition thus removed, Thibaw was proclaimed heir apparent, and by 1st October, when authentic news of Mindôn's death had been received, he had ascended the throne without opposition.

Following the usual custom, King Thibaw made Supayágyi, one of the late King's favourite daughters, his chief Queen, but she absolutely refused to be his consort in anything more than name. So her sister, Supayálat, virtually became chief Queen ; while later on Supayá-galé, the youngest, was likewise raised to queenly rank. These Princesses represented the purest of the pure royal blood. Their father was a son of King Tharrawaddi, while their mother was a daughter of Nanmadaw Mè Nu, chief Queen of Bágyidaw.

But the Dowager Chief Queen had miscalculated. No sooner had she succeeded in crushing anything like power and authority in the case of the Kinwun Mingyi, Minister of Foreign Affairs, than she found herself checkmated in her ambitious designs and forced into the position of an absolute nonentity by her daughter Supayálat. Master-ful to a degree, ambitious, and jealous in every possible way, Supayálat very soon showed that she intended to domineer over her lord and master and to rule the palace, and consequently the national affairs, without permitting either King, Queen Dowager, or Ministers to have very much to say in the matter. And, as might have been ex-pected with such a woman, her opinions and actions were far more influenced by the brutal and ruffianly Taingda Mingyi than by any of the more reputable of the nominally responsible Ministers of the King.

The political situation of the British Resident had by this time become unduly strained. The treaties in force were not respected, while British subjects and their com-mercial interests involved in Upper Burma were wan-tonly injured, redress for wrongs being tacitly refused. Everywhere throughout the country affairs had run riot, and life and property were insecure.

In February, 1879, Supayálat had obtained Thibaw's consent to the " clearance " of many of the Princes who were of political importance, though no conspiracy of any sort was on foot. On the 15th, 16th, and 17th men, women and children of royal blood, all the near relatives of the King and the Queen, were massacred in cold blood at Supayálat's instigation, prompted by the Taingda Mingyi. Neither infancy nor old age afforded protec-tion from the bloodthirstiness suddenly developed. The aged uncle of the Nyaungyan Prince, an old man stand-ing on the brink of the grave, who had been Governor of Pegu in 1852, was among the victims, but these also

included children of the tenderest age. Infants were even
torn from their mothers' arms, and their brains dashed
out against the wall before their parents' eyes. And
"*all this was effected under the superintendence of the
personal followers of the King*," as Mr. Shaw, the British
Resident, reported officially to the Government of India.
The women and children were buried in the jail yard
within the palace precincts, but eight cartloads of corpses
of Princes of the royal blood were borne, wrapped in red
velvet sacks, through the "accursed" western gate and
thrown into the river Irrawaddy according to precedent
and custom. In September more massacres occurred,
and in November of 1879 they were continued, as all
the scions of the royal stock had not yet been cut off.
Among those then released from confinement and thus
freed from their present human incarnation was poor
Supayágyi, the nominal chief Queen by virtue of having
been the *Tabindaing* Princess on Thibaw's accession.
Apparently all along in love with the Nyaungyan
Prince, and maybe the one who sent him a friendly hint
to flee, she had recently attempted to administer poison
to Thibaw and Supayálat, her own half-brother and
sister. But failing in this attempt to stop bloodshed,
butchery, and general oppression, she had to pay forfeit
with her life; for Supayálat was not a person likely to
spare even her own sister after that sort of crime.

While the walls within the inner palace enclosure were
thus being stained red with royal blood, everything was
done to provide mirth and amusement for the citizens
and the suburban population, and to distract their attention
from ruminating over the reports that leaked out about
the carnage going on within the palace. These reports
could not be stifled. The ghastly procession of carts
with the corpses of the murdered Princes could not but
tell its own horrible tale, and corpses of common folks
were even intentionally exposed to public view.

Within the palace the state of affairs was desperate,
and Thibaw, "the Excellent King of the Rising
Sun and Lord of the White Elephant," bullied by the
termagant Supayálat and no doubt horrified by the
bloodshed ordered in a moment of terror, or of alco-

holic excitement, or of both, was probably one of the most miserable of all the men within his kingdom, for at this time, though he had been a *Patama Byan*, or graduate with the highest possible honours in theology, he fell far below the usual standard of Burmese Buddhists with regard to abstinence and self-denial. A few years before he had attained, as a novice, the highest honours at the public examination in religious philosophy held annually in the *Thudamá* hall; and as King he was virtually the head of Burmese Buddhism. Hence, if he had any belief at all in the doctrines enunciated by Gaudama, he must have felt convinced that in the next state of exist-ence he was doomed to fearful torments in one of the lowest regions in hell. No wonder he was dismayed and despairing about his future existence, as well as wretched and miserable about the rung he now occupied in the "ladder of existence."

So he lost faith in everything. Even the *Wèza* or soothsayer in whom he placed most confidence fell into disgrace during the spring of 1879, was degraded, and had to flee from the wrath of the King, while the attend-ant or disciple whom he left behind was thrown into prison. On his flight a rival soothsayer of Minhla, near the frontier, boldly declared that this previously much-honoured personage was no seer at all, but merely a common demon who had been enabled to assume the form of a man by means of the arts of a sorcerer; and this sorcerer was, the new authority affirmed, no other than the supposed disciple now in the royal prison. So the poor unoffending servant was executed at the sug-gestion of the new soothsayer, who also strongly advised a change of capital back to Amárapura. But this was out of the question, for obvious reasons.

Thibaw became almost demented with terror when the British Resident withdrew from Mandalay in the autumn of 1879. Knowing that the political and commercial courses he was pursuing must sooner or later bring him into conflict with the Government of India, he suddenly developed frenzied proclivities for soldiering, which his Ministers were unable to check. And even if he had recollected sufficient of the ancient Jewish Old Testament history—for, when about twelve years of age, he was sent to be taught English and western wisdom at the Mandalay Mission School of the Society for the Propagation of the Gospel—to know that Jehosaphat was promised the throne of Israel for four generations because, in slaughtering the seventy sons of Ahab, "*he had done that which was right in the sight of the Lord*," yet he must have known quite well that *that* piece of ancient history could hardly be considered as parallel with the massacre, in the latter part of the nineteenth century, of about four times as many innocent victims who were his own nearest relatives.

So the state of affairs within the heart of the Golden City was dreadful. Thibaw's mother appealed to the Dowager chief Queen, beseeching her to stay the ruthless follies of Thibaw and Supayálat; but in vain. The royal couple were now quite incapable of being restrained, and the only advice they seemed to listen to was the fatal promptings of the ignorant and brutal Taingda Mingyi, urging them on to conflict with the British.

The story has been told in another chapter of how political and commercial matters gradually drifted from bad to worse within the golden city, and how intrigues with foreign powers, and blunt refusal to submit to proper judicial enquiry certain grave charges raised against an influential trading corporation, ultimately led to the third Burmese war in 1885. How strange it was that the first procession which Thibaw and his Queens made through their capital was when, driven in a cart passing between files of British troops and furnished with a guard of honour of British soldiers, they passed, for the first time since the summer of 1878 and for the first time during Thibaw's reign, through the Red Gate at the east side of the palace enclosure and were conveyed by the southern gate of the golden city westwards to the river bank for embarkation on board the *Thooreah* (*Thuryá*), "the Sun"—appropriate name for the steamer which was to bear the King of the Rising Sun away from his dominions into lifelong exile in a foreign land.

While thus reaping the fruits of his own wickedness and folly, Thibaw was spared the deepest indignity of being made to pass through the "accursed" western gate of the city. But his cup of bitterness and remorse was full enough without that, although the degrading insult of being forced to come and go by that gate had from time immemorial been thought good enough treatment for the various British Envoys and Residents who had visited any of the capitals of the kingdom of Burma during the previous century and a quarter.

Chapter IX

A T the end of 1899, for the first time in her history, Burma was absolutely free from organized dacoity; not a single dacoit gang was known to be in existence within the boundaries of the province. Before that, although the main efforts for the pacification of Upper Burma could be considered as crowned with success by the end of 1890, it was not to be expected that all trouble was then at an end. There still remained a great deal to be done among the frontier tribes inhabiting the forest-clad hills all round the northern borders marching with Siam, China, Assam, Manipur, and Bengal.

Early in 1891 the chiefs of the Shan States of Wunthó and Kalé, lying west of the Irrawaddy and west of the Chindwin, conspired with a view to a general rising along with Manipur, and the Wunthó Sawbwa broke into open rebellion. Both were deposed, and their States were incorporated into the existing districts of Upper Burma.

In the Chin hills raids continued to occur, which necessitated the infliction of severe punishment on the Kanháw and Baungshè tribes. In 1891 many of the Chin chiefs were brought down to Rangoon to be shown the wonders of civilization, and the power and extent of British rule; but some of them were so little impressed thereby that they broke into revolt soon after their return to the fastnesses within their native hills. Columns were therefore sent to explore and subjugate the whole of the Chin tracts, levying and fixing tribute, recognizing or appointing tribal chiefs, releasing slaves

THE HILL TRIBES

kidnapped in raids, imposing fines or burning contumacious villages wherever necessary, and opening out
mule tracks. The only real difficulties encountered by
the military were the physical obstructions offered by the
mountainous nature of the densely forested country
operated in; for the rainy season, during which operations had to be suspended, came early and was late of
ceasing, so that an expedition could seldom complete its
work effectively during one short field season. Thus,
when, in October, 1892, the Siyin and Nwéngal tribes
revolted, and, ambushing a party, killed a Burmese
magistrate and eleven of his men, operations promptly
taken at a cost of casualties exceeding seventy on the
British side crushed the rebellion : but the operations
had to be continued in the following open season before
the rebel leaders were all captured and the tribes
thoroughly disarmed and subjugated. This was, however, effected in due time, and the Chin hills were
brought under the jurisdiction of a political officer
stationed at Falám. In all, about 7,000 guns were
taken from the tribesmen. In 1894 a battalion of
military police was substituted for the military garrison
of the northern posts, and in 1896 a similar change was
effected in the Southern Chin hills; while the increased
security for life and property was naturally accompanied
by an expansion of trade and greater freedom of intercourse with the adjacent districts on the plains.

Among the Kachin tribes much also remained to be
done. Early in 1891 the Kaukkwé valley was quieted,
and a post was established at the Jade Mines, while
columns were also sent south-eastwards from Bhamo to
reduce to order the wild tribes dwelling in the forests
north of the Shweli river. To the north-east of the
Bhamo district nothing had yet been done to bring the
hill tribes under control; but repeated outrages committed by the Kachins, the Alsatian character that this
tract had acquired as a refuge for outlaws and bad
characters, and the necessity of preventing the importation into Burma of illicit opium, liquor, and arms from
Yunnan, involved operations being undertaken in the
open seasons of 1891–92 and 1892–93. As the result

of these expeditions, some of which met with considerable resistance, strong posts of military police were established along the Chinese border at Namkhan on the Shweli river, and northwards at Nampaung, Sima, and Sadôn, or Fort Harrison, as the last was called after an officer who defended it with great gallantry when the small garrison there was besieged by a large number of Kachins. After the military operations civil officers moved about the hills with moderate escorts, collecting tribute, settling disputes, and meeting with little or no opposition.

In 1894 the policy to be adopted in the Kachin hills was definitely fixed. The point where the Malíkha ("good water") and the Maikha ("bad water") join to form the Irrawaddy river, about twenty-five miles north of the flourishing new town of Myitkyina, was taken as the northern limit of active administration, which was to include all the tracts lying south of the Maikha to the east of the Irrawaddy, on its left bank, and on the right bank all the country lying south of a line drawn from the confluence of the Malíkha and the Maikha westwards through the northern limit of Labán, including the Jade Mines. So long as the tribes to the north of this administrative boundary abstained from raiding into the tracts south of it, it was notified to them that they would not be interfered with. In order to carry out this scheme a new district, Myitkyina, was formed in 1895, while the Kachin Hill Tribes Regulation was passed to legalize the procedure previously in force, and was extended to various hill tracts throughout the northern districts. Since then the establishment of law and order has proceeded regularly and satisfactorily, and considerable progress has even been made in the extremely difficult matter of settling disputes between Kachin tribes on different sides of the frontier line separating Burma from China.

Throughout the northern and the southern Shan States satisfactory advances continued to be made in the matter of introducing more orderly methods of administration than had previously been in force. During the open seasons of 1890–91 and 1891–92 the two Superintendents were busy with the work of revenue inspection and house-counting, with a view to making better arrangements for the assessment of tribute, in bringing the distant State of Manglün under regular control, and in visiting Kengtung with a view to placing matters there on a satisfactory footing—for the young Sawbwa was proving far from amenable to the control of the Superintendent. In 1891 the customary law of the Shan States was modified by a short and simple set of rules designed to serve the purpose of Penal and Criminal Procedure Codes among a primitive people. In 1892–93 the demarcation of the boundary between the southern Shan States and Siam was accomplished satisfactorily as far north as Kengcheng, the Siamese Commissioners working in perfect accord with the Superintendent ; while in the northern States an expedition was made into the wild Wa country. In the following year a partial demarcation was made of the boundary between Kengtung and Kengcheng, an assistant political officer was stationed at Kengtung, and steps were taken to promote cordial relations between that State and the Siamese tracts on its borders. As affairs in Kengtung continued unsatisfactory, it was in 1894–95 reduced from occupying a position of subordinate alliance with British India to precisely the same status as the other Shan States, a small garrison was established at the capital, and it was connected with Fort Stedman by a telegraph line and by a mule track capable of being used throughout the year. The young Sawbwa, who had married a daughter of the Thibaw Sawbwa, died in 1895 ; and the State of Kengtung, which had recently been enlarged by the cis-Mekong districts of Kengcheng, was provisionally placed in charge of the late chief's brother till the succession could be decided. The Kengcheng territories thus attached to Kengtung accepted the new situation loyally, and the partition of the State to the west of the Mekong river led to no difficulties with the French, who thereby became our neighbours. Cordial relations were maintained with Siam, and there was no trouble with the Chinese of Kenghung and Möng Lem.

BURMA UNDER BRITISH RULE

The maintenance of peace and order and the abrogation of tolls were already bearing fruit in a considerable expansion of trade throughout the Shan States. In 1894–95 the southern Shan States exports and imports amounted to over £36,666, having more than doubled themselves within the last year or two, and the several chiefs were beginning to take an intelligent interest in the development of the resources of their States. Among other reforms introduced, the financial arrangements of the States were placed on a sound footing. Budget estimates were drawn up and revenue registers kept in specific forms; unauthorized demands were not to be made ; and the inhabitants of each village or circle were to know exactly how much they were required to pay.

In May, 1895, Sir Frederick Fryer, who had acted as *locum tenens* from 23rd May, 1892, to 2nd May, 1894, and had substantively succeeded Sir Alexander Mackenzie in the Chief Commissionership of Burma on 3rd April, 1895, held a durbar at Taunggyi, to which the headquarters of the Superintendent had recently been removed from Fort Stedman. Here, for the first time, chiefs from all parts of the southern Shan States, from the territories beyond the Salween, as well as from *cis*-Salween tracts, and all the chiefs of Karenni came together. Early in 1896 he also held durbars at Tiddim, Falám and Háka in the Chin hills. Many of the more important of the Shan chiefs, as well as a number of Chin chieftains from the western mountain range, had also been present at the durbars held in Rangoon and Mandalay, when Lord Lansdowne visited Burma towards the end of 1893, before laying down his viceroyalty. Representative Kachin chiefs from all parts of the northern hills had also been presented to His Excellency at Bhamo.

Throughout the whole of the more settled and the regularly administered portions of the province a steady advance was being made such as had characterized the province of British Burma before the annexation of the kingdom of Ava. The decennial census taken on the night of 26th February, 1891, was carried out over the whole province without difficulty or disturbance, and probably afforded a fairly accurate record of the population. The enumeration gave a total of 8,098,014 souls, of whom 4,658,627, occupying 869,132 houses, were in Lower Burma, 3,063,426 in Upper Burma, and 375,961 in the northern and southern Shan States. The population of Lower Burma had increased from $2\frac{3}{4}$ millions in 1872, to nearly $3\frac{3}{4}$ millions in 1881, and $4\frac{2}{3}$ millions in 1891; but the maximum and the minimum density of population were both to be found in Upper Burma, with 178 to the square mile in Mandalay district and only 5·23 to the square mile in the wild forest district of the Upper Chindwin. A not inconsiderable share of the increase in Lower Burma was due to immigration from India, especially from Madras, and from Upper Burma, from which large numbers fled during the troublous times following the annexation; but now that the northern portion had been brought into a settled condition, emigrants to Lower Burma flocked back across the frontier to secure to themselves the rights to the land which they had formerly possessed. The removal of restrictions on trade and liberty now also operated naturally to check the stream of emigration from Upper Burma, while the abolition of exemption from capitation tax formerly granted to the newly-arrived immigrant into Lower Burma assisted in the same direction.

When Lord Lansdowne in November and December, 1893, paid a viceregal visit to Burma, towards the close of the tenure of his high office, it was practically decided that the position and importance of the province was such as to render necessary its transformation from a local administration to a local government. After the first Burmese war the ceded sea-board provinces of Arakan and Tenasserim were administered by Commissioners, and after the annexation of Pegu, in 1852, the new territory was also placed under another Commissioner until it had been reduced to order and quietude. On 31st January, 1862, these three commissionerships were amalgamated and formed into a local administration called British Burma, Lieut.-Colonel (afterwards Sir Arthur) Phayre being made Chief Commissioner and

Agent to the Governor-General in Council. It was then placed on the same level as the Central Provinces of India ; but, from early in the seventies, the exceptional importance of Burma as a local administration was shown by the fact that the ablest among the coming men in India were sent to administer the province. The first two Chief Commissioners, Colonels Phayre and Fytche, were members of the Indian Staff Corps ; but, from 1873 onwards, the appointment was filled only by covenanted members of the Bengal Civil Service. The roll of Chief Commissioners included successively the men who achieved Indian fame as Sir Ashley Eden, Sir Augustus Rivers Thompson, Sir Charles Aitchison, Sir Charles Bernard, Sir Charles Crosthwaite, and Sir Alexander Mackenzie. All of these,—with the exception of Sir Charles Bernard, the breakdown of whose health under the strain of the troublous times immediately before and after the annexation of Upper Burma prematurely terminated his brilliant Indian career,—after holding charge of Burma, were subsequently promoted to seats on the Viceregal Council and to lieutenant-governorships of Bengal, the Punjab, or the North-West Provinces.

That the province, now greatly increased by Upper Burma, and the Shan States, stood on quite a different plane from the other local administrations under the Government of India, and involved under higher responsibilities than the other chief commissionerships, had been previously acknowledged by raising the pay of the appointment from 50,000 rupees to 80,000 rupees ($£3,333$ to $£5,333$) per annum, thus giving it emoluments equal to those drawn by members of the Viceregal Council, and by granting to Burma the practical status of a local government with regard to powers of sanction and the control of financial matters in various departments of Government. Financial pressure intervened, however, to prevent the Government of India from taking the necessary steps towards moving the Secretary of State to sanction the transformation of the chief commissionership into a lieutenant-governorship, and to have the necessary legislation carried through. It was, therefore, not until 1st May, 1897, that Burma became a lieutenant-governorship, having a separate Government and a Legislative Council of its own.

The first Lieutenant-Governor, Sir Frederick Fryer, had originally been sent down from the Punjab to Upper Burma in 1886, as soon as it had been decided to incorporate the kingdom of Ava with the British possessions, and bring it under direct administration. After filling for some time a divisional commissionership, he had been selected for the financial commissionership on that appointment being formed in June, 1888, but had subsequently returned to his old province, the Punjab. From May, 1892, to May, 1894, he had officiated as Chief-Commissioner during the absence of Sir Alexander Mackenzie on long leave to Europe, and on 3rd April, 1895, he had substantively succeeded to the appointment, after acting for some time as a member of the Viceregal Council. For a term of five years from May, 1897, the province now became assured of an administrator who had a much more intimate knowledge of the province and its people than had been brought to the task of government by any of his predecessors since the days of the two military proconsuls, Phayre and Fytche.

At the head of the Administration is the Lieutenant-Governor, who exercises the powers of a local government in respect of all the territories forming the province of Burma as constituted by the Upper Burma Laws Act, 1886, and who exercises political control over the wild tribes of the Chin hills and over Karenni, a small independent State in subordinate alliance with the British Government.

The disposal of Secretariat business is conducted by three departments controlled by a Chief Secretary, a Revenue Secretary, and a Secretary, together with Under Secretaries. From these various departments business is transmitted by the Secretary-in-Charge for the orders of the Lieutenant-Governor; but in place of proceeding back direct to each department, the boxes of records filter through the Chief Secretary, who is thus kept in constant touch with what is passing in the other two departments, and has the opportunity of making any suggestions which may occur to him.

BURMA UNDER BRITISH RULE

The various secretaries and the heads of departments have each a specified morning for waiting upon His Honour the Lieutenant-Governor, while in residence at the headquarters of Government, Rangoon, for reporting upon current business, and receiving his instructions as to its disposal. Other responsible officials who have no fixed days for discussion of business can always, when necessary, arrange for a special interview through the Private Secretary. Once a week, at noon, officials at large are afforded an opportunity of bringing before His Honour's notice any matters in which they are personally interested ; for, of course, apart from personal matters, the official communications of subordinate officers with the Local Government must proceed through the prescribed channel, the head of the department and the Secretariat. A Private Secretary and an Aide-de-Camp assist the Lieutenant-Governor in the transaction of business which does not pass through the Secretariat, and in the arrangements for the social, the sumptuary, and the ceremonial duties attached to this highest office in the province. Like all Orientals, the Burmese love ostentation and ceremonial observances not only on public occasions, but even in the every-day routine connected with the high officials ruling over them. In this respect it is far easier for a mistake to be made in the way of omission than by paying strict attention to ceremonial and official display.

For legislative purposes connected with the province the Lieutenant-Governor is assisted by a Legislative Council consisting of nine members, five of whom are appointed by him as official members, and the remaining four are non-official members, selected from among merchants and others. Bills affecting local requirements passed by this Council became law on receiving the sanction of the Governor-General, without being referred to the Indian Legislative Council ; though, of course, the functions of the Council are limited strictly to purely provincial matters.

Owing to differences in legislative status, the primary administrative division of Burma is into Lower Burma, and Upper Burma (including the Shan States). Exclusive of the Shan States, Upper Burma is a scheduled district. While the law in force there is being gradually assimilated to that applied in Lower Burma, there are still considerable divergences. For the executive administration of the province, exclusive of the Chin hills and the States on the Shan plateau, there are eight Commissioners of Divisions, under whom are the thirty-six Deputy Commissioners in charge of districts. As throughout India, the district forms the real unit of administration in Burma. The thirty-six districts are divided, for judicial and revenue purposes, into eighty-one subdivisions, held by Assistant Commissioners and extra Assistant Commissioners ; and these again consist of townships, each under a *Myo Ôk* or "town magistrate," forming the smaller units of regular civil and revenue jurisdiction. Lower Burma is divided into four commissionerships, including twenty districts, with thirty-nine subdivisions ; while Upper Burma also has four commissionerships, comprising sixteen districts, with forty-two subdivisions.

The chief civil officer ranking next in position and authority below the Lieutenant-Governor is the Financial Commissioner. He is, subject to the control of the Lieutenant-Governor, the Chief Revenue Authority, and also undertakes the duties of Chief Customs Authority, Inspector-General of Registration, and Commissioner of Excise and Stamps. His most important work is connected with land revenue and agriculture, in which he is assisted by a Settlement Commissioner, two Secretaries, and a Director of Land Records and Agriculture, with a Land Records Departmental Staff.

As the methods of collecting the land revenues and the system of survey and settlement are elsewhere described (in the chapter on "Land Tenure and the Revenue Settlement") no details need here be given concerning these matters.

During the official year, 1899–1900, the collections of civil revenue in the departments controlled by the Financial Commissioner amounted to £2,878,298, and it exceeded this two years earlier. The principal item towards this total is the land revenue proper of Lower

Burma yielding £928,488, while customs bring in £643,318. Except when years of scarcity occur in the dry central zone of Upper Burma, the *Tháthamédá* or house tax yields over £390,000, while the capitation tax in Lower Burma, assessed at five rupees a head for married men, three rupees for widowers, and two rupees for adult bachelors, brings in nearly £300,000, levied from considerably over one million men. Exemptions from payment of this latter tax have to be made when calamities occur locally from flooding of crops or other causes, and on the average over a hundred thousand persons are thus exempted annually. The incidence of assessment connected with land revenue levied directly or indirectly cannot be correctly stated. The incidence of land revenue per acre of cultivated land is just over two rupees (2s. 8d.) in Lower Burma, while it is close upon two rupees in Upper Burma, or between three and four rupees (4s. to 5s. 4d.) per head of population in the tracts assessed. Fisheries in Lower Burma, chiefly in the *In* or "lakes" formed throughout the low-lying deltoid tracts after the summer monsoon floods have receded, realize from £120,000 to over £130,000 annually. They are usually disposed of by auction, being let for several years to tenants who manufacture on a large scale the *Ngapí* or salted fish, the national condiment eaten with curry and rice. This dainty, beloved by the Burmese, is a loathsome and evil-smelling moist preparation of fish, pickled and pressed with coarse salt; and it is very largely imported along with *Nga-cháuk*, or sun-dried fish, into Upper Burma and the Shan States, where the supply of salt is not so favourable as throughout Lower Burma. Opium, imported from Bengal, though also grown by the Shans in Upper Burma and the Shan States, brings in over £180,000, and excise (including salt) over £190,000. Rents from State lands in Upper Burma, the old "royal fields," bring in upwards of £131,000, while nearly £100,000 more are classified as miscellaneous land revenue. By far the greater portion of this latter sum, over four-fifths of it in fact, is realized from Upper Burma, on account of revenue from fisheries, water rates from irrigated tracts, and royalties from the Ruby Mines and from the petroleum wells of Yenangyaung and its vicinity. Stamps produce an income of nearly £130,000, and income tax £70,000, of which one-fourth consists of deductions from the salaries of officials. With the exception of the town of Mandalay and of civil officers, residents in Upper Burma are exempt from the operation of this unpopular tax, which might well be remitted for all that it brings in. Officials in any case might be exempted, for Burma is admittedly the most expensive province to be stationed in, and the days of exceptionally rapid promotion in any of the civil departments are now at an end ; nor are they likely to return again till some further political move takes place like the Administration of Yunnan, or the Protection of Siam.

Traffic in opium is regulated by the Opium Regulations of 1894. As a general rule the possession of opium in any part of Burma, except for medical purposes, is forbidden to Burmese ; but those who have become habituated to the drug were permitted to register themselves as opium consumers, for the purpose of getting certificates authorizing them to obtain and possess the drug in small quantities. The registration of such Burmese opium consumers was carried on from February, 1893, to the end of June, 1894, when the registers were closed. Since the latter date no Burmese have been registered except such as can show sufficient cause for the omission of registering themselves while the registers were open, such as, for example, absence from Burma during the period allowed for registration. Persons of other than Burmese race are permitted to possess opium in small quantities.

Concurrently with the registration of Burmese opium consumers a census of non-Burmese consumers was also taken, and the twofold data thus obtained were used as a basis for making a rough estimate of the total quantity of opium annually required to supply the requirements of those legally entitled to purchase and possess opium. On this basis the maxima quantities of opium are fixed which may be issued to the twenty-six retail vendors licensed in different parts of the province. These opium shops are mostly in Lower Burma. Those in Upper Burma are only in the chief towns, and along the frontiers, where they are absolutely required to meet the needs of non-Burmese consumers. Even with these arrangements illicit opium traffic is rife along the northern frontier, for opium is grown largely by the Shans and much more largely still throughout Yunnan. The retail-vend licences are sold by public auction in the Deputy Commissioner's court, and are entirely in the hands of Chinamen. The licensed vendor may from time to time obtain from the Government Treasury as small supplies of opium as he pleases, but the total quantity to be supplied to him during the year must not exceed the estimated maximum.

As many opium consumers live in places remote from any licensed retail shop, steps have been taken to provide such persons with the means of obtaining opium legally by permitting the sale of opium at the Government Treasury by, or in the presence of, a gazetted officer to those permitted by law to possess opium. Previous to April, 1894, the maximum quantity of opium permitted to be possessed by any individual consumer was ten tolas (3¾ ounces), but this was then reduced to three tolas (1⅛ ounces), and the possession of opium by Burmese doctors and tattooers for professional purposes was legalized. Early in 1896 the price of Bengal opium was raised by one rupee per *sir* (2⅕ lb.), and the duty on Chinese and Shan-Chinese opium by two rupees a *viss* (3·65 lb.). To defeat a combination of Chinamen the retail shop at Tavoy was closed, and retail sales were made to legal consumers from the Treasury. Stringent measures are everywhere taken to prevent opium smuggling, and the Opium Regulations have been framed and worked so as to prevent Burmese from becoming consumers of the drug; but it is still doubtful if the consumption of opium has really been diminished by the restrictive measures taken.

The Commissioners of Divisions are responsible to the Lieutenant-Governor for the working of every department of the public service, except the Military Department and the branches of the Administration directly under the control of the Imperial Government.

THE DEPUTY COMMISSIONER

They are also *ex-officio* Sessions Judges in their several divisions, and have civil powers under the Lower Burma Courts Act, 1889, and Upper Burma Civil Justice Regulation, 1886, in addition to powers as revenue officers under the Land and Revenue Act, 1876, and the Upper Burma Land and Revenue Regulation, 1889. The Commissioners of the Mandalay and the Meiktila divisions, in Upper Burma, also supervise certain of the minor Shan States adjoining the eastern boundaries of their divisions.

The Deputy Commissioners perform the functions of District Magistrates, District Judges, Collectors and Registrars, and the various miscellaneous duties which fall to the real unit representative of Government. Each has not only his own special and onerous duties as a judge in civil and criminal cases, and as the chief authority in revenue matters, but he has also the control of the Police, the Public Works, and the Forest business throughout his district; for it is laid down that the District Superintendent of Police, the Executive Engineer, and the Deputy Conservator of Forests are the assistants of the district officer in their special departments. There is practically nothing whatever connected with the administration from which the unfortunate Deputy Commissioner escapes responsibilities, some nominal, but others real and heavy, either by direct provisions of the Acts or Regulations, or else by some resolution or executive order of Government. Even if the day were to consist of forty-eight hours in place of merely twenty-four, and if he could toil incessantly throughout the whole of these day after day, it would be next to impossible, except in a few of the lighter district charges, for the Deputy Commissioner to do personally, in anything like a satisfactory and conscientious manner, the multifarious duties prescribed for him. And, of course, the tendency always is to increase these in place of lightening the burdens already put upon him.

Burma is a non-regulation province, that is to say, the Commission is recruited, as in the Punjab and the Central Provinces, by young covenanted civilians appointed from England, by the selection of young military officers from the Indian Staff Corps, and by the nomination of others not belonging to any covenanted or commissioned service; whereas in the regulation provinces of Bengal and the North-West Provinces appointments are now limited solely to the members of the Indian Civil Service.

Before the annexation of Upper Burma, the Burma Commission consisted of 62 officers, but its strength was gradually raised to 123 by the end of 1889. Prospects of promotion in the Burma Commission are now less favourable than in any of the other provinces, as the Commissioners and Deputy Commissioners are all comparatively young men. This is the natural result of the floodtide of promotion which set in after the annexation.

The *Myo Ôk* or township officer is the ultimate representative of Government who comes into direct and close personal contact with the people. Below these in the towns there are headmen of wards and elders of blocks, an arrangement of recent origin and modelled on the Upper Burma village system; while in the rural tracts the village headmen are assisted in Lower Burma by *Séingaung* or rural policemen in charge of ten houses, and in Upper Burma by elders of various designations. In Lower Burma the village system is in a state of transition. Up till 1889 the collection of land revenue and capitation tax was entrusted to *Taikthugyi* or headmen of revenue circles, each comprising several villages, and the headman was remunerated by commission, fixed according to a sliding scale, on the amount of revenue collected within the circle. In the discharge of his revenue work and of various miscellaneous duties the *Taikthugyi* was assisted by the *Kyédangyi* or village headman ("tax collector") and by rural policemen (*Yazawút-Gaung*), each of whom was in charge of several villages. Under this system it was found that the village headman had gradually degenerated into something little better than a village drudge. To improve matters the Lower Burma Village Act was passed in 1889, with a view of bringing affairs more in a line with the village system which had been so successfully retained in Upper Burma as being most in accordance with the national customs and character of the Burmese. While the *Taikthugyi* are being gradually abolished and the office of *Yazawút-Gaung* has been done away with, the position of the village headman has been rehabilitated by making him a collector of revenue, giving him power to decide petty civil and criminal cases, and securing for him the assistance of rural policemen subordinate to his authority. In Upper Burma the village headmen (*Ywá Thugyi*) had always been associated with the collection of revenue.

The judicial administration has only recently been improved by the formation of a High Court for Lower Burma. When Lord Lansdowne visited Burma in 1893, strong representations were made by the mercantile community and the Bar concerning the establishment of a High Court for Burma. It was, however, at that time decided that the matter was not one of the most urgent needs of the province. During Lord Elgin's tour in Burma, in November and December, 1898, the subject was once more considered, and with more favourable results. Proposals for a High Court could not be entertained, as this would have necessitated legislation by the English Parliament. But the establishment of a Chief Court for Burma, to consist of a chief judge and three puisne judges, two being barristers and the other two members of the Indian Civil Service, has been sanctioned by the Secretary of State from 1st April, 1900.

Previous to that the purely judicial officers of the province had been the Recorder of Rangoon, the two Judicial Commissioners for Lower Burma and for Upper Burma, the Additional Sessions Judges for the Pegu and the Irrawaddy divisions, the Judge of Moulmein, the Civil Judge of Mandalay town, and the Judges of the Court of Small Causes in Rangoon. The Recorder was a District and Sessions Judge in the town of Rangoon, and a High Court for all Burma with regard to criminal cases in which European British subjects were accused. He had original jurisdiction in all such civil cases in the town of Rangoon as were not within the powers of the Court of Small Causes. In civil and criminal matters the Judicial Commissioners exercised the powers of a High Court for appeal, reference, and revision of all cases except those for which the Recorder was the High Court. For the disposal of references transferred to it by either the Recorder or the Judicial Commissioner for the trial of such original cases and appeals as were transferred to it by the Local Government, and for the decision of appeals from decrees in civil cases passed by the Judge of Moulmein, a "Special Court" might be formed at Rangoon by the sitting together of the Recorder and the Judicial Commissioner of Lower Burma, with whom might also be associated the Judge of Moulmein if the Local Government so directed in any particular case. In practice this Special Court was found to be a poor substitute for the High Court required by Burma.

Within the limits of his jurisdiction the Judge of Moulmein is a District and Sessions Judge, and has the powers of a Civil Court for the adjudication of any suit without restriction as to value. The Civil Judge of Mandalay has jurisdiction in all civil suits arising in Mandalay town, and in such as may be transferred to it from the district. He has also the powers of a Small Cause Court for the trial of suits up to 500 rupees ($£33\frac{1}{3}$) in value. The two judges of the Court of Small Causes in Rangoon dispose of cases up to the value of 2,000 rupees ($£133\frac{1}{3}$), except as regards cases specially excepted from the cognizance of such courts. At Rangoon, and in some of the other large towns, there are benches of honorary magistrates exercising powers of various degrees. In the different military cantonments there are cantonment magistrates.

In Upper Burma the highest court is that of the Judicial Commissioner, who exercises both original and appellate jurisdiction.

In the administration of the Shan States a successful experiment has been tried. Now, as under the King of Ava, the Shan uplands, extending over more than forty thousand square miles and with a population exceeding 375,000, are divided into a large number of mutually independent States, each ruled by a *Sáwbwa* or Chief appointed by Government, and most likely to become an hereditary appointment whilst good management continues in any given State. Each chief, though no longer a feudatory but a British subject, has the power of life and death, together with an almost unlimited authority in the internal management of his State, so long as this is not characterized by oppression, or cruel and barbarous practices. Two civil officers, called Superintendents, are posted at Taunggyi in the south, and Lashió in the north, to exercise a general control and supervision over the chiefs, their administration, and their relations with each other. There are five large States under the supervision of the Superintendent, Northern Shan States, and thirty-nine under the Superintendent and Political Officer, Southern Shan States. Certain sources of revenue, such as teak timber and minerals, are reserved by Government, as in the time of the kingdom of Ava; but the extraction of timber on liberal terms is permitted to the chiefs in whose States teak forests are to be found. The revenue or tribute payable by each State is fixed at a lump sum, being assessed roughly on the basis of the number of houses. The chief is responsible for payment of the tribute, which he can easily raise without resorting to illegitimate means.

The total assessment is now about £18,000, as compared with a demand of about £30,000 under the Burmese Kings. But there is this difference, that, whereas in 1885 King Thibaw obtained the tribute only from a few of the States adjacent to the plains, the whole amount now comes into the treasury without any difficulty or leakage.

Tribute is paid with commendable punctuality, and in many instances a portion of it is remitted in consideration of expenditure on works of public utility, such as road-making. A simple regulation secures attention to ordinary legal forms and procedure, and debars the infliction of excessive or cruel punishments. The law thus administered in these States is, subject to the extension to them of specific enactments in force in the rest of Burma, merely the customary law of the State so far as it is in accordance with justice, equity, and good conscience, and is not opposed to the spirit of the law in force throughout the rest of British India.

The administration of the chiefs is not the best possible; but it is at once cheap, effective, and better suited to the Shan people than any more elaborate system modelled after the districts in charge of British officers. There is very little crime of any serious description. The principle of local responsibility is strictly enforced. When the offenders in a serious case are not detected, the State in which the crime is committed has to pay compensation. Communications are being rapidly improved, agriculture is flourishing, new crops like wheat and potatoes have been successfully introduced, medical relief and vaccination are being extended, and provisions are being made for veterinary aid and the training of veterinary assistants in the cattle-producing tracts. Though they can hardly be regarded as altogether an El Dorado, the Shan States have shown remarkable improvement under British rule, and present a fair field for future development agriculturally. Internecine warfare has ceased, agriculture is spreading normally at a quick rate, caravan traffic is increasing year by year, the population is growing quickly, and the Shan plateau is now traversed by a railway. The short record of the Shan States is one of peace, prosperity, and progress, which will continue to develop rapidly as communications are opened out by means of railways and roads.

The administration of the Chin hills on the north-western frontier has been since 1892 in charge of a political officer at Falám. After the disarmament, completed in 1896, of the numerous and powerful hill tribes inhabiting these mountain tracts, the conduct of the tribesmen remained for some time satisfactory, and a partial re-issue was made of the guns called in, marked guns being given to licensees on a scale of about one gun for every ten houses for purposes of defence. Serious crimes were now for some time of seldom occurrence, raiding was suppressed along the whole of the frontier, and there was little or no political disturbance within the hills themselves. During 1897 and 1898, however, arms were successfully smuggled in, and disarmament had again to be carried out, about 2,000 guns being seized by the end of May, 1899. A serious rising taking place in consequence of this, the garrison in the hills had to be reinforced; yet on the whole the condition of the Chin hills is as satisfactory as frontier districts usually are. Statistics of trade with the valley of the Chindwin are wanting; but the traffic is believed to be increasing considerably, while the Chins have begun to show readiness in providing labour for transport and public works. The tribute amounts only to a nominal sum of about £1,200, which is easily levied. The Chin hills have been declared to be a part of Burma; but they constitute a scheduled district, for the administration of which a Regulation was passed in 1896. The Political Officer and his Assistant are invested with powers to enable them to keep the peace and to exercise supervision over the chiefs, who are allowed to administer their affairs so far as may be in accordance with their own tribal customs. Since 1897 the Chin hills have been garrisoned entirely by military police.

The Military Garrison of the province had been reduced to 10,727 men in 1898, of whom 4,234 were Europeans, and 6,493 natives. It was increased again to 12,309, of whom 4,656 were Europeans and 7,653 natives, during the following year, but has fallen again to 10,324 in April, 1900 (2,811 Europeans and 7,513 natives). Of the latter, seven battalions are Burma regiments raised for permanent service in Burma by transformation from military police. These regiments, consisting of Gurkhas, Sikhs, and Pathans, are distributed throughout the Shan States and the northern part of Burma.

The Burma district command forming a first-class district, is held by a Major-General directly subordinate to the Lieut.-General commanding the Madras forces. It is divided into two second-class districts held by Brigadiers-General at Rangoon and Mandalay, while the native regiment at Kengtung and the detachment at Fort Stedman in the Southern Shan States are under the separate command of a Colonel on the Staff. The total cost of the garrison during 1897–1898 amounted to a little in excess of £60,000, which may fairly be taken as about the normal cost of the regular troops maintained within the province, now that everything is tranquil. In addition to these regular troops there are close upon 2,500 efficient volunteers in the various towns and on the railway lines, who form a valuable addition to the military forces.

The Police Department had a force of 13,545 civil police and 15,667 military police in 1898, costing upwards of £530,000 a year. It is administered by an Inspector-General of Police, assisted by Deputy Inspectors-General for Civil Police, Military Police, and Police Supply and Clothing. For the control and management of the executive duties of the civil police there is a District Superintendent of Police for each of the thirty-six districts of Burma, while fifty-nine Assistant Superintendents are in charge of the more important subdivisions. The special duties of the military police are controlled by twelve Battalion Commandants and twenty-seven Assistant Commandants, whose services are lent, for periods of five and two years respectively, from the Indian Staff Corps for this specific purpose. The District Superintendents of Police have certain magisterial powers, but in all essential respects they are directly subordinate to the Deputy Commissioner as District Magistrate. Apart from political uniforms worn by members of the Government, political officers, and certain administrative officers having political duties, the police is the only civil department in Burma whose officers are required to wear a uniform.

The military police is in reality a regular military force with only two European officers in command of each battalion; and it is recruited entirely from among the warlike races of northern India, with the exception of a small battalion of between six and seven hundred men raised by enlistment from among the Karens inhabiting the forest-clad hills throughout the central portion of Lower Burma. None of the other hill tribes seem to be suited for enlistment, while both the work and the discipline of this special branch of the Police Department are unsuitable for the Burmese. At Mogôk, in the Ruby Mines district, Panthay or Yunnanese

Mohammedan recruits were enlisted, but proved so unpromising that they had to be disbanded. A similar experiment now being made with the Kachin hillmen may perhaps turn out more successful.

So averse is the Burmese character to discipline and control in petty matters that it is impossible to get really suitable men to enlist even in the civil police. About twenty per cent. of the whole force is illiterate. Training schools have been established in nearly every district, where recruits are grounded in their future work before being drafted into the police force. A feature of the civil police administration is the maintenance of a beat patrol system, one of the principal advantages of which is that it enables the police to keep in touch with the village headmen in rural tracts, and with the headmen of wards and elders of blocks in towns, thus enabling information and assistance to be given by these at a minimum of inconvenience.

The number of crimes of violence in 1897 consisted only of 540, which seems a remarkably low total for a population then probably numbering nearly ten millions. Of these no less than seventy occurred in one district, Tharrawaddy, which has ever been turbulent and inclined to lawlessness. Cattle theft is common (3,442 cases occurring in 1899), though the beat patrol system helps to keep it in check.

Persons suspected of bad livelihood can be called upon to show cause why they should not be made to furnish security for good behaviour. Of 4,574 such cases brought before magistrates in 1897, 3,660 were actually called upon to furnish security. The provisions of the enactments under which villages can be fined, or have punitive police quartered on them at their own special cost, for harbouring criminals or neglecting to take due measures for their arrest, are now freely used in Lower Burma, with the result that much is now done by village headmen and villages to assist the police and prevent anything like the organization of crime. In the matter of ensuring the recognition of offenders previously convicted the Bertillon system of anthropometry was formerly in use, but has now given place to the method of identification by finger-prints, the police being charged with the duty of thus identifying criminals.

The control of the Jail Department is vested in an Inspector-General, who at the same time performs the duties of Sanitary Commissioner, Superintendent of Vaccination, and Head of the Civil Medical Department. The two central jails in and near Rangoon are in charge of special medical officers as Superintendents ; but in all other cases the Civil Surgeon at the headquarters of any district is *ex-officio* Superintendent of the jail there. Thus all the jails throughout Burma are in charge of officers of the Indian Medical Service, except at small stations where the post of Civil Surgeon and Superintendent of Jail happens to be held by a member of the subordinate medical service.

In Upper Burma there were no regular jails till 1887, when one was opened at Mandalay. At other district headquarters a mere lock-up was provided for the accommodation of prisoners, and large numbers of escapes were made from these insecure and inadequate buildings. A scheme was afterwards drawn up for the construction of a central jail holding 1,000 prisoners at Fort Dufferin (Mandalay city) and at Myingyan, with smaller jails at other district headquarters. At that time, too, the jails in Lower Burma became overcrowded and liable to dangers of epidemics. After the wave of crime rose, in 1885, the central jail in Rangoon became chronically overcrowded with nearly 4,000 prisoners, many of whom were men of desperate character. The pressure on sanctioned accommodation was partially removed in 1891 by the release of over 1,500 men, some on security, and some unconditionally, who had been convicted during the disturbed times, and it became further obviated by the opening in 1892 of a jail to hold 2,000 prisoners at Insein, a few miles to the north of Rangoon. There is total jail accommodation throughout the province for over 15,000 prisoners distributed over seven central and twenty-five district jails, and the average daily number in prison throughout 1899 was 12,547 (of whom 12,416 were males, and only 131 females), but the accommodation, still somewhat insufficient, is being enlarged. To

prevent overcrowding special batches of long-term convicts are from time to time sent from Rangoon to the
penal settlement on the Andaman Islands, while, since
1895, the normal annual number of prisoners transported
to the Andamans has been raised from 75 to 200.
Close upon 18,000 convicts were committed to prison
during 1897. This represents the enormous proportion
of about one convict to every 550 of the total population.
Of these 18,000 commitments close upon one-sixth were
prisoners charged with bad livelihood, nearly 3,000 of
whom were imprisoned for failure to give security for
good behaviour. In committing these prisoners to jail the
courts classified altogether 3,227 as " habitual criminals,"
either because they were convicted of offences punishable with three years' imprisonment after having been
previously convicted of an offence similarly punishable,
or else because they were believed either to depend on
crime as a means of livelihood or to have attained peculiar skill in crime. Out of 20,000 prisoners committed
to jail in 1896, over one-eighth of the total number
committed to prison confessed to the habit of consuming
opium, and more than nine-tenths of these were found in
the prisons of Lower Burma. In 1899, 16,917 convicts
were sent to jail. Of these, 3,459 were habitual offenders,
and all but twenty-seven of them were identified before
conviction.

Serious outbreaks in any of the jails are of comparatively rare occurrence, as the discipline maintained is
distinctly good. Among the minor punishments inflicted
for breaches of discipline are the treadmill, shot drill,
and the loss of good marks leading to curtailment of the
time to be served. Whipping was formerly frequently
inflicted, but is now had recourse to only in comparatively rare cases, when exemplary punishment is really
necessary. One of the most effective punishments
for maintaining discipline is solitary confinement with
reduced diet. For juvenile offenders a reformatory is
attached to the central jail at Insein.

As the sanitary arrangements of the jails are infinitely
better than prisoners have previously been accustomed
to, the health of the jail population is usually good,

although the larger jails from time to time become infested by the obscure forms of fever and other kinds of disease peculiarly liable to break out where large numbers of men are confined together in a small space. The daily average number of sick is usually about forty per thousand of the average strength, and the death rate is ordinarily only about eighteen per thousand. In 1896 the death rate was below that (17·93) and sixty per cent. of the prisoners gained in weight during their incarceration ; but in 1897 it increased to twenty-four per thousand, in consequence of cholera breaking out in three jails at towns having defective water supply. It was 18·73 in 1899.

The gross expenditure on jails amounted in 1899 to £52,506, which was reduced to the extent of £22,200 by the gross cash earnings from work done by the convicts. This reduced the cost per head from a gross charge of £4 3s. per annum to a net amount of £2 8s., while it does not take into consideration prisoners' labour employed upon jail extensions and gardens. A garden is attached to each jail for providing anti-scorbutic vegetables to the ordinary prison diet of curry and rice. The jails are employed to the fullest possible extent in meeting the wants of Government departments in furniture, clothing, food, and other articles ; and the problem of finding useful and remunerative employment for the abnormally large percentage of criminals is continually under consideration.

The Public Works Department is under the control of a Chief Engineer, who is *ex-officio* Secretary to the Lieutenant-Governor in that department. The administration is carried out by five Superintending Engineers in charge of circles, four of whom have charge of general works such as roads, buildings, and canals, while one is specially charged with the irrigation works and surveys throughout the central dry zone of Upper Burma. Within these five circles the works are in charge of twenty-three Executive Engineers holding divisions, assisted by Assistant Engineers as subdivisional officers. Appointments to the Public Works Department are mainly made from the Indian Engineering College at Cooper's Hill, in Surrey, though young officers from the

Royal Engineers and the pick of the students at the Thomason Engineering College at Rurki, N.W.P., also receive a small number of nominations. The subordinate service, consisting of Sub-Assistant Engineers and Overseers is recruited mainly from the army and from the lower grade engineering schools of India.

So far as possible the circles of the four Superintending Engineers charged with general works are conterminous with the eight civil divisions held by Commissioners, but they also include the Shan States and the Chin hills. In like manner the divisions in charge of Executive Engineers are conterminous with the one or more civil districts held by the Deputy Commissioners to whom they are in certain matters directly subordinate. Since 1894 all military works except the special defences of Rangoon have been transferred from the Madras Military Works to the Local Government.

When the various portions of the province came under British administration the only means of communication were the tidal creeks of the delta, the rivers and their tributaries, rough jungle paths, and the temporary cart-tracks across the fields when once the crops had been reaped and harvested. Anything like good roads did not exist. Perhaps the nearest approach to highways was the ancient *Minlan* or "royal road" cleared through the jungle following the two belts of laterite running north and south along both sides of the Pegu Yoma, which forms the watershed between the Irrawaddy and the Sittang rivers. Crossed by scores of large streams and smaller watercourses, it could only be used during the dry season ; and its reputation was so bad that part of it running through the Tharrawaddy district was known as the *Thakólan* or "thieves' road." Even down to 1877, after Pegu had been in British possession for a quarter of a century, there were exceedingly few roads ; and none of these were complete with bridges and metal. The only important trunk-road bridged throughout, though not metalled, was one running north and west from Rangoon to Prome, and thence on to the military frontier station at Thayetmyo. Another, going north-east to Pegu and then turning northwards to

Toungoo, the frontier fort on the Sittang side, was un-bridged at all the larger streams, and was therefore only a fair-weather track. The old military road from Toungoo to Moulmein, the extension of the trunk road from Chittagong to Akyab, and that across the Arakan hills from Taunggup to Prome, had been allowed to fall into such disrepair that they could hardly any longer be called roads.

The first real impetus towards the construction and the proper maintenance of fairly good metalled roads was felt about the time of the opening of the Irrawaddy Valley Railway line from Rangoon to Prome in 1877. The necessity for feeder-roads became then, of course, at once apparent. The growing wealth of the agri-cultural population and the rapid extension of perma-nent rice cultivation throughout all the central portion of Lower Burma necessitated the construction of roads to enable the surplus grain of land-locked areas to be brought within easy reach of the rice mills at Rangoon, Moulmein, and Bassein. The impulse thus given to road construction has never been relaxed. After the annexation of Upper Burma the funds for road-making were granted much more freely by the Government of India than previously, with the result that of the 6,220 miles of road maintained by the Public Works Depart-ment in 1900 more than one-half are in the northern portion of the province.

While the internal requirements of the country are satisfied as fully as funds permit, the Government of Burma are anything but unmindful of the desirability of improving existing trade routes and opening up new tracks for the facilitation of traffic and commerce with the countries beyond the frontiers of Burma. More especially with regard to trade routes leading eastwards into Siam and Yunnan the Government of Burma are doing as much as is possible, under the financial limita-tions imposed upon them by the Government of India, in the way of constructing roads and caravan tracks without neglecting the more immediate and pressing requirements of the internal portions of the province. From Myitkyina to Sadôn, and from Bhamo up the

ROADS AND TRADE ROUTES

Taiping valley to Loikaw, roads run to the frontier, whence the tracks converge on Momein. Namkhan, the frontier mart on the Shweli river, has now good road connection direct with Bhamo. From Myitsôn, lower down the Shweli but separated from Namkhan by a long and unnavigable stretch of rocky obstructions, a fair cart-track leads to Möng Mit, and from Möng Mit a good mule-track ascends to Mogôk, the headquarters of the Ruby Mines, whence a good cart-road descends westwards to Thabeitkyin on the Irrawaddy river, while another mule-track trends southwards through Mainglôn to Maymyo and Pyaunggaung on the Mandalay-Kunlôn railway line. Running parallel to this line of railway a good fair-weather road, complete as to bridges or ferries as far as Lashiô, a distance of 178 miles, leads from Mandalay across the Northern Shan States towards the Kunlôn ferry on the Salween river; and from this trunk road feeders extend north and south into the Shan country. From Thazi on the Rangoon-Mandalay railway line a cart-road leads eastwards to Fort Stedman and to Taunggyi, the headquarters of the Southern Shan States, and for seventy miles beyond that to Napôk, thus bringing the whole of the Southern Shan States in the neighbourhood of Möng Nai (Moné) in direct communication with the railway line. And when Möng Nai, in the course of a few years, becomes linked up with the Mandalay-Kunlôn line by a branch railway from Thibaw, this improvement in communications is certain to be immediately followed by a considerable increase in the prosperity of the States, marked as the progress of these has already been since the Shan country came under British rule. From Napôk a good mule-track, which is gradually being improved into a fair-weather road, extends eastwards across the Kengkham ferry on the Salween to Kengtung, where a Burma regiment forms the garrison near the Chinese, Siamese, and French frontiers. Some of these roads have proved enormously expensive. Thus the Ruby Mines cart-road from Thabeitkyin to Mogôk, $61\frac{1}{4}$ miles in length, had cost considerably over £60,000 for construction and maintenance by the end of March, 1894. The metalling of this road is now in course of completion, and when that is done the total cost of this difficult hill road will be close on £80,000.

The actual outlay on communications, exclusive of supervision and tools, in 1899–1900 was £173,350, of which about two-fifths were for original works and three-fifths for maintenance.

The railways in Burma were originally constructed by a special (Imperial) branch of the Public Works Department; but they have, since 1st September, 1896, been transferred to the Burma Railways Company, though the working of the open line was carried on by Government on behalf of the Company till February, 1897. The total capital expenditure on construction up to 31st March, 1898, amounted to £5,915,340, of which £5,127,860 had been incurred by Government before the Company took over the railways in 1896. The total length of line open to traffic on 31st March, 1900, was 993 miles. Further consideration need not, however, here be given to railways in Burma, as they form a subject specially dealt with in chapter xvi.

Among the principal of the earlier Public Works was the construction of the seven lighthouses erected for the protection of shipping along the dangerous sea-coast. One of these unfortunately had an insecure foundation on the Krishna shoal off the middle of the delta, and consequently disappeared one night in August, 1877. Another of the greatest of the Public Works was the embankment of the extreme north-western portion of the Irrawaddy delta by a bund running along the west bank of the main river and along the east bank of its offshoot the Ngawun river, which, after flowing past Bassein, enters the sea near Cape Negrais. It formed an A-shaped embankment running with a cross connection for about sixty to seventy miles along each bank of the apex of the delta on the western side of the Irrawaddy, and was designed to protect the land in the upper portion from disastrous floods occurring annually in July and August. The embankment was completed in 1878 at a total cost of nearly £270,000; but the results realized have hardly been as good as were anticipated. When the settlement of the land revenue was made in the

THE DRY ZONE

Bassein and Henzada districts, in 1884, it was found that while eighteen square miles of cultivated land were protected by the embankment nearly 130 were not protected, and of this area about fifteen square miles (9,500 acres) had been thrown out of cultivation in consequence of the operation of the embankment.

While the rice lands situated in the delta and along the sea-board from Cape Negrais to the Gulf of Martabun are thus liable to inundations capable of sometimes seriously affecting the crops, the whole of the central portion of Upper Burma is exposed to considerable danger from drought, unless a sufficiency of soil-moisture be provided by irrigation.

The central portion of Upper Burma naturally forms a dry zone comprising the whole of the districts of Myingyan and Meiktila, together with portions of Yamèthin, Magwé, Minbú, and Pakkoku on the south, and of Lower Chindwin, Sagaing, Shwebó, Mandalay, and Kyauksè on the north. The moisture-laden winds coming from the Bay of Bengal during the summer months, when the south-west monsoon prevails, deposit the great bulk of their moisture either on the Arakan hills between the Irrawaddy and the Bay of Bengal, or on the Pegu Yoma between the Lower Irrawaddy and the Sittang River, while copious rainfall is at the same time provided by them for the lower portions of the valleys of these two rivers. As these comparatively cool winds, saturated with moisture, travel northwards in the direction of the dry central zone their temperature becomes gradually raised ; consequently their relative humidity decreases and precipitations of rain are less frequent and less abundant. Thus, from a rainfall of between 200 and 250 inches on the coasts of Arakan and Tenasserim, and of about 100 inches in Rangoon, the precipitations in areas lying to the north gradually become less till the dry central zone is reached, within the different portions of which the average annual rainfall varies from about fifteen to thirty inches. North of this again, throughout the hilly and densely wooded districts of the Upper Chindwin, Katha, Ruby Mines, Bhamo, and Myitkyina, the temperature is also lower than what prevails in the dry zone ; consequently the relative humidity of the air increases once more, and the result is frequent copious rainfall varying up to over ninety inches. During the winter monsoon season, when the winds set from the north-east, the rainfall throughout Burma is not much affected, the inconsiderable amount of rainfall due to this particular cause being mainly confined to the thickly-wooded northern districts of Myitkyina, Bhamo, and the Ruby Mines.

The essential climatic features of this central zone are therefore a high summer temperature, with strong, dry winds prevailing from April till October, which but infrequently bring up rain-storms. The only possible means of contending against these natural disadvantages of geographical position throughout the great central portion of the Irrawaddy valley would obviously have been to preserve large tracts under forest, in order to act as huge natural reservoirs for the storage of soil-moisture and to increase the relative humidity of the air for the benefit of agriculture. These scientific precautions were naturally enough neglected in Burmese times. Instead of being preserved, the once existing forests throughout the dry zone have been destroyed, and the result is that, to climatic features already unfavourable for agriculture, there have been added the physical drawbacks that the soil, unprotected by forest growth, gets washed away during heavy rainfall, and that the rain-water is not retained within the soil for the feeding of streams and the effecting of other results beneficial to agriculture. Hence only irrigated portions of the dry zone can be relied on to yield crops with certainty year by year; and rice cultivation within it is confined to tracts obtaining a good supply of water by means of irrigation. Apart from such more favoured portions the food crops grown by the peasantry consist chiefly of maize, millet, and peas, whilst cotton and sessamum are also raised for sale.

As a net result of these climatic disadvantages and of wasted physical features, years of scarcity are of frequent occurrence in this dry zone. Seldom does any year pass without complaints of want in some part of it. In several of the years since the annexation the scarcity has been so great and widespread as almost to verge on famine, and to necessitate the commencement of irrigation works, road-making, and railway earthwork as famine relief measures. Actual famine, however, is hardly now possible, even in the driest parts of Burma, though the memory of the *Thayáwgyi* or "great scarcity" which occurred in 1792, during the reign of Bodaw Payá, still lives in tradition.

In olden times many irrigation schemes had been hatched, and some of them were even undertaken ; but when the kingdom of Ava was annexed, most of these works had long since been allowed to fall into disrepair, and the people were left to their own devices as regards the storage of water for agricultural and other requirements. The chief irrigation systems were in the Kyauksè district and the Salin subdivision of Minbú. These works were some hundreds of years old, but it was hoped that much could be done in the way of improving them by draining the hollows between the canals, strengthening the weirs and main canals, and reducing their number, improving the openings for distributing water so as to prevent wastage, making the larger canals more conveniently navigable, and bringing a much larger area under irrigation.

As soon as the state of Upper Burma permitted it, an officer of the Public Works Department was, in 1890, deputed to examine and report on the existing irrigation works and their condition. As 1891 and 1892 were years of great scarcity a large number of old Burmese irrigation projects were taken up and put in order to provide work for the distressed agriculturists, and in the Meiktila and Yamèthin districts a fair amount of work was done in the way of making tanks and weirs. In 1892 an irrigation circle was formed, and extensive works were commenced in the Mandalay and Shwebó districts, the irrigation canals of the Kyauksè district being already well supplied with water from the hills immediately to the east. These were followed by other large works in the Myingyan and Minbú districts, and by improvements in the existing works in Kyauksè,

Meiktila, and Yamèthin. The Nyaungyan Minhla tank
in the Meiktila district has been restored at a cost of
£30,000, and the Kyauksè tank in the Yamèthin district has been formed at an outlay of over £33,000 ; while
large sums were spent on railway earthwork from Meiktila to Myingyan in 1897 as a special famine relief work.
This has now been open to regular railway traffic since
November, 1899.

In other districts, where irrigation can take place by
means of canals fed from large streams, more costly
operations have been undertaken on major works. These
include a project for irrigating 72,000 acres in the Mandalay district at a cost of over £200,000 ; another in the
Shwebó district to cost more than £330,000, and irrigate
130,000 acres, together with other works in the Minbú,
Mandalay, and Shwebó districts for the irrigation of
other 100,000 acres. These last works are estimated
to cost over £310,000, of which nearly £180,000 have
been expended between 1896 and 1900. When all these
schemes have been carried out, about 420,000 acres or
close upon 670 square miles of land will by irrigation be
capable of sustaining permanent cultivation irrespective
of the rainfall upon the tracts producing the crops.

The total outlay on the various public works throughout Burma during the last five years has averaged more
than £600,000 ; and the new territory of Upper Burma
has very properly had by far the lion's share of this expenditure. It amounted to £623,485 during 1899–1900,
exclusive of £117,648 for payment of salaries, etc., of
Public Works officers.

The Forest Department, administering the enormous
natural wealth represented by the forests of Burma, is
controlled by four Conservators of Forests, two in Lower
and two in Upper Burma, whose circles are conterminous
with the civil divisions held by Commissioners, while the
Shan States are also included within the southern circle
of Upper Burma. The controlling staff consists of
thirty-six Deputy Conservators of Forests, whose divisions are, so far as possible, conterminous with one or
more civil districts. There are also fourteen Assistant
Conservators of Forests, most of whom are drafted into

divisional charges,—consequent on the inadequacy of the sanctioned staff to cope satisfactorily with the constantly expanding work of the department,—as soon as they have qualified for this by passing the prescribed examinations in the Burmese language, forest law and procedure, and land revenue. These officers form the Imperial branch of the Indian Forest Service, to which appointments are now made only after a three years' course of study at the Indian Engineering College, Cooper's Hill, Surrey, including a few months' instruction on the Continent. The provincial branch, or Burma Forest Service, consists of nine extra Deputy Conservators holding minor divisional charges, and twenty-two extra Assistant Conservators for subdivisional work. They are appointed by selection from among the senior Forest Rangers, most of whom now receive their first appointments after undergoing a two years' course of training in the Forest School at Dehra Dím, N.W.P. The Subordinate Forest Staff consists of 687 Forest Rangers, Deputy Rangers, Foresters, and Forest Guards on salaries ranging from twelve to one hundred and fifty rupees per mensem. Appointments are almost entirely confined to natives of Burma. A Vernacular Forest School was opened during 1899 for the purpose of giving selected junior members of the Subordinate Staff elementary instruction in forestry and in departmental work as it is done in beats and ranges.

The Conservators of Forests are responsible for, and have complete control over, all professional, departmental, and financial matters throughout their circles, while the Deputy Commissioner is responsible for the general management and protection of all the forests in his district. For this purpose the divisional forest officer is the Deputy Commissioner's assistant in all forest matters.

As compared with other branches of the Administration, the Forest Department in Burma labours under the great disadvantage of having no real head responsible for controlling the whole of the provincial forest affairs and for submitting matters direct to the Lieutenant-Governor for orders. Each of the four Conservators is an independent head of department in matters affecting his own circle; and he is directly responsible to the Local Government, with which he communicates through the Revenue Secretary. For all matters concerned with questions of general administrative policy, forest settlements, contracts, finance, and matters of routine, the Revenue Secretary exercises an effective control over the four Conservators; but he is no more qualified to criticise or to advise the Lieutenant-Governor on purely professional matters connected with scientific forestry and technical questions than he would be to scrutinise and report on engineering projects submitted by the heads of circles in the Public Works Department. It consequently often occurs that, when important suggestions are made by any one Conservator, the opinions of the other three are taken; and if it should happen that two are for and two against the proposals, the matter is shelved indefinitely.

In other respects efficient and economical, the Forest Department will never be on a really sound footing until, like the Public Works Department, it has a Chief Conservator of Forests controlling the administration of the four Conservators and *ex-officio* Secretary to Government for the disposal of forest business. A department whose gross earnings in Burma for 1898–1899 were £556,726, and showed a net surplus revenue of £399,256, can surely well afford the creation of such a controlling administrative appointment; and to refrain from creating it now is, for various important financial and technical reasons, not an economy.

The work of the Forest Department throughout India has been much abused on the one hand, and much belauded on the other. There can be no doubt that the work of forest conservancy, so essentially important for Indian agriculture, has usually to be carried out under conditions imposing unwelcome restrictions on the wasteful and irrational customs which formerly prevailed. In Burma, however, the opposition to the work of the Forest Department has been considerably less than throughout most of the other parts of India. District officers have on the whole, and more especially since the commencement of Sir Charles Bernard's administration as Chief Commissioner of British Burma in 1879, been favourable to proposals for the formation of reserved forests selected either for financial or for other economic reasons. Men who formerly scoffed at the departmental efforts made for the formation of forest reserves, after seeing the swiftness with which total clearance of forest growth can be accomplished and the evils following as its result, have, personally, recently urged that the last remnants of the forests in the lower delta should be preserved for timber and fuel production. Moreover, Burma is at once the most thickly forested and the most thinly populated province in India ; and the work of selecting, settling, and demarcating the forest areas set apart as permanent reserves could, without any undue pressure on the people, be carried out much more freely in the thinly populated jungle tracts than would have been possible in any other province of India.

The careful manner in which existing rights of the people, even of nomadic cultivators practising the wasteful system of *Taungya* or shifting hill-cultivation, are safeguarded in dealing with such proposals for forest reservation will be found described in chapter xvii. treating of Burma's forest wealth.

The reserves already sanctioned up to the end of 1899–1900, aggregated 17,153 square miles, or just over ten per cent. of the total area ; but the process of selecting reserves will continue for many years yet, especially in Upper Burma. Only in the Hanthawaddy, Pegu, and Tharawaddy districts of Lower Burma has this important work been completed, where about two-thirds of the existing forest-land still at the disposal of Government have been reserved. Outside these reserves enormous tracts of tree-forest and jungle still remain for clearance and cultivation, reservation being for the most part confined to forest land unsuitable for permanent self-sustaining cultivation.

Even in the Shan States attention is now also being given to this matter. The Sawbwa of Thibaw, acting on my advice in 1898, requested the Local Government to depute a forest officer to begin the work in his State, first

of all by the examination and reservation of the best
teak-producing tracts, and then by the selection of other
wooded areas to be reserved for reasons more particularly
connected with the absorption and retention of soil-
moisture for the benefit of agriculture and pasturage. As
the early result of this prudent policy, the Kainggyi
Forest Reserve in Thibaw, the first created in the
Northern Shan States, was constituted during the official
year 1899-1900.

Notwithstanding a departmental reorganization in 1896,
the progress of forest operations is much hampered by
the paucity of officers of all ranks. Classified as a
"*quasi*-commercial department," the Forest Department
is worked mainly on financial principles; and the increase
in the number of administrative, controlling, and executive
officers is not taking place *pari passu* with the rapid
expansion of departmental operations and of the handsome revenue resulting therefrom. Several new divisions,
which it would be advantageous to create, cannot be formed
for want of officers, and all three branches of the forest
service will soon have to be increased unless the capital
value of the enormous forest wealth contained in the
province is to remain partially unutilized or to run the
risk of suffering permanent damage by neglect of the
economic possibilities otherwise attainable. Even assuming, though it is nothing like the reality, that the
whole of the revenue-producing teak and other forest produce were harvested solely from the reserved areas, this
would merely indicate an average annual rate of growth
far less than should be obtained under intensive treatment with adequate supervision. The £399,256 of net
surplus revenue earned in 1898–99 certainly do not
represent more than 1 to 1¼ per cent. of the capital value
of the forests, which may consequently be roughly estimated at from £30,000,000 to £40,000,000; and if a
fair proportionate share of the net earnings were to be
granted annually for the important works of fire protection
of reserved forests, for improvement fellings for the benefit
of teak and other valuable trees, and for cultural operations
in connection with their growth and development, there
would be every probability of both the annual returns

THE CUSTOMS DEPARTMENT

and the capital value of the forests increasing considerably in course of time. A property of this sort having a present actual marketable capital value of at least £30,000,000 to £40,000,000 sterling seems worth developing and improving to a greater extent than has hitherto been the case.

The Ports and Customs, under the Financial Commissioner as Chief Customs authority, are administered by a Chief Collector of Customs at Rangoon, assisted by an Assistant Collector and Superintendent of Preventive Service, and by Collectors at the ports of Moulmein, Bassein, and Akyab. At Rangoon, through which eighty per cent. of the total trade of the whole province passes, there are a Port Officer and an Assistant Port Officer; but at the other ports the Collector of Customs is also Port Officer. The total value of the sea-borne trade of Burma amounted to £20,819,992 in 1899–1900, of which about two-fifths were imports and three-fifths exports. Of the exports over £4,000,000 worth are annually shipped to Europe, the principal articles being rice, teak timber, cutch, and hides. Internal trade between Burma and Siam, Karenni, the Shan States, and Western China amounted to £2,047,314 in 1899–1900. Altogether, the trade of the province (see chapter xiv.) is in a healthy, expansive condition, and is bound to develop normally with the extension and ramification of the railway net and the increase of population and of cultivation.

The Education Department is under a Director of Public Instruction, while the work of school inspection is carried out by four Inspectors, assisted by numerous Deputy Inspectors and Sub-Inspectors. Formerly education was almost entirely in the hands of the *Pôngyi* or "religious" at the monasteries. Lay schools existed here and there, kept by old men leading a semi-recluse life; but these were few and far between. Every male Burmese has, in order to acquire the religious qualification distinguishing him as human and not a mere brute, to wear the yellow robe of a recluse during some portion of his youth; and before he can enter a monastery as a *Maung Shin*, or acolyte, he has previously to receive instruction. As this has always been the case from time immemorial, the monasteries became the national schools of the country, where elementary education was given gratis by the monks (or religious recluses, to speak correctly), who thereby added to their *Kútho* or "religious merit," the attainment of which was their object in leading the humble mendicant life of a "religious." But it was not the custom of the country for girls to receive any education of this sort. As no woman can ascend the path leading towards *Neikban* (Nirvana) till her soul has become incorporated in the body of a man, it would have been premature and altogether unnecessary to inflict upon her, or endow her with, even elementary education. That would all come naturally in due time when once such an amount of merit had been attained by her good works as would enable her to revisit this world in the shape of a boy.

When a small boy enters the *Kyaung* or monastery at about seven or eight years of age, he is given a papier-maché slate (*Parabáık*), or a blackened wooden board (*Thinbôn*) shaped like the pointer of a roadway sign-post, and a pencil roughly cut from steatite or soap-stone. These *Thinbôn* are usually made of the light white wood of the Yamané tree (*Gmelina arborea*). On his board he is taught to write the vowels and the consonants of the alphabet, and is made to repeat them aloud so as to imprint them on his memory. Each day the boards are blackwashed with finely powdered moistened charcoal, and a fresh lesson is set. Having mastered these foundations, advances are gradually made to simple combinations of letters, and then to more complicated words of the language.

There is a regular stereotyped gradation from the simplest consonants to the most difficult syllabic combination in Burmese and Pali : for the language is monosyllabic, and in words apparently consisting of more than one syllable each portion is separate and complete in itself. The course of instruction follows the *Thinbôngyi* or "great basket of instruction," beginning with the initial letters of the alphabet—*Kágyí* ("big K"), *Kágwé* ("crooked K"), etc.—and gradually proceeding up to the most involved combinations of vowels and consonants. The alphabet is interesting, as the consonants have all descriptive names, referring mostly to their shapes. Thus, in place of our bald A, B, C to X, Y, Z, the Burmese youngster learns to know his letters as "humpbacked B," "little G," "pot-bellied T," "elephant-fetter T" (aspirated), "capped P," "water-dipper D," and the like, so that the mastering of the alphabet is not altogether uninteresting and unattractive. Having in some cases four, including aspirated, forms of a consonant almost similar as to sound is, however, rather a drawback to its easy acquisition by the adult European. It also renders correct spelling somewhat difficult in the Burmese vernacular.

Repetition is the basis of the system, and the boys intone their tasks monotonously over and over again in chorus at the top of their shrill, high-pitched voices. Morning, noon and night these lessons go on for a considerable time, thrice daily. After setting the daily tasks the monks can only close their eyes in the calmness of soothing meditation while the Babel of young voices keeps up in full cry. Quietness usually means idleness and probably mischief on the part of the boys, who lie face downwards on the floor each with his own slate in front of him containing the task for recitation. But for this discordant chorus, which is peculiarly irritating about five o'clock in the morning and again during the hottest part of the afternoon, monasteries are fairly comfortable places of residence for officers on tour, as they are generally cleaner and more commodious than any other buildings in the jungle villages. No matter how small it may be, each village usually supports at least one monastery.

This gradual progress of elementary instruction in reading and writing, combined with very simple and rudimentary arithmetic, lasts for about two to three years, by the end of which time the boy is able to read ordinary manuscripts, including the religious books written with an iron style on dried palm leaves cut into strips of about fifteen inches long and two and a half inches in breadth. These palm-leaf manuscripts are formed into volumes by means of two boards of teakwood of similar size, usually lacquered in vermilion and often richly ornamented with designs in gold. In these books the leaves are kept in place by two bamboo pegs, which pass through from board to board, the leaves between which are thus impaled and kept in position. To prevent displacement of the boards the whole is tied up with cords, or with narrow strips of cotton into which sacred precepts are often interwoven. As the books read in the monastery, and the oral instruction given in connection therewith, are invariably of a religious nature, the elementary education given by the monks is essentially religious in its character. Religious notions are gradually imbibed by the young pupils, who thus become generally acquainted with the creed of Burmese Buddhism, and more particularly with the *Zattagá* (Jataka) or "birth-stories" relating to the penultimate and the last existences of Gaudama.

When the British came into possession of the various parts of the province, this simple monastic system of religious education prevailed, and it still exists so far as the monasteries are concerned. There were certain centres of higher instruction in Pali and religious philosophy, of which Mandalay was latterly, and still is, the chief: for in all branches religion was the basis of the nationalization of gratuitous education. The *Patamá Byan*, or highest examination in Pali and philosophy, was held annually at Mandalay until the overthrow of the kingdom of Ava; and it has been reinstituted by Government since 1896, although at first the proposal met with some opposition from the leading monks in Mandalay.

The first efforts of the Government to improve education on systematic lines were made by Sir Arthur Phayre in 1866. For centuries back Roman Catholic missionaries had been at work in Burma, and early in the present century American Baptists also began labouring in the same field, to which they were followed by the servants of the Society for the Propagation of the Gospel. These missionaries, who taught the children of converts while endeavouring to convert adults, had long received grants in aid of education, but nothing had been done to raise the level of education among the people at large who were taught by the monks. No plan had any chance of success if it was likely to interfere with the time-honoured national system of elementary instruction, or if it tended to arouse suspicion or hostility on the part of the monks or the people. It was therefore decided to distribute, to such monasteries as would receive them, elementary works on arithmetic, geography, and land-surveying, and to appoint teachers to go round and assist the monks, with their permission, in teaching the new wisdom; while a Director of Public Instruction was appointed to supervise the work of the lay teachers and report on its progress.

The experiment was at first confined merely to the principal towns; but even there it languished so much that, in 1868, it was proposed to supersede it by the establishment of lay schools. Finally it was decided that both systems should be worked simultaneously, and gradually both monastic and lay schools were brought on a similar footing under the supervision of the Educational Department.

The general scheme of education which thus evolved itself led to the encouragement and development of native lay and monastic schools, partly by lending assistant masters trained in Rangoon, partly by payments of grants in aid or rewards based on the results of inspections or examinations by the Inspectors of schools and their subordinates. Town schools, supported from municipal, town, or district cess funds, were established in all the towns and larger villages, for the purpose of imparting a somewhat higher class of education, partly in Burmese and partly in English, between the mere primary instruction given at lay and monastic schools and that imparted at middle-class schools maintained by the State. Any head of a school could apply to have his school visited and the pupils examined; while, once a year, examinations were held at district headquarters for primary scholarships tenable for two years at a Government middle-class school.

In 1880 the scheme of education was revised, annual provincial examinations being instituted under a special departmental Board of Examiners. There are now nine standards of instruction, and the classes in schools correspond with these standards, while the classification of the school itself depends upon the highest class it contains. These standards are respectively termed lower primary, upper primary, lower secondary or middle, and upper secondary or high. Beyond the ninth standard, which is the matriculation examination of the Calcutta University, collegiate instruction, imparted in arts only, is obtainable at the Rangoon College affiliated to Calcutta University. Scholarships are now given only for middle English and University courses, except in the case of upper primary scholarships confined to Upper Burma schools.

The gratuitous monastic schools, for boys only, still form the backbone of national instruction throughout all the rural districts, and particularly throughout Upper Burma. There is a special set of standards for these indigenous vernacular schools, none of which teaches beyond the seventh or lower secondary standard. In order that such may earn grants-in-aid from Government they must have a working session of at least four months, and an average attendance of twelve pupils, of whom at least four must be able to read and write their vernacular according to the second lowest standard. Non-indigenous schools, mostly established by mission-, ary societies, receive grants-in-aid only when they comply with certain rules as to qualifications of teachers, rate of fees, admission of pupils, accommodation, and discipline ; but in no case is any grant given in excess of the amount contributed from private sources during the previous year for the maintenance of the school.

Educational work was begun in Upper Burma in 1890, as soon as the pacification of the new territory had progressed sufficiently to enable such a step to be taken, and the whole of the departmental rules under which Buddhist priests and other heads of schools may look for assistance from Government were embodied in an education code published in 1891. The policy of Government is rather to assist, regulate and inspect schools maintained voluntarily by monks, laymen, municipalities, or other associations, than to found and manage schools of their own; and the work of the officers of the Educational Department is mainly concerned with such inspection and regulation. Commissioners of Divisions and Deputy Commissioners of Districts are generally responsible for the state of education in their respective jurisdictions, and are expected to do all they can for its promotion. But upon the four Inspectors of schools rests more particularly the responsibility for the state of instruction in their circles, and for the efficiency of the work done by their subordinates. For the special supervision and encouragement of indigenous primary education in monastic or in lay schools each circle of inspection is divided into sub-circles corresponding with one or more of the civil districts, and each sub-circle is in charge of a Deputy Inspector or Sub-Inspector of schools. In Lower Burma a portion of the district cess fund is allotted to the support of indigenous schools, and is divided among the village schools by the Deputy Commissioner, who manages the fund and distributes the grants-in-aid according to the rules laid down in the education code. In the towns of Lower Burma a portion of the municipal fund is similarly allotted to education, and in 1882 the schools formerly managed by Government were, with the exception of the Rangoon High School, handed over to the municipalities. Some of the chief of these, however, make a fixed assignment to the Director of Public Instruction for the maintenance of the schools under technically trained supervision, in place of directly administering and controlling them. As there are no cess funds in Upper Burma, all educational grants are paid from imperial funds; and the only municipalities which are directly connected with education in the towns are those of Mandalay and Sagaing.

The only special Government schools which exist in Burma are the five Normal Schools, where pupil teachers are trained for municipal and aided schools, two Survey Schools in Rangoon and Mandalay under the control of the Director of Land Records and Agriculture, an elementary Engineering School established at Rangoon in 1895, and a Vernacular Forest School for the training of subordinates, established on my recommendation, and opened at Tharrawaddy in August, 1899. There is a law class at Rangoon College, but those desirous of studying medicine have to go to India. The Dufferin Maternity Hospital in Rangoon, however, trains women as midwives, and has thereby inaugurated a work of enormous future importance, considering the barbarous Burmese birth customs.

An Educational Syndicate was established in 1881, consisting of a committee appointed by the Chief Commissioner, and representing all educational interests. In 1886 it became incorporated to enable it to hold property in trust for educational purposes. The deliberations of this syndicate, which is presided over by the Director of Public Instruction, are not merely confined to the management and economy of the Rangoon College and High School under its immediate control, but are also directed towards the furtherance of education generally, and more particularly towards improvements in the conduct and scope of examinations. It advises the Local Government regarding all standards of instruction below those prescribed by the Calcutta University, and undertakes the management of the middle school (seventh standard) examinations, and the educational tests for advocates, township officers (*Myo-Ôk*), land revenue collectors (*Thugyi*), and clerkships in Government offices.

Of late years the progress of education throughout Burma has been rapid and continuous. The total number of schools of all sorts has risen to 17,050, affording instruction to 287,987 children. Nearly three-fourths of these are private elementary schools, while the remainder, slightly exceeding one-fourth, is chiefly composed of primary schools ; but the attendance at the former is considerably less than at the latter. Secondary education, imparting instruction beyond the standard fixed as the qualifications for clerkships in Government offices, is limited to seventeen schools attended by 5,093 pupils in 1900. The progress of university education in Burma is slow, the average attendance at Rangoon College being eighty-nine in 1900. From time to time there has been talk of establishing a university for Burma, but the province is far from ripe for such a new departure. The Rangoon College, affiliated to Calcutta University, and the Baptist College founded at Rangoon in 1895 (with an average daily attendance of nine in 1900), afford quite adequate facilities for all the existing needs in this direction.

A hopeful feature for the future is that the attitude of the monks towards secular education is gradually becoming more favourable, although the method of teaching at monasteries or at village lay schools is of course not ordinarily in conformity with any of the standards of the Education Department. There are 341 girls' schools, and the total number of girls receiving instruction is 32,468, or more than one-eighth of the total number of children attending schools. It is hardly possible to over-rate the importance of this advance; for the women of Burma are the true heads of the households, are naturally gifted with keen trading instincts and business acumen, and are probably, as a rule, considerably better endowed with intellect and mental power than the men, notwithstanding the higher rung occupied by the latter on the "ladder of existence" according to Buddhistic religious philosophy. The movement towards the education of girls is, as might be expected, most noticeable in the more thickly populated parts of Lower Burma.

The expenditure on education amounted in 1899–1900 to £107,197, of which £72,257 were contributed by Government, the largest share in the cost of developments being borne from the provincial revenues. Progress in primary and middle vernacular education has been somewhat hampered by the want of good textbooks, but steps are being taken under a Textbook Committee to substitute carefully prepared translations of sound books of instruction for the rather badly arranged and unskilfully compiled works hitherto in use. The Shan, Kachin and Chin hill tribes have hardly as yet been touched by the operations of the Education Department; but Tamil schools for the children of Madras immigrants have been brought under inspectors, and education has made marked progress among the Karens, mainly under missionary guidance.

BURMA UNDER BRITISH RULE

The Accounts Department is under a Comptroller-General, assisted by five Assistant Comptrollers. For the regulation of financial matters between the imperial Government of India and the provincial Government of Burma, a contract is entered into every five years. The provincial Government receives for its own requirements fixed proportions of the revenues as derived from various sources, and has to transfer the remaining portions to the Government of India for imperial purposes. When unforeseen calls upon provincial funds occur, the financial equilibrium is restored temporarily by advances from the imperial revenues; but such advances are repayable. From the very outset this provincial contract system, which began to operate on 1st April, 1882, proved disadvantageous for Burma, as had been predicted by the local Administration, because the proportions of revenue allowed were insufficient to meet the rapidly expanding requirements of a young and prosperous province. During three out of the first five years the provincial balance sheet closed with a deficit, which had to be made good from the imperial share of revenue. For some years before the annexation of Ava, Lower Burma had each year to hand over to the Government of India more than a crore of rupees (£666,666); and this gave rise to the outcry of the merchants that British Burma was being made a "milch cow" for India, and that money which ought to have been spent on roads, railways, and other communications in Burma was being misappropriated through bestowal on other provinces. Out of gross revenue receipts amounting to over £1,820,000 in 1885–86, the imperial net surplus share, after deduction of expenditure for liabilities, was nearly £743,000, against a total provincial allotment of only £828,000 (which proved insufficient), the remainder being local and municipal rates excluded from the terms of the provincial contract. In 1886–87 India claimed a net revenue of over £900,000 as her share under the contract, leaving only £966,666 to cover all provincial expenditure.

With the expenditure of the third Burmese war to be provided for, Burma of course had to receive special imperial assistance. From military outlay amounting to

THE "PROVINCIAL SETTLEMENT"

£190,000 for Lower Burma in 1884–5, the charges for the troops in Upper and Lower Burma in 1885–86 bounded up to £635,000; and they increased to £1,230,000 in the following year. But the purely military expenditure incurred on the pacification of Upper Burma, and the cost of the garrison during the following years, have already been shown in a footnote at the conclusion of chapter v. (see p. 149).

As affairs were still in a state of transition when the first provincial contract lapsed in 1889, a provisional contract, following the lines of the previous one but with certain modifications, was made for one year on slightly fairer terms for Burma as estimated by a Finance Committee. In 1888 this provisional contract was extended for another year with new modifications, and then continued for other three years without further change. A new provincial contract was made with Lower Burma for five years from April, 1892 ; but it was considered that the time had not yet come for extending the provincial contract system to Upper Burma, where large special outlay had to be incurred on railways, roads, irrigation, buildings, and other public works of various descriptions.

At length, in 1897, a new quinquennial contract, called the " Provincial Settlement," was made with the Government of India. Hitherto Upper Burma finances had been purely imperial, the annual excess of expenditure over revenue being met by the Government of India and not by the local Government of Burma ; but now Upper and Lower Burma were amalgamated and unified for financial purposes.

Under the terms of this settlement the provincial share of land revenue and excise, hitherto one-fourth, was raised to two-thirds and one-half respectively, to permit of enhanced outlay for the development of the province being met from the expanding receipts under these two chief sources of revenue.

During the first year of its operation, in 1897–98, the net outcome of the provincial transactions under this new settlement resulted in a surplus of £113,513, after remitting to the Imperial Treasury its full share of the total sum representing the net revenue of the province for the year.[1]

Adding to the whole Civil Expenditure the total Military Expenditure disbursed from Imperial funds by the Government of India, as shown in the table previously given at the end of chapter v. (see p. 149), it will be seen that Burma has already more than recouped all the outlay expended upon it from imperial and provincial sources since the third Burmese war. Since the end of 1891, indeed, it has more than paid its own way; and for the last few years it has been again yielding a large and rapidly expanding surplus revenue. Moreover, the expenditure includes the cost of State railways throughout Burma, which up to the 31st August, 1896, when they were transferred to the Burma Railways Company, represented a capital outlay of £5,248,334, yielding a net return of 4·4 per cent. a year.

[1] The financial prosperity of the province may be gauged from the following abstract of revenue and expenditure since the annexation of Upper Burma (converted at rate of 1s. 4d. per rupee) :—

Year.	Revenue, in Pounds Sterling.			Civil Expenditure (including State Railways and all other Public Works), in Pounds Sterling.			Surplus, in Pounds Sterling.
	Lower Burma.	Upper Burma.	Total.	Lower Burma.	Upper Burma.	Total.	
	£	£	£	£	£	£	£
1886–87	2,266,000	148,667	2,414,667	1,259,334	518,666	1,778,000	636,667
1887–88	2,252,000	334,667	2,586,667	1,317,333	1,096,667	2,414,000	172,667
1888–89	2,186,667	551,333	2,738,000	1,477,333	1,245,334	2,722,667	15,333
1889–90	2,625,334	746,666	3,372,000	1,604,000	1,338,000	2,942,000	430,000
1890–91	2,838,667	808,000	3,646,667	1,535,333	1,292,667	2,828,000	818,667
1891–92	2,901,334	804,000	3,705,334	1,592,000	1,339,334	2,931,334	774,000
1892–93	3,190,000	798,000	3,988,000	1,748,667	1,243,333	2,992,000	996,000
1893–94	3,045,334	852,000	3,897,334	1,910,667	1,263,333	3,174,000	723,334
1894–95	3,267,334	916,000	4,183,334	1,956,667	1,172,667	3,129,334	1,054,000
1895–96	3,494,667	924,000	4,418,667	1,935,334	1,194,666	3,130,000	1,288,667
1896–97	3,338,666	875,334	4,214,000	1,864,667	1,351,333	3,116,000	1,098,000
1897–98	(Amalgamated)		4,564,704	(Amalgamated)		2,989,864	1,574,840
1898–99	Ditto		5,212,913	Ditto		3,253,140	1,959,773
1899–1900	Ditto		5,241,619	Ditto		3,420,407	1,821,212
Totals			54,183,906			40,820,745	13,363,160
							£54,183,906

MUNICIPALITIES

The Comptroller-General is also Commissioner of
Paper Currency, for which an office was first opened at
Rangoon in August, 1883. The notes are issued for
sums of five, ten, twenty, fifty, one hundred, five hundred,
one thousand, and two thousand rupees, but the circulation is of course almost entirely confined to pieces up to
one hundred rupees ($£6\frac{2}{3}$). Considerably more than
one-half (83,304) of the 148,720 notes in currency in
1900 were for ten rupees. Owing to extensive forgeries
of five-rupee notes in 1891 the circulation of these
became very limited, and seems to show little sign of
improvement (7,916 in 1900).

The District Cess Fund in Lower Burma and the
District Funds in Upper Burma, derived from
bazaar rents, ferries, and the like, form incorporated
local funds taken into consideration in the provincial
contract; while Town, Cantonment, and Port Trust
funds are excluded therefrom. A commencement was
made with municipal administration in 1874, when the
Municipal Act was passed and applied to several of the
larger towns. There are now forty municipalities
throughout Burma, to which members are nominated by
the Lieutenant-Governor, except in the case of twelve
towns where a portion of the members is returned
by election so as to represent the various sections
of the community. In Rangoon the President of the
municipality is a senior Government official, whose
services are lent specially for five years, while members
are elected to represent Europeans, Burmese, Chinese,
Madrasis, Hindus, and Mohammedans, in addition to
the members nominated by Government. In all the
other municipalities the Deputy Commissioner, the Sub-
Divisional Officer, or the Township Officer is elected
President, according as each municipality happens to be
the headquarters of a district, subdivision, or township.
The twenty-five municipalities in Lower Burma are
administered under the Burma Municipal Act, 1898,
while the fifteen in Upper Burma are under the Upper
Burma Municipal Regulation, 1887.

The Rangoon municipality has an income and an
expenditure each over £200,000 a year, but is burdened

by a debt of £272,167 (in 1900) incurred chiefly on water works and on the installation of the Shone sewage system. In 1884 large water works were opened in the anticipation that they would prove sufficient for many years to come; but for the last ten or twelve years, consequent on the rapid growth of Rangoon after the annexation of Upper Burma and the introduction of the Shone drainage system, the question of providing a further supply of water has been forcing itself more and more prominently on public attention. Experiments have been made with artesian tube wells for temporarily augmenting the water supply, though without obviating the necessity for heavy expenditure on additional water works. The construction of high-pressure works has mitigated the inconvenience of a short supply since 1893, and in 1896-97 the pumping engines raised 766 million gallons of water. The other municipalities have incomes aggregating about £140,000 a year, which is a sufficient revenue to cover their expenditure. The incidence of municipal taxation is a little over five rupees (or 6s. 8d.) per head in Rangoon, and about one and one-seventh rupees (or 1s. 6½d.) in the other municipalities.

In seven of the smaller towns in Lower Burma, Town Committees are appointed to consult about local affairs and the utilization of the town funds. Curiously enough, considering the Burmese character, some of these show a disposition to hoard the incoming money in place of expending it on useful works.

The Telegraph Department is administered by a Chief Superintendent in Rangoon, and two Superintendents in Akyab and Mandalay, assisted by Assistant Superintendents in charge of subdivisions. In 1898 there were 5,183 miles of telegraph lines open, with 12,786 miles of wires. From 118 Government offices, 76 of which are combined post and telegraph offices, 666,983 messages were despatched in 1899-1900; but there are also 144 railway and canal offices, and 154 smaller offices not open for paid telegrams. The maintenance of communications often involves exceedingly arduous work for the telegraph officers and subordinates, as interruptions from windfall trees are frequent on many of the jungle lines during the south-west monsoon period.

Postal affairs are administered by a Deputy Postmaster General, assisted by seven Sub-Superintendents and three Inspectors. In addition to the railway mail service, inland mails along the Irrawaddy and its chief affluents are also served by the Irrawaddy Flotilla Company under a five-years' contract running from 1st August, 1896; and since 1st October, 1896, the weekly ocean mail service between Rangoon and Calcutta, performed with great efficiency and punctuality by the British India Steam Navigation Company, has been supplemented by an extra steamer in each week. Mails to and from Europe could be expedited if a quicker steamer service were arranged for between Rangoon and Madras; but the British India Company, to which no inconsiderable share in the development of Burma's prosperity has been due, has not yet been induced to place upon the Madras run for this purpose a better class of steamer with a higher rate of speed. A direct mail route from Rangoon viâ Colombo to Naples or Marseilles will no doubt come in time as the commerce of Rangoon expands, but it is hardly yet a matter of urgency.

Even in the outlying portion of the province postal arrangements are decidedly good. A daily service of runners passes from the railway line to Lashio, the headquarters of the Northern Shan States, and four times a week mails proceed from Thazi railway station by cart for about thirty miles to the foot of the Shan hills, and thence by mules to Taunggyi, the headquarters of the Southern Shan States, whence they are despatched further eastwards to Kengtung and Möng Hsing. Mogôk, the headquarters of the Ruby Mines, has its mails brought up by mules thrice a week from Kinu on the railway line; and during 1899 a service by runners was initiated between Bhamo and Talifu, the trade emporium of the central Yunnan plateau.

During the year 1899-1900 nearly eighteen and a

quarter million articles were delivered through the 287 post offices; and of the fourteen and a half million letters and postcards therein included, nearly one-fourth were in Burmese and Chinese characters. There is probably no place in the world where a more polyglot correspondence has to be dealt with than that passing through the Rangoon Post Office. During the same year money orders were issued to the extent of £1,748,135, and were paid to the sum of £727,925. Upwards of ten per cent. of these latter issues are in the shape of telegraphic remittances, a convenient system which has long been customary throughout India. Under the orders of the Government of India, the system of paying money orders in sovereigns was introduced into Rangoon in March, 1900.

Another postal convenience arising from the conditions of Anglo-Indian life is the system of value-payable parcel post, by which articles ordered of tradesmen can be received through the post on payment of cash before delivery, the Post Office paying the declared net value to the sender after collection. This is a very doubtful benefit, as obvious drawbacks are inherent in the system. Savings banks have been opened at 173 of the post offices, and showed balances amounting to £550,768 in 1900. Another benevolent use made of post offices is for the sale of small packets of five-grain doses of quinine to counteract the effects of malaria. Made at the Government factories, the quinine is thus distributed at a price of one-third of a penny, which a little more than covers the cost of manufacture and contingencies; and in 1899-1900, 148,384 such doses were purchased. The sale is increasing largely each year, as the Burmese know and appreciate the properties of the *Séká* or " bitter medicine " in warding off and curing the malarious fever so prevalent in all jungle districts during the spring and autumn.

Ecclesiastical matters are administered by the Bishop of Rangoon, assisted by an Archdeacon, the diocese having been formed in 1877. There are eleven Chaplains on this provincial branch of the Bengal Establishment, while five clergymen of the Additional

MISSIONARY SOCIETIES

Clergy Society receive allowances from Government for holding religious services at places where, there being no European troops, chaplains are not stationed. The Roman Catholic Church, whose missionaries, at work in Burma since the fifteenth century, are scattered all over the country and farther north-east into China, is represented by Bishops at Rangoon and Mandalay; while the American Baptist Mission, the Society for the Propagation of the Gospel, and the Church Missionary Society have their teachers resident in many of the healthier parts of the province.

Chapter X

UNDER the ancient and original land system among the Burmese, as detailed in the opening portions of the eighth section of the Laws of Manú, the complete title or "perfect proprietary right" was restricted either to land given to soldiers and royal servants, or to grants and assignments made by the monarch in measured allotments for the support of civil officials, or else to land which had descended by hereditary succession, had been long in the possession of the family, and was now in use for the cultivation of food-grain. Such areas were called *Myéthé*, while all others were *Myéshin* lands having an incomplete title or "imperfect proprietary right, liable to dispute." These latter comprised lands received in gift, land purchased from those in whose family it was hereditary, land reclaimed from the forest, abandoned land cultivated for upwards of ten years with the knowledge and tacit consent of the owner, and land allotted to cultivators by civil officials or village headmen. In any of these cases the title held good during the lifetime of the buyer or cultivator; but the land could be redeemed by the original owner, or by his heirs, on the decease of the person temporarily in possession or on his wishing to dispose of it.

Theoretically and legally the Kings of Burma were not, like most of the sovereigns in ancient India, absolute lords of the soil. They received a share of the produce of the land; but to the land itself the people could originally obtain a clear title conveying absolute proprietorship, subject only to contribution for the purposes of the State, by the clearance and cultivation of forest tracts. The title to land was therefore essentially allodial. The

OLD LAND TENURES

Burmese agriculturists were peasant proprietors. The land was held in fee-simple, and the right and title vested in the original occupier, and his heirs and assigns, as owner. To this general allodial possession, however, there were two exceptions, although they really did not apply to anything like vast extents of cultivable land. These were the Crown lands, and the lands held under the various kinds of service tenures. Apart from these two classes of land, the Kings of Burma laid no restrictions on the cultivation of waste land. Any person was at liberty to make a clearing in the jungle ; and on bringing this under cultivation, he became its owner. In this case there was no tenure, no holding from an overlord. Clear primitive titles of this sort could, of course, only be obtained in a country where the amount of cultivable land was far in excess of the requirements of the population. But this right of private property in land descended in Burma as unaltered, as certain, and as absolute as could be expected under any oriental despotism, and under the rule of autocratic Kings upon whose will the lives and property of their subjects were practically dependent.

The feeling of attachment to the land is strong within the Burmese peasantry, and so long as the members of a family continue to reside in the vicinity of their ancestral holdings they will not willingly relinquish the claim they have upon the title to it. Even if a holding were temporarily abandoned, the Burmese customary laws sanctioned its being claimed again by the original clearer, unless the party in possession could prove that he had been in undisputed enjoyment of it for ten years of constant occupation. Thus, from ancient times down to the present, sales of land outright have never been customary. Though agricultural lands were frequently conveyed from one person to another for valuable consideration, through a transaction much more closely resembling a sale than any mere mortgage, yet there always existed a right of re-purchase, and a disability on the part of the purchaser to re-dispose of the land without the consent of the original seller. What seems at first sight to clash with any deep-rooted affection for hereditary lands is the fact that, in the great majority of cases, the holdings of peasant families do not usually date back for many generations. This is, however, easily accounted for by the constant state of anarchy and mal-administration, and the slackness of the control exerted over the provincial Governors for centuries back. Thus the normal course of residence, generation after generation, on the family holdings originally acquired by clearing in the primeval forest was, probably time after time, interfered with by social disorders necessitating the abandonment of lands already cleared and migration to fresh clearances, which were at all times very easy to make. But, at the same time, the Burman has no sense of duty towards the land. A creature of whim and caprice, he will often only cultivate a part of his holding, leaving the rest untouched. The Upper Burman is particularly uncertain in this respect. He may take it into his head to try Lower Burma for a year or two, sell off his plough cattle, and abandon his fields for a time; or he will go down to the delta, and work as a coolie for a season; or he may rush improvidently to the opposite extreme of hiring labourers and trying to cultivate an area altogether beyond the means really at his disposal.

The existing land system found in force when the Burmese Empire crumbled away during the last three-quarters of a century, and fell piece by piece under British rule, consisted, therefore, either of *Crown lands*, the property of the King, or of *service-tenure lands*, set apart as appanages in support of officials of various ranks, or of *petty allodial properties*, held in private ownership.[1] All the rest was *waste land*, either in the shape of un-

---

[1] The monasterial and pagoda lands (*Wuttagán*) are so comparatively small that they may practically be left out of account. Regarding the tenure of such lands, some doubt exists as to the holder in trust under the State. Lands, buildings, and gifts of all kinds to the religious body, may be dedicated in three different ways. The formula used may apply only to an individual recluse (*Pagalika*), or to several monks conjointly (*Ganika*), or else to the whole religious body present and future, and for public use (*Singika*). Pagodas, chapels, and rest-houses are invariably, while monasteries and monastic lands are usually, dedicated in this last way (*Singika*); and in this case the holder in trust may be presumed to be the *Sadáw*, or chief of the religious body

reclaimed forest jungle or of land which, after having been cleared and occupied, had been abandoned and allowed to revert into jungle.

On the annexation of the provinces of Arakan and Tenasserim in 1826, and of Pegu and Martaban in 1852, the first two classes of land were allowed to disappear, their occupiers being placed on precisely the same footing as the cultivators of other lands; but after the annexation of Upper Burma in 1886, the British Government took possession of the Crown lands and service-tenure lands, and introduced a law regulating the proprietorship and the tenures of all classes of land, State or non-State. Waste lands thereupon became the property of the British Government, and the acquisition of new land for cultivation thenceforward took place by means of tenure direct from the State.

The practice which sprang up in Lower Burma, after 1852, was based on the customary law of the country as to the clearance of waste lands being open to any new comer. Any one could select a piece of land at his pleasure, clear it, and cultivate it, paying the Government land revenue demand upon it when the time came for the circle *Thugyi* or Revenue Collector to measure it for the annual assessment of land revenue. If the clearer and cultivator desired to hold the land free of revenue for some years, until it was brought into a thorough state of cultivation, he could make written application to the *Thugyi* for a grant up to five acres, to the subdivisional Magistrate if above five and under fifty acres, and to the Deputy Commissioner in charge of the district for an area over fifty acres in extent. The grants applied for usually varied from about five to sixteen acres. After the land had been surveyed, a grant was issued, cultivation being allowed rent free for a term of years, varying according to the nature of the jungle which had to be cleared and the obstructions to be overcome in bringing

in the district, who usually appoints a head monk to the monastery in case of the death of its occupant. Under either of the first two forms of dedication (*Pagalika* and *Ganika*), the giver and his heirs and representatives are in practice considered the holders in trust of such property.

the soil into a state of thorough cultivation. For rice cultivation the period of exemption varied from one to seven years, the latter being in high tree-forest, the roots of which took long to rot and were hard to remove; while for orchard cultivation rent-free tenure was permitted up to a limit of twelve years, in proportion to the trouble of clearing and the time when the fruit-trees would begin to yield returns. Special periods of exemption were also permissible in the case of land requiring extra expenditure beyond mere clearance, as in tracts needing irrigation works to make them productive, or needing embankments to protect them from inundation.

The modes of acquiring ownership of land in the rural tracts of Lower Burma are prescribed in the Burma Land and Revenue Act, 1876, which gave the force of law to the above system based mainly upon the customary modes of acquisition found current when the province came under British rule. Under this enactment, ownership in land may be acquired either by squatters' rights, exercised over the same piece of ground for twelve years without interruption, or by a specific grant from the State made through the district officials and to the extent above indicated. The first of these modes of acquisition prevails in all the more settled parts of the country, where permanent villages and hamlets have long maintained their position, and where there is consequently a more advanced state of cultivation ; for under such circumstances the margin of waste land still available continually tends to decrease, and the holdings of individual cultivators are gradually increased by extending the existing clearances for permanent cultivation. When single households or small communities of two or three families cut themselves adrift from their old associations, and go elsewhere to make fresh clearances in the forest with a view to permanent cultivation and residence, the exercise of squatters' rights is also a not unusual method of acquiring a title to the land cleared; but, in the majority of cases, new settlers in remote jungle tracts usually secure the speedier and more formal and direct ownership by obtaining a *Patta* or grant from the State. As clearances of this sort are almost invariably under

five acres per individual holding, the great bulk of the
ordinary grants for new cultivation were formerly issued
by the *Thugyi* of the revenue circles into which each
township of a district is subdivided ; but under new
rules, sanctioned in 1897, all power of making grants
has now been withdrawn from *Thugyi*, whose position
exposed them to the temptations of land-jobbing. The
tendency of these new rules was to prevent unnecessary
applications for land grants, and to secure a more exact
scrutiny of the terms upon which land is granted, care
being taken to try and check acquisition by mere speculators. During 1895–96, 70,150 acres (109 square miles)
of land were granted free of revenue for a term of years
under the Act in Lower Burma ; while in the following
year the areas granted fell to 34,070 acres (53 square
miles), mainly in consequence of the check then given to
land speculation, and of greater care in issuing grants.
In 1898–99 the grants rose again to 55,870 acres (87
square miles), and in 1899–1900 they increased to 68,534
acres (107 square miles).

Larger grants of land, amounting actually in some
cases even to upwards of thirty square miles in extent,
had formerly been made by Government throughout
Arakan, Pegu and Tenasserim, with the object of
enabling capitalists (*Thuté*) to bring these great estates
(*Thuté Myé* or "rich man's land") speedily into cultivation by means of imported labour. All such grants
were made under the old Waste Land Rules, which were
superseded when the Land and Revenue Act came into
force in 1876. The results anticipated by Government
in creating estates of this nature were, however, not
realized, even although exceedingly liberal terms of
exemption from rent or revenue had been attached to
these tenures. In some cases the grantees applied for
and obtained great stretches of forest land apparently
rather for the purpose of working out the existing stock
of mature timber—other than teak, the proprietary right
over which vested solely in Government—than with any
bonâ fide intention of investing capital in trying to bring
their grant-lands speedily into permanent cultivation.
This endeavour to create large agricultural estates proved

rather a failure. Many of the grants were from time to time voluntarily surrendered, or were resumed owing to non-compliance with the conditions under which they were held, such as failure to bring a certain proportion under cultivation within a certain period, or failure to pay the revenue demand when the land in due time became assessable thereto. In 1897 the number of existing grants, dating from the time of the Waste Land Rules, was one hundred, the total area held under which amounted to 159,859 acres, or 250 square miles. All these have already become assessable to land-revenue except nine grants; and, of these nine, four will ultimately become assessable, while five were granted under conditions exempting them from such liability.

The provisions, above sketched, for the extension of permanent cultivation throughout the plains do not apply to the shifting *Taungya* or temporary "hill-clearings" practised for rice-cultivation by the Karens and other jungle folks inhabiting the low, forest-clad hills of Lower Burma—a wasteful, primitive, nomadic system, which is elsewhere described in detail (*vide* chapter xvii.). Subject to the payment of an annual *Taungya* tax, these hill-men can migrate from year to year, clearing, burning, and cultivating patches of forest not included either within State Reserved Forests, or in tracts preliminarily notified for inquiry and settlement, with a view to proposed reservation. The killing or injury of teak and certain other reserved trees, and permitting fire to spread into Reserved Forests are also prohibited, and are made punishable under the forest laws; but the latter are, in these particular respects, applied only with leniency and discretion. In many of the Reserved Forests *Taungya* tracts have been set apart exclusively for the practice of this form of agriculture by the Karens located in or near these at the time of reservation and settlement. Thus, of the 17,153 square miles of Reserved Forests throughout Burma in 1900, 865 square miles were burdened in this manner with *Taungya* rights or privileges.

In some parts of the country, as, for example, among the inhabitants of the higher hills between the Sittang and the Salween rivers, the pressure of population has

LAND AND REVENUE LAWS

led to the tacit recognition of definite tribal or communal tracts within which shifting cultivation is carried on with a definite and regular system of rotation. The Land and Revenue Act recognises the necessities of the jungle tribes with regard to this hereditary mode of cultivation, and provides for *Taungya* tracts being formally assigned to communities which make application to this effect in order to keep newcomers away from the localities where the applicants have been accustomed to exercise *Taungya* rights. The importance of this shifting hill cultivation in Burma may be estimated from the fact that about six per cent. of the total male population is engaged in it. Endeavours are being made, by offers of land and of advances for the purchase of plough cattle, to induce the hill-men to take to permanent cultivation on the plains fringing the hills. In course of time many will thus change their habits ; but in a country like Burma there will always remain a large number who prefer the freer and rather romantic nomad life in the forest to the more monotonous existence in villages surrounded by permanent cultivation on the plains.

When the lines were fixed upon which the administration of Upper Burma was to be conducted, the law regulating the land system was embodied in the Upper Burma Land and Revenue Regulation, 1889, which differs in many respects from the Act in force in the older portion of the province. A primary division of all land was made into *State land* and *non-State land*. The former included all the Crown lands of different denominations (*Lèdaw, Ayádaw, Lamaingmyé*—as previously described in chapter vi.), all lands held under service-tenures of various kinds, all waste and forest land, and all land which had been abandoned after being brought under cultivation, and to the ownership of which no claim was preferred within two years of the enforcement of the Regulation, *i.e.* up to 13th July, 1891. The non-State Land comprised all lands held in private ownership, and included pagoda or monasterial lands (*Wuttagán*), hereditary lands (*Bóbábaing*) in possession of the descendants of persons who cleared them, or of those who obtained them by purchase from the original owner (clearer) or his descendants, or the ownership of which had been conveyed under a written grant from the King, and lands cleared and reclaimed (*Damáguyá*) before the enforcement of the Regulation and still in the possession of the person who thus brought it into cultivation. These non-State lands are allodial possessions already alienated from the ownership of Government. They are consequently held as freeholds, and not under tenure of any description, the peasant proprietors of all hereditary and reclaimed lands being merely burdened with the *Tháthamédá* or house-tax as their direct contribution towards the support of the Administration.

In the case of the Crown lands and the lands held under service-tenures, the British Government simply assumed the rights previously enjoyed by the Burmese Kings. But with regard to all waste lands, and lands which had been allowed to revert into jungle after once being cleared for cultivation, they did much more than this in declaring all such waste land to be the property of Government and decreeing that no such land may be cultivated except in accordance with rules framed under the Land Regulation. A system of land-tenure was thus introduced in place of the previously existing allodial peasant proprietorship. These rules provide for the grant of leases of waste land for any period not exceeding thirty years, and for the grant of permits to occupy such land temporarily. Cultivators wishing to occupy waste land can adopt either of these methods of acquisition. The rules, modelled on those in force in Lower Burma, provide for the levy of revenue on areas leased and occupied, and for the temporary exemption from revenue of areas which have first to be cleared of grass, scrub, or tree-jungle before they can yield remunerative crops. In 1895–96 leases of waste land were granted only to the extent of 9,806 acres (15 square miles) in Upper Burma, as the majority of new cultivators preferred to do without leases. In the following year the area leased sank to 6,154 acres (9¾ square miles) owing to the rules being amended by a provision expressly prohibiting the transfer of any lease of State land to a non-agriculturist or a non-Burmese without the permission

TENANTS IN UPPER BURMA

of the township officer; for the Upper Burman was thus paternally protected against usurers of his own race and the more rapacious Indian money-lenders. In 1898–99 the area rose to 11,236 acres (17½ square miles), and it fell off again to 9,761 acres (15¼ square miles) in 1899–1900. Some of these State lands were put up to auction for sale of the occupancy rights. Thus, in 1896–97, 4,163 acres of rice land were sold in the Mandalay district; but such sales of the right of occupation are now infrequent, owing to the restrictions applied with regard to the transfer of the tenant's interest.

It will thus be seen that while a simple uniform land system sprang up in Lower Burma under British administration, a more complex system is in force throughout Upper Burma. In the latter case there were not only large stretches of *Lèdaw* or "royal lands" let out to tenants of the Crown paying a rental varying in amount up to one-fourth of the produce, at which share it was usually fixed, but also a class of landowners in the persons of those, or of their descendants, who had received grants of land through the special favour of the King. Tenancy under landlords was therefore, and still is, much more common throughout Upper than in Lower Burma. The tenants occupying State land have the incidents of their tenure, and their rights and privileges, laid down in the rules under the Land Regulation. Fixation of rent is provided for on a consideration of the market value of the produce and of the amount of the customary rent. Provision is also made for the eviction of tenants after notice and on payment of compensation for improvements, or on further additional payment for disturbance in default of due notice to quit. Tenancy under private landlords is not privileged with any fixity of tenure, nor are there any legal limits to the rents which may be demanded. In these respects the position of tenants of private individuals is similar to that of tenants in Lower Burma.

Although the normal condition of the Burmese agriculturist is that of a peasant proprietor, yet the number of tenancies which have recently sprung up in the centres of rice-production is already considerable, and the class

277

of tenants appears to be growing quickly. It is mainly recruited from persons who have formerly possessed the land but have had to part with the ownership owing to debt, and who now occupy as tenants the holdings they originally held in fee simple. Other tenancies are often also held, particularly in the deltoid tracts, by newcomers from other districts and by young men setting up house; for on marrying it is still not unusual for a young man to live for two or three years in the house of his parents-in-law and to work for them, or to be a tenant on a portion of their land, before he and his wife found a separate household of their own.

As registration of transfers of land is not in every case compulsory, a precise estimate cannot be made as to the extent to which land is being year after year transferred from its original owners to their creditors. But such transfers are annually increasing in all tracts within easy reach of trading centres in Lower Burma, and there is a corresponding steady increase in the area of land cultivated by agriculturists who have descended to the position of tenants having no statutory rights. As a cultivator acquiring land under the Land Revenue Act has transferable rights in his holding, borrowing money on mortgage of these is thus rendered easy in all localities where land has obtained a market value; and money-lenders are usually to be found ready to make advances by means of which they can ultimately secure to themselves the ownership of land which they will probably be able to let at six rupees (eight shillings) or more per acre, the former owners being often left in possession as tenants. The condition of tenants is on the whole prosperous, even although they have no fixity of tenure and there is no legal limit to rents. The only safeguards against rack-renting, and they have hitherto proved efficient, are the facts that there is a considerable competition for tenants, that a fresh tenancy is not difficult to obtain, and that in most districts fresh land for cultivation under direct holding from Government can generally be had on easy terms by moving elsewhere to less populous tracts.

The rent fixed by custom in parts of the Bassein and

LAND MORTGAGES

Henzada districts in the extreme west of the Irrawaddy delta is ten per cent. of the gross produce, measured after harvest, *plus* the land revenue.   Under this custom the tenant only pays rent on the crop he has reaped. As the actual amount of the rent is thus only known after the harvest, partial relief is practically afforded to the tenant in case of any circumstances operating to prevent him from obtaining the full quantity of crop usually yielded by the land, and any loss thus arising is distributed between landlord and tenant.

Increase of population and increase of cultivation in all the districts within easy reach of the centres of the rice-export trade naturally tend to diminish the area of cultivable waste land capable of being reclaimed for permanent cultivation ; and this of course tends to establish a marketable value for land, which is much more likely to rise in the future than to remain stationary or to fall.   It is naturally therefore in tracts of this description that foreclosures on land mortgages are most numerous.   Creditors usually prefer to make further advances to their debtors in order to induce the latter to hold on to their fields, rather than foreclose and take possession of land which they cannot cultivate themselves, and for which it is at present difficult to get tenants.   A decided movement is, however, gradually taking place in the direction of tenancies throughout the richer portions of Lower Burma, where nearly twenty-one per cent. of the whole occupied area is now held by tenants.   This tendency may be seen from the following statistics, even though these data are not complete :—

Year.	Land Sold. Acres.	Land Mortgaged. Acres.	No. of Tenants.	Area occupied by Tenants. Acres.	Average Rent per Acre. Rs.
1887–88	106,037	36,202	30,791	—	—
1891–92	263,686	63,326	46,971	—	—
1895–96	304,580	96,237	—	1,112,510	6·88
1896–97	338,983	89,289	—	1,229,917	7·83
1898–99	—	—	—	1,459,386	—
1899–1900	473,768	—	—	1,560,942	8·15

The improvidence of the Burmese tends to drive agriculturists into the hands of money-lenders; and this has resulted in the formation of a class of non-agriculturist landlords, which now numbers over eighteen thousand in Lower Burma. But at the same time agriculturists with money at disposal are purchasing holdings largely, so that it cannot at present be said that the land has yet passed to any large and serious extent out of the hands of the agriculturist class. Yet in some districts, as in Tharrawaddy, such a danger exists; and an experimental Tenancy Bill is now under consideration with a view to checking abuses of their rights by landlords.

As the rent is usually paid in kind, the rental value of land fluctuates from year to year with the current price of paddy or of the other crop raised. Thus the apparent increase in average rental value of rice lands, which rose from 6·88 rupees in 1895–96, culminated in 1898–99, and then decreased slightly to 8·15 rupees in 1899–1900, was solely due to fluctuation in the price of paddy, and not to any variation in the actual rental value of land from competition among tenants. A favourable market for paddy also enables landlords to find tenants for land which would otherwise remain uncultivated if the price of paddy seems likely to be low during the next shipping season. The market value of land became temporarily reduced a few years ago, partly on account of lower prices for paddy being anticipated, and partly also through Government assessing at full rates all fallow lands held by non-cultivators, for the purpose of imposing a check on land-jobbing and the wholesale transfer of land to non-agriculturists in the deltoid districts. The more careful application of the rules concerning the fallow rate has on the one hand deterred professional money-lenders and traders from being too eager in acquiring the proprietorship of land, while on the other it has impelled them to seek tenants for such land as they hold already. As uncropped land belonging to an absentee landlord is now assessed at the full rate of revenue instead of at the fallow rate, it has thus been rendered less profitable for money-lenders to hold large areas of cultivable land as a mere speculation for a rise in price.

LAND SURVEY SYSTEM

The enforcement of a stricter practice with regard to fallow rates has further had the very beneficial effect of inducing some persons to relinquish land which they were unable to cultivate themselves, and has thus thrown open areas for occupation by other cultivators who take up the land under direct tenure from Government.

Land in towns in Lower Burma is held partly under grants or leases made in accordance with rules promulgated from time to time, and partly by squatters; and there is no law under which fresh rights in town lands can now be acquired. In Upper Burma there is also no special law on the subject of town lands, though rules modelled on those in force in Lower Burma were issued in 1890 for the grant of leases and were extended to the principal towns.

The land survey system adopted about twenty years ago by the Agricultural Department in Lower Burma was a cadastral survey consisting of an exterior survey by theodolite, in connection with which there is an interior field-to-field survey. The country under survey being first of all divided into large circuits or polygons, the geographical position of each of these is carefully fixed and the included area ascertained. Each circuit is subdivided into minor polygons, whose geographical position and area are likewise carefully determined. Within these minor circuits come the *Kwin* or local circuits of cultivation, forming polygons rarely exceeding one to two and a half square miles in area, which are dealt with in a similar exact manner as to boundaries, position, and area. These *Kwin* are simply compact blocks of rice cultivation and waste land of convenient size, situated near each village or hamlet,—the word *Kwin*, meaning "a cleared plain" or also "a circuit, a ring," having from time immemorial been used to denote something like the village or communal lands, as if enclosed in an imaginary ring-fence.

When the accuracy of the survey has been proved by repeated check processes, resulting in the perfect agreement of the smallest, the intermediate, and the largest circuits, the field (*Lè*) is entered upon it as the unit of survey. This is a square or rectangular piece of paddy land enclosed by low ridges thrown up for the purpose of keeping in the water, upon a large supply of which the rice-cultivation is dependent. These ridges are called *Kanzinyò*, which literally means " straight walls forming a water-tank." The fields thus divided vary in extent from about a quarter of an acre in the drier districts of Prome and Thayetmyo, above the apex of the Irrawaddy delta, to about an acre in extent throughout the great moist alluvial plains within the deltaic zone. Until the aggregate of the field areas corresponds with the area of the *Kwin* polygon, the field survey is not accepted as correct. Accuracy of detail is thus guaranteed by the cadastral survey, before further operations can be commenced for the settlement of the land revenue.

The experience acquired during the last twenty years has shown that the adoption of the field as the unit of survey was a prudent measure, for the field-to-field survey is the most efficient and the cheapest method that could be adopted. Any attempt to artificially enlarge this convenient and practical, though small, unit would only increase the cost of the detailed survey without being compensated either by greater rapidity in survey or greater precision. As the field is after all the practical unit of cultivation, and of all movement and change in cultivation, no artificial limitation or determination of the unit of survey could prevent the field from stamping itself as the main practical unit on the map. Even with fields averaging only one-third of an acre in area, a cadastral survey party can in a working season turn out field-maps for from seven to eight hundred square miles of country. Begun in 1879, the cadastral survey has now been completed throughout all the districts in Lower Burma.

In the maintenance of the cadastral maps and the settlement registers from year to year a supplementary survey is employed, whose operations cover the whole area surveyed, and consequently extend to almost the whole of the regularly cultivated tracts throughout the older portion of the province.

When any part of a district has been surveyed and settled, it is transferred to the charge of this Supplementary Survey and Registration Department, which undertakes the survey and mapping, on fresh copies of the original village maps, of all changes and extensions ; and it also prepares and maintains registers showing the areas of these changes and extensions, holding by holding, and their resulting changes in the assessments. The methods adopted are similar to those of the cadastral survey and the settlement, so that the work of this department practically consists in an annual revision of the areas and the assessments of the old cultivation, together with an annual survey and assessment of the new cultivation.

Apart from the administrative advantage of having, in a conveniently arranged form, the mass of well established facts which this department is constantly collecting year by year, its operations are rendered necessary in consequence of the law and custom governing the acquisition, cultivation, and assessment of land in Burma. As the land is free, any person can, after obtaining the requisite permission, and without further let or hindrance, take up practically as much new land as he or she pleases and is able to bring under cultivation. Old fields may be surrendered in whole or in part, or may be left fallow, or may be let out to tenants. The Government, as overlord of the land taken up under grant, does not interfere with regard to movement in any of these directions. The revenue demand depends on the area of land actually cultivated or from which profit is derived, fallow rates being imposed, as previously mentioned, only in the case of land-holding non-agriculturists, and for the express purpose of trying to check land-jobbing by speculators. In order to adapt the assessment to this custom of free cultivation, the entire area under cultivation has therefore to be annually examined, each and every change in the old cultivation that can effect the revenue demand being carefully noted, and the assessment for the current year modified accordingly. The ground broken for new cultivation has also to be examined, surveyed, and plotted on the maps ; the respective areas have, holding by holding, to be computed ; and the new assessment rolls have to be prepared.

BURMA UNDER BRITISH RULE

The system of settlement for the assessment of the land-revenue demand was also begun in 1879, and has since then been carried out continuously, until it has now been almost completed for Lower Burma. The principle adopted consisted in acre rates based upon the ascertained productivity of the chief varieties of soil and fixed for a term of years, in annual survey of the changes taking place in area, and in corresponding adjustments of the assessment on each individual holding. Thus, while the rates remain unaltered throughout a term usually fixed at fifteen years, the assessments on individuals may vary from year to year with changes in the areas of their holdings.

Settlement operations are conducted by selected junior members of the Commission, who remain for several years deputed on this special duty. The control and administration of operations are vested in a Settlement Commissioner, who is directly subordinate to the Financial Commissioner. At the time of the settlement, the holding of each cultivator is registered field by field, and a record is made of the cultivator's status, in which it is shown whether he be a landholder by prescription (from original squatting rights), a grantee, a lessee, a tenant, or a mortgagee. The area of each field and the total area of each holding are also noted. All these details are entered in a principal settlement register, which practically forms a basis for all subsequent statistics as well as for readjustments of the assessments on each holding. This settlement register, in fact, represents the exact state of each holding during the year in which the settlement takes place.

In the year following that in which the settlement is carried out, the duty of maintaining the land records is assumed, as already described, by the Supplementary Survey and Registration Department, which ascertains any changes that have taken place in the state of each holding, and records them in a register which is the counterpart of the original settlement register. Should it happen that the cultivator has enlarged his holding by bringing some of the existing waste land under the plough or by purchasing a field from a neighbour, he is assessed on the increased area, while a corresponding reduction is made in the case of a cultivator who has meanwhile sold or surrendered any portion of his former area under cultivation. The original settlement and the subsequent annual supplementary registers and assessments thus record from year to year the entire history of each holding. By this simple process of addition and subtraction each holding should, at the end of the term for which the rates have been fixed, be found just as correctly recorded as the original holdings were when the settlement operations were first carried out.

The rates of assessment fixed at the time of settlement are arrived at after careful inquiry by the settlement officers over wide and varied tracts, and are based on the actual quality and productivity of the land as ascertained by careful harvesting and measurement of the grain in several hundreds of fields. The results thus obtained in kind are then transformed into their money valuation at rates deduced from the average prices of produce for several years back. Wherever substantial differences are found in the quality or crop-producing power of the soil, the patches of inferior land are marked off from those of superior quality, and separate rates are fixed in proportion to the ascertained differences in productive capacity.

Until within the last few years it had been the custom in Lower Burma that the cultivator should only pay the full assessment rates on the area actually under crop. He could leave uncultivated as much of his holding as he liked, and on this uncultivated portion a merely nominal rate of assessment of two annas or twopence an acre was imposed as a sort of quitrent, upon payment of which the cultivator retained all his rights in the land. It was thus fallow only in the obsolete meaning of this agricultural term, because it was unsown and neglected ; but it was not ploughed and left an open fallow as the term is now used in England. A fallow field in Burma is one that is left untouched after a paddy crop has been reaped from it, and remains unploughed till the cultivator feels inclined to take another crop from it. The usual reason for letting land lie idle in this way is that the owner is either unwilling or unable to cultivate it. This low two-anna rate on so-called fallows is still maintained, though the extent of its application has been considerably curtailed owing to the increase in the value of land and the growth of a landlord class. The two-anna rate is consequently now only levied on the whole or any part of a holding which is left uncultivated either for the purpose of allowing the soil to recover from slight temporary exhaustion or because the owner is unable to cultivate it through causes beyond his control, such as illness, deaths in his family, loss of cattle, or the like. An assessment varying from two annas per acre up to the normal rate for cultivated land is, at the discretion of the Deputy Commissioner, now levied from land left uncultivated for grazing purposes, or which remains uncultivated in any year after having been generally sublet during the previous five years, or which, after having been granted with exemption from revenue for a term of years, has not been brought under cultivation within a reasonable period, or which has otherwise been a source of profit to the owner during the year of assessment. That full rates of assessment have within the past few years, with the view of checking land-jobbing, been demanded on all fallows held by non-agriculturists and all uncropped land belonging to absentee landlords, has already been mentioned.

When crops have been wholly or partially destroyed by inundations, or drought, or any other cause beyond the cultivator's control, remissions of land revenue are granted. No remission is made unless the damage to the crop causes a loss exceeding one-third of the estimated average full crop of the holding. If the whole, or nearly the whole, of the crop has been destroyed, the whole of the revenue is remitted ; but, otherwise, the remission is proportioned to the extent of the partial loss. Though quite distinct from abatements on account of fallows, the two kinds of remission often coincide in practice.

The system of settlement thus sketched has been carried out in strict accordance with the agricultural usages of the province, the customs of the people being duly recognized and placed on record. While no restrictions, not previously imposed, have been placed on the free exercise of their rights and privileges, all that is traditional and of advantage to the peasantry has been maintained and properly regulated. A villager may cultivate as much land as he likes ; but he only pays land revenue on the area which he crops, or from which he derives rent or other profit or advantage. The system of annual supplementary survey and registration introduced ensures prompt adjustment of the assessment according to changes in the area cultivated each year ; and by thus ensuring due elasticity in the land-revenue demand, it also permits of free exercise of the individual right to extend or curtail cultivation according to personal circumstances for the time being.

In Upper Burma the system of survey is practically the same as in the lower portion of the province, the field being again taken as the unit. The only important difference is that, in place of a *Kwin*, the unit of assessment is the *Ywá* or " village," consisting of the collection of houses forming the hamlet or village proper, together with the land belonging to the villagers and under the jurisdiction of the village headman.

The work of the cadastral survey in Upper Burma was commenced in the Kyauksè district in November, 1889, under considerable difficulties. The native Indian subordinates, new to the country, and in constant fear of being attacked and cut up by dacoits, were most reluctant to venture out of their camps, and large numbers of the surveyors and chainmen were unable to work owing to malarial fever. The nature of the country and the novelty of the peculiar circumstances under which work had to be done also retarded progress at first; for the village boundaries were usually irrigation channels, the banks of which were clothed with a thick fringe of dense scrub jungle, while all through the dry season the rice-fields were flooded by irrigation.

The system of supplementary survey and registration in Upper Burma is practically the same as in Lower Burma, but the system of settlement differs considerably owing to the local circumstances and customs. In Lower Burma one settlement officer deals finally with an area of about six hundred square miles in each year; but in Upper Burma, aided by several assistants, he deals with an area of three to four times that extent, over which his operations extend for three years. During this time he and his assistants record tenures, harvest and measure crops from sample areas, and collect agricultural statistics over the whole area, fresh test measurements and fresh statistics being collected over the same area in each year. At the end of the third year the settlement officer submits his report embodying the information collected and the conclusions drawn by him therefrom, and proposing rates for assessment.

With respect to details in procedure the work of the settlement officer also differs considerably from the practice in force in Lower Burma, being much more difficult and varied. In Lower Burma there are practically only one agricultural season, from June till December, only one kind of crop, paddy or rice, and only one kind of tenure, peasant proprietorship, to be dealt with ; and the field operations of the settlement officer are restricted to the dry season from December till April or May, while he has no direct concern with the non-cultivating classes of the people. In Upper Burma, however, there are at least three separate agricultural seasons for rice-cultivation alone—the *Kaukkyi* or ordinary rainy season crop, grown on land watered by rainfall or irrigation ; the *Kaukti*, grown on irrigated lands, usually as a second crop on the *Kaukkyi* land, between February and June ; and the *Mayin* or hot-weather crop, grown on swampy land and reaped in May. There are also many varieties of field crops (rice, maize, chillies, peas, grain, wheat, etc.) and several kinds of land tenure to be considered ; and in most districts, owing to the comparative lightness of the rainfall, field operations can be conducted throughout the whole twelve months of the year. And, finally, an important part of the work is to adjust, with reference to the non-agricultural classes, the *Tháthamédá* or house-tax to be levied from the trading and non-cultivating portion of the population.

THE THATHAMÉDA TAX

This tax, introduced by King Mindôn into Upper Burma, was retained by the British Government on the annexation, and still forms the principal tax there. Its incidence usually amounts to ten rupees (13s. 4d.) per house, though in exceptional cases it is less than this. Thus, the Shan communities in the Bhamo district pay only five rupees (6s. 8d.) per household, in consequence of this special rate having been fixed in Burmese times. Residents in two townships of the Kyauksè district were accustomed to be assessed at a reduced rate of six rupees (8s.) per house, owing to their being required to turn out and repair breaches in canals without receiving remuneration for their labour; but this unsatisfactory system was abolished in 1893. Those cultivating above seven acres of royal land were altogether exempt from the tax. Throughout the hill tracts inhabited by Karens in the Yamèthin district the rate varies from three to four rupees (4s. to 5s. 4d.) per house.

The tax is now assessed in much the same manner as formerly. The *Thugyi* or village headman reports the number of houses in his village. This statement is checked by the *Myó Thugyi* or headman of a circle, in districts where there are such officers, or else by the *Myó Ôk* or township magistrate, the *Akunwun* or native revenue officer of the district, and the district officer and his subdivisional assistants. The sum due from each village having been fixed, *Thamádi* or assessors (lit. " ascertainers of truth "), corresponding to the village elders, determine the amount to be contributed by each householder; and, as a rule, there are no serious objections raised to the individual incidence of the tax under the operations of the assessors. Special exemptions are given during years of scarcity, or whenever exceptional reasons exist for not demanding the usual full amount; while religious recluses, public officials, and all persons incapable of earning their own livelihood are exempt from any contribution.

The revenue law of Upper Burma provides for the levy of *Tháthamédá* on all classes of the population, for the assessment of rent on State land, and for the assessment of revenue on non-State land. But as no revenue was assessed on land of the latter class by the Burmese Government, the British revenue law recognizes this fact by authorizing that when revenue is levied on such land the owners of the same may obtain exemption from or reduction of the *Tháthamédá*. The work of the settlement officer in Upper Burma is therefore threefold, namely, (1) to draw up a record of rights and occupation in land, (2) to propose rates for the assessment of all cultivated lands, in the form of rent for State land and revenue for non-State land, and (3) to submit proposals for the adjustment of the *Tháthamédá* on the non-agricultural classes and on those classes whose livelihood depends only partly on agriculture and mainly on other sources.

The first section of these settlement duties includes the ascertaining and recording of the exact area of land owned or occupied by each person, and the kind of tenure upon which it is held or occupied. These facts are entered in registers and become the records-of-rights which have under the Land Regulation to be maintained throughout Upper Burma.

The assessment of rent and revenue is based upon deductions drawn from the information collected as to the productivity of the soil, the cost of cultivation, and the value of the produce. With reference to the final section of the settlement officer's duties, information is collected as to the occupations and means of livelihood of the people with a view to determining what amount of *Tháthamédá* can equitably be demanded from them after revenue has been assessed on non-State land. The main principles that have been laid down for his guidance are, firstly, that persons dependent solely on agriculture are to be exempted from the house-tax; secondly, that persons who, though partly dependent on agriculture, derive the substantial portion of their income from other sources, are to pay *Tháthamédá* at a reduced rate; and, thirdly, that persons who derive the whole of their income from other sources than agriculture are to pay the house-tax to the same extent as before the settlement.

Following these principles, the settlement officer utilizes the statistics he has carefully collected in drawing up proposals for exempting the purely agricultural section of the population altogether from the *Tháthaméda*, for reducing it in amount in the case of those partially dependent on cultivation of the land, and for assessing to the full amount those earning their livelihood by trades, handicrafts, and the like. The rates thus fixed at settlement include the rent rates assessed on State land, the revenue rates assessed on non-State land, and the house-tax rates assessed on income derived otherwise than from agriculture. These rates vary from about one rupee to three rupees (1s. 4d. to 4s.) per acre on the different qualities of rice lands, due consideration being of course given to the various localities and their lines of communication with the great centres of the rice export trade.

The proposals made by the settlement officer for the assessment of the land revenue are not accepted without the most careful scrutiny, or without measures being taken to safeguard the interests of the people on the one hand and of the Government on the other. The settlement officer submits his report to the Commissioner of the division, who forwards it with his remarks and criticisms to the Settlement Commissioner. Here it is again scrutinized very carefully before being submitted for the consideration of the Lieutenant-Governor and for the requisite orders as to notification in the official gazette when sanction has been accorded to the proposals. How great is the care bestowed on this important work may be judged from the fact that the settlement proposals for the Mandalay district, in which operations were begun in 1890, were only sanctioned at the very close of December, 1896; and before sanction had been accorded the whole matter had been twice submitted by the Chief Commissioner to the Government of India, once in the form of a minute by Sir Alexander Mackenzie, and again in the shape of a note by Sir Frederic Fryer. And when finally sanctioned, the rates of assessments were only approved for a term of five years in place of the usual fifteen years for which the settlement is generally fixed.

In this case of the Mandalay district, however, special conditions and circumstances obtained. It was the first

BURMA UNDER BRITISH RULE

district coming under settlement in the new province; and it was the first time in the history of the land-revenue settlement that what might be called a precarious tract of country had to be dealt with, where the rainfall is ordinarily small and capricious, and where, except in a comparatively limited area under irrigation, a remunerative paddy crop could only be reckoned on once every two or three years. And yet so strong is the hold of custom on the Burmese cultivator that he prefers persisting in the effort to grow paddy rather than change to the cultivation of other cereals, for which the climate and the physical conditions of the soil are really much better adapted, and for which a fair market demand exists. Save in the alluvial tracts and the lands under permanent irrigation, the condition of agriculture throughout the Mandalay district was therefore at the time of the recent settlement little better than chaotic and uncertain. The average size of the holdings was extremely small, ranging from about three to five acres only, and in consequence of this the mass of the peasantry found themselves forced to supplement their earnings from agriculture by other occupations. Thus, in the vicinity of Mandalay, the cultivators would in bad years readily abandon their fields for work of any description, such as earth-work on roads or embankments, cartage, grass-cutting, and fuel-chopping.

The care and consideration given to the first settlement operations in the Mandalay and the Kyauksè districts were necessitated by the fact that the Government recognized the land-revenue settlement to be at the time a matter of vital and permanent importance to the people of Upper Burma. The general standard of living had, of course, to be carefully considered. This not only varies greatly from year to year, but also fluctuates from week to week, being highest just after the harvest has been reaped and garnered. On the whole, however, it is below the average standard throughout the settled tracts in Lower Burma. In 1891–92, when several districts in Upper Burma suffered from scarcity of food owing to insufficient rainfall, the standard of living in the poorer townships of the Mandalay district fell to a very low level indeed. There was no actual starvation, for a district with so many resources as Mandalay could hardly sink to anything like complete destitution, but the effects of a succession of poor harvests were nevertheless distinctly noticeable. In the rural parts of the Lamaing and Amárapura townships luxuries had to be eschewed, silk clothes being dispensed with, and but little betel or tobacco being consumed; while in the poorer tracts the peasantry were driven to live on the very margin of subsistence. The rice for food was eked out by adding one-fourth to one-half of millet; and to this change of fare the chief objectors were the *Póngyi*, or monastic body of religious mendicants wearing the yellow robe of poverty and professing contempt for all the material comforts of life. The people themselves bore their trials well; and the mixture of millet and rice was in itself palatable enough. By 1893 the standard of living had again risen, though not to the fair degree of comfort which is reported to have obtained while King Mindôn held court in Mandalay, the time to which the high level record is ascribed. During Thibaw's reign fluctuations took place from year to year according to the rainfall and the harvest. The revenue settlement and the irrigation works now in course of construction should, however, raise the general standard considerably above what it has ever been.

Reference has already been made to the transfer of the land, particularly in the deltaic tracts of Lower Burma, from the hands of agriculturists to those of traders and money-lenders, which may be looked upon as practically synonymous terms, for these men never cultivate the land themselves. Within the richer tracts opened up and brought within easy reach of large towns by railway and river-steamers, a standard of luxury previously unknown has gradually been asserting itself. Though still as frugal as formerly in his food, the Burmese cultivator is now more lavish in his expenditure on clothes and household comforts. Besides his cheap cotton garments for ordinary work-a-day use, he invariably has one or more holiday suits, always of silk and often of rich pattern and costly texture, while his wife and children are decked with gold ornaments on holidays and festivals. In place of a bamboo house roofed with thatch-grass, he laudably endeavours to build a substantial wooden house, and often roofs it with corrugated iron; but he makes the mistake of generally becoming tainted with a tendency towards humble imitation of English manners and customs, in which respect he is merely following the lead of his more advanced relatives in the towns. Though the peasant has not yet taken to wearing socks or stockings and patent leather shoes, like most of the up-to-date Burmese in Rangoon and the other great trading centres, yet he apparently feels impelled to acquire tables, chairs, bedsteads, lamps, glasses, and the like, for the adornment of his house. Curiously enough, this tendency is nowhere more noticeable than among the *Pôngyi* or religious body, the ultra-conservative devotees of Buddhism vowed to a life of poverty and extreme simplicity, whose monasteries are often filled with articles of luxury, the use of which was formerly quite unknown to the Burmese.

Though as a rule happy, contented, and fairly well off on the whole, the Burmese agriculturist can seldom be said to be in anything like affluent circumstances. As soon as he sells the surplus of his crop he spends his money freely, either in works of religious merit for his own personal benefit in the next life, or else in jewellery, clothes, amusements, or gambling. He rarely forms any reserve of savings to fall back upon when temporarily embarrassed, and usually has nothing in the shape of capital except his land, his house, and his plough-cattle. The rest of his possessions, such as agricultural implements and household chattels, have little or no market value. Very frequently the best evidence of the prosperity of the Burmese cultivator is to be found in the number of cattle he possesses; for he can always hire them out at substantially profitable rates during the ploughing season, if he does not require them for his own land. The Karens who have settled on the plains in the Bassein and Thôngwa districts are of a much more saving and careful disposition. This is no doubt mainly owing to their being mostly converts from spirit-worship

to Christianity, neither of which involves the expenditure
of large sums on works of religious merit so essential to
the equanimity of the Buddhist Burmese. Besides
lavish outlay on priests, monasteries, pagodas, shrines, etc.,
and on dress, the prosperous Burmese agriculturist will
generally soon dissipate his ready money in theatrical
performances in the open air during the period immediately following the garnering of the grain between
December and February. At this season boats and
carts conveying troupes of performers are everywhere to
be met travelling from village to village. They obtain
as much as 300 to 400 rupees ($£20$ to $£26\frac{2}{3}$) for two or
three nights' entertainment at villages or hamlets, which
at a cursory glance might be described as poverty-
stricken collections of huts. Throughout the country
generally the appearance of a village is no criterion of its
wealth, squalid houses being found as frequently in the
richer as in the poorer tracts.

Thus, even when otherwise really well off, the Burmese agriculturist suffers from a chronic want of ready
money, occasioned partly by his hereditary improvidence,
vanity, and love of amusement, and partly by his
religious impulses. When in want of cash to pay
labourers, to meet the capitation-tax during the rainy
season, or to purchase commodities like salt, salted fish,
tobacco, and so forth, he finds little difficulty in borrowing from traders, brokers, or professional money-lenders
(*Chetties*). Interest is usually at the rate of four to five per
cent. per mensem, although in some localities loans
can be obtained at a lower rate consequent on the
facilities for borrowing offered by a larger number of
traders. The lowest rate of interest, about three per
cent. per mensem, is obtainable on deposit of gold
ornaments exceeding in value the amount lent. In such
a case the creditor can easily obtain an additional profit
by lending out the pledged gold ornaments at a remunerative rate on holidays and festivals. Cattle disease,
inducing exceptional mortality, is often the direct cause
of indebtedness, as well as extravagance and gambling;
but the great facility with which loans can be obtained,
even although at an exorbitant rate of interest, is in

itself, next to the hereditary and characteristic improvidence of the Burmese, the chief cause of indebtedness.

These inordinately high rates of interest even induce speculators to borrow from capitalists on pledge of gold at thirty to forty per cent. for the purpose of lending out to cultivators on mortgage of land. Self-denial and thrift finding no place in the Burmese character, if the cultivator wish for money he will pay an exorbitant rate of interest for it. As money can be laid out in many ways with certainty of excellent profit, there is practically no competition among small money-lending capitalists ; and so long as this state of affairs exists the usual percentage is little likely to confine itself within anything like reasonable limits. The rates of interest sanctioned by the Laws of Manú, the ancient statute law, were one per cent. for poor agriculturists, two per cent. for cultivators in general, four per cent. for those who were well to do, and five per cent. for traders in any large way of business.

The average amount of indebtedness among the majority of agriculturists who are unable to make both ends meet during any given year varies from about 100 to 150 rupees ($£6\frac{2}{3}$ to $£10$). Though not in itself a large sum, this is just sufficient to hamper them considerably, through the high rate of interest current. Where the land is fertile, the cultivator can usually easily extricate himself from his difficulties, because a good harvest enables him to discharge the liabilities incurred during the previous year. If he cannot manage to free himself in one year, two or three good harvests should see him again unencumbered. But when the soil is poor, or when there is heavy mortality among cattle, matters become complicated. The land then hardly yields enough to support the cultivator and his family, and there is no surplus crop available for the clearance of debt. Renewal of the old loan, and perhaps even the additional burden of a new advance, weigh him down more heavily in the following year, and he gradually falls into a chronic state of indebtedness from which he can only escape by giving up his property to his creditors, or by abandoning his lands and home and making a moonlight flitting to break fresh ground in another part of the country in the hope of there being free from his creditors. But cases of absolute insolvency are fortunately, however, of exceptional occurrence. In this respect Burma happily differs essentially from the more thickly populated portions of India. Such cases of hopeless indebtedness as do occur, and mostly for comparatively small amounts, are generally due to illness of the cultivator and his family, loss of cattle through disease, and gambling, or to a combination of these or similar circumstances.

As yet the Burmese agriculturists have practically no legal protection against the usury of money-lenders. Excessive as the customary sixty per cent. rate of interest is, the money-lenders not infrequently make their creditors sign extortionate bonds acknowledging the receipt of sums amounting even to three or four times the money actually advanced, and the usurers thereupon proceed to register these documents under the Registration Act. After the harvest the creditors generally obtain repayment as soon as the paddy is threshed, before the grain is removed from the threshingfloor, the rate per hundred baskets having been determined beforehand. Thus, the results of inquiries made about December or January invariably show a much smaller proportion of indebtedness than statistics collected before the harvesting and threshing of the paddy crop in these months. If the seizure of the crop in this way leaves little or no margin for the requirements of the cultivator, the creditors will often promise to lend money for the payment of the land-revenue demand and other ordinary expenditure. But when the time of collection comes, they refuse to fulfil their promises; and the cultivator, having no crop to sell, either sinks deeper into debt or sees his land sold up to satisfy the rapacity of the money-lender. Owing to want of ready money, to loss of credit, and to the inconvenience of leaving their homes at harvest-time, the agriculturists generally refuse to apply to the civil courts for redress; for they believe that the false and extortionate bonds signed by them must have, in consequence of registration by the usurers, received the formal sanction of Government, so that they cannot be disputed or cancelled. Moreover, such a procedure would hardly be consistent with Burmese notions, for the Burmese peasant has hereditary and intuitive knowledge of the enormous difficulty of proving a negative. It would seem much easier and far more reasonable to him to bring a dozen or a score of witnesses to prove that he repaid the money with interest to his creditor, than to attempt to show that he had actually received only one-fourth or one-third of the amount for which the money-lender forced him, under pressure of want of money, to sign a receipt or to make his mark by way of acknowledgement.

In the interests of the Burmese peasantry it is much to be regretted that the Registration Act in Lower Burma should have been extended to the interior of districts where the rural population is exceedingly ignorant and quite incapable of understanding the objects of such an enactment. Its effects have certainly been to enable unscrupulous men of the trading and money-lending class to enforce fraudulent contracts against their more ignorant neighbours and other borrowers.

To obviate fraud in this way and to enable the cultivators to obtain advances for specific purposes, as, for example, the purchase of plough cattle after loss through epidemic disease, agricultural advances are obtainable from Government at a low rate of interest. But much more than that is required to place matters on a sound footing. There can be no doubt that the greatest blessing which could be bestowed at present upon the Burmese peasantry is, in addition to the Tenancy Bill now under consideration, a well managed Land Mortgage Bank duly approved by Government, and owned and conducted by Englishmen, from which loans could be obtained by approved applicants at a fair rate of interest considering the circumstances of the country. In all the settled districts, where each man's holding and the nature of the tenure are at once clearly recorded in the Land Record Registers, a business of this sort could easily and profitably be worked on a sound and secure basis. Operations would of course have to be first of all confined to selected portions of the districts immediately in communication with the centres of the rice export trade, for it is only in such favoured localities that the requisite security could be found justifying business on a large scale at a moderate rate of interest. Conducted by men thoroughly conversant with the Burmese language and character, personally known and trusted by the Burmese, and personally acquainted with the rural conditions of the districts forming their particular sphere of operations, such a Land Bank would prove the greatest and most undisguised blessing to agriculturists while giving good returns to the shareholders. It probably would, within the course of a few years, become a potent factor in connection with regulating the market price of paddy, in which respect it might also perhaps contribute in no inconsiderable degree towards obviating fluctuations in the onward progress and development of the province.

During the settlement of the Bassein and Tharrawaddy districts it was found that, although tenancies were numerous, there was hardly what could be called a tenant class in contradistinction to an absentee landlord class; but there were distinct indications that such classes had already begun to form themselves even seventeen or eighteen years ago. In most cases, however, the tenant of one holding was generally the owner of adjacent land, and was not a man of separate class or different social standing from his landlord. Tenants of this sort usually held only for one year, and paid a rent of ten per cent. of the gross produce of the fields in addition to the land revenue. When yearly tenancies of this sort ran on for several years, the tenants were generally relatives of the landowners, sons paying rent to their parents, or one heir paying rent to the co-sharers of the unpartitioned estate. Temporary illness, the death of his wife, a lawsuit, or any circumstance of this description is considered by the Burmese quite a sufficient reason for reposing from his labours for a year, provided he can find any neighbouring cultivator who will work his fields upon payment of the land-revenue demand and giving him a share of the grain harvested.

BURMA UNDER BRITISH RULE

Some such system would be almost certain to spring up wherever the owners of the soil are peasant proprietors : but it is probably found to a greater extent in Burma than elsewhere, owing to the peculiar disposition and characteristics of the people. The growth of a landlord class consisting of traders and money-lenders must of course naturally be slow in a rich but thinly populated country, where the still large amount of cultivable waste enables tenants to be very independent.

In Upper Burma tenants of ancestral land (*Bóbábaing*) usually pay a rent of one-fourth of the gross produce, which corresponds with the nominal land revenue fixed for State land (*Ayádaw*). But as under Burmese rule the measurement of the private areas generally approached nearer to accuracy than in the case of the royal lands, the rent of leased tracts was consequently in effect higher than the revenue on *Ayádaw*. No provision was made against partial failure of the crop, and the tenant had just to take the risk of this. In the majority of cases, however, a reasonable remission was made during bad years. The water-rate for irrigated tracts was usually paid by the landlord out of the rent, unless a special arrangement had been made about this matter. As the relations between the owner of large ancestral lands and his tenants were very much the same as between the State and the tenant of royal lands, the agriculturist's preference for *Bóbábaing* or *Ayádaw* holdings was mainly dependent on his relations with the landowner in the one case, or with the village headman and assessors in the other. Up to the present date there is little or no rack-renting with regard to ancestral lands ; for the tenant can always move to State land, of which an abundance is still available for cultivation. Hence there is as yet no urgent necessity for protecting the tenant against his landlord, although matters are inevitably tending in this direction.

Land is seldom sold outright in Upper Burma. The usual conditions of mortgage are that the borrower shall not disturb the mortgagee's possession for a period of three to five years, after the expiration of which term the mortgage may be redeemed. The price fixed for redemption is usually the same as the amount originally advanced, the usufruct of the land being considered as the equivalent of interest. Mortgages of this sort are occasionally converted into bonâ fide sales by payment of a small additional sum of money. In the vast majority of cases the mortgagee is an agriculturist. When this is not the case, the mortgagor usually works his own holding as the tenant of the former. Interest is, however, paid when the mortgage is merely an advance of money without the ownership and possession being temporarily pledged ; and here again, as in Lower Burma, a poor man without substantial credit generally has to pay about sixty per cent., while the man with a good holding can pledge his possession temporarily, paying merely rent as a tenant but nothing in the shape of interest on the loan. Within the last eight or nine years the custom of recording these transactions on stamped paper has gradually sprung up. Having occasionally been taken in through not understanding the status of such local tenures, Chetties of the Indian money-lending class are now very cautious about accepting mortgages of land in the vicinity of Mandalay.

While it is as yet difficult to form any clear idea as to the extent to which land has been, and is being, transferred by sale or mortgage from the persons with whom the revenue settlement was made to others, yet it appears certain that in the neighbourhood of the large trading centres such transfers are frequent, and that the area of land cultivated by persons in the condition of tenants paying rent to middlemen is already extensive. And it is rapidly increasing. Bengalis in Akyab, Chetties and Burmese brokers and money-lenders in the neighbourhood of Rangoon, and Chetties and Chinamen in Moulmein, are to a certain extent displacing the original landowners. Considering the facilities for borrowing, and the improvidence of the Burmese people, this result, though much to be regretted, is perhaps inevitable.

The incidence of the total demand for land revenue, capitation tax, and export duty on rice taken together amounts merely to between three and four rupees (4s. to 5s. 4d.) per acre. Land cultivated with paddy pays, on the average, less than two rupees (2s. 8d.) direct revenue per acre, and the incidence of the export duty on sea-borne rice comes to a little over one rupee (1s. 4d.) for the produce from the same. This duty, being paid only when there is a surplus for export, varies on the total cultivated area with the gross quantity exported. The rice crop in Burma is certainly as abundant as that produced from the best irrigated land in Northern India; yet for this the cultivator will pay his landlord a rent of at least between five and six rupees (6s. 8d. to 8s.) per acre, although he has to bring from the canals of the Irrigation Department, at a further cost of six rupees (8s.) an acre, the water which the Burmese agriculturist obtains gratuitously from the rain-clouds driven inland from the sea by the south-west monsoon winds. Rain-water is also more fertilizing and stimulating than water of irrigation.

The Government land-revenue demand in Burma is therefore nothing more than a light rate, which does not amount even to one-half of the actual rental value of the land. As the cultivator has transferable rights, it would be unreasonable to expect that under such circumstances he would refrain from borrowing; nor is it surprising that well-to-do neighbouring cultivators, as well as paddy-brokers, traders, and general money-lenders of the trading centres, are able and eager to acquire large areas of land which they can probably let to the former owner at a rent of six to eight rupees (8s. to 10s. 8d.) or more per acre, while they have only to pay the Government land-revenue demand, amounting to less than one-third of that: for the capitation-tax and the export duty on rice do not affect the landowner. In point of fact, the land-revenue demand in the rich tracts of Lower Burma is extremely light; and, indeed, the financial loss thus voluntarily incurred by the State is hardly compensated by any permanent gain to the actual cultivator.

Chapter XI

AGRICULTURE AND RURAL CUSTOMS

THE cultivation of the land is by far the most important industry in Burma. Less than twelve per cent. of the people can be classified as urban.[1] Nearly two-thirds of the total population are either directly or indirectly engaged in agriculture, or else are dependent for their livelihood on the occupations immediately connected with it ; and nearly one-third of the whole population is classifiable under the heading of land occupants cultivating, including dependents. The overwhelming predominance of the agricultural class may be gauged from the fact that the category next in importance, which comprises fishermen, grain-dealers, fruit and vegetable sellers, butchers, and a whole tribe of petty bazaar stall-keepers, distributed among about forty separate occupations concerned with the preparation and supply of food, amounts only to a little under ten per cent. of the population. The butchers comprised in this latter class are principally Chittagonians and other non-Burmese nationalities, as the slaughter of living animals for food is a deep offence against the Buddhist religion. Being a hunter or a fisherman, or being engaged in rearing silkworms and harvesting the cocoons, is hardly looked on as following a quite respectable calling ; but to breed and fatten cattle for the slaughter-house is a pursuit that no self-respecting and consistent Burmese would admit to be the occupation upon which he depends for his livelihood. He will gladly eat his bullock if it happen to die a natural death, and will even feast gloriously on the carcass of a dead elephant ; nor does he feel any

[1] The data given here and in the following chapter as to population and its distribution follow the census of 1891, as the results of that of 1901 are not yet available.

compunction or inconsistency in partaking of fish, flesh, or fowl that has been caught and killed by another. He is not his brother's keeper, and his religious principles involve neither personally nor indirectly any responsibility for the sins of another.

The rural population is distributed in villages having, on the average, forty-three houses, each occupied by seven souls, this proportion being remarkably equal both in Lower and Upper Burma. The total area under actual crop-cultivation throughout Burma in 1899–1900 was 10,556,104 acres, which is rather less than one-fifth above the acreage under corn crops alone in the United Kingdom. But there are still more than $24\frac{1}{2}$ millions of acres of land suitable for permanent cultivation, which only await the advent of population by natural increase or by immigration from the congested areas in India. Nearly two-thirds of the cultivated area are situated in Lower Burma (6,857,898 acres), and of this total over ninety per cent. are under rice crops (6,277,678 acres); while less than fifty per cent. of the total area under crops in Upper Burma (3,698,206 acres) are devoted to rice cultivation (1,818,962 acres), rather less than one-third being under millets, maize, and pulses (1,141,955 acres), about one-seventh under sessamum and other seeds for the manufacture of oil for cooking purposes (527,825 acres), and between four and five per cent. under cotton (153,734 acres). Wheat is not cultivated in Lower Burma ; and, although the climate and soil are suitable, only 15,813 acres are as yet cropped with it on the plains of Upper Burma. Its cultivation has also been successfully introduced into the Shan States, where enormous stretches of good land could be made to produce wheat if any favourable market existed for its sale.

For the cultivation of the lands on the plains oxen and buffaloes are used, the former for ploughing the higher lands with light soils, and the latter for the heavy wet tracts and marshy lands. Throughout the greater portion of Upper Burma bulls and bullocks form the bulk of the plough-cattle ; but in all the central and deltaic tracts of Pegu, Martaban, and Tenasserim buffaloes, which here obtain splendid development, form a very large proportion of the agricultural stock. Massive, unwieldy, and slow, buffaloes are less suited than oxen for cartage purposes along roads, but they can be used on fairly level ground for dragging timber and supplementing the work of elephants, as well as for ploughing the fields. A pair of ordinary buffaloes in their prime is worth between 150 and 200 rupees ($£10$ to $£13\frac{1}{3}$) on the average. Fine, heavy, well-grown animals, however, run up to three to four hundred rupees ($£20$ to $£26\frac{2}{3}$), which is a far higher price than is ever paid for a yoke of bulls or bullocks, except for cart-racing purposes.

Of the whole mature agricultural stock of Burma, aggregating, in 1900, nearly three million oxen and buffaloes fit for the plough, about one-fourth consists of buffaloes, and considerably over two-thirds of the total number of these are to be found in Lower Burma. As the returns of the Agricultural Department show about nine hundred thousand ploughs and harrows to be in use, this gives one such implement for every $11\frac{2}{3}$ acres, and one yoke of cattle for every seven to eight acres, allowing for a small proportion of the transport required for the four hundred thousand carts in the country being withdrawn altogether from agricultural employment. The young immature stock is estimated at nearly a million and a quarter. With the exception of the cattle in the Akyab district, which are of a very inferior breed, and, being specially ill-cared for, contrast badly with those in other parts of Burma, the agricultural stock is decidedly good in quality.[1] The buffaloes, which, like the elephant, form

[1] AGRICULTURAL STOCK RETURNS.

1899–1900.	Bulls and Bullocks.	Cows.	Bull Buffaloes.	Cow Buffaloes.	Young Stock.	Ploughs and Harrows.	Carts.
Lower Burma .	576,127	317,358	276,620	231,588	594,034	478,388	199,181
Upper Burma .	687,823	697,439	109,953	98,581	638,724	415,630	239,101
Total . . .	1,263,950	1,014,797	386,573	330,169	1,232,758	894,018	438,282
Grand Total	2,278,747		716,742		1,232,758	894,018	438,282

BURMA UNDER BRITISH RULE

rather a link with the pleistocene geological age than a characteristic type of the existing fauna, are constitutionally much more delicate than might be expected in the case of such powerful and finely developed animals. They have comparatively little faculty of resisting disease and can hardly be reckoned on for use throughout more than from three to four or five seasons on the average owing to the abnormally heavy percentage of mortality from epidemic diseases. Otherwise, a buffalo may be calculated to work for about fifteen years. This delicacy of constitution is also peculiarly characteristic of the larger and more powerful elephant.

Burmese buffaloes are by no means of a gentle disposition. In the deltoid tracts, where they attain their finest development, they are often suspicious and prone to attack the European even though unprovoked. This may probably be more due to fear than to natural savageness of disposition. The appearance of any unusual object, like a European riding on a pony across the fields in which they are grazing, will excite them, causing them to raise their nostrils, sniffing suspiciously, and to move towards the object of fear or dislike, gradually quickening their pace as they approach. When once buffaloes begin to scent in this manner there is no way of obviating the impending attack except by either riding away quickly or else charging the still hesitating herd and emitting a war-whoop, a manœuvre that is usually successful. As a Burmese pony is fleeter of foot than a buffalo, one can in such cases easily escape with only the risk of a false step on the broken ground bringing the rider within reach of further inconvenience. Any little Burmese urchin near the buffaloes would, however, be easily able to restrain the animals from an attack, as they would then retain equanimity in the presence of the unknown object. At the same time they have a certain strain of innate savageness, which is even cultivated in Tavoy and the other southern districts of Tenasserim in training the animals for buffalo fights.

The oxen, though small, are hardy and active. They belong to the *Zebu* or humped class, having a large, soft, fleshy protuberance above the tips of the shoulder-blades.

TREATMENT OF CATTLE

They are well-shaped, and have good clean limbs. When anything like well cared for, their short coats are sleek and glossy. In the Amherst and Thatôn districts of Tenasserim selected pairs are trained to race in light carts, and can travel very rapidly over the rough roads. Few or no attempts are made to improve the breed by the selection of good sires, the breeding taking place promiscuously, as also in the case of buffaloes, while the cattle are pastured on the grazing grounds. The stock of oxen is largely recruited from the Southern Shan States and Siam, where the upland pastures are well suited for cattle-breeding. But the plains of Burma are very favourably adapted to the raising of cattle, if the people would only bestow attention on the matter. The supply of ponies is also mainly obtained from the Shan States, but elephants are bred in a state of semi-captivity in the eastern tracts of Tenasserim bordering on the Siam frontier.

Notwithstanding their utility in general, their actual necessity for agricultural operations, and the fact of buffaloes and oxen being perhaps the fairest standard by which their owner's prosperity can be measured, the Burmese peasant bestows but little care on his cattle. The hire of a yoke of buffaloes for the season is usually at the rate of 100 to 110 baskets of paddy, though it is sometimes as much as 200 baskets, or nearly ten baskets an acre for the area they can plough; and this is not very far short of the market value of an ordinary pair. But the hire is paid in grain on the threshing floor, and an actual purchase means ready money early in the year. All risks considered, the cultivator often prefers to hire the cattle rather than borrow money to purchase them outright.

From August till January, or between the ploughing and the threshing seasons, the cattle are driven out into the grazing grounds, generally at some distance from the village. Here they are nominally herded by a villager, who gets paid five baskets of paddy for each animal. After the crops have been cut in December, the herds are allowed to stray over the fields foraging for themselves. When the wisps of soft rice straw and the herbage on the fields get dried up and burned off during the hot spring months, the cattle have often difficulty in picking up a sufficiency of food, unless there is scrub jungle in the vicinity of the village, or unless grazing grounds have been set apart for providing shade, shelter, and forage during the hottest months of the year. Such grazing grounds have been extensively formed during the last fifteen to seventeen years, and the work of selection and demarcation is still going on. Originally it was endeavoured to provide for grazing in the fuel reserves, administered by the Forest Department, in the vicinity of the railway lines; but such provision was found to be quite inadequate, and to be opposed in several ways to the interests of the peasantry. The grazing grounds now being formed for the benefit of villages in their vicinity are scattered as equally as possible over the different districts, and are under the direct control of the Deputy Commissioner. Unfortunately, in many of the richest parts of the province steps were not taken in this direction till most of the tree-forest, which formed the original covering of the soil, had been denuded. Hence, with regard to some of the grazing grounds, it will take many years before a new growth of trees will spring up spontaneously—for planting would be too expensive—and be capable of affording suitable shade and shelter during the hottest period of the year. When the "mango showers" in March, and the first rains in April and May cause a rank flush of coarse, unnutritious grasses, the poor hungry animals are allowed to gorge themselves with the succulent, toothsome food. The most the cultivator does in the dry season is to fire his fields and the surrounding jungle of *Kaing* or elephant grass, so as to bring out an early growth of young grass during April.

This want of shade and shelter, combined with insufficiency of food and of water from February till May, is the main cause of the grievously heavy mortality among cattle in Burma. The death rate is indeed quite abnormally high. In Lower Burma alone the mortality was 69,424 during 1894–95, estimated at 22½ lacs of rupees in value (£150,000), and in the following year it was recorded as 116,794 : but this apparent enormous increase was stated to be partially due to improvements in the system of registering deaths of cattle, and not solely to the virulence of infectious diseases.

The chief forms of cattle disease are dysentery, anthrax, rinderpest, and foot-and-mouth disease; while in the Akyab district in particular sheer debility, caused by absolute neglect of the poor animals, contributes very largely to the annual bill of mortality. During 1895–96 and 1896–97 the loss of cattle in Akyab district alone amounted to over 60,000. When once anthrax effects a foothold in any locality, it is exceedingly difficult to prevent the recurrence of the disease during the following years, as the bacillus infects the grasses to the height of about two feet around the spots where carcases have rotted. To secure anything like immunity from infection it would therefore be necessary to cut fodder for cattle at the height of more than two feet above the ground : and it would indicate total misconception of the Burmese character to think of such trouble being habitually taken. Even elephants engaged in timber operations frequently succumb very rapidly to anthrax if they happen to graze near such infected spots.

The Burmese have of course their own fantastic notions as to the causes of disease. Thus they say that cattle turn seriously ill when they happen to eat a soothsayer insect or praying mantis along with their food, and that ponies die if, while grazing, they happen to nibble grass upon which frogs' spawn has been deposited. The most common treatment given to cattle and ponies, when in bad condition from over-exposure, is to inject into the eye a mixture of betel-leaf, cloves, tobacco, and salt, which is specifically known as " eye-medicine."

To try and curtail this big annual bill of cattle mortality, which weighs heavily on agricultural prosperity and on the more rapid extension of permanent cultivation, Government in 1896 framed rules for the prevention of cattle disease, and enforced them for several districts in both Lower and Upper Burma. A Veterinary Department has been at work on a small scale since 1876, and sixty-four trained assistants were employed throughout the province during 1900. But a more hopeful sign regarding the practical utility of the department than can be represented by mere statistics is the fact that villagers are now beginning to apply for the services of veterinary assistants whenever cattle disease breaks out epidemically. The benefits which this small department can bring to the people would be hard to over estimate, since cattle murrain may cause the entire savings of the more thrifty to disappear in the course of a single season.

The abnormally heavy mortality among stock would no doubt be very considerably lessened if the people could be induced to take more care of their cattle. Allowed to forage for themselves during the scorching months of the dry season, and so poorly nourished that their strength becomes reduced before the coarse fresh grasses spring up on the advent of the early rains, the cattle blown out with large quantities of new grass during May, and out of condition in every respect, are put to the plough in June and worked heavily for several hours a day. When not yoked to the plough they are turned out to graze, without shelter being afforded from the rain or dry ground being assured to them for lying upon. Immersed knee-deep and often more in mud and water, they soon fall into a condition little capable of resisting diseases of a febrile or dysenteric nature. Large numbers of oxen die off from these causes, but the buffaloes are less liable to be affected by exposure to damp and immersion in water.

Many portions of the Pegu and Hanthawaddy districts are almost treeless tracts of which the parts not actually under cultivation are overgrown by coarse elephant grass (*Kaing: Saccharum spontaneum*), twelve to fifteen feet in height, and with a stem about an inch and a quarter across, which dries and hardens in the hot season. These tracts become arid except where watercourses traversing them here and there still retain some water in their channels, while during the rainy season the whole of the plains are covered with water to such an extent that in July and August one can proceed in a bee-line across country in boats. Vast stretches of country are then often inundated for weeks at a time. Men and boys fish with rod and line in the ditches on each side of the Public

CATTLE IN RAINY SEASON

Works roads, and large boats of forty or fifty tons capacity are poled along their ditches in places where during the hot weather no water is ever seen except what is drawn up from deep wells for domestic purposes.

At midsummer the villages on the plains are inundated unless they happen to be built on rising ground, and progress from house to house is by means of canoes. This is one of the main reasons why houses in Burma are always built on piles, like the ancient lake-dwellings of Switzerland. Here one frequently finds the buffaloes and oxen tied on small mounds raised above the level of the water, usually without any protection from the wind or rain. In the centre of the mound there may be a smouldering fire of damp wood, whose smoke helps to keep off the swarms of mosquitoes, but that is about all the protection afforded to them. In the Pantanaw and Yandôn townships of the Thôngwa district, notorious for their plague of mosquitoes, the buffaloes are habitually placed at night in open sheds and protected by the smoke of fires, while the oxen are kept in closed sheds walled in with bamboo mats plastered with mud, within which fires are kept smouldering. The more careful cattle-owners even place their bullocks and cows under large bamboo frames covered with muslin to protect them from the fretful irritation caused by the myriads of mosquitoes. In parts of Thôngwa liable to be flooded during July and August the cattle have, when the river is highest, to take refuge on ant-heaps, hummocks, and knolls in order to get above the floods. In places where standing ground of this sort is not available, they have sometimes to remain for days together in the water.

Things are better now at Maúbin, the headquarters of the Thôngwa district, since the island was embanked; but twenty years ago it was, on account of the insect plague, the most horrible of places to have to reside in even temporarily. The Deputy Commissioner and the Superintendent of Police were the only two European officers then stationed there. To escape from the awful torments of mosquitoes, the former dined before sundown in a framework of muslin mosquito-netting, and remained inside this room within a room till it was time

BURMA UNDER BRITISH RULE

to go to bed, there again to be protected in similar manner, as is usual all over Lower Burma ; while the latter, living in a wooden house built on piles like the ordinary Burmese dwelling, had a fire of green wood lighted below his dining-room, the smoke from which came up through wide chinks between the floor planks and, filling the room, drove off large numbers of the mosquitoes that buzzed around. The Deputy Commissioner's pony had even to be protected by a framework of mosquito-netting to enable it to obtain sleep. These are no mere myths, but actual facts within my personal knowledge.[1] Maúbin, so called from a tree (*Sarcocephalus Cadamba*) was selected in 1874 as the chief station of a new district by Mr. (afterwards Sir Ashley) Eden : and it soon gained an unenviable reputation as "the Garden of Eden."

Further north, in the Prome and Thayetmyo districts, and throughout the dry zone forming the central portion of Upper Burma beyond that, the climate is drier. There

---

[1] This perhaps seems like making a mountain of a mole-hill, or, at any rate, a great fuss about a mere flea-bite. But all of the European officers first stationed at Maúbin became eccentric, and some even completely unhinged in mind. Here, too, is the much earlier description given by Major Symes in his *Embassy to Ava*, 1800, pp. 452, 453—

"We had now reached the place where in going up we had been so severely teized by mosquitos, and again felt their venomous influence ; they even assailed us in the daytime, and in such numbers that we were obliged to fortify our legs with boots, and put on thick gloves, whilst by continually flapping with an handkerchief we endeavoured to defend our faces. But no sooner had darkness commenced, than these troublesome insects redoubled their attacks in such multitudes, of such a size, and so poisonous, that I am persuaded if an European with a delicate skin were to be exposed uncovered to their ravages for one night, it would nearly prove fatal ; even the Birman boatmen, whose skins are not easily penetrated, cannot repose within their action ; and my Bengal servants actually cried out in torment. I lay in boots with my clothes on, and a double napkin over my face, and even thus could procure no rest."

Some twenty years ago an artillery officer told me that when, under his charge, a draft on the way up to Thayetymo first halted for the night in the delta, the torment of mosquitoes was so bad that one of the men jumped overboard in frenzy and was drowned. On the following night, higher up the river, fireflies flitted about when it became dark, and the wit of the draft exclaimed : "Be jabers, here's the bloodthirsty villains following us with their lanterns now." Only a strong word will adequately express the torture which myriads of mosquitoes can cause : and that particular word must vary in each several case according to the personal equation of the individual as to forcible language.

the oxen thrive well, and are much healthier. It is too dry indeed for buffaloes, which are only to be found in the villages along the banks of the main rivers and their tributaries.

These climatic variations from constant annual rainfall exceeding 200 inches near the coast to a precarious tithe of that in the centre of the dry zone, the nature and extent of which have already been elsewhere referred to (chap. ix. p. 243), of course necessitate great differences both as to the modes of agriculture and the crops raised. As all the methods of cultivation are, however, simple enough to be classed as rather primitive, and as the implements used are much the same all over the country, there is no great variety in agricultural operations. The permanent cultivation is everywhere known as fields (*Lè*), in contradistinction to the shifting cultivation, (*Ya*, or on hills *Taungya*) practised for one to three years on land cleared for the purpose and then abandoned and allowed to revert to jungle. Another class of temporary but more or less recurring cultivation (*Kaing*), principally of tobacco, tomatoes, chillies, and other garden produce, is that taking place on the rich and fertile banks of mud deposited along the inner bends of streams, which are planted up when the waters subside after the rainy season. But all garden produce of these and other varieties, and orchards of fruit trees grown on permanent holdings on the high ground are included within a specific term (*Uyin*) applied to all lands enclosed with bamboo fencing for such purposes. There are no hedges separating field from field, but merely small ridges of earth (*Kazinyo*) to retain water for cultivation.

Throughout the whole of the moister parts of the province the agricultural season is the wet period of the south-west monsoon, which sets in towards the middle of May, and usually extends till November ; and the bulk of the crops consist of rice. In some parts of Lower Burma a hot-season crop (*Mayin*) is also grown with the assistance of irrigation during the spring months ; but this is not nearly so widespread a custom as in those districts of Upper Burma which have only a comparatively light or precarious rainfall.

In the moist localities comprising the rice-producing tracts *par excellence*, the fields are ploughed in June or early in July, as soon as the thirsty, sun-baked, and deeply fissured soil has become so saturated and soaked with rain that a layer of water covers the surface of the field. In many localities, however, it is sometimes delayed from one cause or another until early in August, so that the ploughing may be taken to extend over about two months. The ridges (*Kazínyo*) round each field are carefully repaired to prevent the off-flow of this surface-water, which is essential to the healthy development of the rice-plants.

The first ceremony of all is to consult the village sooth-sayer (*Bédin Sayá*) and ascertain from him the most auspicious day for the commencement of ploughing operations. For each individual every month has two very unlucky days on which it is dangerous for him to set forth on a journey or to undertake any new work. These the astrologers can divine from his horoscope, and it is inadvisable for him to break soil with the plough while these unlucky days are in the ascendant. Nor must land be ploughed upon the days when evil spirits lie beneath the earth, which can also be revealed by astrological calculations (*Pyetkadein*). To make up for these two unlucky days each month contains one gloriously auspicious "royal day" (*Yetyazá*) upon which it is most proper that the chief enterprise of the year should be entered upon. If for any reason it be inconvenient to await this day of days, then at all events the phase of the moon must be awaited in which this lucky day is in the ascendant.

Until within the last twenty or twenty-five years the implement used throughout the wet tracts near the coast for breaking up the soft rain-soaked soil was a primitive harrow (*Tundón* or "plough-log") rather than a plough. It consists of a stout round pole or transverse bar, about seven to eight feet long, usually with seven broad tough wooden teeth made of Cutch wood, or Padauk for preference, fixed in at intervals of about nine or ten inches and long enough to stir up the surface soil to about the same depth in buffalo ploughs, and about two inches shorter in bullock ploughs. The former is used on heavy

BURMESE PLOUGHS

marshy land, the latter in lighter soils and on higher ground. A tough bow was bent over the top of this from near one end to the other, so as to form an arch against which the cultivator could lean when driving the bullocks or buffaloes, thus sparing himself the fatigue of wading through the oozy mud, while adding his own comparatively light weight towards rendering the work of the harrow more effective by weighing down the teeth into the soil. The two buffaloes or oxen are loosely attached to a long thin pole fixed in the centre of the "plough-log," being united by an easy yoke stretching across this and over their necks. The guiding is done by means of a thin rope attached to a hole made in the nostrils of the cattle. There being no metal work about it, the whole harrow could easily be made by a peasant in less than a day, without any assistance. In and around the central zone of precarious rainfall, where the constant annual struggle with nature naturally led to the use of better implements in preparing the soil for the reception of seed or plants, a primitive but fairly effective form of plough (*Tè*) has long been in use for breaking up the soil before using the harrow. This has gradually been introduced into many parts of Lower Burma for turning the sod in the preliminary operations, without, however, driving out of general use the harrow with which alone the soil has been lightly and superficially worked from time immemorial. Another implement introduced from Upper Burma is a clod - breaker (*Kyandôn*), consisting of a number of straight thin iron blades revolving on a common axis, sometimes used for the preliminary breaking up of the soil. The *Tè* has a share consisting of a piece of iron raised in the middle with slightly curved edges, terminating in a point, and fixed to a shaft. The simplicity of this plough may be imagined by the fact that the iron share only costs about a rupee (1s. 4d.) locally, while those taken down to Burma are sold at about two and a half rupees (3s. 4d.). Efforts have been made by Government to introduce a light kind of metal plough (the "Kaiser" plough), but in view of the force of hereditary custom and the enormous *vis inertiae* with which the Burmese can resist innovations not resulting directly in amusement, the introduction of improved agricultural implements and of more advanced agricultural methods can only be expected to be very gradual. The *Tè* is certainly an improvement for the first and second courses of ploughing in so far as it partially inverts the soil, in place of only scraping and stirring it up slightly like the *Tundôn* or harrow.

It would be of vast economic benefit and would give a great impetus to the more rapid extension of permanent cultivation if the use of any light plough for the first breaking up of the soil could be made general, and if strong, light, simple harness could be used, such as is in common use for plough oxen throughout Upper Bavaria. This only costs about five shillings a set, and could surely be locally reproduced more cheaply in Burma; while, yoked with it, a single buffalo or bullock, exerting its strength through the steady pressure applied to the padded band passing across its forehead just below the horns, would perform work more quickly and effectively than can at present be achieved by a pair of loosely yoked cattle. Specimens of these could very easily be obtained through the British Consul in Munich, and experiments in this direction are certainly worth a trial.

An auspicious day having been fixed for the commencement of operations, the plough is drawn across the field in parallel straight lines either from east to west or from north to south, according to the advice of the astrologer. When this has been done, the plough is then turned at right angles to its former track, and the whole area again ploughed in parallel lines, thus throwing it into small squares (*Légwetcha*) like those of a chessboard. Young buffaloes are then turned into the fields and driven up and down "to stir up" the soil (*Hmwéthi*) till it becomes worked into a mass of soft mud. In the Amherst and Tavoy districts, where the wet season sets in early with heavy rainfall, it is no uncommon sight about the beginning of June to see twelve or fifteen buffaloes being thus driven in a line up and down the fields. After this the land is again ploughed twice diagonally (*Daungdan*) to the original

lines, and buffaloes are once more turned into the field
to stir up the mud. Again the plough is drawn across
the field still more slantingly (*Yásaung*), and the young
buffaloes turned in to liquefy the soil and obtain a
smooth surface of mud on the water-sodden field. If
the cultivator has no young buffaloes to stir up the mud,
ploughing is again performed at still another angle
(*Nánsaung*) before the ploughing operations are considered to be completed.

There are thus eight complete courses (*Sat*) of ploughing for each field, four being in given directions, and the
other four at right angles thereto, every operation
comprising two courses or *Sat*, having each its own
technical name. When young buffaloes are turned in to
assist in preparing the soil only six *Sat* are performed;
but otherwise the whole eight are usually carried out.
In low-lying tracts, however, it often happens that only
four *Sat* are ploughed. Sometimes even less trouble
than that is taken in very wet tracts, while on rather
drier land as many as ten or twelve courses are
adopted. Working with the customary Lower Burma
plough, the *Tundón* or harrow, two *Sat* or courses at
right angles to each other can easily be accomplished
over an acre during one forenoon's work lasting for
about five to six hours. The preparation of the soil
consequently claims a total of about four days' work per
acre of the holding cultivated; but intervals are allowed
between each two courses to kill off the weeds by
immersion. Sometimes after the fourth or the sixth
ploughing, when much water is standing on the field,
this is drained off after the weeds have been killed
and before the remaining courses of ploughing are
carried out.

Ploughing operations being completed, the seed is
sown broadcast, after being steeped for two days in water
and allowed to germinate, or else the field is planted up
with paddy transplants raised in nurseries. Broadcast
sowing between the middle of June and the middle of
July is of course cheaper than transplanting, but the
latter method gives a much larger crop. A basket of
paddy sown broadcast over the fields is said to yield

fifty to seventy baskets at the harvest, according to the soil; whereas each basket sown in nurseries gives from eighty to a hundred bundles of transplants, and each bundle will yield one basket of paddy.

Simultaneously with the ploughing a few fields are prepared as nurseries (*Pyógin*) for the paddy plants. Without any knowledge of vegetable physiology, the Burmese cultivator knows by experience that the medium class of land, neither the wettest nor the driest in his holding, is that most suitable for selecting as nurseries for raising the healthiest and most vigorous transplants. These nurseries are ploughed first, and in some very few cases are even manured with cowdung, before the seed is sown broadcast thickly over the soil. In some parts the best sheaves harvested are kept for sowing in the following season, being stored in bamboo baskets coated and closed with mud and cowdung to keep it dry. When required, it is put into a large basket and covered with straw, which is kept wet till germination begins; then it is sown broadcast. As a general rule, however, no attention whatever is given to the selection of good seed, the only precaution taken being to see that the seed grain is of one uniform kind, as there are many individual varieties of paddy which each require different periods of time for their development and ripening.

Transplanting usually takes place in July or August, by which time the whole of the ploughing operations are at an end and the young paddy plants in the nurseries have grown to about a foot or eighteen inches in height. When rainfall is late in coming in sufficient quantity, when the first planting is destroyed by inundations in August, or when agricultural operations cannot be taken in hand till after the floods subside, transplanting is continued during September, and sometimes even into October; but fields planted so near to the end of the rainy season seldom yield a good crop.

When wanted for transplanting, the young plants are pulled in wisps out of the soft wet mud and tied together in bundles (*Pyólet*) containing about 1,300 plants each, which are carried away on bamboo poles and distributed over the fields to be planted up. Here they are inserted with the right hand into the soft mud at distances of about a foot apart, two or three plants being inserted each time in the soil. Roughly speaking, it may be estimated that about 100,000 paddy plants are required for planting up each acre, and that these are put in at a foot apart (43,560 wisps per acre). As this work is continued from early morning until evening with an interval for a meal, *i.e.* about ten hours' actual work, as it takes five women nearly a whole day to plant an acre, and as the planting hire is a basket of paddy a day with the morning meal thrown in, the cost of planting an acre with hired labour costs about five baskets of paddy. Transplanting is usually done by the wife and children of the cultivator, assisted perhaps by neighbours, or else by hired hands ; for it would really be too much to expect the cultivator himself to incur the fatigue of constantly bending down to dibble in the young plants. As holdings are small, there is only a very slight proportion of the population which can be classified as regular farm labourers ; but field-workers, crop-watchers, and reapers, who are hired by the job, number close upon 700,000.

For some time after being transplanted the young paddy wilts, turning yellow and sickly in appearance. With abundance of water, however, it gradually recovers and assumes a fine, healthy, deep-green colour. When wilting appears to be due to insufficiency of water, any neighbouring ditch is dammed up and the water scooped into the field with a big shovel made of bamboo matting. Little or nothing is done in the way of weeding. Rank vegetation is often allowed to grow up with the paddy to the prejudice of the future crop. The most that is done in this direction is to hack down with a long bill the high grass that rises above the water, till the paddy sown broadcast comes up. In all such important matters as selection of seed, manuring of soil, and weeding the crop, the Burmese cultivator is exceedingly negligent and apathetic, whereas such Karen and Shan as have left the hills to settle on the plains are much more diligent cultivators, ploughing their fields carefully and taking great trouble to keep the crops clear of weeds.

BURMA UNDER BRITISH RULE

Although for long essentially hill tribes, and dependent entirely on shifting cultivation (*Taungya*), the Karen have come down in fairly large numbers to found villages and engage in permanent cultivation in the various districts abutting on the hilly ranges. The original, or at any rate very early, inhabitants of many portions of the delta, they had first to retreat before the Peguans and were completely driven into the hills by subsequent Burmese incursions. Now, however, they are distinguishable by language into the two main branches Pwo or Talaing Karen and Sgaw or Burmese Karen. Both are good cultivators. As the former select their clearings in heavy tree jungle, they obtain the most fertile land; but they are often compelled to part with it later on, owing to their unfortunate propensity for drinking and gambling. Nominally they are Buddhists, but in reality they are very superstitious, and chiefly worship spirits to whom they make offerings at different seasons of the year. The Sgaw Karen, though less fond of heavy work in clearing their holdings, are more intelligent and enterprising than the Pwo. Most of the Sgaw tribe have been converted to Christianity by American Baptist or Roman Catholic missionaries. Their villages are generally well laid out, their houses spacious and substantial, and the cultivators themselves thrifty and careful.

The Talaing Karen make offerings of fowls and liquor to the spirit of the field at the time of ploughing, and again when the paddy has been planted out. These offerings are continued for three years in the case of new land, when the spirit is supposed to be propitiated and willing to watch over the crops. When the threshing ground is being prepared, offerings of eggs are made during the first year, of fowls in the second, and of pigs in the third year, to secure the continuous goodwill of the spirit. Though only deemed essential for three years, it is considered politic to make the offerings every year; and the practice even finds much favour in the eyes of the Burmese cultivator. The festivals during which these spirit-offerings are made usually last for three days, throughout which no food can be carried out of the cultivator's house nor any guest allowed to depart therefrom.

They have also many superstitious ideas as to the shape of their fields. They object to their land touching that of any cultivator living in a different village, even though he be one of their own race ; and unploughed fallow strips are left to prevent such holdings touching each other. They likewise object to the field of a neighbour forming an acute angle with their own land. In a small field such a projecting piece is left untilled, but if the field be large a plough's breadth of land is left between the two holdings to avert the evil that might otherwise ensue. Not altogether so unreasonably, he also objects to his holding being situated between those of near relatives, such as father, uncle, brother or sister, son or daughter, and nephew or niece, an objection which is shared by the Burmese, and, even more reasonably still, applied to houses in towns with regard to the nearest degrees of relatives.

Another of their curious customs is the payment of *Ashaung* or compensation for certain acts supposed to be productive of evil consequences. If any cultivator or his cattle cross fields on which an offering to the spirits is deposited, he has to pay *Ashaung* to the owner of the field. For various other acts which would not appear objectionable to an ordinary individual, but which fall under something like the *Taboo* of the Maoris, this sort of compensation or fine has to be paid. Thus there is an *Ashaung* for happening to let a knife or bill drop in another man's house, or for descending from his house without touching the last step of the ladder. The compensation is usually only of some such trifling amount as a fowl or four annas (6*d.*), but it is paid without demur even by Christian Karen or Burmese who may profess not to believe in the evil influence of the act. The heaviest *Ashaung* is demanded when a cart happens to touch a house or a heap of paddy. Then it varies from five to thirty rupees (6*s.* 8*d.* to £2) in amount, being supposed to be equivalent to the value of the house or of the paddy. The evil influence thus roused can be dispelled if the cart-driver will allow the owner of the house to pour water over his cart ; but the man at fault is hardly ever bold enough to face the unknown possibilities which might lurk behind so mystic a ceremony, and almost invariably prefers to pay a fine.

Most Burmese cultivators, and the unconverted Sgaw Karen, have similar superstitious ideas with regard to the shape of their fields. They also believe implicitly in the evil influence of a cart colliding against the posts or other portion of a house, but they affect disbelief in most of the other kinds of *Ashaung*. Fines for careless driving were even prescribed in the Laws of Manú. If the cart struck the posts of the steps, or of the landing near the steps, the posts were merely to be replaced ; but if any of the eight chief posts of the main portions of the house were to be driven against, new posts were to be put in and three tickals of silver forfeited "to promote the flow of the pure waters of friendship." The propitiation was the same in the case of driving against the steps, because the steps are a material part of the house. " But if the owner of the house shall throw water on the cart, nothing shall be paid as forfeit." If cartmen driving at night in a walled royal city ran against a house, they were to suffer the infliction of forty stripes with a rattan in addition to punishment as above. Such was the ancient statute law of the Burmese.

After transplanting, little more is done until the grain is in ear, when the fields are watched by the cultivator or by his children, or else by hired hands, who sit on raised platforms in the fields and drive away the flocks of sparrows, green parrots, and other birds that feed on the tender crop. Occasionally one sees conventional scarecrows made of a bamboo cross covered with rags to impersonate a human being, but the most usual method is for children to fire small mud-balls, like diminutive marbles, from a pellet-bow into the flight of birds. And there is naturally a good deal of shouting in the fields at this time of the year.

A very ingenious method of scaring birds from the crop is to be seen in the *Taungya* or shifting cultivation of the Karen and other hill tribes. Surrounded by the

THE KAREN ORACLE

tree forest in which the clearing is made for the year, these patches of temporary paddy land are liable to be preyed upon to a very injurious extent by enormous swarms of green parrots. While the grain is ripening the cultivator usually resides on his clearing in a small hut raised high enough above the ground to be secure from night attacks of tigers, which infest most of the thick jungles. To scare birds effectually, and to accomplish this desirable object with the minimum of effort, but the maximum of effect and of conservation of energy, the wily Karen constructs a system of thin cane lines, like telephone wires, from his hut as a central point and radiating in all directions towards the limits of his clearance. These thin wire-like canes are loosely supported on long bamboos stuck into the ground, and a kick with the foot or a tap with a stick instantly sends them swaying and jangling for some time, and throwing off scintillating flashes of reflected sunlight from the glossy surface "smooth with nature's varnish." This simple and ingenious method is a most effective means of scaring away the parrots, which are not very timid birds.

The manner in which the Karen selects the patch of forest to be cleared is peculiar and interesting. During the month of January or early in February each cultivator prospects and fixes on what seems a suitable locality, two or three cultivators usually selecting their patches together in small areas of about three to five acres per man. Before commencing to clear the heavy tree-jungle, the traditional oracle has to be consulted to find out if the spirits of the air, the earth, and the forest approve the cultivation of the spot selected for the particular year. The oracle for this is the *Kyetyotó* or "puncture of the fowl's bone," as it consists in trying to pierce the larger end of the thigh-bone of a fowl with a small sharpened piece of bamboo. If the piece of bamboo can be inserted and driven home into the bone, the spirits approve the clearance and cultivation, but otherwise the patch selected must remain uncleared, and fresh areas sought till the approval of the spirits has been won. As the fowl is sacrificed and boiled before

323

the oracle is consulted, it practically rests with the operator to decide whether he is personally in favour of the patch selected being cleared or not. This oracle is consulted with much secrecy. Although for very many years my work in the forests lay among the Karen and was specially connected with their *Taungya* cultivation, yet I never was encouraged to ask if I might be present at a consultation: nor have I ever heard of any brother officer being witness of the ceremony. Perhaps a *Dô*, or a *Thwéthauk* who had "drunk blood"—the equivalent of the beer "Bruderschaft" of German students—might be allowed to be present without vitiating the solemn procedure.

The area selected being approved of by the spirits, the trees and bamboo jungle are felled and left for a few weeks to dry. Towards the end of March or early in April this mass of inflammable matter is fired, and the operation repeated to make the clearance as effectual as is practicable. Thus richly manured, the rice sown at the advent of the rains yields a good return.

On the Shan hills another effective form of scarecrow consists of a tailed windmill, which is set automatically by the breeze in such direction as will enable two wooden hammers to play upon a small hollow trough of wood like an inverted cattle bell. It makes a harsh, unpleasant noise, but is of course inoperative except when there is a certain amount of breeze, which, however, seldom fails on the pleasant Shan uplands.

Except as regards crop-watching, the cultivator has little or no call upon his time between the seasons of transplanting and harvesting. Those who have small holdings, or whose crops have been damaged by floods or destroyed by drought, occasionally cut fuel or bamboos for sale, or catch fish for their own consumption. Those who are more fortunate, as often as not pass the time in gambling away what remains of their last year's gains ; but the really industrious and frugal can often earn thirty to sixty rupees (£2 to £4) by cartage.

About the end of November in the earlier and drier tracks, and elsewhere in December, the harvest commences. The crop is cut with a sickle, bound in sheaves, and left for a few days to dry, before being brought to the threshing-floor on sledges or on carts. In the Talaing tracts of the delta before reaping commences an effigy of straw covered with a woman's garments and bearing a pot of cooked rice is placed in a cart and driven round the fields to propitiate the *Pônmaso Nat* or "guardian spirit of the earth." The rice is then eaten by the village children, and the effigy is placed on the grain shed.

The threshing-floor (*Kauktalin*) is generally made in the fields, or on the outskirts of the village in the case of cultivators whose lands are close by. The ground being smoothed off for a space of about twenty feet square or more, this is covered over with cow-dung and beaten to a hard surface, in the centre of which a stake is driven into the ground. The grain having been brought on sledges or carts to the threshing-floor and piled in a stack near it, the rows of sheaves are laid two or three deep, and with their heads together in circles round the central stake. Then cattle are driven round and round this to tread out the grain. Slowly the heavy buffaloes or the bullocks toil round the stake, pressing out the grain from the ear, and lazily lifting up a few straws which they chew as they perform their circuit. For the ancient law of the East, recorded by the Israelites for their own national guidance close upon thirty-five centuries ago (Deut. xxv. 4), still holds—even like this primitive method of threshing itself—by immemorial custom the position of an unwritten law among the Burmese, "Thou shalt not muzzle the ox when he treadeth out the corn."

When the weary rounds of the cattle have been continued to a sufficient extent, the grain is winnowed. The simplest process consists in one man throwing it up into the air from a large shallow tray of light bamboo mat-work, while five or six others stand around and fan away the chaff with similar trays before the grain falls to the ground. Another common method is to raise a platform of bamboos at a height of five or six feet above the ground, and to shoot the paddy into the air, the good grains falling on a sloping mat and settling in a

heap while the chaff and straw dust are wafted away by
the light breeze which usually springs up in the morning
and towards evening. In some of the more advanced
tracts of the delta the use of hand-winnowing machines
(*Hát*) of simple construction has during the last twenty
years or so been gradually spreading; for the Burmese
cultivator does not object to any useful innovation which
has the great advantage of reducing his personal labour
while bringing material benefits at the same time. Any
innovation which causes him individually more trouble
is, however, a violation of the unwritten law of " custom,"
and a thing to be avoided and opposed. The hand-
winnowing machine consists of fans fixed to a revolving
spindle, and enclosed in a light casing of wood. Poured
in at a hopper on the top the heavy grain passes down
between the revolving fans, driven swiftly by an outside
handle, and comes out clean from a bell-shaped spout at
the lower end of the machine, while the light grain and
straw are blown out of the open ends.

As soon as winnowed the paddy (*Sabá*) is ready for
sale or for storing in the granary (*Sabăgyî*). But first
of all the wages of any labourers employed in ploughing,
transplanting, or reaping have to be measured out, for
these are usually paid in kind. Debts to creditors are
also generally paid on the threshing-floor at rates per
100 baskets as previously agreed on; and only the surplus that then remains forms the cultivator's net return
for the year.

Out of this balance a sufficient quantity is laid aside
for the food of the family and of next year's agricultural
labourers, and is stored in small granaries consisting of
a large round frame-work of woven bamboo bedaubed
with a thick waterproof coating of cowdung and mud,
the whole being raised on posts about three feet above
the ground, and roofed in with thatch to protect it from
wet. As a rule cultivators do not store up their surplus grain, but sell it to the paddy-broker on the threshing-floor, and the latter makes his own arrangements for
carting it to the river or the railway. When the cultivator sells the paddy with delivery at a stream or a railway station, he can always, if he likes to take the trouble,

earn about four to six rupees (5s. 4d. to 8s.) per 100 baskets over the rate obtainable on the threshing-floor.

When the grain is being removed either for storage in the village or for transport to one of the great rice-consuming centres, the fields gradually become cut up by small temporary cart-tracks, when once the ground is dry and hard enough to permit of sledging or cartage. The small ridges or embankments formed round the edge of each field to keep in the water during the period of growth are cut through to allow the easier passage of the cart, and gradually a more defined and better worn track becomes formed as the manifold trails converge on the village. It is thus, too, that in the purely rural districts cart-tracks are formed from village to village each dry season, which soon become entirely obliterated and impassable during the following rains.

Throughout the ploughing and planting season, from June to October, the buffaloes are let loose near the fields during the day without any herdsman, and are allowed to wallow in what is called the grazing ground, even although it may be inundated with water; but they are tied up at night near the cultivator's house. As every cultivator is employed on his fields in the daytime, he is supposed to watch his own interests, and to drive away cattle that stray near his land. It is consequently not customary among cultivators to pay compensation for damage done by cattle during the daytime, as the negligence is attributable to the landowner not driving off the animals; but damage done by night is compensated, as the fault lies with the cattle-owner in having neglected to tie up his beasts securely. The buffaloes are not sent to the grazing-ground, properly so called, till the ploughing is finished; and they are left there until the reaping is over, when they are required to tread out the grain upon the threshing-floor. While at the grazing-ground, a good deal of promiscuous breeding takes place, though nothing is done systematically for its improvement by the selection of good sires. After the threshing the cattle are turned loose to graze in the fields.

In accordance with a generally recognized custom,

cultivators of holdings surrounded by other fields have a temporary right of way through the holdings of their neighbours surrounding them. Until the end of the planting season a path must be left open of a width sufficient to allow a yoke of buffaloes to pass abreast along it. As the planting season approaches its end the strip is planted up, so that no material loss is caused to its owner. Great doubts have arisen as to the validity of this custom owing to decisions of civil courts; but without some consideration being shown in such a matter it is difficult to see how the owners of interior fields could otherwise reach their holdings for cultural purposes. The want of any definite *modus operandi* in such cases is often the cause of frequent quarrels among cultivators.

During the dry season the clayey or stiff loamy soil becomes fissured with deep cracks through the sun's heat. Towards March, when the hot season is commencing, the tufts of paddy straw left standing to the height of about a foot or more are set fire to in accordance with immemorial custom, and the atmosphere becomes hazy, oppressive, and laden with tiny bits of charred straw which ascend and are carried long distances with the currents of air. A good deal of this burned rice-straw finds its way into the cracks in the soil, and this, together with the casual droppings of the cattle grazed there after the harvest, constitutes all the manuring ever given to the fields. The burning of the straw seems, however, to be customary rather with a view to speeding the plough than to enriching the soil; for, though soft and perishable, the wisps of straw do not decompose rapidly enough with the first showers of rain to prevent them catching in the teeth of the harrow and interfering with its progress when ploughing operations are commenced.

When the fields have been fired in this manner, the glare of heat reflected from them is intense, while the hot haze rising from the ground makes objects at any little distance appear as if they were quivering in the fierce tropical heat. Survey and levelling operations during March and April are consequently difficult; for the numbers on the levelling staves look as if they were dancing about in never-ending restlessness.

In low-lying lands, which form lakes during the rainy season till the water runs off at the beginning of the dry weather, the land is cultivated for a dry-weather crop (*Mayìn*). The soil is ploughed about November, and the paddy reaped during March or April. The fields have no marginal bunds, only small spaces of un-ploughed land being left to separate them.

Apart from the dry central zone of Upper Burma, where cultivation is either partially or solely dependent on water from irrigation channels, a hot-weather crop is also obtained in the tracts having only a comparatively small rainfall for Burma, by a simple temporary system of irrigation either through damming up a stream and diverting its flow, or else through the use of a self-acting water-wheel driven by a large, deep stream. These water-wheels (*Yehát, Yìt*) are only to be found in the Thayetmyo and Toungoo districts of Lower Burma, but they are not uncommon in the Katha district of Upper Burma, the former Shan State of Wuntho; while their use extends across the Shan country into Siam. They seem thus to be a Shan method of cultivation only infrequently practised in Burma. Except the Y-like posts and the axle resting on them, these water-wheels are made entirely of bamboos, lashed with cane where joints have to be tied. Unless the current of water in the stream be strong enough, the wheel has to be worked by a man. It is about twelve feet in diameter, —though this, of course, varies with the height of the bank above the water-level,—and consists of a double row of bamboos, each about three feet long, a node forming the base and the top end being open. The open mouths of this double row of bamboo buckets point up-wards towards each other at an angle of about 40°. As the wheel is moved in the direction of the flow of water, the bamboo buckets descend empty into the stream, fill themselves, and are borne upwards on the other side. In tipping over again on reaching the top, the bamboos empty themselves of their contents, the water falling into a hollow palm-stem or wooden trough which feeds the irrigation channel that leads off the water to the fields.

The total area of the land irrigated in Lower Burma is extremely small, amounting only to 5,069 acres, or less than eight square miles ; whereas in Upper Burma the area irrigated extended in 1899–1900 to 799,021 acres, or 1,248 square miles. Over two-thirds of this latter total is irrigated from private canals, tanks, wells, and other sources ; but when once the Government canals are completed and in operation, the area under irrigation will become enormously increased (*vide* chap. ix. p. 246).

Throughout the dry tracts with precarious rainfall in central Burma the methods of cultivating rice are in the main similar to those above described for the moister localities. From climatic causes, however, the varieties of rice grown are not only much more numerous,—numerous enough though they be even in Lower Burma,—but the range of different crops is also much greater. Black, red, green, white, and yellow kinds of paddy are subdivided into long, short, round, rough, or smooth varieties, according to the peculiarities of the husk or the grain ; and each has its distinctive name. Of the other crops grown, millets, peas, sessamum, and cotton are the chief.

Speaking broadly, three agricultural seasons may be distinguished in the central dry zone, but it should be borne in mind that they are all in ordinary years to a greater or less extent dependent on irrigation, while in years of abnormally light rainfall they are practically entirely dependent on such artificial water supply. The *Kaukgyi*, or "rice which takes long in growth," the south-west monsoon crop corresponding to the paddy grown throughout moist localities during the rainy season, is cultivated from June or July to December or January. The fields are then left fallow for about two months or more, before being utilized for the hot-weather crop of *Kaukti*, or "rice that soon ripens," which is harvested in June. The successful cultivation of *Kaukti* depends on an uninterrupted flow of irrigation during the months of March, April, and May, and on early monsoon rain in June. Where irrigation is not obtainable, dry crops of millet, peas, etc., are grown during the four to five months when the land is not required for the *Kaukgyi*, the chief crop of the year.

As in Lower Burma, the *Mayín* or dry-season paddy is generally grown in swamps within the line of river floods subsiding in October and leaving bare the land near the marshes. When water is not available from the swamps it has to be obtained by irrigation from tanks or dammed-up streams, or by means of a water-lift. The approved method of cultivating *Mayín* is to give water frequently, but in small quantities. The hot sun of early spring is apt to make the plants run to straw, but this tendency can be checked by cutting off the water supply and leaving the base of the plant bare for a few days.

The outturn of rice, even in the best irrigated tracts, is not so manifold as in the more fertile tracts of the Irrawaddy delta. For *Kaukgyi* the average crop yielded varies from about thirty to sixty nine-gallon baskets per acre; for *Mayín* it is from thirty to forty, and for *Kauktí* only about thirty baskets. That is to say, the hotter the season of the year and the lower the atmospheric humidity, the smaller is the outturn in grain yielded by the crop then in cultivation. And these smaller results, too, are only obtained with better agriculture than is practised in the districts blessed with never-failing copious summer rainfall. Inverted first of all with a plough (*Tè*), broken up with a clod-crusher (*Kyandôn*), worked with a harrow (*Tundôn*), diligently weeded with hoes (*Pauktu*) and spades (*Taywin*), and sometimes also manured with cowdung, burnt straw, and wood ashes, the soil is altogether poorer and less productive, even when abundant supplies of water are available, than the rich fertile alluvial deposits forming the lower portion of the Irrawaddy valley near the sea coast. There is a struggle with nature which is unknown to the careless cultivator of the richer tracts, which are not only endowed with greater productivity as to soil, but also enjoy more favourable climatic and physical conditions for the cultivation of rice. And in consequence of this struggle the agricultural methods of central Burma are better and more intensive than in the wet tracts.

Without ever having heard of nitrogen or having been told that in its descent rain carries down from the atmosphere small supplies of nitrogen, oxygen, carbonic acid, and ammonia dissolved from chlorides, sulphates, and nitrates of sodium, calcium, and ammonium—without having any technical education in agriculture, or any knowledge of agricultural chemistry—the ignorant cultivator in the dry zone of Upper Burma knows, from his own observation, that rain-water is, measure for measure, more valuable than irrigation water, and that at certain stages of the growth of the paddy-plant rainfall is particularly beneficial, namely, when the ear is first forming inside, and when it is on the point of bursting from its covering sheath. Throughout the whole country a proverb is current that " Tazaungmôn (November) rain is worth one hundred thousand ticals of pure gold." When once exposed to the air, the ear does better without rain. He has also learned from experience that the more labour he expends in tillage of the soil, the larger will be its yield. The good effects of thorough ploughing, harrowing, and weeding are more prominently conspicuous than the advantages of manuring.

Before breaking up the land it has to be irrigated with about five inches of water, and as each double course of ploughing and cross-ploughing or harrowing takes place a similar additional supply of water has to be provided. All the lower-lying and favourably situated land is planted, while broadcast sowing is adopted in the case of land that is higher and more remote from the irrigation channels, as on these lands the season of growth is shortened by the later arrival of the water supply.

When the transplants are set out in the fields, a dressing of about four or five inches of water is given to the soil, and subsequently flushes of about the same depth are given every seven to ten days as required. A clear sky, a hot sun, and a drying wind of course necessitate more frequent demands for irrigation by causing rapid evaporation of the water and stimulating transpiration in the plants. Sometimes, however, it is necessary to withhold water temporarily in order to check any tendency to run to straw, but this expedient has only to be adopted on the best classes of soil.

In *Kaukgyi* crops the ear begins to form about sixteen to nineteen weeks after planting. A fortnight later it is clear of its protecting sheath ; and three weeks after that it is ripe. The last irrigation is given while the ear is forcing itself clear of its case, about twenty-five days before harvest, and after that the field is allowed to dry up gradually as the time for reaping approaches.

The total quantity of water required for ploughing and harrowing five times in double course, and for watering once every eight to nine days during four and a half months of growth,—flushes of water being each time given to the depth of five inches,—amounts to between 100 and 105 inches.

For the *Kaukti* or hot-weather crop nurseries are planted near the main irrigation channels or large tanks. These are at their lowest water-level during February and March, and remain low till they are filled up again from the second half of April onwards by the early rains falling on the hills forming the water catchment area. Transplanting takes place during March, or broadcast sowing a little earlier. The great solar heat, the hot winds, and the low relative humidity of the intensely dry atmosphere during the fiercely hot months of April, May, and June, cause the *Kaukti* paddy crop to make large demands on the water supply. On the average an inch of water is required daily during the seventy days which elapse between transplanting and the final disuse of irrigation water ; and during the three to four months it occupies the soil, the total demand for water made by the crop amounts to about ninety inches.

Taking the average rainfall in the precarious tracts as being twenty inches a year, distributed in about the ratio of twelve inches during the *Kaukgyi* and eight during the *Kaukti* season, those crops would appear to require about 114 and 98 inches of water, or an annual

total of 212 inches for the land cultivated. About one-
third of this being irrigation water supplied from
December to the middle of May, there remain about 140
inches of combined rainfall and irrigation water necessary for paddy cultivation during the south-west monsoon
period, lasting from about the middle of May till the end
of November. If the rainfall be deficient, the success
of cultivation must mainly depend upon such shortage
of water being met by supplies from irrigation canals.
Allowing for the rapid evaporation caused by hot dry
winds, and for the enhanced transpiration of the paddy
plants induced by isolation, these 140 inches of water
just about represent the equivalent of the 90 to 120
inches of rainfall which the south-west monsoon bestows
gratuitously upon the fields in many of the most productive portions of Lower Burma.

As in other parts of the country, various tracts have
their own superstitions and ceremonies with regard to
cultivation. Formerly the Kings of Burma performed,
along with the Princes and Ministers, a ploughing ceremony (*Lètun Mingala*) in the month of Wasó, or
" beginning of Lent " (about June or July) in each year,
as is still done by the Minister of Agriculture in Siam,
and also in China. But the practice fell into abeyance
during King Mindôn's time, and was entirely discontinued after his death, for King Thibaw never had
courage to leave his palace for any such ceremonies.
The royal ploughing took place in a portion of the
Lèdawyá, or "royal fields," a little to the east of the city.
Its object was to secure a favourable rainy season for the
rice-crops.

Around Mandalay, where transplanting from the
nurseries into the fields is often delayed till late in
August, owing to scarcity of rainfall and uncertainty as
to irrigation being secure from the large neighbouring
tanks or lakes, planting operations take place to the
accompaniment of clarinet, gong, and cymbals. The
cultivators can, or will, give no other explanation of this
except merely to assert that it assists in making the
subsequent harvest abundant; but the idea of pro-
pitiating or scaring away evil spirits seems very distinctly

indicated in the din and clamour thus raised. Frequently, too, in accompaniment to this rude music, a woman sways to and fro in an excited, semi-frenzied state, being apparently worked up into this condition for the purpose of providing an asylum for the evil spirits, as once of yore in the case of the herd of swine. In other parts, the women adorn themselves with flowers and sing whilst planting the fields, and rough practical jokes are played upon any stray members of the male sex who may chance to come near them while thus employed.

A peculiar system, known as *Kow Chow* cultivation, is practised by the Kachins on the alluvial lands in the Mosit valley (Bhamo district) during every year following one in which the harvest has been bad. The tall elephant grass being cleared and fired, the roots are also cut out and burned, and the soil is roughly gone over with a small iron pick attached to a bamboo handle. With the pick in his right hand, and grain in his left, the cultivator stoops down and makes a series of rapid strokes in front of and to each side of him, the seed-grain being dropped into each hole as it is made. Advancing with short quick paces, he kicks up his legs at each step, much in the manner of a hen scratching in search of food, and keeps shrieking and yelling all the while. The outturn from this method of cultivation is only about twenty to twenty-five baskets of paddy per acre, as compared with thirty to thirty-five commonly yielded there by the ordinary *Taungya* cultivation ; but the harvest is reaped within four months under *Kow Chow*, whereas five months are requisite before *Taungya* grain is ripe for cutting.

On the whole, paddy-crops enjoy comparative immunity from fungous diseases and insect enemies, though the latter sometimes cause considerable damage, particularly during the month preceding harvest, in seasons during which the growth of the crops is less vigorous than usual. Some of these insects, attacking either the root, the stalk, or the leaves of plants standing in deep water, can be got rid of by cutting through the marginal bunds and letting the water run off temporarily ; while others, later on, gnaw through the stalk or attack the ear and the grain. Small land-crabs also at times do a great deal of damage in the dry zone by nipping the paddy-stalks, as well as by burrowing through the small mounds dividing the fields and thus letting the water out. The great ally of the cultivator against the enemy is the crow, which hunts the crab and pecks a hole in his back. In some of the districts fringing the sea-coast myriads of other small crabs come up out of the sea, and spread over the land, destroying the seed-grain while it is germinating or the young plants which have sprouted from it. They infest the fields during June and July, before returning to the sea in August. The cultivators affect to believe that paddy sown in fields infested by these crabs will not germinate; but in any case it is necessary to get rid of them by running or, if necessary, baling off the water from the fields and carefully repairing the marginal bunds. Wild elephants, wild pigs, and deer often do much damage in tracts abutting on forest jungle. Large herds of elephants sometimes devastate the cultivation and terrorize the villagers to such an extent that rewards have to be offered by Government for their slaughter, even though there is an Elephant Act in force in Lower Burma for the special protection of these animals, so useful for timber-dragging and commissiariat transport purposes.

The usual size of agricultural holdings varies considerably in different parts of the country and even in the different parts of the several districts forming each civil division. Thus the Revenue Settlement operations show that in some localities the average size of the holding does not exceed ten to fifteen acres, while in other places it varies from fifteen to twenty, and in others again from twenty to twenty-six acres. In that portion of the Tharrawaddy district which was settled during 1882-83 the average holding was found to be as low as $6\frac{1}{2}$ acres: but this is about the most thickly populated part of rural Burma, and the people do not look to agriculture alone as a means of livelihood. Taking the statistics for the whole province, the average holding would be about sixteen acres.

BURMESE CHILDREN

Throughout most of the villages in the rural tracts men, women, and children all take part in the agricultural occupations, although in riverine villages whole families often support themselves from the retail sale of petty commodities and eatables.

The average number of the cultivating family is five souls, consisting of the cultivator, his wife, and three children. To be barren is a reproach, and the laws of Manú lay down that a childless wife should be divorced. Only less despised is a woman who bears no more than one child. A woman who has two children enjoys a fair measure of respect, but it is not until she bears her third child that the Burmese matron is considered to be both praiseworthy as a wife and crowned with honour as a woman. As the birth customs are rather barbarous, this probably explains the fact that more than three children are seldom to be found in Burmese families. More are born, but owing to want of care and to bad food the mortality among children is high.

Up to the age of six or seven years the every-day attire worn by small children consists only of a pair of silver anklets worth a few rupees or a silver amulet of nominal value hung round the neck by a piece of dirty string, but more commonly they are allowed to run absolutely stark naked. On ceremonial days, holidays, and festivals, however, they are gaily clad in tiny garments like those worn by their parents. Thus attired, they for the time lose their natural gaiety, and look like preternaturally solemn little caricatures of grown-up people. During the rainy season the children play about in the rain and the water to such an extent that it seems marvellous how any of them escape death from fever or dysentery. Perhaps it is owing to such Spartan treatment that the Burmese are, on the whole, a remarkably sound and healthy race ; for the weaklings must either get killed off or else become strengthened in constitution. For the next six or seven years, up to about twelve years of age or so, the village children usually wear the cast-off clothes of their parents, cut down to suit them ; but as the whole costume only consists of a waist-cloth, a cotton jacket, and a handkerchief turban, the question of every-day clothing is extremely simple. After performing his religious duty as a *Maung Shin* or novice at the village monastery, the young lad comes back to worldly life as one fitted to enter in due course upon the duties of manhood. Young men usually marry about the age of sixteen to eighteen, and then either go to reside for a time with their parents-in-law, or else found a new household and begin cultivation on their own account. The girls generally marry about the age of fourteen or sixteen.

Formerly the custom universally adhered to was that the son-in-law should get broken in to the yoke of married life by residing for two or three years under the roof-tree of his father-in-law, working for him till the time arrived when, sanctioned by usage, he and his wife could build a house for themselves and the firstfruits of their marriage, and set up on their own account. The little expense which setting up house and beginning cultivation necessitated was easily covered by the share of the out-turn from the fields which was earned by the young man for the assistance given to his father-in-law. A gift of cattle, money, or land was also commonly made by the parents-in-law. Like many other old national customs, this ancient usage is now rapidly falling into desuetude, especially in the more civilized localities near the sea-board and the trading centres, where young couples are now apt to show a preference for assuming at once the responsibilities of a separate household and an independent existence. There is thus, as a rule, now only one male adult cultivator in each household; and this explains the fact that the extensive employment of hired labour is necessitated wherever the holding exceeds about twelve to fifteen acres, this being the average area which the ordinary family is able to cultivate without assistance.

The preparation of the soil with plough and harrow being completed by the agriculturist, his wife and children assist in the cultivation of the holding by taking the young paddy plants from the nursery and transplanting them in the fields in midsummer and by reaping and winnowing the grain five or six months later.

In the towns the standard of living has risen, as might

MODE OF LIVING

naturally be expected, and it is still rising; but in the interior of the country the mode of living remains unchanged as yet in its extreme frugality so far as food is concerned. This consists simply of boiled rice, with salted, fresh, or dried fish, salt, sessamum-oil, chillies, onions, turmeric, boiled vegetables, and occasionally meat of some sort from elephant flesh down to smaller animals and fowls, by way of condiment. Even the secundines, or after-birth of cattle, are often eaten, and this is sometimes referred to in disputes as proof of the ownership of the animal. The staple article of diet is boiled rice (*Tamín*), while all the rest of the meal is classed as curry or condiment (*Hin*), and "to eat rice" is the only expression used with regard to a meal. The rice is produced on a man's own land, the vegetables are grown around his house or are simply wild herbs gathered in the jungle, and the fish are often caught by himself or his children; so salt, salted fish, and curry stuff are all he needs to buy. His every-day clothes and those of his family are made of coarse cotton, and are generally woven by his wife or daughters. The only articles of apparel bought in the bazaar are, as a rule, the silk waist-cloth and the gaudy silk kerchief worn as a turban on high days and holidays. His house is built with posts and beams of common jungle-wood or bamboo, with plank or bamboo flooring and walls, and a thatch-grass roof. In most cases the cultivator builds it himself, and he generally cuts the grass (*Thekké*; *Imperatum cylindricum*) and prepares the thatch and other materials for its repair from year to year. Except his cart and his strong, steel-faced, iron *Dá* or bill, without which the rural Burmese seldom goes abroad, his agricultural implements are simple and of little value, and are generally both made and kept in repair by himself.

The Burmese agriculturist usually has two meals a day, the first about nine o'clock in the morning, and the other between three and four o'clock in the afternoon. At these times all the members of the household eat together, squatting on the floor around the large flat lacquered tray (*Byát*) whereon the potful of freshly boiled, well steamed rice has been poured and the dishes of curry and condiments stand, from which they help themselves with their fingers. Rice is rarely eaten cold except when some member of the household is late in coming to the meal, or when travelling. For the use of those making a journey "rice-sticks" (*Tamìndôk*) are prepared by filling a piece of bamboo tightly with a specially glutinous and nutritious kind of rice, and then roasting it. When required for use, the woody-fibrous covering of bamboo is torn away to the length required, while the thin inner cuticle adheres to the cooked rice and gives the "rice-stick" the appearance of a thick white sausage. Milk is not used as an article of diet. This may perhaps in some measure account for the general excellence of the cattle under somewhat hard circumstances as to fodder during the hot months of the year.

The clean rice is obtained from the paddy by husking with pestle and mortar made of hard wood and worked either by hand or foot. This task is invariably performed by the women of the household. The white rice thus prepared is preferred to that husked by machinery in the steam rice-mills of the European firms; and in many villages the women carry on a large retail trade in white rice prepared in excess of their own household requirements. The amount of rice consumed is estimated at one nine-gallon basket a month for each male adult, one half basket for each woman, and one quarter basket for each child. As two baskets of paddy yield, when husked, one basket of rice, the average family consisting of five souls would, during the course of the year require from fifty-four to about seventy baskets of paddy according to the age of the children.

The average actual cost of living to the agriculturist varies, of course, very considerably in different parts of the province. Concerning this, one might say that it varies in the inverse ratio of the distance of any given locality from any of the great trading centres, and that it probably amounts to 90 or 100 rupees ($£6$ to $£6\frac{2}{3}$) a year in the poorer rural tracts, and 125 to 150 rupees ($£8\frac{1}{3}$ to $£10$) in the richer districts, exclusive of the land-revenue demand. The average value of the paddy required for rice will be about forty to fifty rupees ($£2\frac{2}{3}$

to £3⅓) locally, though higher near the large towns; salt and salted fish, curry stuffs, and oil, and tobacco and betel will cost from twenty to thirty rupees (£1⅓ to £2). Clothing will usually range from about fifteen to fifty rupees (£1 to £3⅓); while the capitation tax of five rupees (6s. 8d.) for each married adult male, religious offerings, and contingencies may be put down at about fifteen to twenty rupees (£1 to £1⅓). To provide for such subsistence, and for the payment of land revenue, the requisite minimum holding is one that will yield about three hundred baskets of paddy; and, allowing for fallow, this will usually be an area of about nine or ten acres of land of average quality. For a twenty-acre holding the cost of living would probably be at the rate of a little over six rupees (8s.) per acre, or about 130 rupees (£8⅔) in all. Where the holding is less than about ten acres, as in some parts of the Tharrawaddy and the Prome districts, other means of livelihood, such as cartage, fuel-cutting, or petty trade, must be adopted to make both ends meet and to maintain the cultivator in a solvent and secure condition.

On such a ten-acre holding the actual cost of cultivation would be about five rupees (6s. 8d.) an acre, exclusive of any monetary estimate being made as to the wage-earning capacity of the cultivator and his family. The cost of cultivation depends chiefly on the amount of hired labour which the cultivator has to employ for his assistance. Some labourers are employed for the whole period of cultivation extending over about nine months from the commencement of ploughing operations to the storing of the grain. In this case two men are usually hired, the skilled hand who ploughs the land getting about 150 baskets of paddy, and the help, who cuts the long grass, weeds the fields, and herds the cattle during the ploughing season, getting 100 baskets, in addition to his food during the time of service. For labourers employed only for the four to five months which cover all ploughing and planting operations the hire is generally about 100 baskets for a skilled man and fifty to sixty for ordinary hands. For the reaping season, to the storage of the winnowed grain, the pay is usually

fifty baskets of paddy. For daily labour the rate is a
basket of paddy and the morning meal. Where the
holdings are large and the cultivator has to hire both
cattle and labour, the cost per acre may rise considerably
above what it is where the holding is small and the
whole of the work can be done without hiring cattle,
ploughmen, planters, and reapers.

All items of necessary expenditure being taken together, the total cost of rice cultivation throughout Lower
Burma varies from about twelve to twenty rupees (16s.
to £1⅓) an acre, distributable between cost of living at
six to eight rupees (8s. to 10s. 8d.), cost of cultivation at
five to nine rupees (6s. 8d. to 12s.), and land revenue at
one to three rupees (1s. 4d. to 4s.) per acre. Whatever
outturn in paddy the land yields beyond the quantity
required, calculated at current local rates for grain to
cover such outlay, therefore represents the profit derived
from cultivation. This surplus is soon converted into
money and spent, the family expenditure easily becoming
doubled in any year when the harvest has been good.

In the dry zone of central Burma the standard of
living is lower, while the actual cost is higher owing to
the frequent scarcity of rice. It may perhaps be taken
at about 120 rupees (£8) as the bare cost of food and
clothes, even though the usual size of the family is
rather smaller than five souls. The average cost of
cultivation is also higher than in Lower Burma, varying
from about six to twelve rupees (8s. to 16s.) an acre;
while the outturn, despite the more laborious and intensive methods of agriculture, falls far short of what is
yielded by the fertile land of the delta.

On the whole, the condition of the Burmese agriculturist can fairly be considered prosperous and comfortable. Taxes and land revenue are light; markets for
the disposal of produce are constant, and prices good;
while fresh land can still in most districts be obtained on
easy terms by those wishing to increase their holdings.
These favourable conditions, combined with the careless,
happy-go-lucky, amusement-loving character of the
people, make Burma anything but a distressful country.
In comparison with any of the other provinces of the

BURMESE FRUITS

Indian Empire, with perhaps the sole exception of Assam, which resembles Burma in several important respects, the lot of the Burmese peasantry is one that may well be envied, and more especially by those crowded together in the congested districts of India. To assist them to tide over bad times loans are made to agriculturists on easy terms by Government. In this way nearly £25,000 were lent in 1897-98, nearly the half of the advances being made in the eastern portion of the dry-zone districts in order to enable cultivators to purchase seed and replace the cattle which they had lost during the time of scarcity from deficient rainfall. These advantages are fully appreciated by the people. With one or two favourable seasons there should be no difficulty in paying off such advances.

With regard to minor forms of cultivation of the land there are over four hundred thousand acres or six hundred and forty-four square miles of orchards and gardens, nearly nine-tenths of which are to be found in Lower Burma. The great bulk of these are for the cultivation of plantains, while the betel-palm or areca-nut is largely grown at the base of hills where water can easily be procured for irrigation. The cultivation of succulent fruits consists chiefly of large pine-apple groves and orchards near Rangoon, and of custard-apple (*Anona squamosa*) plantations on the hills near Prome, which, seen from the deck of a river steamer, remind one of the vineyards on the Rhine. The other chief fruits are the Guava (*Psidium guyava*), the Durian (*Durio Zibethinus*) of Tavoy, which tastes like a fine custard spoiled by an after flavour of garlic, and the Mangosteen (*Garcinia mangostana*) of Mergui. Oranges of excellent quality are grown largely on the Karen and the Shan hills, and in Mandalay fine grapes for table use are produced in the gardens under the supervision of the French and Italian missionaries. Wild apricots, peaches, and quinces grow all over the Shan hills, and fruit culture can easily be carried on there extensively whenever the Shans may see that it will be profitable.

Experimental gardens have been established by Government at Taunggyi and Maymyo on the Shan hills for the cultivation of European and selected Indian fruits, the demand for which would be large on the plains of Burma if good supplies could be sent down regularly at reasonable rates. The vegetables required by the European community are chiefly obtained from gardens cultivated near the large towns by Chinamen, but better and more varied supplies should soon become available now that the Shan hills have been brought into direct communication with Rangoon by railway.

Chapter XII

MINOR RURAL INDUSTRIES

ONE of the most characteristic sounds heard in the morning or towards evening in any Burmese village is the dull thud of the wooden pestle and mortar with which rice is cleaned for domestic consumption. The raw paddy is first of all husked by being ground in a hand-mill or quern (*Kyeiksôn*), consisting of a heavy, solid, round block of wood, cone-shaped and grooved at the top, and ending in a central pole. Fitting over the top of this is a hollowed block of wood, whose base, also grooved, fits upon the upright cone of the solid block. This upper portion is either moved to and fro horizontally by straight wooden handles at the sides of the upper movable block, or else kept turning continuously in one direction by means of an arm about seven or eight feet in length fixed to the top of it. For easy working this long arm is supported from above by a rope fixed near the end of the handle, so as always to maintain it at about the same level. The raw paddy is poured in at the top of the upper hollowed block and issues husked at the sides when it has been slightly crushed and rubbed by the play of the movable upper block upon the fixed lower one.

The roughly husked paddy is then placed in a large wooden mortar, and is beaten with a heavy pestle, also made of wood, to complete the hulling process. The pestle may be worked by hand, or the mortar may be fixed in the ground and the pestle worked by foot through the leverage obtained by treading on the short arm of a horizontal wooden bar, also fixed near the ground at its fulcrum, to the long end of which the pestle is attached, like the head of a hammer. By treading with the foot on the short end of the lever the pestle is raised by the weight of the body ; and on the latter being removed, the pestle descends again heavily into the mortar filled with grain.

For working the hand-mortar, hollowed out of a block of wood about two and a half feet high, pestles of about three feet long, narrowing in the centre to give a good hand-grip, but symmetrical above and below this for greater effectiveness, are raised up high with both hands and brought straight down with considerable force. Very frequently these hand-mortars are worked by two women, whose pestles alternately ascend and descend in rapid strokes like the piston-rods of a steam-engine.

Rice-cleaning with the foot pestle fixed in the ground below the house is a comparatively easy sort of work, with which smoking and gossip can be combined; but the use of the hand-quern means hard exercise, unlightened by frivolity. Stripped to the waist for freedom in using the arms, the rapid alternate rise and fall of the long wooden pestle means hard work for the young women. The rough-husking is sometimes, though not usually, done by men ; but the rice cleaning and pounding with the pestle is almost invariably women's work, quantities far in excess of domestic requirements being often prepared for sale. There is a large trade in half cleaned rice (*Lôndi*) and white rice (*Sán*) along all lines of communication by road or river, the hand-cleaned rice being, as an article of food, much preferred to the white rice turned out by the steam-mills at seaports.

The fact that no inconsiderable retail trade in hand-cleaned rice still maintains itself throughout the rural tracts, despite the competition of machinery and of improved communications, is mainly due to the strong trading instincts with which Burmese women are endowed. As regards petty trade of all sorts, they are keen and eager, though, of course, they have a leaning to those branches in which their natural volubility of speech is likely to give them any advantage. The men are less gifted in this respect, although even with them the trading instinct is in some ways strangely apparent. For these, however, the trading operations must, as a rule, be untrammelled by personal exertion entailing bodily fatigue. That

SIFTING FOR GOLD-DUST

"time is money" is an aphorism which would be completely devoid of sense to the Burmese mind, for all the hereditary ideas and personal notions and experiences on the subject have never trended in the direction of equating or in any way correlating these two factors. Another consideration having great weight with the male Burmese is his love of independence, and his dislike of being tied down to perform specific duties at or within given times. It is therefore by no means uncommon to find him engage in trading operations which, measured by their monetary gains, sometimes appear hardly worth the time and trouble expended upon them. For example, he will sift the sands in the beds of streams for gold-dust, even though this does not yield him half the amount he could easily earn by a comparatively light day's work as a labourer. But then he would not be his own master, and that makes all the difference to him. While engaged in these and various other operations with a like object he will often undergo much personal inconvenience and physical discomfort, provided always that it is not combined with really hard muscular exertion. To digging, in any shape or form, the Burman has a strong objection, the digging of a well being classed as one of the most laborious of tasks.

There are not, and there never have been in Burma, any guilds connected with trade. Nor is there any restriction, either legal or social, requiring given classes or individuals to pursue certain callings, trades, or professions. There is absolute free will and free trade in this respect, although heredity and custom exert strong power in the matter. In all Burmese towns there were specific streets or quarters in which handicraftsmen following, almost invariably hereditarily, one branch of trade were located; and even in the anglicized municipal towns this is still traceable in streets whose names, when translated, mean "potters' quarter," "blacksmiths' row," "carpenters' row," and the like. In similar manner there is "China Street" and a "Shan quarter," wherever traders of these nationalities carry on their avocations in or near the chief towns.

BURMA UNDER BRITISH RULE

One of the great minor industries followed throughout the whole province is weaving. This is carried on entirely by the women-folk, and forms more particularly the work of the girls of the household. Seated at the loom under the house, there is good opportunity for looking around and gossiping with any passer-by, whilst lightly throwing the shuttle across the warp by hand and plying the treadle by foot to cross the strands and fix the thread of the woof. It is an occupation of the day time, after the rice has been husked and the morning meal has been prepared and partaken of.

Under Burmese rule every household had its own loom, for nearly all articles of clothing were practically home-made, and the loom was the absolute and inalienable property of the wife. The Laws of Manú even laid down that if a woman unreasonably insisted on separating from her husband without having any just cause of complaint against him, she was still entitled to take away, as her personal effects, a skirt, shawl, jacket, and loin-scarf as clothing, together with cloth woven and rolled up on the loom, the loom itself, the shuttles, and other implements belonging to it. The loom is a very simple wooden framework, of comparatively slight monetary value. Flowers and petty offerings to the spirits are often hung on it in order to speed the shuttle.

The introduction of cheap cotton and silk fabrics has dealt a blow to hand-weaving from which it can never recover, and weaving is no longer so profitable as it once was. It still may, however, be ranked as one of the chief occupations of women in the rural tracts. Both silk and cotton cloths are, though coarser in texture, more durable when home-made ; and the mother engaged in housework knows her daughter cannot be up to much mischief while the monotonous click-clack of the loom is heard without interruption from below the house. As a means of livelihood weaving now brings in but a mere pittance, so that it is still followed far more as a means of occupying spare time than for any actual profit derivable from it.

Although silkworm breeding and cotton production form occupations among the Yabein class of the Burmese peasantry, yet raw silk and cotton yarn are largely imported for weaving. Thus, in 1898–99, the imports of raw silk amounted in value to £123,910, in addition to £268,677 worth of pure and mixed silk piece-goods, while cotton twist and yarn was imported to £298,019 in value, besides nearly £740,672 worth of cotton piece-goods, and woollen goods to the extent of £247,728 in value. And under some of these headings the imports had been larger in the previous year.

The best silk-weavers are to be found at Amárapura, near Mandalay. There large numbers of people follow this occupation as their sole means of livelihood, whereas silk and cotton weaving throughout the province generally is carried on mostly by girls and women whilst unoccupied by other domestic duties. Rich, heavy, brocade-like silks are produced by Manipuris who have settled in the Henzada district of Lower Burma. Since the downfall of the Court of Ava the trade in high-class silks has been in rather a depressed condition. Made to order, strong and very beautiful shot silks, consisting of warps of red, green, or yellow woofed with lighter tints, or with white, cost about sixteen rupees (£1 1s. 4d.) per piece measuring eight yards long and twenty-two inches broad. Silks woven in blue are not common, for they contrast badly with the dark olive Burmese complexion; while certain definite mixtures, like light green and dark green, are never made on account of being unlucky. Pink, and especially rose-pink, is the predominating colour in silk manufactures, and next to it comes yellow.

It is seldom, however, that only a single shuttle is used, as in the case of shot silks made to order for European tastes. To suit the native idea, fond of brightness and variety, the pieces woven are usually bright with patterns of gay colours forming tartan-like checks or wavy zig-zag lines of various colours and shades. Some of the *Lôn Pasó* or short wavy-lined waistcloths worn by men, though only about fifteen feet long and two cubits in breadth, cost anything up to two or three hundred rupees (£13½ to £20) according to the intricacy of the pattern and the number of shuttles (*Lôn*) used in making them. But the woman's waistcloth (*Tamein*), a single piece composed of a narrow upper part, a broader lower portion, and a border of different patterns, measuring in all about four and a half feet long by a little over five in breadth, lends itself even more effectively to elaboration of wavy-lined patterns and deft shuttlework.

The handweaving of artistic silks, as most of the many-shuttled cloths unquestionably are, is one of the first rural industries which feels the ebb and flow of agricultural prosperity. When times are hard the demand for rich and costly waistcloths for men and women at once falls while the cheaper and usually gaudier inferior import silks hold the market. A bumper harvest in Lower Burma will, however, as in 1896–97, bring back a revival of prosperity for the time being to the looms of Amárapura and give a fillip to home silk-weaving throughout the province.

But fashion in women's dress is now becoming subject to change even in so conservative a country as Burma. There has been a marked tendency of late years, especially in Lower Burma and more particularly in the vicinity of the seaport towns, towards the adoption of uniform colours such as maroon, brown, olive, and dark green for women's skirts or waistcloths, in place of the bright variegated *Lŏn Tamein* of stiff, heavy texture. Though neat and not unpleasing in effect, this change in fashion as regards the national costume for women seems only one of the many indications everywhere noticeable of the gradual decay of art-feeling which appears to be the inevitable outcome of contact with western civilization.

A curious custom obtains among the Kachin hill tribes with regard to weaving the narrow dark blue cotton cloths which constitute one of their principal articles of dress. The women sit on the ground with their legs fully extended, the threads of the warp being fixed to a piece of bamboo held in position by their toes, while the other end is passed round their waists. The body itself thus forms the loom, the shuttles being plied by the hands across the warp extended between the loins and the feet.

The decline of hand-weaving has naturally led to curtailment in the preparation and use of dye stuffs which abound throughout the province. The rural agricultural population still use barks and other simple forest products for dyeing their cotton of home growth, but to a certain extent the native vegetable dyes have been displaced by gaudy aniline dyes, the imports of chemical products and dye stuffs amounting to £30,404 in value during 1899–1900. Formerly, for the weaving of finer cloths, the raw floss-silk was bought locally, wound off, twisted into thread, boiled in soap and water, then dyed and reeled off again for use ; but now the silk yarns imported are coloured and ready for immediate use on the loom.

The principal colours used in dyeing are red, yellow, and green of different shades, orange, and pale blue, while light blue, dark blue, brown, and black are also in use among the forest tribes and the Shans. White silk is largely used both in the piece for jackets, and for variety in check and other patterns. If white thread is wanted, the thread is boiled in a lye of soap and water, or of earth containing potash, and then beaten clean on a slab of smooth wood or a flat stone. For red, the thread is dipped into boiling water in which powdered stick-lac has been thrown, or seeds of the tamarind tree, or chips of the wood of the Thitsi or black varnish tree (*Melanorrhœa usitata*). For yellow and orange, saffron (turmeric) and the wood of the Jack-tree (*Artocarpus integrifolia*) are largely used, the latter being exclusively employed for dyeing the robes of the monks or religious. A soft and very beautiful shade of reddish orange is obtained by rubbing the seeds of the Thidin or Panbin (*Bixa orellana*) between the palms of the hand in cold water and then boiling it. This shrub used to be largely grown around houses for this specific purpose. Green is obtained by boiling yarn, already dyed yellow, in a decoction of the leaves and twigs of the Mènwè creeper (*Marsdenia tinctoria*). Blues are obtained from wild indigo and similar plants, and black from decoctions of the berry of *Diospyros mollis* (Shan black), the drupes of *Terminalia chebula*, and other trees. When necessary for fixing the dyes, the chief mordants are alum, lime juice, tamarinds, and barks of trees or shrubs, including species of *Terminalia, Eugenia, Kandelia*. The printing of patterns on cotton, so common in Upper India, is almost unknown in Burma, and the cotton pieces woven are all thicker than what is known as the muslin type.

The forest wealth of Burma includes vast quantities of dye-stuffs and tanning materials, which are at present waste products of the woodlands without marketable value. Of other waste products one may perhaps be deserving of notice, as it is obtainable free of cost in considerable quantities at the sea-ports of Moulmein, Tavoy, and Mergui. This is the large, thick fibrous skin enclosing the dainty succulent seeds of the Mangosteen (*Garcinia mangostana*). Enormous quantities of these husks are thrown away as refuse during the spring of each year; and it seems at any rate worth ascertaining their commercial value for tanning by having them artificially dried and sent home for chemical analysis and for experimental tests of a practical nature.

The total number of people engaged in the manufacture and conversion of textile fabrics of any description, including clothing, silk, cotton, flax, coir, etc., amounts (according to the last census figures available) only to about 375,000, or rather less than one-twentieth of the population; and nearly three-fourths of those thus employed are of the female sex. The fact that, despite its far lower total population, about twice as many are classifiable in this category throughout Upper Burma as are to be found in Lower Burma, gives some idea of how much more rapidly as compared with the tracts far inland the people in the delta are abandoning what once ranked next to agriculture as the chief rural industry in the country, and are now supplying their requirements with the produce of the steam-power looms of Europe and Japan. From this movement, onward in a commercial sense but downward as to artistic effect and aesthetic feeling, there can be no retrogression; for the time must gradually come when the plying of this ancient handicraft will be a thing of the past, and the click of the weaver's hand-loom will only be heard in lonely hamlets amid the recesses of the jungle.

The manufacture of pottery forms another rural industry, which, though only giving employment to some forty thousand people, or less than one-half per cent. of the population, is very widely carried on. The women employed in this trade also outnumber the men following it, although not to any overwhelming extent. As might be expected from the nature of the articles manufactured, the bulk of which are thin pots or jars for holding water, cooking rice, and so forth, potters are to be found distributed over the whole of the plains of Burma, though most numerous, of course, in the more thickly populated tracts of the delta. In Upper Burma, Sagaing and Shwebo are the chief seats of the industry, while in Lower Burma, Bassein, at the western limit of the delta, has attained the highest position in this branch, and produces large numbers of terra-cotta articles which may be classified as art pottery. These latter productions may, however, more appropriately be referred to along with wood-carving, lacquered articles, brass ware, and silver work in the chapter dealing with art and art-work. The manufacture of porcelain is unknown, only earthenware being made.

The pottery manufactured for general use varies, of course, according to the specific purpose to which it is to be put. The chatties or pots for carrying water and boiling rice are only about one-sixth of an inch in thickness below, though thicker and stronger towards the grooved neck and wide open mouth. Consequently they are rather brittle, and become very much so after long usage. The clay used is carefully selected, and a little fine clean sand is added to strengthen the puddle. Similar pots for boiling brine and *Sha*-chips in the manufacture of salt and cutch are much thicker and contain a greater proportion of sand. Still larger vessels of the ordinary jar shape are made for holding crude earth-oil and similar substances while in transit, and these are usually glazed with a mixture of rice-water and galena. Some of these, known as "Pegu jars," have a capacity up to over a hundred and fifty gallons.

The puddled clay being placed on the potter's wheel, this is turned rapidly by a pedal while the pot is fashioned by hand. After being sun-dried, the pots are built up, mouth downwards, in the form of a cottage-shaped kiln covered in with bricks and mud, the kilns usually being about twenty feet or more in length by about twelve feet in breadth and ten feet high along the central line. During the process of firing large numbers of pots get cracked or broken owing to their thinness and fragility.

Fisheries and fish-curing, both along the sea-coast and in inland tracts, afford employment to over sixty thousand adult males, and yield the means of livelihood to about one hundred and seventy thousand souls, or considerably over two per cent. of the total population; while rents for fishery leases and licences for fishing bring in a revenue exceeding £150,000 a year. As salted fish forms, along with boiled rice, one of the chief articles of food among the Burmese, this rural industry continues to flourish and to yield a steadily increasing revenue even although the rapid spread of cultivation, the protection of low lands by embankments, and the drainage of water-logged swamps tend to very materially reduce the area of the tracts worked as closed fisheries (*In*). The reduction in the area of the swamps is leading to improved methods of working the fisheries; and as the price of salted fish is gradually rising with the prosperity and purchasing power of the population generally, this industry is on a very sound basis. As might of course be expected, the extent and value of the fishing industry is much greater throughout the delta and along the sea-coast of Lower Burma than in the inland tracts of Upper Burma. The chief seat of the industry is in the Thôngwa and Bassein districts, where the income from the leased fisheries on individual streams and their tributaries sometimes amounts to between six and seven thousand pounds a year.

A Fishery Act in Lower Burma and a corresponding Regulation for Upper Burma regulate the sale of fisheries and the license of nets and traps. Net fisheries, worked by license-holders in the principal rivers and along the sea-shore, are not nearly so valuable or so profitable as the closed fisheries (*In*), which are from time to time sold by auction for fixed periods of years. Fishery and fish-salting can only be carried on during the dry season of the year. For sea-fishery a funnel-shaped bamboo

FISHERIES

trap (*Damin*) secured by a rattan rope to a stake fixed in the mud, is chiefly used ; while for inland river and lake fisheries weirs (*Sé*) are formed, thin bamboo screens (*Yin*) being extended from side to side to keep back the fish while allowing the water to pass through. About September, towards the end of the rainy season, whilst the low-lying tracts of country are still swamped with water, the *Inthugyi* or lessee of an inland fishery erects a strong weir across the main stream of the fishery near its lower end in the case of a stream, or near its outlet if a lake. This weir usually consists of strong posts, firmly fixed in the mud and held in position by stout struts, to which longitudinal poles are lashed. Against this solid framework the loose screens made with narrow strips of split bamboo, woven together with stout twisted cord, are lashed tightly so as to withstand the pressure of the current. The lower portions of the screens rest on the bottom of the creek or lake, while the upper part rises about three or four feet above the water-level in order to prevent the large fish jumping over and escaping. Towards the centre of the weir a long projecting trap, with a sloping floor of split bamboo, is fixed about the water-level, and as this forms the only exit downwards from the waters above, the fish are here easily caught and taken ashore. In some cases, however, the weirs erected across the beds of streams consist of solid earthwork thrown in between retaining walls formed of stout posts and bamboo wickerwork.

These weirs and screens are kept in position till nearly all the water has drained off, leaving a number of shallow pools simply swarming with fish which can be easily taken by net or thrown out by means of shovels made of split bamboos. Large inland ponds are often divided into smaller sections by low mounds at this stage, the water being baled out if necessary for the more effective capture of the fish.

As the water gradually disappears through evaporation and percolation during the dry season the fish remaining uncaught become embedded in the mud and remain dormant there till the following rains flood the country again, while cattle are grazed on the now dry plain. It seems otherwise impossible to account for the undoubted fact that as soon as hollows, absolutely parched and dried up in the hot months from March to May, become filled with rain-water early in June they abound with fish which cannot have been brought by river-water into the swamps; because these latter are often entirely cut off from direct communication with streams till the high flood season sets in during July and August. The spawn of very large numbers of such fish must also be laid on the mud or around the roots of coarse grasses, for the first heavy showers of rain call countless myriads of tiny fishlets into active existence.

Certain of the lake fish of Burma, of somewhat perch-like general appearance, are endowed with locomotive powers by land, though probably incapable of exercising them over any distance exceeding a few hundred yards. Once, during the hot weather of 1884, whilst taking a morning ride round the Royal Lake, near Rangoon, I was astonished to see, at the extreme north-east end of the lake, a fish of about five or six inches in length crossing the road, then thick with fine pulverized dust, and making its way slowly and with exhausting efforts towards the water of the lake. Over the shoulder of the low hill which extends to the north-east at this part there is a shallow pond which becomes dried up during the hottest time of the year, and presumably this fish had instinctively made an effort to reach the big lake distant about two or three hundred yards down hill; for in this case there was probably little or no mud, as in large swampy tracts, in which any natural process of embedding could take place for a fish of that size. The locomotive process could hardly be termed walking. The fish, lying on the ground, laboured to inflate strongly its swimming bladder, and as soon as this was accomplished it moved with something of a seal-like motion, combined with jumps and jerks, for about two or three feet before the inflation of the air-bladder gave out and re-inflation became necessary for further progress. Although perch-like in general appearance, such peregrinatory fish may possibly belong to the smooth-skinned cat-fishes (*Siluroidae*), which usually have their home in muddy surroundings and are characteristically long-lived after being taken out of water.[1]

I should hardly venture to narrate this personal observation but for the fact that an exactly similar phenomenon was again noted during April, 1888, on the road which skirts the southern side of the lake to the west of Toungoo ; and as regards this latter occasion corroborative evidence to the fact can be given by those who were with me at the time—my wife, and Surgeon-Major G. B. Hickson, A.M.S., then in medical charge of the British troops at that station. Many other strange phenomena relative to wild life observed in the jungles could be given as having come under my own personal observation ; but some of them might appear so improbable that, in the absence of unquestionable corroborative evidence, the description of certain wonderful provisions of nature will remain untold.

The inland fisheries vary greatly in value, and in the manner of working them. Some are only small ponds or stream-channels, workable merely for a short time at the beginning of the dry season, whilst others are large lakes, creeks, and navigable channels, worked by complicated systems of weirs, screens, and nets. Many fisheries in the creeks of the delta, though small in area, are of specially high value from including the spots where fish collect in large numbers in burrows (*Tu*), whence they can be removed without difficulty. These burrows are supposed to be made first of all by eels ; but fish soon oust the latter from them, and then enlarge the originally small and tortuous excavations so as to suit their own peculiar requirements. Some of these burrows extend inland for a considerable distance from the bank of the streams, air-holes being opened at short intervals to the surface for supplies of fresh air. Profiting by this peculiarity of the fish, fishery lessees enlarge and

---

[1] The peregrinatory fish above referred to is not a known species of either of the genera *Antennarius* or *Halicutaea* of the family of walking fishes (*Pediculati*). These are marine genera, both of which are found on the coast of Burma ; whereas the two cases here referred to concern a land fish, which could not by any possibility be migratory from or to the sea at any time of its existence.

improve the burrows, though this sometimes leads to quarrels and litigation with the neighbouring cultivators, whose interests lie in a different direction.

Heavy rainfall during October considerably affects the remunerativeness of many of the inland fisheries. Becoming suddenly filled with water, the channels empty themselves a few days later with equal rapidity, the strong current carrying away many fish. But when the waters subside gradually and normally towards the close of the rainy season, the fish collect in shoals and seek the quiet waters as feeding and spawning grounds; and then the catches are heavy and profitable.

Agriculture and inland fisheries are in many respects antagonistic. And, of course, in the struggle that must ultimately ensue, the former is bound to maintain itself as the supreme interest; while the latter will become confined more and more to perennial lakes, tidal creeks, and the sea-coast. Earthen weirs and bamboo screens have a very injurious effect when thrown across the beds of streams. By checking the flow of the water they cause the bed of the stream to become silted up, and are thus, in low-lying tracts, often responsible for changes in the direction of the river-bed. This is more particularly the case in places like the plains lying to the west of the Sittang river (Pegu and Toungoo districts), where the silt-laden streams issuing from the hills gradually raise the level of their beds and of their banks until the latter are higher than the plains on either side of them. Anything which tends to favour rapid silting up of the bed of the stream is at the same time very likely to lead to diversion of the current and the flooding of cultivated tracts situated below where the outbreak occurs.

A survey, made about twenty-five years ago, from north to south between the Sittang river and the Pegu Yoma range of hills showed that the highest land was invariably the banks of the large streams flowing eastwards in parallel lines from the hills to join the main river; and some of these, the Yenwè in particular, were in the habit of every now and again becoming silted up, and overflowing their banks in search of a new channel. Fallen trees forming snags, dead bamboos, reedy grasses, and other jungle rubbish were usually the natural causes of such deviations, but they were also often occasioned solely through the weirs erected for fishery purposes. The closure of timber-floating streams in this manner is prohibited under the forest rules, but this prohibition alone would not be effectual to prevent the silting up of the hill-fed fresh water streams flowing through the plains if it were not actively assisted by the drifting and floating operations of the departmental timber contractors. Everything in the shape of snags or rubbish is likely to cause silting ; and silting of the bed of the stream means obstructions, which must be removed before the floating and extraction of timber can be profitably effected. It is mainly owing to the regular and extensive floating operations of the Forest Department that the streams throughout the rich Tharrawaddy district of Lower Burma are kept free from silting, and from consequently overflowing their banks from time to time and doing much damage to rice-crops and agricultural holdings.

The lower portion of the delta was formerly well wooded, the banks of the tidal creeks and rivers being lined with a deep fringe of trees which stretched back to where the forest had been broken into and cleared for agricultural occupation, temporary or permanent. As permanent cultivation began to extend, however, the tree-forest was gradually cleared away and long stretches of almost treeless fields took its place. Along the banks of the streams a fringe of trees and shrubs, chiefly mangroves, growing on muddy land, too low and too much subject to inundation to be selected for clearance, protected the banks from erosion and formed valuable spawning grounds for the migratory kinds of fish which came up from the sea for their breeding season. To arrest the rapid process of denudation and to protect this valuable fringe of jungle against fuel-cutters, agriculturists, and even the fish-curers themselves, a rule was made a few years ago prohibiting the cutting of trees within two chains of the banks of streams.

Sometimes the damming up of a stream and the poisoning of the waters so as to catch the fish more

easily form an annual festival in which the whole population of the country side takes place. Such used to be,
and probably still is, the case on the Thaukyegat river,
a very large and important tributary of the Sittang
coming from the hills to the east and joining the main
river about five or six miles below Toungoo. This
river, the name of which means " whence the drinking
water is drawn," is a broad, pellucid stream, with a
shingly bottom, flowing between beautiful hill ranges
whose covering of tree-forest is only broken here and
there by the *Taungya* or "hill cultivation" of the
Karen tribesmen.

During the month of April, when the stream, then at
its lowest level, had sunk to about three feet in depth, a
strong weir of wooden posts and bamboo screens was
thrown across it at the lower end of a fine long reach of
deep water about half a mile in length, just above the
village of Chaungmagnè, "where the main stream
narrows." In this weir, stretching from bank to bank,
numerous exits were made at the water level, each
ending in traps whence the fish could be easily lifted as
soon as caught.

Here, at the full moon of *Tagù* (about April), the last
and hottest month of the dry season, the whole of the
hill-tribesmen and the villagers from all the hamlets in
the vicinity collected and commenced a slaughter of the
fish for the purpose of supplying themselves with a stock
of dried fish to last throughout the whole of the next
twelvemonth. For three nights—the night before the
full moon, the night of the full moon, and the night after
it—the catch continued, large fish being leistered while
smaller ones and half-grown fishlets were caught in the
traps. During the daytime and the afternoon the waters
of the long reach above the weir were poisoned with
lime, pieces of a woody climber called *Hôn* (*Anamirta
cocculus*), the bark of the scandent *Suyit* (*Acacia pennata*),
and barks and roots of various kinds of trees, shrubs, and
other climbers.

After sundown hundreds of men went in canoes to the
top of the reach, and torches, made of chips of wood and
wood-oil, were lighted. Then the waters were beaten

with rods, and the half-stupefied, drugged, and terrified fish were driven down stream into the traps of the weir or speared in the torchlight by the men in the canoes. For three nights this leistering and wholesale destruction went on from about seven o'clock in the evening till far into the small hours of the morning, the lighted boats plying to and fro, and the men at the bamboo-traps in the weir busy lifting out fish measuring up to a couple of feet and more in length. Many of these were mahseer, or Indian salmon, a fish that gives first-class sport to the fly-fisher. It was a weird, beautiful sight to see the broad river, enclosed between the thickly-wooded hill-sides, bearing the vast moving mass of torchlit boats and almost nude figures, while the whole scene was flooded with the silvery light of the full moon shining in an intensely clear and cloudless sky. In the warm, relaxing air of a tropical April evening it might have seemed more like a scene in fable or fairyland than anything else, but for the ceaseless shouting and chatter of the men, and more especially of those who lifted the fish from the traps and handed them to boatmen on the lower side of the weir for transport to the shore as soon as each canoe was filled. Gutted, scraped, and salted in the daytime, the fish were soon dried by exposure to the scorching rays of the fiercely hot April sun.

The *Ngapi*, or salt fish condiment, made at the regular fisheries is extremely offensive in smell and altogether loathsome to western ideas. Immediately after being caught and brought to land the fish are either scaled by hand or have the scales roughly brushed off with a frayed bamboo, and are then thrown into a wooden trough, the larger being gutted and deprived of head and fins. After being rubbed with salt they are packed in baskets and pressed down by means of a board weighted with large stones. Next morning they are unpacked and again rubbed with salt, then spread out on thin bamboo mats to dry in the sun until the afternoon of the following day, when they are packed alternately with layers of coarse salt in large earthenware jars placed in the shade. To retard the process of liquefaction of the salt, the powdered bark of the Ôndôn tree (*Tetranthera lauri-*

folia) is mixed with it; but, during the three to five weeks this rough method of pickling is allowed to continue, the oily brine oozing to the top and evaporating, sometimes becomes so full of maggots before drying up that fresh supplies of salt have to be added. The scaleless siluroid mud-fishes are those most easily treated in this way.

Greater care is taken in the preparation of *Ngathalauk* (*Clupea palasah*), the Hilsa of Indian rivers, which are simply gutted, but not otherwise cleaned, and then salted and sun-dried before being spread between thin bamboo mats and pressed for about three days. These dried fish (*Ngachauk*), the daintiest of Burmese condiments, are both in preparation and in transport handled separately, whereas the stinkingly offensive *Ngapi* is sold in bulk, in baskets and sacks. Both varieties are cooked by roasting or frying when used to flavour the meal of boiled rice.

Along the Tavoy and Mergui coast a finer quality of fish-paste is made with shrimps and prawns, which are worked up with salt when half-dried in the sun. As this is eaten uncooked, it is termed *Seinsa* or "raw food." The more carefully prepared paste, made with selected small prawns, is frequently used with curry and rice as a chutney by Europeans all along the Malay coast, where it is known as *Balachong*; and of recent years it has competed with caviare as a *bonne bouche* in the boulevard restaurants of Paris.

Extensive though the salt-fish industry be, it fails to supply the existing demands of the population; for in 1897–98, nearly 12,500 tons of *Ngapi* were imported from the Malay Peninsula, although home production is protected by a duty of six annas (sixpence) per maund of 80 lbs.

Within a couple of years of the annexation of Tenasserim, in 1826, divers were brought from Madras to test the resources of the pearl fisheries which were known to exist among the islands of the Mergui Archipelago; but as only seed-pearls were found, the fisheries were abandoned as unlikely to yield the large revenue which had been anticipated. The fisheries continued, however, to be worked in a very primitive and spasmodic way by the Selungs or Salones, an aboriginal tribe inhabiting the islands, and subsisting chiefly by fishing and by the collection of edible birds' nests formed by a glutinous exudation from the mouths of swifts (Peale's Swiftlet, *Collocalia spodiopygia*; *C. esculenta*, and others), and used for the preparation of soup as a delicacy for rich Chinamen. But it was not till 1892 that the pearl-oyster beds began to be worked on any considerable and systematic scale, when divers with scientific apparatus were employed on the work, with capital raised in Singapore. In the autumn of that year the pearl fields were divided into five blocks and leased for three years at a rental of £1,784 for the first year, and £2,217 for each of the two succeeding years. The services of an expert from Queensland were then obtained to examine the fisheries, and work is now carried on under lease by Australians and Manila divers; but the industry can hardly be said to be in a flourishing condition. In 1895, three pearl-beds were discovered off the Bassein coast, only to prove unremunerative after a couple of years' working. The pearls found in the Mergui Archipelago are of good colour and fine lustre, but the fishery season only lasts for about five months owing to the exposed nature of the coast and the very early advent of the south-west monsoon winds.

Salt-boiling is an ancient industry all along the coastline, and until about thirty years ago this trade formed the principal source of the salt supply for Burma. Brine-wells occur in the Katha, Shwebo, and Sagaing districts of Upper Burma, where salt-boiling forms the occupation of the poorest of the poor; but the northern part of the province, together with western Yunnan, has ever been practically dependent on Lower Burma for this essential commodity. Since about the middle of the sixties, however, salt of home production has been in great measure supplanted by imports from Europe, cargoes of salt being brought in place of ballast by ships coming under charter for rice or teak timber.

Local salt production is taxed by a duty on the vessels used in its manufacture, which is intended to be equivalent to the import duty of one rupee (1s. 4d.) per maund (80 lbs.) levied on foreign salt arriving at any seaport. In this branch of import trade Rangoon possesses a practical monopoly, as most of the salt used in Arakan and Tenasserim is of local production, although in the rest of the province foreign salt is now almost exclusively used both for domestic consumption and fish-salting. The endeavours made to equalize the rates of composition for salt duty with this customs import duty are rendered very difficult through the power which the local industry possesses of increasing production so as to meet increases of rates on vessels used. In 1895 the rates on cauldrons and pots were revised and enhanced, and in 1897 salt-boiling was limited merely to specific tracts in certain districts. The only result of this restriction, which would be unintelligible but for the very poor quality of the home-made product, was to reduce the number of pots and cauldrons used, and to throw the industry almost entirely into the hands of professional salt-boilers, without seriously affecting the gross outturn ; for salt-boilers were led to improve their methods of manufacture in order to make up for the enhancement of taxation. During 1899–1900, over 22,000 tons of salt were manufactured locally, upon which the salt-excise revenue demand was £15,883, while import duty amounting to £81,614 was collected on clearance from bond of portions of the 49,703 tons of foreign salt imported. In 1899 fully one-third of the salt consumed was of local manufacture, while the sources of supply of the remaining two-thirds were almost exclusively England and Germany, and respectively in the proportions of twenty-seven and thirty-four per cent. of the total amount. German salt is cheaper than English; and in Upper Burma the former is said to be preferred to the latter. The whole revenue actually received from salt in 1899 amounted to £96,414.

Along the sea-coast iron cauldrons are used for boiling sea-water and brine from land flooded by the sea, until the contents have evaporated into dryness. In the inland tracts, where the soil, the subsoil water, and the streams are brackish, fields are divided into compart-

ments, ploughed, pulverized, and levelled, then filled with
water which is afterwards drawn off into large tanks
before being evaporated in great, thick earthenware jars
kept over a steady fire. Operations are confined to the
months of February, March, and April. The salt thus
crudely manufactured is apt to be much discoloured and
of poor quality, and cannot possibly compete on anything
like equal terms with the foreign imports.

Twenty years ago the chief luminant used after dark
throughout the rural tracts, except those of the dry zone
within easy reach of the central petroleum fields, was a
small torch about a foot and a half long made of chips of
dead wood and the resinous oil of the Kanyin or
wood-oil tree (*Dipterocarpus alatus, D. turbinatus*) rolled
in palm-leaves. Known in Chittagong and Bengal
under the name of Gurjan oil, this oleo-resin was at one
time used as a specific for leprosy. It can also be used
as a thin varnish for interior woodwork, but turns white
on exposure to wet. These *Kanyinsi* torches were sold
in bundles in every bazaar. While burning they emitted
incessant smoke and a strong oily smell, pungent and
differing vastly from the European idea of fragrance.
At one time the manufacture of these torches formed an
industry wherever the wood-oil trees abounded ; but
now, in consequence of improved communications and
of large imports of kerosine at low rates, torch-making is
only betaken to in jungle tracts in order to eke out the
means of livelihood during bad years, when the shadow
of misfortune darkens the household. Although of the
541,076 acres of sessamum or til (*Hnan*), nearly
nineteen-twentieths are cultivated in Upper Burma, yet
there are comparatively few villages which have not
their own oil-press (*Sizôn*), as this is the only means of
preventing adulteration with the cheaper oil obtained
from ground-nuts, and largely imported from Madras for
this very purpose. The seed is stored up till the hot
weather, when it is warmed in the sun for a few days
before being pressed by mortar and pestle, worked by a
bullock. A large log having been sunk deep into the
ground so that only about four feet of it remain above
ground-level, it is hollowed out for nearly a couple of feet

in such manner that a heavy revolving pestle can press closely round the sides. The upper end of the long pestle is fixed to a wooden cross-bar, to the extremity of which a bullock is yoked and made to trudge round the mill. The oil is either run off through holes in the side of the mortar, or obtained by the very primitive method of dipping cloths into it and wringing them out when saturated with oil.

Sugar (*Thagyá*) or Jaggery (*Tannyit*) is largely made from the juice of the toddy-palm (*Tan* ; *Borassus flabelliformis*), which grows all over the province and is sometimes planted solely for this purpose, from below Prome northwards to the mouth of the Chindwin river. The manufacturing process simply consists in boiling the juice till it becomes thick, and then spreading it out on thin bamboo mats to harden into a dry brown cake. A superior kind of tablet of brown sugar (*Kyantagá*) is made in similar manner from the juice of the sugar-cane (*Kyan*) after this has been pressed out in wooden presses like those used for extracting sessamum-oil. The sugar-cane is grown on the rich alluvial deposits left on river bends when the summer floods subside, but the total area thus cultivated only amounts to about 12,500 acres, nearly half are in the district round about Moulmein.

The toddy-palm, whose juice is collected in earthenware pots fastened to the spadices of leaves where these have been cut through to tap the sap in flow, gives employment to over 26,000 adult males, and affords the means of livelihood to about 90,000 souls. About half of those dependent on this industry are to be found in the Myingyan and Pakôkku districts of Upper Burma. Allowed to stand and ferment, toddy soon becomes an intoxicating drink, but the great bulk of it is formed into jaggery. The smooth stems of the tall palms, which run up to fifty or sixty feet before bearing their coronal tuft of sparse fan-shaped leaves, are ascended by means of small thorny bamboos lashed to the stem. A certain monkey-like agility, combined with a cool head and good hands and feet, is required for their ascent; and the Burmese are adepts at this kind of tree-climbing.

FELLING TIMBER

It is, however, perhaps in woodcraft and the extraction of timber that the Burman excels most of all. With regard to this, although he is careful to put himself to no unnecessary personal exertion, he cheerfully undergoes a vast amount of continuous exposure under troublesome and depressing circumstances. He possesses a considerable natural bent in this direction, united to hereditary association with jungle work. For the felling of the largest trees he uses no implements save a heavy bill (*Da*), an axe (*Pauksein*), and a sort of chisel-axe (*Kyettaung*) having a movable head. The *Da* has a slightly curved blade of about a foot and a half in length, which varies up to one-fourth or one-third of an inch in thickness along the back, and is fixed firmly into a rounded slightly convex wooden handle of nine or ten inches in length. A heavy and well balanced bill, it is a very effective instrument, used for everything in the way of cutting, from the whittling of a small shred of bamboo for a toothpick up to the felling of giant stems from three to five feet in diameter. The *Pauksein* are usually flat-headed axes with straight shafts, as improved English and American instruments find no favour with the woodmen. The undoubtedly greater effectiveness of the latter is dependent solely on greater personal exertion in using them; and this is a fatal drawback in the eyes of the Burman. The *Kyettaung* or "fowl's feather" is an extremely interesting implement, because it forms the hitherto missing link between the methods of the stone age and those of modern advances and developments. It consists of an iron head about nine or ten inches in length, the upper part of which is conical and tapering to a point, while the lower steel-faced portion becomes broadened and flattened like a thin chisel having a cutting edge of about two inches or slightly more. This chisel-axe is fastened to a long slightly curved handle made from the branch and stem of a sapling *Kyetyo* (*Vitex alata*) or other light, tough tree, the branch forming the shaft and the short section of the stem being hollowed out to form a bed for the lower half of the conical top of the chisel-axe. The latter is held in position by being firmly laced down with strips of cane. The peculiar advantage possessed by this quaint and very effective implement is that the cutting edge can be set at any angle desired, by simply displacing the head and turning round the conical portion in its casing of cane and wood. While easily moved and fixed in any new position, there is no practical danger of its flying out of the case during use.

No Burman in the rural tracts ever goes out of the house without his *Da* in his hand, and at an early age he acquires marvellous dexterity with it, while the effectiveness of these simple tools is heightened by means of almost universal ambidexterousness in their use.

With these primitive wood-cutting implements many hundreds of thousands of trees are annually felled for extraction and sale, or for the mere clearance of the soil for temporary rice-cultivation by the hill tribes. When large trees are strongly buttressed near the base, as often happens on steep hill-sides, the wood-fellers erect a bamboo stage some feet above the ground and work in a leisurely manner at the part where the girth seems to them of more reasonable dimensions. Stumps of large trees containing valuable timber are thus often left from five or six to ten or even twelve feet high, greatly to the vexation of the Forest Officer. The foresting contracts stipulate that felling is to take place within three feet above the ground; but this clause cannot always be enforced in hilly country where labour is difficult to procure.

The more economic process of felling by use of axe and saw is only now being found capable of introduction under the immediate supervision of European foresters; and even for the logging of felled stems the Burman will naturally prefer to use his bill and axe unless forced to cross-cut with the saw. Hereditary custom possesses enormous force in this, as in other matters, among the Burmese. Time is to him of far less consideration than the avoidance of innovations which seem to entail more personal exertion; and as for the greater economy with regard to timber, that is absolutely the very last idea with which he would trouble his mind. As an example both of what can be done with such simple implements and of the waste of good timber in so richly wooded a

TEAK TIMBER

country as Burma, I may record, as having come within my own personal knowledge, the felling and logging, with such small bills and axes only, of an enormous hard Pyingado or ironwood tree (*Xylia dolabriformis*) in the Bassein district which yielded a log measuring sixty feet in length and having a girth of thirteen feet measured at the middle. This was rough-hewn or wastefully chipped away at the sides so as to form merely one long thick plank for use as the keel of a sea-going boat. All the rest of the timber was wasted; and this is a fair sample of the sort of thing that goes on all over the country.

The most important forest work is connected with the teak timber (*Tectona grandis*), for which Burma is renowned. When felled it is logged in as large dimensions as can be extracted under local circumstances, for the value of sound logs increases largely with their dimensions. The largest recorded teak log was one of $82\frac{1}{2}$ feet in length by 10 feet mean girth, which was launched into a tributary of the Shweli river, in 1898, by Messrs. Darwood & Co., foresting there under a purchase contract with Government. It girthed over 12 feet at the base and over 7 feet at the top end, and contained 517 cubic feet or $10\frac{1}{3}$ tons of timber. Logs of anything like even two-thirds of that length are, however, exceptional; and the great bulk of the timber extracted varies from about 20 to 30 feet in length. Logging of stems is partly dependent on the formation of the bole and the occurrence of large branches, but one of the main considerations guiding the timber contractor has of course reference to the dragging power at his command.

On fairly level or merely undulating ground buffaloes are used extensively for dragging. Yoked together in pairs by means of a stout wooden beam, from which a chain is attached to dragholes cut in the log, from one to four or five yoke of strong buffaloes drag the timber to the floating stream or to collecting places whence it can be conveyed on rough little timber carts (*Gindeik*). To make dragging easier it was, and to some extent unfortunately still is, the wasteful custom in Upper Burma to "snout" the thick end of the logs with the axe so as to make them offer less resistance in being dragged along the ground. Logs thus fashioned are called *Ngalú Gaung*, from their resemblance to a carp's head (*Ngalú*; *Labeo angra*)

The timber-carts are small strong tumbrils consisting merely of two broad wheels and a large central block of wood hollowed to form a bed for the log and keep it from rolling off on either side. Loading takes place by the laborious though ingenious method of raising the butt end of the log by means of a chain suspended to stout poles attached to the yoke at the end of the cart-shaft and resting on the wooden block above the axle-tree. The end of the shaft is raised high up in the air when the chain is passed under the head of the log; and on men pulling it down again the leverage obtained with the axle as fulcrum enables the head of the log to be brought on the cart. It is then easily levered forward with poles so as almost to balance, when it is lashed down to the shaft. A huge well-balanced log can thus easily be carted by a pair of buffaloes. Work of this particular kind by buffaloes is of course confined almost entirely to the dry season and the early part of the rains.

Wherever the local configuration of the soil is unfavourable for buffalo-dragging, as well as during the height of the wet monsoon months, and for all work in the floating streams, elephants are required; and powerful tuskers now command prices varying from two to three thousand rupees (£133 to £200). Females are also largely employed; but they have neither the weight and strength of the males, nor can they without tusks " handle " the logs in the way the males are taught to do. The intelligence of elephants—and the Burmese elephant is no doubt about the cleverest, though perhaps the smallest of the genus—seems much overrated. The apparent intelligence in handling timber is solely due to training and to the guiding of the mahout or *Uzi*, " the man riding on the head," who directs movements by voice, knee and toes, and enforces his directions with the pointed arguments of a sharp heavy iron spike fixed to a thin wooden handle about two and a half feet long. The spike is curved or slightly hooked, so that it can be hung over the elephant's ear in more peaceful moments.

ELEPHANTS WORKING TIMBER

As a matter of fact the elephant hates dragging and hard work just as much as his Burmese master does ; and when made to exert all his strength in moving heavy logs sticking fast in the mud, he trumpets and roars as loudly as ever he can. For timber extraction during the rainy season, however, when the ground is a mass of deep mud, elephants are indispensable, though in course of time some other motive power will have to be introduced owing to the gradual diminution in their numbers. Large wild herds still roam about many of the forests and lay waste cultivation in parts of the more thinly populated districts ; while breeding is carried on among animals maintained in a semi-captive state in the forests of eastern Tenasserim and western Siam ; yet the steady increase in the price of elephants has arisen not only through competition for their possession, but also from failure of the supply to meet the growing demand. And as timber operations are expanding throughout the province, this demand is certain to become enhanced throughout the great forest tracts of the country.

For dragging work the elephant is lightly harnessed with a broad breast-band made of twisted liber of the Shaw tree (*Sterculia villosa*), to the ends of which the heavy iron dragging chains are fixed, the latter being held up in position by another *Shaw* rope passing over the back behind the shoulder-blades. The backbone is protected by a skeleton saddle of wood or by rounded blocks of light wood resting upon a thick pad of folded skins and *Shaw* bark. Logs of ordinary size—about twenty to thirty feet in length and six to seven feet in mean girth—can be dragged by one elephant ; but for long large-girthed timber two, three, or more are set to work simultaneously on alternate sides of the log. Including dragging, launching into the creeks, and bringing into the fair channel such logs as have got stranded or stuck, an elephant can work out from about 70 to 150 logs a year according to the class of animal and the given local conditions under which the work is done.

The work of felling, logging, and dragging commences in November or December, and is continued till the great heat and the want of water—for all except the main streams dry up during the hot season—bring work to an end with the month of March. The early rains find the lumberers again at work; and dragging, drifting, and floating operations continue all through the rainy season, the largest deliveries of timber at Rangoon taking place between November and February.

Logs are launched singly into the bed of a floating stream and allowed to drift along as each heavy fall of rain brings down a freshet. Near the sources of the small tributaries, and even in many of the main channels having broad, shallow, sandy watercourses, these rises and falls occur very suddenly, and cannot be utilized to full advantage unless elephants are at hand near the launched logs to push them into the main current. This is done by the elephant applying its head, just above the root of the trunk, to the end of the log and making the latter slide forward over the wet mud or sand into the deep water, or into the position required. To *aung* or "overcome" obstructive logs in this way the aid of the elephant is essential; buffaloes are of no use for the purpose.

It not infrequently happens that in drifting down loosely in the floating streams logs get stuck in shallows or obstructed by snags or jungle rubbish and drift refuse from the forest; for the banks of the streams are much subject to erosion, when trees and bamboos growing at their edge fall into the current and are swept down till their course is perchance arrested by snags, or through the subsiding of the waters. Care is therefore taken to patrol the floating streams and keep them clear of snags and jungle refuse; but sometimes in the course of a single night large obstructions are formed by the jamming of hundreds of logs. For the breaking up of such obstructions (*Taik*) formed of logs and jungle drift (*Taikthayáw*) elephants are again essential, and both animals and their intrepid drivers incur no little danger while loosening the logs and setting free the vast masses of firmly wedged timber and bamboos that dam up the waters behind them.

Many streams give a vast amount of trouble in this respect. The most troublesome are perhaps three large streams draining an extensive forest area along the western

TIMBER-FLOATING OPERATIONS

slopes of the Pegu Yoma in the Tharrawaddy and Prome districts of Lower Burma. After reaching the plains these streams all converge near the boundary between the two districts and form the Myitmaka or Hlaing river leading direct to Rangoon. During the flood months of July to September the Myitmaka meets here with the flood waters of the Irrawaddy, which then rise and inundate the whole of the country from Myanaung, on the western river bank, eastwards to within four or five miles of the Rangoon and Prome railway line. As the hill streams come into the slack water thus formed during floods the heavier sandy portion of the silt becomes deposited and a bar or sandy obstruction is formed which tends not only to impede timber-floating operations, but also to cause inundation of the surrounding rice-lands, destruction of crops, and deviation of the watercourse. After nearly a quarter of a century of wrangling between district and forest officers, and of repeated consideration of this problem by the Engineering Department, it has been proved that the best and indeed the only practicable way of obviating these annually recurring dangers at this particular locality is to maintain a clear watercourse and to keep it open by timber extraction. This necessitates the cutting in each dry season of a narrow channel about two or three hundred yards in length through the sandy bar, and keeping it open continuously by means of elephants dragging or "*aung*"-ing logs across.

At the end of each rainy season all the floating streams are examined, and stranded logs are placed in a favourable position for being drifted down with the early floods of the following season.

On reaching the main rivers the drift-logs are caught at convenient centres and formed into rafts, which are floated down to the great timber marts of Rangoon and Moulmein. The method employed is simple and effective. A thick rattan cane (of the genus *Calamus*) is stretched loosely across the stream and firmly fixed at each end. Being run through the drag-holes of a series of logs, it is kept just on the surface of the water, and forms a boom (*Kyódan*, "rope line") to catch the drifting timber,

BURMA UNDER BRITISH RULE

which is taken out from below by men in canoes and removed to where the rafts (*Paung*) are made up. Though varying much in size, the rafts are all constructed on the same principle. The logs of about equal length are arranged in sections, being lashed together fore and aft by transverse poles fixed with split rattan to the drag-holes of the logs, and each section is connected by strong twisted rattan to the sections before and behind it. On the Sittang river, where floating operations begin early and the current is very strong, the rafts consist only of forty to fifty logs in about four to six sections, while on the Irrawaddy river the rafts from Mandalay, which do not start on their 500 miles' river journey till early in October after the flood period is at an end, are three or four times as large.

The number of men employed specially in the extraction and handling of timber in the rough cannot be estimated with any approach to accuracy, but the extraction and preparation of forest produce afford employment to between fifty and sixty thousand adult males and yield a livelihood to over a quarter of a million souls or about three per cent. of the total population. These bald figures, however, hardly bring home to one's mind the national and economic importance of Burma's vast forest wealth. This may perhaps be better exemplified in the statement that the outturn of timber and fuel in 1897-98 amounted to 58 millions of cubic feet, whilst 157 millions of bamboos were extracted, besides minor produce of various sorts. The gross income from forests during 1899-1900 was £556,726, while the net surplus revenue was £399,256.

One of the chief of the jungle industries connected with the utilization of minor forest produce is cutch-boiling. Three men usually work together in one camp. One of them fells the *Sha* or cutch trees (*Acacia Catechu*) and drags them to camp, while another hews off the pale sapwood and cuts the dark red-brown heartwood into small chips of about an inch square and a quarter of an inch thick, and the third looks after the boiling of the chips in earthenware pots and iron cauldrons. Round earthenware pots, of about three gallons capacity, and to the number of about twenty or twenty-four, after being tightly packed with chips and filled up with water, are placed over narrow earthen trenches in which fires are kept constantly burning. Near these trenches are placed the central fires in holes dug in the ground, above which iron cauldrons of about twelve gallons capacity are hung. By the time the pots full of chips have boiled for nearly twenty-four hours the liquid they then contain has been reduced to about half its original quantity. From the pots it is next poured into the iron cauldrons and boiling is continued, with stirring, till the liquid attains a viscous consistency. After the removal of the cauldron from the fire stirring has to continue so as to let the cutch cool equally throughout its whole mass in place of forming a hard solid cake on the top. When cool enough to be handled, it is poured out in moulds, like brick moulds, lined with large leaves to prevent it from sticking to the sides. Fresh chips are used each time the earthenware pots are filled and placed on the trench fires. During the rainy season boiling takes place under an awning of thatched grass, to protect the fires from the rain. The method is crude and wasteful, for a cubic foot of *Sha* wood weighing between sixty and seventy pounds only yields on the average about $3\frac{2}{3}$ pounds of cutch when thus primitively treated.

Cutch-boiling forms the chief means of livelihood of a large number of the poorer classes in the Prome and Thayetmyo districts of Lower Burma, who work for Chinese that furnish them with the money for obtaining licenses. But it also affords to many more in these districts, and in the Upper Burma districts of precarious rainfall, a subsidiary means of eking out a subsistence during times of scarcity. In some of the driest portions of the central zone, as in Pakôkku, Myingyan, and Meiktila, where the cutch tree does not attain the same dimensions as in tracts blessed with a rainfall of about forty to sixty inches, recent years of scarcity have, combined with improved communications by the railway opening out the land-locked interior, effected the exhaustion of marketable trees within the cutch-producing area. It grows quickly, however, and reserves and plantations are being formed by the Forest Department for the provision and maintenance of future supplies of this valuable tree.

Of recent years the reputation of Burma cutch has been lowered through adulteration, and measures have been taken by Government to try and obviate this. The chief adulterants are bark extracts made from various kinds of trees, and more especially from those of the genus *Terminalia*. Astringent to a degree, these bark extracts are perhaps worthy of commercial attention for the preparation of tanning extracts ; but their admixture depreciated the cutch trade.

Charcoal-burning forms the occupation of comparatively few, and it is followed in a most wasteful manner. Open pits are dug, fire is placed in these, and wood thrown on which is allowed to char. The preparation of charcoal is generally confined to the wet season, as otherwise the wood would be completely consumed, leaving only the ashes as the product of combustion. As it is, the outturn is of course of a very poor description, and consists mostly of small pieces.

Conversion of timber at all seaports, and at a few mills in the forests, takes place by means of steam power, but hand-sawing is still general in all the towns and larger villages, and even in the heart of the jungle, throughout the province. There does not exist, however, within the whole length and breadth of the country any sawmill driven by water-power ; nor has the Burmese mind apparently ever risen to the possibility of utilizing water-power in this manner.

With continuous progress in the formation of permanent roads since the British occupation, the manufacture and the use of carts have increased enormously. There are now 438,282 carts in the province, or about two for every five households on the plains. Radical changes have also at the same time been made in their construction, to suit them for roads metalled—when metalled at all—mostly with balls of burned brick apt to be easily pulverized during the hot season. Good greenstone road-metal is only to be found in the seaports and their immediate vicinity, where it is obtainable from ships that have brought it out as ballast from Europe.

In former times, before the era of road-making, the country carts had to be so constructed as to be capable of travelling over very rough ground. The cart-tracks began in the fields whence the grain was brought on sledges or carts to the hamlets and villages, and gradually those single threads converged to form the main lines of communication, as small tributary streams are gathered together in the main watercourse.

Two heavy, round, convex-sided, untyred wheels about three feet in circumference, made out of a solid block of hard wood, or else in two or more frequently three pieces, having been fashioned and fitted to a hard tough axle-tree, a shaft is formed of two poles extending in an upward curve for some feet behind this and reaching forward for about ten or twelve feet. These being lashed together at the front end, the bed of the cart is formed either of boards or of stout bamboo strips loosely interwoven, the sides being a rough wooden framework let into the poles forming the shaft. From the yoke, fixed by a leather thong to the front part of the two-poled shaft, the framework slopes down to the axle-tree and then curves up behind, thus necessitating the selection of poles with symmetrical bend. For ornament the poles jut out behind, and to finish off the cart in front a piece of wood pointing upwards is lashed to the end of the shaft and carved to represent the neck and head of a paddy bird or white heron (*Herodias alba*). Even when no attempt is made to adorn this piece of wood it is always called the *Hgnetyôk* or "image of the bird," and to it is always fastened the wisp of flowers, the ears of grain, or the simple twigs placed as an offering to the spirits of the air when carting home the harvest or setting out upon any journey by road.

The carts drawn by buffaloes are larger and heavier than those meant for bullocks, but in all essential features the indigenous form of Burmese cart formerly used all over the country, though now only to be met with off the beaten tracks of main communication, differed only in dimensions and not as regards the lines upon which they were constructed. There is no metal work about them. Wheels, axle-boxes, axle-trees, lynch-pins, shafts, body, and sides are all made of wood, and are jointed, mortised, and tenoned with wood, wherever necessary. For the wheels *Padauk* (*Pterocarpus indicus*) is the wood preferred ; and as creaking is considered melodious instead of being looked on as a defect, a fine well-toned pair will fetch as much as thirty rupees (£2). The favourite woods for axles are the hard, tough *Gyo* (*Schleichera trijuga*), *Petwun* (*Berrya mollis*), Cutch (*Acacia Catechu*), and Ironwood or Pyingado (*Xylia dolabriformis*), while *Yindaik* (*Dalbergia cultrata*), Petwun, and Mangroves in the tidal districts are most prized as shafts.

Such primitive carts were well enough suited to the extremely rough work for which they were required before the country began to be opened out by permanent roads. They could stand very rough work better than carts of more complex construction, and could be repaired without the aid of any blacksmith or wheelwright. But they soon cut up the earthen roads, and by the middle of the hot season, when all the moisture had completely evaporated from the soil, the ruts became so deep that the carts sank nearly up to the axle in the pulverized earth. This did not matter much, however, as the roads became impassable during the rainy season and were opened anew each year when traffic overland became once more practicable.

Whenever a string of carts passed along, a thick cloud of fine dust was raised which hung long in the hot air. From afar off the monotonous, high-pitched creaking and groaning of the wheels against the broad wooden axle-boxes could be heard increasing in intensity as they approached, and then passed, and gradually lessened and faded away, something like the well-known arrangement of the "Turkish Patrol." During the hottest season, from the middle of March till the middle of May, when cartmen go by night to avoid exposing their cattle and themselves in the daytime, sleep was almost out of the question to the unfortunate traveller whose camp happened to be on any of the much frequented tracks.

CARTS AND BOATS

To protect the driver and the load from the effects of sun, dew and rain a thin bamboo mat is often stretched across the top of the cart in the form of a semi-circular awning. When thus slowly wending their way along at less than two miles an hour the cartmen take the leading position by turns, and the driver of the first cart is supposed to keep awake and guide the party while the rest enjoy repose in sleep. The wakefulness of the leading cartman is usually, however, merely nominal; he, too, generally goes to sleep, and the bullocks wander on just as they list.

With the formation of municipalities and the licensing of carts plying for hire in urban districts, it soon also became necessary to insist on the use of spoked and iron-tyred wheels for traffic along Government roads. The use of country carts with solid wooden wheels has not been exactly suppressed in rural districts, but under Public Works Departmental orders they are supposed only to go along the berme, leaving the prepared roadway, whether metalled or unmetalled, for carts of improved construction. Wooden wheels get worn away unevenly and then jolt fearfully, throwing much extra work on the buffaloes or bullocks. Hence the gradual disappearance of this picturesque remnant of primitive Burma is hardly a matter for regret. Carts of light and graceful construction are used for bullock-racing in the Thatôn district; while light single-pole carts, with enclosed sides and a considerable quantity of carving around them, do duty as carriages in Mandalay.

Boats, however, approach much more nearly than carts to being an essential requisite of life in Burma, and especially so in the delta and in all districts having heavy rainfall. For two or three months of the year vast stretches of country are deep under water, and locomotion is confined to boats. Many of the villages on the plains become inundated so that movement even from house to house has to take place in canoes; and during July and August large boats can be poled up, far inland from the streams, in the ditches at the side of the Public Works roads.

Except as regards the comparatively few sea-going

craft built with heavy keels of ironwood, boat-construction follows very much the same main lines, no matter whether a small fifteen to eighteen feet canoe or a large boat for transport of earth-oil or rice be in consideration. The former consists simply of a "dug-out" or hollowed stem; while in the latter a dug-out forms the hull or base upon which ribs and crooks are fixed for the support of washboards and side-planks. The country boats are consequently of shallow draft, and can be easily lifted or poled off when they happen to run on any mudbank or sandy shoal.

The most highly prized and valuable hulls are those made of *Thingan* (*Hopea odorata*) or Teak (*Kyûn*; *Tectona grandis*), which are said to last about thirty years. *Pyinma* (*Lagerstroemia flos reginae*) and *Lèza* (*L. tomentosa*) are also much in demand; but the largest number of canoes is made from the less durable *In* (*Dipterocarpus tuberculatus*), which is the most abundant tree throughout Burma and can easily be obtained of large girth and free from branches to the required length. Under the Forest Rules timber, except teak and a few other reserved kinds, can be cut free for boats required for bonâ fide domestic and agricultural use, though all such as are made for trade purposes have to pay revenue.

The green log having been roughly hollowed out, with due consideration to the future shape of the hull when completed, a light fire is applied all round it and the sides are gradually stretched outwards by means of wooden hooks and strong wet cords fixed to stout pegs in the ground, which contract slightly in drying. More hollowing out then takes place, and further stretching apart; and so on till the sides are fully opened out, and the work of adzing, smoothing, and fashioning the dug-out can be completed. The operations extend over a considerable time, to obviate any cracking which would render the hull practically worthless.

When large boats are built, the bows are kept low, while the stern runs up behind to form an elevated stage for the helmsman, which is often very richly ornamented with carving in teak. Some of the carvings on the sterns of large boats on the Irrawaddy are of a high artistic order, though somewhat rough in execution. The helm consists of a huge paddle lashed to the port-side and moved by a short handle from the steersman's bench. The *Pènin* who "treads on the stern" is the man in authority on board ; and this term is often applied to the petty officials in up-country hamlets. The oarsmen row standing up. They generally have small foot-rests against which they press with one foot when giving the weight of their bodies to the stroke, while they remove this foot and give it a backward swing when bringing forward the oar again for another stroke.

Among the *Inthá* or "lake-dwellers" around the *Inle* lake near Fort Stedman in the southern Shan State of Nyaungywé, the men row their canoes standing up with the leg wound round the long oar which passes down the inner side of the knee, then across the tibia, and past the outer side of the foot.

For rowing small canoes, and long *Laung* or racing skiffs, used also in conveying priests from place to place and generally kept under the village monastery, light, pointed paddles with long narrow blades are used, while the steersman guides the boat with a long and broad sweep. Paint is not used on boats or canoes, which are smeared from time to time with dark-brown crude earth-oil to preserve and beautify them. The racing skiffs form, however, an exception, as they are almost invariably coated over with black varnish both inside and outside.

On the Irrawaddy enormous lug sails of thin white or light-brown cotton are used to carry the boats up stream during the hot weather and the monsoon season, when strong winds usually blow inwards from the sea-coast. The mast is formed of two giant bamboos (*Wabó : Dendrocalamus Brandisii*) bolted and lashed to the hull, and spliced together in the top portion. On this a yard consisting of bamboo is raised having pulleys at the ends through which cords pass, so that by hauling these the sail extends by running on rings along the smooth bamboo yard on both sides of the mast. As the boats are smooth-bottomed, without any ridged keel, and the sails are only adapted for running straight before the wind, little or no tacking is possible. When the wind fails or is unfavourable, rowing in slack water or poling along the bank must be reverted to. When not in use, the mast is lowered down on to the roof of the arch covering the dwelling part of the boat.

During April, May, and June, before the Irrawaddy becomes so swollen with flood water as to have a swift current, the wind blowing up stream is often so strong as to impede the progress of large boats making the downward journey, and water-sails are then lowered to catch the under-currents and carry the boat down stream in spite of the wind. A fleet of large Irrawaddy boats sailing up stream under their enormous expanse of white or light-brown sails, forms a very pleasing and graceful addition to Irrawaddy river scenery often extremely picturesque and beautiful in itself.

For the conveyance downwards from Yenangyaung of crude earth-oil, carried in large glazed earthenware jars, boats (*Peingaw*) of special construction are built. They usually consist of two broad, straight, punt-like dug-outs lashed together, and have a bamboo gallery extending along both sides to facilitate poling up stream whenever the bamboos have to be taken in hand for this purpose. These *Peingaw* are not to be met with except on the Irrawaddy. The royal barge or "great golden raft" at Mandalay—which was never used after the Myingun Prince's rebellion in 1866, because the King was afraid to leave his palace and go on the river—was of this class. It was profusely decorated with tinsel, coloured glass, and gilding, and was finished off fore and aft with wild leogryphs picked out in gorgeous colours, the gilded and glass-mosaiced pavilion occupying the central position being surmounted with a seven-tiered pagoda-like roof.

For some distance immediately in front of the steersman's perch the hind part of the ordinary Burmese riverboat is covered with an arched awning of bamboo mat so as to form the dwelling-place of the crew. Here the cooking is done on a shallow box filled with earth, and here the men sleep at night. The deck of the boat is formed by thick bamboo mats or coarse framework placed over the cargo, for loading does not take place above the gunwale.

Notwithstanding the competition of railway and steamers, there is still a vast amount of petty and local traffic conveyed by boats ; and the floating population employed in this, as well as in timber-rafting operations, includes no small proportion of the worst classes of thieves, gamblers, and opium-smokers to be found among those of pure Burmese nationality.

In all jungle hamlets, and in most villages, a man builds his own house, his neighbours helping him to raise the posts and place them in position. It is only in larger villages that the assistance of a carpenter (*Letthama*) or "handy man" is required for house-building. In the heart of the jungle, indeed, the houses are made of poles, bamboos, and grass, without any rails or iron-work being required in their construction.

Mat-weaving with thin strips of bamboo is universal, but the preparation of a fine quality of mat from the outer portion of the *Thin* rattan (*Maranta dichotoma*) forms a speciality in various parts. They are often woven in patterns with strips dyed black for this purpose in a decoction of the bark and leaves of the *Zibyu* tree (*Zizyphus jujuba*), the work of this finer class forming the occupation of women. The best mats are made at Danúbyu in the Henzada district, where mat-making has almost entirely displaced the weaver's hand-loom. The mats known as *Thinbyu* are used all over the country for sleeping on, a Burman's bed consisting merely of a blanket or cotton coverlet (*Saung*), and a small pillow rolled up in one of these flexible mats and tied with string. The *Thin* grows in great abundance throughout the lower delta. After being steeped in water it is split, and the rind is peeled off in two layers which are woven separately. The smooth outer strip forms the fine upper portion of the mat, while the rougher inner rind is plaited for the coarser lower part. When stitched together, the finished mat, consisting thus of two layers, mitigates the discomfort of sleeping on the ground or on a flooring of plank or bamboo. A *Thinbyu* mat spread on a bed is the coolest resting place during the hot season of the year.

The heart of the *Thin* rattan is used for rope-making. But there are many excellent fibres of far better quality suitable for this and for other textile purposes, many of which have as yet no marketable value. All along the coast coir or cocoa-nut husk is extensively picked and twisted into cordage for mats and ropes, and this forms an important industry in all the large jails. But in the rural tracts tree-fibres are in general use, the most important being supplied by species of *Shaw* (*Sterculia*). On the rope-walk a simple wooden framework containing spindles worked by a crank handle is all the machinery that is employed for turning out well twisted, stout cordage and ropes. The fibre-yielding shrubs and grasses may become of considerable economic importance in the future, but thus far the other resources of the province have proved so abundant and remunerative that little or no attention has yet been given to the former commercially.

Blacksmiths are to be found plying their trade all over the country, though their number is very limited. Of the less than 6,000 males following this occupation, the great majority find employment in the manufacture of *Da.* Apart from the shorter heavy bills (*Damá*), varying up to about four pounds in weight, used by agriculturists and wood-fellers, sword-like blades (*Dáshe* or "long Da," and "*Dalwe*" or "*Da* suspended from the shoulder"), considerably lighter, though of greater length, are made in large numbers. These latter, as well as short daggers (*Damyáung*) are cased in a sheath formed of two pieces of light wood slightly hollowed and bound together with fine cane, or with bands of brass or silver. The finest blades are manufactured at Pyawbwè, at the base of the Shan hills near the eastern limit of the great central dry zone. Some of these, beautifully damascened, are really works of art. The blacksmith's crude bellows consist of two sections of a large bamboo or of cylinders of wood, up and down which loosely fitting pistons are moved to expel the current of air from small holes at the base. It seems almost incredible that there should be so few blacksmiths among a population numbering $7\frac{1}{2}$ millions;

but, except as regards their *Da*, the Burmese have very few requirements in this respect. As a nation they possess no mechanical ability. Of the 894,018 agricultural implements in the country classifiable as ploughs, probably less than a mere tithe have any iron-work about them; while everything in the shape of nails, except the largest mushroom-headed spikes (*Hmó*) used for house-building and other constructive purposes, are imported from foreign countries. As the Burmese do not use brass or copper vessels for cooking, the few brass-founders and coppersmiths in the province are almost entirely employed in art-work, such as founding images of Gaudama, making gongs and similar articles.

As a rule the people go about bare-footed when at work, but almost every man, woman, and child has at least one pair of sandals (*Panát*), and the number of sandal-makers is about three-fold that of blacksmiths. The sandals are usually made of soft, light, white wood, *Yamané* (*Gmelina arborea*) being the most highly prized, though thick dyed felt is also much used in the towns. They are kept in place by two thongs meeting between the big toe and extending thence, the one behind the ball of the toe and the other round the base of the instep to the sides. The wooden sandals are merely clogs, the middle portion of the lower part of which is cut out, except near the toe and the heel, so as to keep the feet out of the mud and water on the ground. Priests and Shan travellers most frequently wear leather sandals; and wayfarers as a rule walk barefoot in order to save their sandals. On entering a house or a monastery, or when approaching any religious shrine to make obeisance and repeat the religious precepts, the sandals are invariably doffed in token of respect.

In the towns the use of patent leather shoes, and also of hose or socks, has for years past become the customary attire of the up-to-date young Burman, and this is more particularly the case among petty officials and clerks; but that is merely a very minor item among the many changes, which are often anything but improvements, taking place among the Burmese coming more directly in contact with western civilization.

BURMA UNDER BRITISH RULE

Paper being imported from India in large quantities, though of course the finer qualities come from Europe, the native manufacture is now confined mainly to the preparation of *Parabaik*, or paper-slates used at monasteries, and of umbrellas. The inner fibre of soft bamboo shoots or the bark of the *Mahlaing* or paper-mulberry (*Broussonettia papyrifera*) being pounded into a pulp with water, and half its weight of lime being then added, it is boiled with water until nothing but the pulp is left. This is pounded and spread thinly over a coarse cotton muslin framework, and allowed to dry in the sun. It now forms a rough grey parchment, about a cubit in breadth, which is folded up in alternating folds of about nine inches wide. When coated with finely powdered charcoal dust mixed in glutinous rice-water, it is ready for being written upon with pencils of steatite or soapstone.

Umbrellas are made of the same sort of parchment-like paper, glued to spokes of thin split bamboo, and fastened to a stem made of the *Tiyowa* or "umbrella-handle bamboo" (*Thyrsostachys Siamensis*). They are usually coated with an oily waterproof varnish which gives them, when open, a diaphanous yellow appearance; and such alone may be held over priests and other "religious;" but, for umbrellas used by ordinary folks, a coating of black varnish is often preferred as forming a better protection against the sun. Workers in the fields and the jungle frequently wear shield-like coverings (*Kadú*) for the head and shoulders, made of leaves and cane, or else large conical Shan hats (*Gamauk*) with broad convex rims, about a couple of feet in diameter. Made of bamboo node-sheaths stitched together with cane, these are very light. Completely waterproof, they act both as sunshade and umbrella. The Burman does not mind getting wet so long as his hair is kept dry, but he feels sure he will be attacked with jungle fever if he allows that to get damp; for his coarse black locks, long as a woman's, are not easily dried.

Most of the paper umbrellas in use in the more populous parts near the sea-board are of Chinese manufacture, imported from Singapore, yet the umbrella-making in-

386

dustry is still largely followed up country, and particularly around Mandalay. The tide of fashion has here also begun so to modify and alter past custom that cheap umbrellas of European make are gradually ousting the still cheaper indigenous article. But the young Burmese woman of a few years ago, with her wavy-lined *Tamein* and a paper umbrella, had a more attractive and artistic picturesqueness than her present successor, wearing a dull maroon skirt and carrying a black umbrella, or a red or green parasol.

No short account of the minor rural industries can be considered complete without reference to cheroot-making. Every Burmese female can roll a cheroot, and all throughout the province cheroot-making is followed either as a profession or else to eke out other means of livelihood.

Though tobacco of good quality is grown on alluvial deposits in the bends of streams, and though cultivation is capable of extension far beyond the 71,015 acres now under this crop, yet most of the tobacco consumed is imported from Madras. Before use it is damped and softened with cocoa-nut water, which mellows the otherwise highly saltpetrous leaf.

The cheroot (*Séleik*, "rolled tobacco") made entirely of tobacco is, however, an innovation of comparatively recent date. The real Burmese cheroot consists mostly of other ingredients. It is a mixture of finely chopped wood,—the dry, dead wood of the Ôkhnè tree (*Streblus asper*) being preferred wherever available,—jaggery, chopped tobacco, and other herbs, rolled up in a casing of leaves or of the thin, soft inner skin of the sheaths growing round the nodes of large bamboos. Some of these cheroots are eight to nine inches in length and four to six inches in circumference at the thick end. They have a harsh, dry, pungent flavour, a liking for which can only be an acquired taste. But the Burmese are initiated to it at the earliest possible age, and it is not altogether an uncommon sight to see sucklings being given a smoke immediately after having been fed at the breast. Altogether, however, the Burmese infant receives peculiar treatment. Kept at his mother's breast so long as she is able to nurse it, or till its place is usurped by a later arrival, the child is not infrequently passed from breast to breast round a circle of matrons when chatting of an evening, just as the cheroot is passed on from mouth to mouth for a whiff to assist the flow of conversation.

When a half-smoked cheroot is not required for immediate further use, the lighted portion is quenched, and the stump stuck like an ear-ring in the loose pierced lobe of the ear, if the Burman should not happen to be wearing a jacket containing a pocket ; and when at work he is seldom encumbered in this latter way.

Even the primitive Burmese cheroot of chopped wood and tobacco is probably doomed soon to become a thing of the past. The consumption of cheroots of pure tobacco has been gradually extending during the last twenty years ; and now at all the large towns throughout the whole length of the land, from Rangoon to Bhamo, small cigarettes, onomatopœiacally called *Ségalé*, are being made with shag and tissue paper and sold in the Bazaars and at the corners of the streets.

Tobacco was originally introduced and regarded purely as medicine, as its name (*Sé*) indicates. But other narcotics are also euphemiously covered by the same term. Thus, while the smoking of tobacco is "drinking medicine," "inhaling" and "eating medicine" are polite terms for smoking and eating opium,—opium (*Bein: Sénet*) being called "black medicine," and ganja or Indian hemp (*Bin: Séchauk*) being spoken of as "dry medicine." Fortunately, however, the preparation and sale of these drugs cannot as yet be numbered among the rural industries followed by the Burmese, though their neighbours on the north-east, the Shans and the Yunnanese, grow the white opium largely as a field-crop and are habituated to the use of the drug. Nor can the preparation and vend of fermented or distilled liquors be classed in such a category ; for the whole of the traffic in such stimulants is in the hands of Chinamen and natives of India, although the Chins and some other hill-tribes brew a sort of rice-beer (*Kaung*), which is largely consumed at their tribal festivals.

Chapter XIII

MINERAL RESOURCES

BURMA is rich in minerals of various kinds, though the two which usually form the surest foundations of national prosperity, coal and iron, have as yet nowhere been found in large workable quantities or of superior quality. Down both sides of the Pegu Yoma range of hills, extending northwards from near Rangoon for more than two hundred miles, and skirting the Paunglaung hills to the east of the Sittang river, there run broad belts of ferrugineous laterite which have in past times been worked for iron. These abandoned workings can still be seen in the forests, and in some cases—as at Thanseik, "the place for shipping iron," about twelve miles north of Shwegyin on the Sittang river—the names of villages sometimes seem to imply that there was formerly a regular trade in iron from them. But imports of iron are so cheap, and the requirements are altogether so slight with regard to this commodity, that the iron ores which have been found in various parts of the province have never proved of economic importance. Nor have the Burmese apparently ever acquired the art of transmuting iron into steel.

Coal is found in the Thayetmyo, Upper Chindwin, and Shwebo districts, and in the Shan States, as one of the Eocene or early Tertiary rocks forming the Nummulitic group, whose chief economic products are petroleum, limestone, coal, and brine. It also occurs in Mergui in the Tenasserim group of rocks of doubtful age, though probably belonging to the Tertiary period. The fuel of the country has always been wood, coal never yet having been utilized for any purpose by the Burmese themselves. King Mindôn apparently gave some pass-

389

ing attention to possibilities with this product, for in
1886 a Shan chief and a village headman assured Sir
Charles Bernard, the Chief Commissioner, that they had
seen large specimens of coal taken from a pit on the
Panlaung river (Sittang) and carried to Mandalay.

As yet no great trade has sprung up in coal-mining,
though efforts have from time to time been made on a
small scale. The best coal-tracts are probably to be
found amid the limestone hills of the Shan country, and
will be brought to light when the tracts are traversed
by the railway lines now under project and in course of
construction. During the past twelve or thirteen years the
coal-mining work carried on has not yielded very satisfactory results, nor has it in any perceptible degree freed
the province from its dependence on sea-borne coal, imported in 1899–1900 to the extent of 33,998 tons, valued
at £35,914.

In 1886 negotiations, begun three years earlier, were
entered into with a Calcutta company for a coal-mining
lease for thirty years in the Thayetmyo district, the
company covenanting to pay a nominal rent on the land
actually worked and a royalty of two annas or twopence
on every ton of coal extracted after 1st January, 1895.
After very feeble attempts work was abandoned in 1888.
Though renewed in 1894, negotiations in a similar direction led to no results.

A more energetic attempt was made at the Lingadaw
or Kabwet coal-fields in the Shwebo district, which were
leased to a local syndicate in 1891. Work was begun
about four miles to the east of the Irrawaddy, with
which connexion was opened by a tramway, and the
Burma Coal Company was formed in 1893 to develop
the fields. The coal was used on the Burma State
Railway, and on the steamers of the Irrawaddy Flotilla
Company and of Government, The output reached
23,000 tons in 1896, but was reduced to the half of that
in 1897 owing to work being interfered with by flooding.
Declining still further, the outturn was only 6,975 tons
in 1898, and 8,105 in 1899. The coal is of fair quality,
and the fields have an advantageous position with
regard to rail and river. The average selling price is

ten rupees (13*s*. 4*d*.) a ton. The young industry is hampered, however, by want of capital.

Most of the coal-fields discovered as yet have some drawback or other to their profitable working. In the Chindwin district, the Kalé fields, on the Myittha river, yield an excessively friable coal; while those on the Nantabin and Paletwa drainage have the seams embedded in soft clay, and are therefore difficult to work. What is obtained from the Panlaung river, east of Yaméthin, at the foot of the Shan hills, yields a dull flame, making it unsuitable for furnaces. In the Lashio and Namma valleys, in the Shan State of North Theinni, now approached by the Mandalay-Kunlôn railway, seams have been found up to thirty feet in thickness; but unfortunately the deposits resemble lignite rather than true coal, being very light and liable to crack when dry, so that they cannot be considered of the first quality. In the Laikha State lignite deposits have also been found.

So far as mere reports of officers of the Geological Survey are concerned, the Tenasserim valley in the Mergui district appears to be one of the richest localities in coal deposits. Examined in 1892–93, coal was found of two distinct ages, belonging to the upper Carboniferous and the Tertiary systems. The former, though the more widely distributed, is economically worthless; but the Tertiary coal, found at two places (Kyámithwé and Kamapyin) on the western bank of the river, is said to be of very superior quality, and is estimated to be capable of yielding close on a million tons. There is no market for coal in that immediate vicinity, however, and the labour difficulty would be so great that coal from Bengal could probably be laid down in Rangoon or Moulmein cheaper than the produce of mines up the Tenasserim river.

More recently still a perhaps more important discovery of coal of good quality has been reported from Lawksawk in the Yatsauk territory of the Southern Shan States, a tract drained by the Zawgyi river and within comparatively easy reach of the Rangoon and Mandalay railway line. The coal is said to lie near the surface, and to extend over a large area. As Lawksawk consists mainly of a table-land varying from 2,500 to 3,000 feet above sea-level, the climate is said to be exceptionally good for this part of the world, the heat, even in the hottest season, not being excessive for Europeans.

Petroleum occurs in various parts of the province, the Arakan oil being clear and limpid, while the Upper Burma product is dark, thick and viscous. The Kyauk-pyu oil-fields of Arakan were the first to be worked directly by European agency. About 1878 the Boronga Oil Company obtained concessions in the Kyaukpyu district, and commenced operations on a large scale in the low hills a few miles from that small coasting port. Experts were brought over from Canada, and the work of boring into the rock was pushed on in the face of many discouragements. In a climate notoriously malarious for more than the half of each year, the Canadian miners, during intervals between attacks of fever, pushed downwards with the deep borings through rock. In June, 1880, when I visited these oil-fields, they were working with tamping-rods at a depth of nearly 800 feet without having struck an oil-flow, while natives working with rude appliances in comparatively shallow pits near at hand were having an output up to twenty barrels a day. Despite patient, persevering efforts, and the outlay of a very considerable amount of capital, the Company had to go into liquidation in 1885. Since then operations in Kyaukpyu and Akyab have been carried on merely by local agency and with varying success. The largest yield was in 1892, when 308,091 gallons were obtained ; in 1899 it was 167,227 gallons.

Sometimes eruptions of petroleum, accompanied by spontaneous combustion, take place in the sea off the Arakan coast. Of one such I was an eye-witness early in April, 1882, whilst being rowed out from Sandoway to the mail steamer moored in the offing. Far north on the horizon, in the direction of the island of Cheduba, a vast pillar of fire burst suddenly from the sea, shooting up for an immense height and ending in great volumes of dense smoke. This phenomenon continued for about four to five minutes before the column of fire subsided.

THE PETROLEUM FIELDS

The Upper Burma oil-fields, scattered over the Magwe, Minbu, Pakôkku, and Myingyan districts, which form the south-western portion of the central dry zone, are partly the property of hereditary well-owners (*Twinza* or "well eaters"), and partly the property of the State. Earth-oil royalties formed one of the seven main heads of revenue in the time of the Burmese Government, the trade in this product being in the hands of a Rangoon firm, which bought the oil from private well-owners and worked the royal wells by direct agency, paying a royalty of eight annas (8*d.*) per 365 lb. in the former case, and of one rupee twelve annas (2*s.* 4*d.*) in the latter. This contract lapsed in 1891, but was renewed for another twenty years to the Burma Oil Company on payment of a fixed royalty of eightpence per 365 lbs. (100 viss).

The most important of the Upper Burma oil-fields are those near Yenangyaung ("where earth-oil flows"), and Yenangyat ("earth-oil barren"), situated along the left bank of the Irrawaddy in the Magwe district. Estimated to extend over about eighty square miles in all, this oil-tract forms a fairly level plateau, ranging from 260 to 300 feet above the low-water level of the Irrawaddy, but much intersected by deep, narrow ravines. The strata consist for the most part of laminated and clayey sands, while pebbly beds occasionally occur along with layers of sand or gravel cemented into rather a hard bed of conglomerate. The Yenangyaung fields yielded 22,111,514 gallons in 1899, and the Yenangyat 10,030,790 gallons, while the whole output for Burma was 32,309,531 gallons, yielding a revenue of £27,179.

Within the tracts leased to the Burma Oil, Minbu Oil, and Burma Petroleum-Producing Companies in the Magwe, Pakôkku, and Minbu districts, the rights of native workers owning wells in the vicinity of State wells have been duly secured by the publication of rules defining the areas within which the native workers may work, and the rights which they possess. The richness of some of the tracts is shown by the fact that experiments made in 1893 at Yenangyaung showed that new wells can be sunk at a distance of sixty feet from existing wells without reducing the output of oil from the latter.

Large oil-producing tracts are still available for leasing, and the fixation of the rate of exchange at 1s. 4d. per rupee has now placed this industry in a much more hopeful position than formerly. But speculative it must always remain to a certain extent, as the sinking of a deep shaft does not invariably result in a flow of oil. A boring sunk to a depth of 700 feet in the Minbu field by the Burma Oil Company in 1896 failed to strike the oil known to exist there. Further borings made by the Minbu Oil Company to a much greater depth proved equally unsuccessful, and the field was abandoned in 1899.

About a couple of miles from the town of Minbu are the well known curious mud volcanoes or "dragons' scratching pits" (*Nagagyit Dwin*). From about fifteen to twenty feet in height, they continue in a ceaseless state of mild activity, throwing up small quantities of hot liquid mud with gaseous exhalations which can be ignited. The whole country round about there exhibits indications of oil-producing strata in the rocks below the surface.

The Burmese method of working the oil-wells is very primitive, and has undergone little or no change for generations past. A shaft of about four feet square is sunk at what is considered a likely spot, though the upper soil gives no practical indication of what may be expected deep down below the surface. Propped with posts of cutch (*Acacia Catechu*), which yields excellent timber though of rather small dimensions in the dry zone, the shaft is sunk till the oil-bearing stratum is tapped or boring has to be abandoned. Above each well and supported by two side posts is a crossbeam, having a central wheel over which a rope passes attached to an earthenware pot that is let down to fill itself with oil. When first brought up, the petroleum is a thin, watery fluid, but it soon thickens and becomes viscous. It is of a dirty-brown colour, with a somewhat greenish tinge, and has a pungent odour, as is pointedly indicated in its Burmese name, *Yenán* or "fœtid water." The majority of native wells vary from about 200 to 250 feet, and the deepest are only slightly in excess of 300 feet; but the output is largest from deeper wells worked by European agency. The oil-bearing stratum itself is known to be about 200 feet in thickness at Yenangyaung, although it may perhaps be considerably thicker.

The bulk of the outturn from the petroleum wells of Burma finds its way to the refining works of the Burma Oil Company in Rangoon, where it is prepared for the market. Rich in paraffin wax, Burmese petroleum is of great technical value as a lubricator. Most of it is consumed in India, as the foreign exports in wax and oil only amounted to £114,159 in 1899, and that was a large advance on previous exports. As a luminant it cannot compete in purity with Kerosine, of which 4,740,657 gallons, mostly from America, valued at £167,052 were imported into Burma in the two years 1898–1900.

Tin, found in the granite of the Tavoy and Mergui districts, has long been worked. Over three hundred years ago it is said to have been exported largely to India. Operations in more recent times have been carried on with varying results, though on the whole with comparatively little success. The mine-workers are mostly Chinese. Owing to want of an adequate water supply during the dry season, work is chiefly confined to the unhealthy rainy months; and this, added to want of capital and inability to control the truculent and quarrelsome labourers efficiently, has hitherto proved an insurmountable difficulty to anything like real progress in the industry. The Maliwun mines near the southern extremity of Tenasserim were leased to a Rangoon firm for fifteen years from 1873; but after three years the lease was resigned, the physical difficulties of the country, the malarious nature of its climate, and the absence of communication with the civilized world for weeks at a time during the busiest season of the year all proving serious drawbacks to successful enterprise. In 1892 a lease was granted for five years, with provision for extension for other twenty-one years, a royalty of five per cent. being paid on the value of tin exported. This advantage was not claimed, however, and mining had again to be carried on merely on a small scale by native workers. A lease of 400 acres has recently been given to a European firm which proposes to introduce hydraulic appliances. The industry is of no great commercial value, however, the largest output having been 1,339 cwt. in 1897, valued at about £4,345. As tin is also worked in Karenni, north-east of Toungoo, from ore similar to that obtained in Mergui, it seems not improbable that the stanniferous belts of granite may be found occurring all throughout the hills between the Salween and Sittang rivers : and if this can be proved, the fact may perhaps become of considerable commercial importance.

Silver and lead have been worked from time immemorial, as there was no coinage in Burma until after the annexation of the coast tracts of Arakan and Tennaserim by the British in 1826. Till the reign of King Mindôn (1852–1878) the kingdom of Ava had no coinage, payments being made in bullion of gold, silver, and lead. Even within the last twenty years payment was made almost everywhere north of the capital in ingots and bullion of recognized standards of quality. The whole of the trade at Bhamo with Shan and Yunnanese caravans was adjusted by such means, in addition to direct barter of goods. Mindôn endeavoured to introduce both a silver and a gold coinage, modelled on the rupee and the sovereign respectively ; but the attempt was on the whole a failure, as there was no security for the quality of the metal, and as this currency was not made legal tender. Hence the bulk of commercial transactions were regulated by the weighing and assaying of silver.

Silver was practically the standard, gold being considered about seventeen times as valuable, while lead had only about one-five-hundredth part the value of silver. Payments to the royal treasury took place in "flowered silver" (*Gnwébwin*), the purest description of silver bullion containing only from two to five per cent. of alloy. This derived its name from the flower-like crystallization setting in on its surface when cooling after being poured out of a crucible. There were various recognized degrees of impurity, varying up to about twenty-five per cent. of alloy. The weighing and the assaying of gold and silver were in the hands of *Pwèza* or "brokers," and each assay reduced through fees and wastage the capital value by two and a half per cent. Hence forty mercantile transactions sufficed to dissipate any given capital under this crude substitute for a minted coinage.

In many parts of the Shan States, and in Karenni, this primitive system still obtains, and interesting specimens of the "flowered silver" used in place of coinage are often procurable in the bazaars. In bargaining, silver to about the amount required is poured out from a crucible on to a flat stone, and during the process of haggling perhaps a few drops more are added after the quantity originally poured out has cooled, these drops remaining as round blobs or excrescences. In the next transaction a piece may perhaps have to be cut off, if a smaller payment has to be made. The red Karen and Shan who used to come in from their forest wilds to Toungoo bazaar about ten years ago, generally brought well-wrought bowls of silver, which they exchanged against their weight of British rupee coins in order to enable themselves to make their purchases in a market where barter was no longer the method of trade.

Galena, rich in silver, is obtainable in various parts of the Paunglaung range of hills immediately to the east of the Sittang river, but the chief lead and silver mines worked of recent years are those at Bawzaing in one of the Southern Shan States. After the annexation of Upper Burma this industry dwindled, as the miners could find no market for the lead in consequence of the prohibition of its import into the plains of Burmah whilst the work of pacification was in course of progress. Since 1890 this restriction has been removed, and the mines are worked to a small extent by a Chinese lessee, who pays a royalty of three rupees (four shillings) per 365 lb. (100 viss).

There are many localities throughout the province which are capable of yielding gold, yet the great bulk of this metal used in Burma for making jewellery, gilding pagodas and sacred shrines, and for other purposes, comes from China in the shape of leaf-gold. This is bought in the bazaars at ever-varying current rates, and is melted down to form heavy solid articles like bangles, necklaces, and ear cylinders.

Gold is washed down in small particles by many of the streams, and in several places the sifting of gold dust from the sands forms an industry on a small scale, yielding rather a meagre and precarious livelihood. The washings are generally carried on in the beds of hill streams, the alluvial gold-bearing deposit being panned out in the crudest manner possible in shallow round wooden trays.

All over the country local names are met with which indicate at any rate past operations with regard to gold washing. Shwegyin, a large town on the eastern bank of the Sittang, receives its name from the "gold sifting" still carried on in the bed of the Shwegyin river. In various parts of the country are to be found hills called Shwedaung or "hill of gold," and inquiries will invariably elicit reliable information that gold was formerly worked there either by merely washing the dirt from alluvial deposits or else by sifting earth dug out of shallow pits and trenches. Thus, at the Shwedaung near Tavoy, gold deposits were found by a Ceylon planter who settled there some years ago. Neglecting his plantation for the gold which he had not capital enough to work, he died in poor circumstances in 1897, rendered miserable by the knowledge of gold being within his reach while he was without the means of actually obtaining it. Searching for the matrix of gold-bearing quartz and digging into the solid rock appear to have been methods quite beyond the Burmese, whose acquaintance with minerals is altogether extremely scanty, even as compared with the knowledge of metallurgy obtaining among their near neighbours, the Shan.

It is by no means improbable that, as regards the precious metals, the greatest mineral wealth in Burma will be found in the Paunglaung range of hills forming the eastern watershed of the Sittang river, and spreading thence northwards and eastwards across the Shan hills. Tin, copper, and gold have been found at various localities throughout the range. I have myself found gold-bearing quartz, in outward appearance and structure

THE WUNTHO GOLD-FIELDS

closely resembling the matrix of the Mysore gold-fields, in a locality within easy reach of the Rangoon and Mandalay railway line, and with abundant supplies of water close at hand for all possible requirements.

In the Shan hills gold deposits are also known, and fields of great magnitude and richness (*omne ignotum pro magnifico*) are said to occur further to the north-east, in the wild Wa country, which will be brought within somewhat easier reach when once the railway line has been opened from Mandalay to Lashio, on the way to the Kunlôn ferry on the Salween river.

The only place where gold-mining is as yet being carried on in any practical business-like manner is at the gold-fields in a portion of the Katha district, which formerly formed the Wuntho Shan State, lying to the west of the Irrawaddy river. Since December, 1895, the quarrying and crushing of gold-bearing quartz has been in progress at the Kyaukpazat Mine, situated about twelve miles from the Nankan station on the Mandalay and Myitkyina line of railway. Abundance of wood and water being procurable, operations were begun with the erection of a ten-stamp mill worked by a portable engine of sixteen nominal horse-power. The yield has hitherto been small, only 1,196 ounces being obtained in 1899; but this yield will now be increased by the introduction of the cyanide process, in 1900, for dealing with the tailings. The outturn could, however, be very largely increased if the capital of the small company were sufficient to enable operations to be conducted on a much more extensive scale.

The Wuntho gold-fields extend over a considerable area, the different tracts having specific names derived from neighbouring streams or villages. After visiting the Kyaukpazat Mines in 1898, I also examined portions of the Panzit and Legyin tracts further to the north. Here also gold-bearing quartz is undoubtedly obtainable. "There's gold there, lots o' gold," said one of the prospecting licensees—a working miner and philosopher, more richly endowed with experience in toiling for the gain of others than with lucre and worldly possessions of his own—after he had shown me over the spots where he had struck the ore within the area of which he wished to acquire the lease, "but to work it *properly* needs at least two lacs of rupees (£13,333); and if I had two lacs of rupees, I shouldn't be here looking for gold in Burma."

This is a very correct indication of one of the two main reasons why gold is not already worked to a large extent in Burma. Beyond doubt there are many parts of the province rich in gold; but it nowhere exists in large pockets and nuggets, in a form which permits of wealth being literally picked up. It will have to be quarried in subterranean mines, and crushed and won at considerable expense. Capital is requisite, and the industry may be safely expected to yield a fair interest for concerns of this nature, say about ten to twelve per cent.; but there is little likelihood of shares in any such concern rushing up to enormous value in consequence of immense harvests of gold easily and inexpensively won from the rocks.

Without being undertaken in a solid, business-like manner supported by a sufficiency of capital, gold-mining is never likely to make much progress in Burma; but otherwise it should soon be able to establish itself on a sound footing as a profitable business resting on a much safer basis than most mining enterprises. Hitherto, however, most of the mining leases taken out in Burma have been applied for by speculators who never had any intention of working them except by floating companies for drawing other peoples' money into their own pockets. During 1899–1900 several exploring and prospecting licenses were issued, and four syndicates, each formed with a capital of £5,000, began prospecting operations. The gold is there; of that there can be no doubt.

Another cause tending to operate very forcibly against the establishment of gold-mining on a proper basis in Burma has been the limitations of the mining rules. Under the mining rules obtaining in 1898 no lease could be given for more than 160 acres, or one quarter of a square mile. The practical effect of this is that, for example, in the Panzit and Legyin tracts, it would be impossible to find a sufficiency of water for crushing and other requirements on the leased area or within reasonable distance of it. Both at Panzit and at Legyin, although convinced that the rocks were auriferous, I was equally convinced that gold-mining could not be profitably carried on as an industry on a large scale unless the 160 acre restriction were cast aside, and one lease given for each area. If this were done, then crushing works could be located on large main streams having an ample perennial supply of water, and the ore could be brought by tramways from the various mine-shafts to the crushing mills. It is only thus that Government can reasonably expect capital to be attracted towards and invested in gold-mining in Burma ; and it is only thus that such investments can be made to yield a fair dividend of about ten or twelve per cent.

With more liberal rules, however, there are various auriferous localities in the Pegu, Toungoo, and Katha districts, within easy access of existing railway lines, which could yield remunerative returns in gold if reasonable inducements were offered to attract capital for the introduction of this industry on a considerable scale. The new Mining Rules of May, 1899, revised the royalties on gold and silver, and reduced them to $7\frac{1}{2}$ per cent. ; but it is equally important that they should authorize the Government of Burma to deal more promptly and liberally than hitherto with syndicates having bonâ fide intention of investing capital in mining enterprises, because this must be the first essential step towards making mining operations possible under conditions favourable for utilizing the great mineral wealth known to exist in Burma.

Jade-stone, which formed another of the many monopolies of the Burmese Government, and was retained as such by the British, is found in large quantity about the headwaters of the Chindwin and the Mogaung tributaries of the Irrawaddy between the twenty-fifth and twenty-sixth parallels of latitude. The mine-workers are wild Kachin tribesmen, while the dealers in and users of jade are Chinese merchants ; and the exports, averaging some 4,000 cwt. a year, valued at nearly £50,000, are almost all shipped to Singapore, for distribution thence to Chinese and Japanese ports. Very small pieces of jade of the purest colour and best quality sometimes fetch fancy prices, while great blocks of inferior quality have little or no value in the connoisseurs' eyes.

The most celebrated of all jade deposits is a large cliff called the Nantelung or "difficult of access," overhanging a tributary of the Chindwin river at a place distant about nine days' journey from where the latter receives the waters of the Uru from the north-east. But the guardian spirits there have been ill-disposed for nearly a generation back, in consequence of which work has long remained in abeyance. The most productive mines at present are those in the country of the Merip Kachin tribe, where some of the largest quarries run up to about fifty yards in length, by forty in breadth, and twenty in depth. Quarrying operations are confined to the dry season, being undertaken from November till May. Even then the best quarries are generally flooded, which greatly increases the labour of working out the stone. During February and March, when the floor of the quarry or pit can be kept dry for a few hours by means of hard baling, large fires are lighted with wood at the base of the stone. Despite the tremendous heat evolved, a careful watch is kept to detect the first signs of splitting in the rock. As soon as these become noticeable, the Kachins attack the stone with pickaxes and hammers or insert levers in the cracks and thus detach portions of the rock. Mortality is high among the jade-workers, as the heat is almost insupportable and the labour severe ; but the Kachin are jealous of their sole right to quarry the stone. Burmese and Shan brokers arrange prices for the quarried stone between the Kachin miners and the Chinese traders, all payments being made in coined silver. From the quarries the blocks of stone are carried by coolies to Nanyaseik, whence it is transported by water in dug-out canoes to Mogaung, on the railway line leading southwards to Mandalay and Rangoon.

When the British began administering this part of Upper Burma, the Burmese system of annually farming the right of collecting duty on jade was continued, the sale realizing £3,333 for 1887–88. The local chief of the jade-producing tract levied 3s. 4d. on every load of jade leaving his territory, and also received from the miners ten per cent. of the sums they obtained from the jade-purchasers. The headman at Nanyaseik levied 1s. 4d. on each load, and the farmer of the right of collection for the year claimed an *ad valorem* duty of 33⅓ per cent. In 1893 this system was slightly altered by extending the period of farming the collection of duty from one to three years, for the business was found to be of so speculative a character that even Chinamen, addicted as they are to all forms of gambling, hesitated to pay a long price for holding the pool merely for one year. The revenue had consequently sunk to only £2,400 a year, but at once rose to £3,474 on a three years' lease being sold by auction.

The blocks of jade are mostly taken to Mandalay to be sawn up. There has always been a good deal of smuggling of stone, to evade payment of the heavy royalty to the farmer of the duty. To try and check this, a subordinate officer on the temporary establishment of the Forest Department was stationed on the railway line between Mogaung and Mandalay during 1898—for jade-stone is classed as "minor forest produce," though the revenue obtained from it is credited to "land revenue." The salary of this temporary Forest Ranger was disbursed from money lodged by the farmer of the jade revenue; but, as the Forest Regulation and Rules permit no power of search extending to goods, luggage, or persons in transit, it is difficult to see what useful purpose he could serve. The jade-farmer himself desired this, however, after extensive smuggling had been discovered in 1897. Moreover, he particularly requested that the post should be filled by a *Baungbe Wut* or "trouser-wearing man" and not given to any mere Burmese, Shan, or Chinaman, who, though infinitely better fitted for detective purposes, would not fill the hearts of the smugglers with awe and dread, or show so clearly that the revenue-farmer was determined to put an end to such malpractices.

The way in which the large blocks of jade are mani-pulated may be seen any time one drives along China Street, the long road leading from the southwest corner of the walls of Mandalay city southwards to the Arakan pagoda. They are sawn through by hand with piano-wire, strung tightly across a bent piece of wood, under the action of water constantly dropping from a vessel hung above the block. To assist the process fine sand is strewn on the stone where the wire-saw works. The exterior of the blocks is oxidized to a greyish-brown colour, but the ooze trickling down on both sides of the stone as the saw passes backwards and forwards is of the green colour that one would expect from jade. The exterior of the block seems to give absolutely no indication of the quality of the jade lying at its core, and in so far the traffic in rough blocks is about as complete a mercantile example of buying a pig in a poke as can be imagined.

The Ruby Mines and their produce also formed another of the monopolies of the Burmese King, which was likewise retained for the State under British administration. Rubies and spinels are found in several parts of northern Burma, as near the jade mines above Nanyaseik in the Myitkyina district, and at Sagyin, about twelve miles north of Mandalay. But the country around Mogôk, the headquarters of the Ruby Mines district, is by far the richest ruby-producing area that has yet been discovered. As the inhabitants of this tract were said to possess certain undefined rights of working the mines, subject to their selling all the outturn to Government or to farmers of the royal monopoly, one of the first duties of the civil officer on the occupation of the district at the end of 1886 was to verify what the rights or privileges of the people actually were, and to ascertain in how far these could be supported by acknowledged custom or by actual concessions from past rulers of Ava. All rubies above a certain weight were claimed as royal perquisites, and this led to the secretion or breaking up of the largest and most valuable stones. The Ruby Regulation was passed during 1887, and rules were framed under it for the control of mining for rubies and precious stones generally, and for fixing and realizing the revenues obtainable from such sources.

The great Ruby Mines, forming the Mogôk, Kyatpyin, and Kathè circles of the Ruby Mines district, are situated at an elevation of about four to six thousand feet on the southern face of a spur trending westwards from the main watershed between the Irrawaddy and the Salween rivers, and forming the drainage between the Shweli on the north and the Myitngé on the south, both tributary to the Irrawaddy. At the time of the British occupation the ruby-producing tracts were found to be inhabited by a motley crew of Burmese, Shan, and Chinese, together with local hill tribesmen of Chinese extraction called Palaung and Lishaw. Whilst the measures to be adopted for the future working of this tract were under consideration, they were allowed to mine for rubies by their own customary methods on payment of small fees for licenses. Operations were primitive, resolving themselves into three different methods. A *Hmyáw Dwin* or "cutting made by the flow of water" might be formed on a spot chosen on any hill-side, a stream of water being led over it and a gully formed in which the ruby-bearing soil (*Byôn*) that collected was carefully turned over and searched. Or miners would go down a *Lu Dwin* or "man pit" formed by a natural fissure or a small cave in the hills, and dig out the soil at the bottom of this, a method confined solely to the dry season of the year. Otherwise *Twinlôn* or "dug pits" were sunk to a depth varying from about twenty to thirty feet, so as to tap the stratum of *Byôn* or ruby gravel in the low-lying alluvial deposits where this is found.

The mining is purely a matter of chance. Whoever turns over and carefully examines the largest amount of *Byôn* or ruby matrix has the best chance of reaping a harvest of rubies and spinels, though chiefly the latter. The whole of the small plain of Mogôk is dotted over with the *Twinlôn* of the native miners, while the hill-sides are scored and marked by the water-channels of the *Hmyáw Dwin*. In some cases water for these latter is brought from a considerable distance, and at a small village called Kyaukpyatthat, near the extreme west of the ruby-producing tract, a piece of very interesting rough Burmese engineering may be seen in the construction, with bamboos alone, of a primitive aqueduct conveying water from one hillside to another across a miniature valley between the two slopes. The intervening space from the water-trench on the northern hill to that on the southern is bridged over with a trestle-work of big bamboos lashed together to form a series of scaffold-like supports upon which bamboos, with the solid internal divisions at the nodes perforated, are laid as water-pipes, the thin end of each being fitted into the thick end of the next bamboo. There is a good deal of leakage, but the water is conducted across in sufficient quantity to serve the purpose required, so that the object in view is attained. Speaking merely from recollection, this rough bamboo aqueduct must be about a couple of hundred feet in length, and from forty to fifty feet high where the gully below was deepest.

Towards the close of 1899 arrangements for working the Ruby Mines were completed by Government, a concession being granted for seven years at an annual rental of four lacs of rupees (£26,666) to five licensees, who floated the Burma Ruby Mines, Limited, on the London market. The concession was in the form of a lease granting the right to mine rubies by European methods and to levy royalties from native miners working by indigenous methods. It was some considerable time before work could be advanced beyond the preliminary stages, much time and labour being spent in the first year in bringing up machinery to the mines. From Thabeitkyin, on the Irrawaddy, to Mogôk, a distance of sixty miles, the road passes for the most part through heavy jungle, pestilential with malaria from the time the first showers of rain fall in May until the soil dries up towards the close of the year. The road is not yet completely metalled, but up to the end of 1897-98, only two-thirds of it had been metalled, and cart traffic had to be suspended from May till October. During these months drafts to or from Bernardmyo—a small military station ten miles to the north of Mogôk, where the left wing of a European regiment is stationed for the protection of the Mogôk and the Ruby Mines district generally—are not allowed to proceed up or down the road on account of its unhealthiness and of difficulties connected with transport. There is no danger to the Europeans in Mogôk from having the troops at some distance, for the Govern-

THE RUBY MINES

ment officers and the Company's European employés form a volunteer company having a strength of over forty and well able to defend themselves temporarily in case of necessity. In the early days of 1889-90, when the Ruby Mines Company began their operations, these drawbacks and difficulties of communication were much greater than they still are ; for the district was unsettled by bands of dacoits, headed by Paw Kwe, a late official of the Burmese Government and a man of great local influence. Even when these organized gangs were broken up, dacoities and robberies on the road were still unduly frequent. And at Mogôk and Kyatpyin, the centres of the industry, the initial operations of the Company not unnaturally excited the apprehensions and the ill-will of the native miners who had hitherto held a practical monopoly of the working of the mines.

During the first year of their lease the Company experienced considerable friction with the native miners ; but, about the end of 1890, better relations were established through an arrangement being come to by which the latter were freed from most of the restrictions on the traffic in rubies, in return for fixed monthly payments to be made by them to the Company. A license system was then introduced under which, subject to certain restrictions, the licensed miners could dispose of rubies and spinels to whom they pleased in return for monthly license fees paid to the Company as Government lessee of the whole mining tract.

From various causes the results of the Company's working were not so remunerative as had been anticipated by those who competed eagerly for shares when the lists were opened for subscription in London. Experience had to be bought and dearly paid for, and several years passed before so important a primary condition of success as the determination of the best system of mining had been fully considered and acted on. In 1895 the system of boring mines into the hill-sides, in order to tap the pockets or strata of ruby earth found there, was discarded in favour of open quarries from which the *Byôn* was extracted. Under this method the

whole of the surface soil is removed over considerable
areas till the matrix of ruby earth is reached at a depth
of about twenty feet, when this is dug up, trollied to the
steam cleansing-mill, washed, sieved, sorted, and examined, so that the rubies and spinels may be extracted
from the clean gravel. The machinery used for washing
is similar to that employed in the African diamond mines.
Abundance of water for washing away the clay and dirt
from the *Byôn*, and fuel to feed the mill-furnaces or other
motive power, are essential requisites for the industry.
As the forests around Mogôk and Kyatpyin have been
much exhausted by fuel-cutters,—for at an elevation of
4,000 to 6,000 feet natural regeneration and reproduction
are not vigorous,—the maintenance of an adequate fuel
supply has hitherto been both expensive and difficult,
even although steps were early taken by the Forest
Department to provide for present and future requirements by the reservation of the areas still under forest,
and by working them on a simple plan. To minimize
these drawbacks, and to work in the most economic
manner possible at Mogôk, the headquarters of the
mining industry, waterworks have now been constructed
in the neighbouring hills to provide for improved pumping machinery as well as for the generation and installation of electricity on a scale sufficient to supersede the
use of wood-fuel and luminants to any considerable
extent. This now enables the central mill to work day and
night, because the chance of reaping a rich harvest of the
precious stones is directly proportional to the quantity of
ruby gravel washed and examined. Operations have
thus been extended considerably, while working has at
the same time been made more economical.

When the picked stones have been sorted in flat
trays according to size, the work of closer scrutiny and
classification goes on in the offices. The rubies are
distinguished from the mere spinels by means of an
ingenious small instrument, like that used by surveyors
for measuring offset angles, in which each stone is placed
for examination. The ray of light passing through the
stone, being polarized in the instrument, comes to the
eye as a pure red ray in the case of a true ruby, whereas

the less valuable, though equally beautiful, spinel exhibits a blue tinge.

Although the Ruby Mines of Burma are perhaps the most productive in the world, the number of pure stones found of good quality and high value appears to be singularly small judging from the official returns. Thus the whole of the export of unset precious stones and pearls to Great Britain amounted in value only to £2,000 in 1896–97, and was *nil* in 1897–98, the total exports to foreign countries for these years being respectively £3,380 and £540, although the stones found in 1897 by the Company alone, exclusive of the outturn by native licensed miners, were valued at £53,497. The only exports of unset precious stones and pearls from 1898 to 1900 were to Singapore and to quite small amounts of £842 and £2,267. Practically, therefore, the whole of the output from the Ruby Mines, with the exception merely of a fine stone now and again, is absorbed by the Indian market, or is at any rate despatched to India, for distribution thence to other countries, so that these gems are not recorded among the exports from Burma. The necessary consequence of this is that the prosperity of the ruby mining industry ebbs and flows in accord with the prosperity and the general economic conditions of India.

The impoverishment of the general population, and the dislocation of trade throughout India on account of plague, famine, and frontier warfare in 1897 and 1898, reacted at once on the industry in Burma by causing cessation in the demand for low-grade stones. This depression became at once appreciable through the fees drawn by the Company from licenses to native miners sinking from £27,370 in 1896 to £9,919 in 1897, but they soon rose again to £14,292 in 1898, and £18,265 in 1899.

On the expiration of the Company's lease in 1896 this was renewed for a term of fourteen years at a rent of £21,000 *plus* a share of the profits. Since this arrangement was entered into the new mining rules of May, 1899, have been issued, revising royalties and fixing those on precious stones at thirty per cent. on the net profits

annually. Under new arrangements concluded in 1899
the whole of the debt owed by the Company to Government, amounting to £26,666, has been wiped off and the
rent reduced to £13,333 a year, while the Government's
share of the Company's net profits has been increased
from twenty to thirty per cent. This seems a very
profitable arrangement for the Company, as in normal
years the fees received from licenses amount to considerably more than the annual rent covenanted to be paid to
Government. The dividend of five per cent. announced
at the eleventh ordinary general meeting of the Company
in London on September 25, 1899, was the first dividend
declared, and the chairman then announced to the shareholders that he thought they might reasonably anticipate
a dividend twice as large next year, as all the Company's
difficulties had at length been overcome. This predic-
tion has been amply verified by a twelve and a half per
cent. dividend in 1900. The value of the stones won
by the Company reached £90,848, including three very
valuable rubies, one of seventy-seven carats being valued
at £26,666.

Except in so far as their operations are on a much
smaller scale than the Company's work, the licensed
native miners have an equal chance with the latter in
discovering stones of value ; and, as a matter of fact, the
largest ruby that has ever been known at Mogôk was
found in a native mine early in 1897. Speaking from
memory, this stone was, as I saw it in May, 1897, rhom-
boidal in shape with a superficies of about 2½ by 2 inches
and a thickness of about ¾ inch. It seemed good in
colour, but was so cracked and flawed that it could only
be expected to yield a comparatively small stone of good
quality. No value could be attached to it locally, as no
stone of that size had ever been previously seen or heard
of in Mogôk. On my asking the owner why he did not
send it to Europe to ascertain its value, he said there
was only one man in the province whom he would trust
to take it there, and that was the Lieutenant-Governor
of Burma ; but, he added thoughtfully, at times he didn't
feel at all sure that he could trust even him with it.
And yet this priceless ruby was kept, wrapped up in

many rags of dirty cotton, in rather a casual way in the owner's house.

Tourmaline is found in the Shan States of Möng Mit and Mainglôn (Thibaw), immediately to the north and south of the Mogôk ruby tracts, and plumbago and mica are worked in the Twinngé township of the Ruby Mines district. But these are,—like the ruby and the amber mines of Nanyaseik, the alabaster quarries of Sagyin near Mandalay, the marble rocks of Amherst and the islands of the Mergui Archipelago, the steatite quarries in the Chin hills and near the An pass crossing the Arakan Yoma from Minbu to Akyab, and the limestone pits worked at many places throughout the province,—mining industries of so trivial a nature as to be unlikely ever to affect the material wealth of the country to any appreciable extent. Nearly all of these mines and quarries are in places where labour is scarce and dear.

The province is rich in mineral resources, of which the chief are petroleum, coal, and gold ; and now that fixation of the rate of exchange has been achieved, mining prospects are of a much less speculative nature than was previously the case. The important amendments made by the Government of India during 1899 in the mining and prospecting rules now afford reasonable facilities to all persons, syndicates, and companies really desirous of operating, while the widely increased powers granted to local Governments in dealing with applications obviate the delay which had before then been unavoidable. By granting permission to transfer prospecting leases and by the revision of the royalties, so that gold and silver will pay seven and a half and precious stones thirty per cent. on the net profits annually, Government appear to have shown their desire to facilitate the development of India's mineral resources generally ; and Burma seems worthy of receiving a fair share of the attention which private enterprise may feel disposed to bestow upon mining concerns.

In its three chief mineral products—earth-oil, coal, and gold—Burma offers a very fair field for enterprise, but nothing more. It is not the inexhaustible treasure-land that will attract those who hanker after untold mineral

wealth extending beyond the dreams of avarice; for its
main wealth lies—as in the past, so also in the future—
in its fertile alluvial plains, its damp climate and copious
rainfall during the summer monsoon months, and its vast
forests, rather than in its carboniferous deposits or the
auriferous rocks of its hill ranges. At the same time,
however, there can be no doubt that the more liberal
policy of the present Viceroy and Governor-General of
India, Lord Curzon of Keddleston, should attract capital
towards Burma with regard to mining enterprises, as
well as in respect of various other commercial openings
—such as branch railways, timber, rubber-plantations,
cotton, a Land Mortgage Bank, and many other schemes
—offering fair prospects of reasonable profit, and capable
of achieving great success under good, prudent management.

Chapter XIV

TRADE AND COMMERCE

AS might of course have been expected from a fertile tropical country traversed by an enormous river like the Irrawaddy, Burma has throughout all historic times carried on a considerable amount of trade with foreign countries.

In the earlier periods Arab *dhows* and other native Asiatic craft maintained traffic with it, while direct contact with Europe was introduced by the Portuguese before the close of the fourteenth century, although Marco Polo had previously visited Burma before the end of the thirteenth century. During the fifteenth and sixteenth centuries the country was visited by Russian and Italian travellers. The first English trader who visited Burma, in 1586, was Ralph Fitch. More recent details of trade and of the country generally are given in the well known *Account of the Burman Empire*, by Father San Germano, a Barnabite priest, who lived in Burma from 1783 to 1806.

The trade possibilities offered by the natural fertility of the rich delta of the Irrawaddy were, however, incapable of being taken proper advantage of owing to the internecine warfare almost constantly being waged there since the beginning of the fourteenth century, which was indeed one of the main causes of the present scantiness of population throughout this fine alluvial tract.

The first trading connexion between Burma and any European country was in 1519, when a treaty was concluded by Antonio Correa, on behalf of Portugal, with

Byanyaran, King of Pegu, for the establishment of factories at Martaban and Syriam (a corruption of *Thanlyin*), a few miles to the south-east of the present city of Rangoon. Towards the close of the sixteenth century, or early in the seventeenth, the Dutch obtained a footing on the island of Negrais, at the extreme western point of the Irrawaddy delta, and subsequently also established factories at Syriam and at old Bhamo (*Bamáw*) on the Taiping river, some distance above the present town situated just below the confluence of that tributary with the Irrawaddy.

Early in the seventeenth century (1612) the East India Company established factories and agencies at Syriam, and gradually extended their business with branches at Prome, Ava, and Bhamo. Disputes soon sprang up between the trading agents of different nationalities, and between these and the Burmese; and about the middle of the seventeenth century all the European merchants were expelled in consequence of a quarrel between the Burmese Governor of Pegu and the Dutch agent. In 1680 and 1684 unsuccessful overtures were made by the English for the re-establishment of factories, and in 1687 they took temporary possession of Negrais. In 1688 the Governor of Syriam invited the British merchants at Madras to re-establish a factory at Syriam, but it was not till 1698 that factories were rebuilt at Syriam and agencies established at Bassein and Negrais. The Dutch and the Portuguese never returned. The French, however, settled at Syriam, and became the rivals of the British merchants.

During the first half of the eighteenth century trade went on briskly between Syriam and the British factories at Bengal and Madras, even although this was a period of warfare between the Burmese dynasty of Ava and the Môn Kings of Pegu. During the short period of Môn supremacy trade was less hampered than under the Burmese rule of Ava. But on a new Burmese dynasty being founded by Alaung Payá, in 1755, he succeeded in uniting his countrymen and overthrowing the Peguan monarchy during the following year. The Peguans or Môn were thereafter called the *Talaing* or " down-trodden race " as a term of contempt, a name they still bear and apply to themselves instead of their proper racial designation. At the same time, to commemorate the victory of the Burmese arms, he founded a new capital, in place of Syriam, near the great Shwe Dagôn pagoda, and called it "Rangoon," pronounced *Yangôn* in Burmese, which means " the conclusion of the war."

As Alaung Payá would not permit the establishment of any factories within his territories, trade at once became much restricted. Towards the end of the eighteenth century it began to spring up again, though under somewhat unfavourable conditions : for the export of gems and precious metals was prohibited, while commercial transactions were burdened with vexatious transit dues, port charges, and commissions.

During the war between the Burmese and the Môn, both the British and the French had tried to run with the hare and hunt with the hounds. The British merchants at Syriam on the whole gave the larger share of their encouragement and assistance to the Burmese, while the French took the opposite course and pinned their faith on the ultimate ascendancy of the Môn ; but the rival merchants all tried to keep on favourable terms with the other side whenever events seemed to show that this might ultimately prove the successful party in the struggle for dominion throughout Pegu. Unfortunately for the French, Alaung Payá's arms were victorious. In 1756, after Alaung Payá had returned to Ava, the Talaings revolted and attacked Rangoon ; but the Burmese King returned, invested Syriam, and rased the town to the ground, leaving unscathed only the golden pagoda and the other sacred buildings.

While the conqueror was endeavouring to crush out, with a terrible outpouring of blood, the last efforts of the Talaing resistance in the Syriam district, he found that the French had been assisting them with warlike stores, so he put all the Frenchmen to death. Though it was discovered that they also had at times assisted the Talaings, the English received more favourable treatment, being permitted to occupy the island of Negrais and to establish a factory at Bassein, in consideration of their having furnished Alaung Payá with munitions of war during the two previous years. In 1758 the Talaings again revolted in the south-western portion of the delta, and in October of the following year the factories at Bassein and Negrais were destroyed, and the English agents and employés massacred, on suspicion of having been in communication with the rebels and having supplied arms to them.

On the death of Alaung Payá, in 1760, the English obtained permission from his successor, Naungdawgyi, to re-establish a factory at Bassein ; but redress for the massacre of the previous year was refused point-blank.

The ports which were then open along the coast of Burma are those which still exist. Commencing from the north-west, Akyab, at the mouth of the Koladán river is the chief seaport in Arakan, the other two being Kyaukpyu and Sandoway lower down the coast. Bassein, about sixty miles up the Ngawun river, the most westerly branch of the Irrawaddy delta, and Rangoon, about thirty miles up the Rangoon river, the most easterly branch of the delta, are the two ports of Pegu. Moulmein, near the mouth of the Salween, Tavoy, about thirty miles up the Tavoy river, and Mergui, on the coast further south, are the seaports in Tenasserim. Rangoon, Moulmein, Bassein, and Akyab are the principal ports, which are all good harbours affording safe anchorage.

From its position, however, Rangoon was naturally bound in course of time to become the greatest trading centre. Even under the Burmese rule Rangoon consequently became not only the principal port, but also the only one of any real importance for foreign export trade. Early in the last century Rangoon was a sort of Alsatian emporium, resorted to by desperate and reckless adventurers of almost every nationality. European countries were represented by a few English, French, and Portuguese residents, along with whom Armenians, Parsis, and Moguls shared the trade : but all were looked down upon, harassed, and greatly restricted in their operations by the Burmese.

TRADE IN 1826

The chief articles of sea-borne commerce consisted then of imports of sugar and muslin from Bengal, of linen and white and coloured kerchiefs, used as headdresses, from Madras, and of miscellaneous iron, brass, glass, and woollen goods from Europe ; while the chief exports were teak timber, lac, cutch, petroleum, and vegetable oils. Of these teak-wood, valuable on account of its essential oil, which preserves iron or steel embedded in it in place of corroding it like the tannic acid contained in oak timber, was by far the most important. Large quantities were exported as planks for shipbuilding, and two or three shipbuilding yards had been established at Rangoon by Englishmen and Frenchmen. This industry, and the export trade generally, was perhaps stimulated by the curious prohibition against export of specie from Burma. Import duty was charged at the rate of twelve per cent., ten of which were supposed to go to the royal treasury, the remainder being divided as commission, in lieu of salary, among the local officials. The export duty on timber was only one per cent., but on all other exports it amounted to five per cent. *ad valorem*. In the early part of the century the number of ships annually sailing from Rangoon averaged less than twenty-five. This had doubled by the time Tenasserim and Arakan were ceded to the British in 1826. But, as Pegu was then restored to the Burmese, the trade of Rangoon advanced much more slowly than would otherwise have been the case. From 1826 to 1852, the period between the first and the second Burmese wars, the average number of sea-going craft of all sorts arriving at and departing from Rangoon annually was merely 125. Of these only twenty were European ships, the rest being coasting schooners, Chinese and Malay junks, and *Kattu* or native craft.

When Arakan and Tenasserim came under British rule in 1826, they were both found to be in a very thinly populated condition. Towns which had formerly been large and populous had either become reduced to the status of mere villages and hamlets, or only existed as ruins.

After Akyab became a free port, in 1826, British ships

soon began to bring cargoes of muslins, piece-goods, cutlery, and crockery from Bengal, carrying away rice, hides, and horns on their return voyages; and the seaport soon became regarded as the chief town instead of Myohaung, the "ancient capital," inconveniently situated far inland on the Lemru river. Restrictions on trade being removed, and security for person and property being assured under British rule, the inhabitants soon returned to cultivate their holdings on the rich alluvial plains watered by the Koladán and the Lemru rivers, from which they had been driven by their Burmese conquerors. As these fertile plains, producing the finest rice in Burma, are intersected by a labyrinth of tidal creeks, their produce could easily be brought down to the seaport by the cultivators. Akyab therefore soon multiplied its trade, and became the centre of the rice export business from Burma. A large trade also sprang up there in salt, which was purchased from local manufacturers and stored in Government *Gola* or sheds until it could be shipped to Bengal.

At Moulmein, on the other hand, trade had to be created. Previous to the cession of Tenasserim, the port on the Salween river had been at Martaban, of which province (comprising the present Thatôn and Toungoo districts, and part of the Pegu district) the Burmese retained possession until 1852, when they lost both Pegu and Martaban, and with these provinces the whole of the sea-board. The kingdom of Ava thus became a purely inland country, the mere *Hinterland* of British Burma.

For many years previous to 1826 English ships had ceased to visit Martaban; and in establishing a port at Moulmein, a little lower down on the opposite or left bank of the Salween, there was practically no trade in view except what could be created. Although located in a very favourable position near the mouth of the Salween—a river considerably longer than the Irrawaddy, which rises in Thibet, traverses Yunnan from north to south, and receives the drainage from north-western Siam—and although the other portions of western Siam are watered by the Thaungyin, Gyaing, and Atarán rivers, which join the Salween above the new seaport, Moulmein has, owing to the rocky obstructions which render water communication with upper Siam, the Shan States and China impossible by way of the Salween, none of the great natural advantages possessed by Rangoon as a seaport and as an emporium for the collection and distribution of commercial produce. The trade which developed at Moulmein was at first mainly confined to teak timber. Sawmills sprang up, and shipbuilding yards were established, 123 vessels being launched therefrom during the quarter of a century between 1830 and 1855. Shortly after 1830 a commencement was also made with the exportation of rice; but, when the second Burmese war led to the acquisition of Rangoon and Bassein by the British, the staple export trade of Akyab was in rice and of Moulmein in teak timber. There was no export of teak from Akyab, as the teak tree is not indigenous to any part of Arakan.

After the annexation of Pegu and Martaban in 1852, trade increased rapidly at all the ports. The chief impetus to commerce, however, was given at Rangoon, through the removal of obstructions to free mercantile transactions. The whole of the seaboard having been lost to the kingdom of Ava, Rangoon and Bassein became almost the only outlets for the produce of the interior of Burma, and the only inlets by which merchandise could reach the upper valley of the Irrawaddy, the Shan States, and western China. Trade therefore soon increased, woollen articles, cotton and silk, piece-goods, iron-ware, salt, and miscellaneous articles being imported; whilst rice, teak timber, cutch, petroleum, hides, and horns formed the principal exports. In 1854 the Sea Customs Department was established, and from 1st January, 1855, dues were levied at all the seaports, while the import and export returns then established soon showed how great was the lion's share of trade Rangoon had even then secured against all the other seaports combined. And this was bound to be the case, considering the extremely advantageous position occupied by Alaung Payá's town nestling at the foot of the Shwe Dagôn pagoda.

Rangoon, from being a small and comparatively in-

significant place, has within less than half a century risen
to be the third seaport in British India, being only surpassed by Calcutta and Bombay in the volume and
extent of its trade. At the census of 1891 it had a
population of 180,324 souls, showing an increase of
over one-third on the previous decennial census returns;
and its present population is now 232,236, according to
the preliminary return of the census of February, 1901.

The approach to the Rangoon river, the main eastern
branch of the Irrawaddy delta, from the sea is not
difficult or dangerous at any season of the year. The
southern sea-face of the province, from Cape Negrais
eastwards past the Rangoon river, up to the estuary of
the Sittang, and down to Amherst below the mouth of
the Salween, is nowhere rocky or dangerous from
numerous sunken reefs. Flat and shelving, the shoal-
banks off the mouths of the main branches of the delta
are the chief sources of danger to shipping, and these are
guarded against by a good service of lighthouses and
lightships. After passing the Eastern Grove lighthouse
marking the entrance to the Rangoon river, the approach
to Rangoon, situated about thirty miles up stream, is
easy. The town lies on the left or northern bank of the
Rangoon river, just above where this receives, on the
same bank, the waters of the Pazúndaung river from the
north and the Pegu river from the north-east, which unite
in debouching almost at the same point into the main
stream. In consequence of this a huge silt deposit,
known as the Hastings Shoal, is formed, which hinders
the entrance or exit of large ships during the ebb-tides.
This is not, however, anything like so dangerous an
obstruction as the notorious James and Mary Shoal in the
Hooghly river, while the distance between Rangoon and
the sea is only about one quarter of that between Calcutta and the Bay of Bengal. Nor are cyclones and
dirty weather anything like so prevalent around the
approaches to Rangoon as they are along the ocean
tracks leading to the capital of Bengal. Above the
Hastings Shoal, within the port of Rangoon, there is
good accommodation for a large number of steamers and
other kinds of shipping. From where the Pegu and the

RANGOON

Pazúndaung rivers join the Rangoon river the port itself extends upwards in a gentle curve for seven or eight miles to where the Hlaing river from the north, joining the Panlaung creek from the north-west, forms the Rangoon river. Throughout this stretch the river is about a mile to a mile and a quarter in breadth, so that during the busiest season of the year, lasting from December to April, large quantities of shipping can be accommodated without danger or inconvenience. And the anchorage is also good and safe throughout the south-west monsoon.

The original Rangoon founded by Alaung Payá has during its recent expansion absorbed all the small villages lying to the north-west and south-east of it, which have now become incorporated as sections of the city; while the settlements on the right bank of the river have also been transformed into busy suburbs, resounding with the ceaseless clang of machinery, the noise of hammering in the shipyards, the dull droning whirr of rice-husking, and the higher-pitched hum from the timber sawmills.

No other point in Burma could have such unrivalled advantages for trade and commerce as are enjoyed by Rangoon. The anchorage is better than could be obtainable off Syriam, near the mouth of the Pegu river, the seaport in Peguan times.

Good, broad, deep, and easily negotiable tidal creeks bring to Rangoon the produce from the Irrawaddy, itself navigable up its main branch for upwards of a thousand miles, and gathering in through its tributaries the whole of the trade possible throughout an enormous extent of rich territory. From the rice-producing districts to the north-east and east grain naturally found its way to Rangoon down the Pazúndaung and Pegu rivers; and even from the valley of the Sittang it could be brought by means of the Kayasu creek joining the lower portions of the Sittang and Pegu rivers, and navigable for large country boats whenever the fortnightly flood-tides were in flow. Thus, even before railways had been opened in Burma, Rangoon had been able to expand its commerce far beyond what was possible in the case of any of the other seaports. In 1899–1900, out of a total trade for the province valued at £20,819,992, £16,239,884, or eighty per cent.[1] passed through Rangoon. Since the opening of the first short railway from Rangoon to Prome in 1877, thanks to the construction of a main trunk line of nearly 800 miles in length, opening up land-locked areas in Upper Burma, the commerce of Rangoon has far more than trebled itself in extent, while the normal expansion of trade at other ports has not done very much more than double itself.

The first view obtained of Rangoon, on approaching it from the sea, gives but little idea of the busy port that is soon to be entered. About halfway up the Rangoon river the golden spire of Syriam pagoda is observable a little to the east, that having of course been spared from religious motives when the Môn capital was destroyed by Alaung Payá. Soon after this the great golden pile of the Shwe Dagôn pagoda is seen right ahead to the north, surmounting the knoll overlooking Rangoon, while the town itself is more or less hidden by trees, above which the smoke from the steam mills is wafted by the breeze. When the forts and submarine defences have been passed, and the Hastings Shoal is being rounded, the tall chimneys of the rice-mills and the corrugated iron roofs of their outbuildings, and of the many other hideously ugly and unromantic shrines of industry, become more plainly visible. Rounding the Hastings Shoal and nearing Monkey Point, the tip of the tongue of land forming the south-eastern limit of Rangoon, the rice-mills can be seen dotting the Pazúndaung river, extending northwards along both banks, and sending out long wind-borne streamers of dirty smoke from their chimneys. Above this, Botataung is soon passed with its rice and timber mills, its earth-oil refinery, and the many wharves and yards having river frontage. Approaching the heart of the city, the central portion on the river's bank, within which are congregated the chief shops and merchants' offices, the great municipal Bazaar, the Customs House, Treasury, banks, post and telegraph offices, law courts, and Government offices, the din and noise afford very

[1] All monetary data have been converted into sterling at the rate of one shilling and fourpence per rupee.

apparent indication of the traffic and bustle of a great city. Before the steamer has been brought alongside of any of the numerous quays, or the harbour-master has had time to assign to it moorings out in the stream, opportunity is given of looking around from the centre of the port and noting the evidences of commercial activity that everywhere surround one. Where Alaung Payá, in 1755, built a few rows of starveling houses or mat huts on a swampy mud bank, which each ebb-tide left exposed as a foetid mass of oozy slime, there now stands a stately and opulent city, whose broad streets are lined with large solid brick buildings, and whose river frontage is dotted with quays and wharves, from which merchandise can either be stored in huge "go-downs" or else be at once loaded on railway trains for despatch into the interior. In this central portion, this heart of Rangoon where the pulsation of business is strongest, there are no mill yards, as land has long since become too valuable for that. On the annexation of Upper Burma, the value of land in the business centre of Rangoon increased with an enormous bound. A small piece of land in Merchant Street occupied by a ramshackle one-storied building, which changed hands in 1885 for between five and six thousand rupees, was sold within a year for over fifty-five thousand rupees : but this unhealthy phenomenal unearned increment fortunately soon abated, although of course the value of land has increased and must continue to rise normally as the city grows in commercial importance.

In all the suburbs the whole of the available river frontage is occupied by mills of one sort or another; while up, and down, and across the river steam launches are continuously conveying merchants' employés or messengers to and from the mill-yards. All along the left bank of the Rangoon river, from Pazúndaung and Botataung past the city itself, and northwards beyond Alôn to Kyimyindaing, where the central Government timber depôt is located,—a distance of about eight miles —there is no frontage available which is not taken up by wharves, or mills, or buildings of some sort ; while on the opposite bank, the Dalla side, in addition to rice-mills there are the great timber yards of the Bombay-Burma

Trading Corporation and other firms, and the docks and shipbuilding yards of the Irrawaddy Flotilla Company, whose large fleet of magnificent river steamers has done so much for the expansion of the trade of Rangoon and the development of commerce over all the river-highways of the province. During the busy season, which commences when the new rice-crop begins to come in about the end of December and lasts till the burst of the south-west monsoon in May, the pool forming the port of Rangoon presents a busy and a noisy scene, unsurpassed and even unequalled in any other port of India except in the Hooghly river off Calcutta.

Equally characteristic as the river-steamers and flats of the Irrawaddy Flotilla Company are the black funnels with two narrow white bands indicating the British India Steam Navigation Company's steamers, which throng the port of Rangoon and practically monopolize the interportal trade along the coast of Burma and with British India. This powerful Company, possessing one of the largest fleets of mercantile steamers in the world, has grown *pari passu* with the development of Burma, towards whose material progress it has assisted in no small degree, and with the coasting trade of which in particular the Company's interests have been most intimately associated. They have the mail contracts between Rangoon, the ports along the Burma coast, Calcutta, Madras, and Singapore, which are all worked with exemplary regularity. Twice a week good steamers ply between Rangoon and Calcutta at a fair rate of speed; and, if sufficient inducement were offered by Government, no doubt the energetic Company would soon organize a better service direct with Madras, which is a far preferable passenger route to Bombay than that viâ Calcutta, with its ascent of the Hooghly and the longer railway journey across the Indian continent.

For many years this was the only ocean steamship company which had any direct connexion with Burma or did anything for the development of the trade of the province. And even now the only competitors it has are the Asiatic Steam Navigation Company, which has run between Calcutta, Rangoon, Port Blair (Andaman

Islands) and Madras for the past twelve years, and the Bibby line of steamers running once every three weeks direct to and from England by way of Colombo and Marseilles.

Though only of metre gauge, the Burma railways are well suited to the present requirements of the country, and should easily cope with a much larger amount of traffic than they have yet been called upon to convey. Although enormous quantities of rice are now brought down from Rangoon by railway from land-locked areas, yet the auxiliary methods of bringing this raw produce to market by means of country boats have hardly been appreciably interfered with by competition. The rapid expansion in the trade of Rangoon during the past twenty years is, however, beyond doubt mainly due to railway construction, and not merely to the addition of Upper Burma and the Shan States to the British territories ; and as the railway net expands and ramifies throughout the province and beyond its frontiers, so will the trade of Rangoon increase and multiply. Rich and opulent though Burma may already be considered, yet its future prospects are brighter still by far. As each decennial census will record a steady growth in population, so, too, will the trade statistics of Rangoon mark a continuous development of commerce commensurate therewith and with the activity in railway construction.

From early in January till late in April the streams and tidal creeks leading from the rural districts to the various seaports are thronged with boats of from below twenty to about fifty or sixty tons capacity, all heavily laden with " paddy " for delivery at the rice mills. Here the grain is measured out in baskets and poured in great heaps on the floors of the grain sheds, in a comparative silence only broken by the tally-men calling out "*cho*" whenever a notch has to be made in the *Gayó* or "tally-stick" of split bamboo to mark the pouring out of every tenth basketful of rice. Enormous piles of grain are thus brought daily into the " go-downs " or sheds of the mill-yards, and the whirr of the machinery goes on ceaselessly day and night all through the week, except for the twenty-four hours succeeding midnight on Saturday.

The Sabbath day of rest, during which the noise of the husking machinery is stayed, is utilized in examining and overhauling the engines and mill-plant.

The scores of thousands of teak logs converted in the timber yards of Rangoon and Moulmein are almost entirely brought down by river in rafts of forty to sixty logs or more. They frequently take two or three, and sometimes even four years or longer to float out from the small streams in the forests into main channels, whence they can be more easily extracted during favourable freshets. During floods they are allowed to drift down the smaller water channels till they reach collecting stations on the larger streams, whence they can be formed into rafts and floated down to the timber yards. Both in dragging logs away up in the forests, as well as in arranging them in the timber depôts and in stacking the converted timber in the mill-yards, elephants perform tasks that seem wonderful to the casual observer. It is one of the sights of Rangoon to see these huge animals at work in the timber yards.

Teak trees have always in Burma been royal property, and the ownership of all teak trees growing in any of the forests, reserved or unreserved, is vested in the Government. Even the chiefs of the various Shan States containing teak forests have no proprietary right over such trees, but can only work out teak timber either on payment of royalty to Government as lessees, or else merely as contractors of the Forest Department, which is closed as a " quasi-commercial " branch of the Revenue Department of the Government of India.

Trade in teak timber from Burma on any large scale first of all sprang up in Moulmein, and until recent years the exports of this staple from Moulmein continued in excess of those from Rangoon. But as the forests of Siam, Karenni, and the Southern Shan States drained by the Salween river are now, after decades of reckless felling, gradually approaching exhaustion, while those lying within the drainage of the Irrawaddy and its tributaries are being worked on strictly conservative principles and in accordance with the provisions of definite working plans, the export of teak timber from

TEAK TIMBER EXPORTS

Rangoon was naturally bound in course of time to come level with that from Moulmein, and ultimately to exceed it considerably. The high-level marks of the Moulmein timber trade were reached in 1888–89, when 93,465 tons of teak valued at nearly £515,000 were exported, and in 1892–93, when 106,850 tons, valued at £483,000, left the port. The statistics of the teak export trade for the seven years ending on 30th June, 1900, are as follows :—

Year.	From Moulmein.		From Rangoon.		Total.		Average Value per Ton.
	Tons.	Value in Pounds Sterling.	Tons.	Value in Pounds Sterling.	Tons.	Value in Pounds Sterling.	
		£		£		£	£ s. d.
1893–94	85,722	402,628	85,623	438,698	171,345	841,226	4 18 2
1894–95	84,456	391,235	106,810	555,644	191,226	946,979	4 19 0
1895–96	84,363	389,614	120,494	626,869	204,857	1,016,483	4 19 3
1896–97	75,298	406,588	115,854	656,668	191,152	1,063,256	5 11 3
1897–98	65,986	361,433	207,405	1,229,165	273,391	1,590,598	5 16 4
1898–99	66,002	373,647	202,281	1,142,970	268,283	1,516,617	5 13 3
1890–1900	62,983	365,628	209,303	1,159,169	272,286	1,524,797	5 12 0

There will probably be a temporary check, and most likely even for some years a falling off in the exports of teak from Rangoon, owing to causes which will be subsequently referred to ; but this will be followed by a steady expansion of the trade on a sounder basis than now exists, and the future exports will to a certainty be far in excess of what they now are.

The rise of the teak trade in Burma possesses an interest of its own apart from the purely financial and commercial aspect. Owing to the impetus then given to shipbuilding, both mercantile and naval, the supply of oak timber for the dockyards of Britain began to get exhausted throughout Scotland and England towards the end of last century, and great difficulty was felt in supplying the demands of the naval dockyards. This drew attention to the good qualities of teak timber for shipbuilding, and regular supplies of it were drawn into the dockyards of Bombay from the forests along the western coast of India. In a comparatively short space of time these first sources ran dry, but soon the cession of

Tenasserim to the British, in 1826, opened out fresh opportunities, which British merchants were not slow to avail themselves of. Many firms obtained leases of forests on payment of low rates of royalty; and the timber thus extracted was supplemented by what was brought down from the Siamese, Shan, and Karenni territories drained by the Salween. Most of these leases within British territory lapsed in 1896, and the great bulk of the timber now converted in the Moulmein saw-mills consists of what is rafted down the Salween by Shan and Siamese foresters. This is, however, supplemented by auction sales of timber extracted by direct Government agency through contractors of the Forest Department. At Kado, a few miles above Moulmein, a large depôt is maintained by Government, in which all timber arriving is stored until it is sold by the owners and cleared from the depôt after payment of the Government royalty, or after the levy of a duty of seven per cent. *ad valorem* on all such teak timber as has been imported from foreign territory.

As soon as free trade was rendered possible at Rangoon by the annexation of Pegu and Martaban, in 1852, the British merchants who established themselves in trade there soon turned their attention to timber operations. As in Tenasserim, they here also obtained leases for forests on payment of a small royalty per ton to Government, and floated down the logs to their mills. Simultaneously with this system direct Government extraction was also introduced by means of contractors usually resident in the vicinity of the forests, who delivered their timber at the central Government depôt near Rangoon on payment of contract rates varying according to the dimensions of each log. Frauds in connexion with girdling operations, for the seasoning of the teak trees before felling, having resulted on a large scale about 1870, the Government of India in 1873 prohibited the issue of fresh leases; but, owing to the circumstances obtaining with regard to the working of the Upper Burma forests on the annexation in 1886, by far the greater portion of the teak milled in Rangoon was until 1900 extracted from tracts still held under lease. While these leases, chiefly held by the Bombay-Burma Trading Corporation, were current the Government found it expedient to allow other European firms to obtain contracts for working certain forests at comparatively low rates of royalty so as to enable them to compete at all, though even then on very unequal terms, with this wealthy Corporation. While these leases and purchase contracts were still concurrent in Upper Burma, most of the forests throughout Lower Burma drained by the Irrawaddy and the Sittang rivers were worked by direct departmental agency with contractors for extraction, and this system is also being gradually introduced into Upper Burma.

The timber thus extracted by contractors in Lower Burma, and the best of what is brought out from the forests to the north of Mandalay, are chiefly disposed of by public auction at sales held monthly in Rangoon ; but the very pick of the finest logs goes, as it ought to go, for the supply of the Bombay dockyard and for other Government requirements in Calcutta and Madras. What seem the best logs are carefully put on one side on arrival in the Government depôt at Rangoon, and are subsequently examined very carefully so that only the best timber of the year is issued in supplying the dockyard and other Government indents ; while tenders are usually called for with regard to the sale of the remainder as selected batches of first-class timber. About 25,000 tons of teak are thus annually disposed of from the Rangoon Government Timber Depôt, but this amount is not sufficient to supply even one-tenth of the quantity now annually exported from Rangoon. Under the leases granted to it in 1887, in continuation of those held from King Thibaw, the Bombay-Burma Trading Corporation was in the happy position of being able to secure enormous quantities of timber at such extremely low rates of royalty as did not leave other firms paying considerably higher rates of royalty any fair chance of carrying on a successful and healthy competition. This abnormal state of affairs terminated when the Corporation's lease for the Chindwin forests lapsed on 31st December, 1900, though extraction at the exceptionally low rate of royalty is permitted till the end of 1901 under the agreement; but it will not be until the vast stock of teak timber accumulated at abnormally low and favourable rates by the Corporation in their great timber depôt at Dalla has become exhausted that the timber trade of Rangoon will stand on a really sound and healthy commercial basis. When this takes place, the position of the teak timber trade will probably be that the leading firms will do a certain amount of foresting work under purchase contracts with Government, while the supply of timber thus obtained will have to be supplemented by purchases made at the monthly auction sales held at the Government timber depôt, the bulk of the extraction taking place by the contractors of the Forest Department. The timber trade that will probably be thus conducted is capable of great expansion in the future, and it should always remain free from the taint of mercantile gambling with which the rice business is infected.

But rice has long been, is, and will always continue to be, the great staple export from Burma. At first the work of the mills was confined merely to rough husking and the preparation of what was called " 5-parts cargo rice," in which the proportion of the husked grains was only one in five; but gradually the treatment improved, the cargo rice showed only about one unhusked grain in five, and finally millers engaged largely in the preparation of white rice. In consequence of the local development of the white rice business large quantities of rice bran are now exported as manures, 135,642 tons, valued at £215,494, having been shipped to foreign countries during 1899–1900. Large quantities of rice of all sorts are now usually exported annually to Europe, America and Singapore, the regular course of the trade in which is only liable to be temporarily deflected during periods of famine such as have recently occurred in India and Japan. Thus, during 1900, over one million tons of rice were shipped to India owing to the famine there. The magnitude of the steady expansion of the existing trade in this staple may be estimated from the following returns of exports of rice from Lower Burma during the last twelve years :—

RICE EXPORTS

Year.	To Europe and America. Tons.	To India, China and Singapore. Tons.	To Upper Burma. Tons.	Total. Tons.
1889	708,930	245,129	58,504	1,012,563
1890	749,564	430,079	53,838	1,233,481
1891	852,799	303,423	77,840	1,234,062
1892	824,151	242,367	152,804	1,219,322
1893	778,223	523,453	116,678	1,418,354
1894	729,965	594,504	36,531	1,361,000
1895	801,450	450,999	25,447	1,277,896
1896	768,242	435,199	102,974	1,306,415
1897	698,273	837,499	not recorded	1,535,772
1898	843,037	975,904	,,	1,818,941
1899	867,415	684,016	,,	1,551,431
1900 (for 10 months)	708,804	1,197,934	,,	1,906,738

England takes by far the greatest share of Burma rice, though large quantities are also consumed in Germany, at Bremen and Hamburg, while France, Belgium, and Holland likewise absorb a considerable amount. More than half of the quantities annually exported, however, are cleared as bound for Egypt, where, in passing through the Suez Canal, instructions are issued to the captains as to the final destination of the cargoes. Even then, more frequently than not, the usual instructions are "to the English Channel for further orders." The total quantity of rice exported to foreign countries during 1895–96, the last year before the Indian famine, amounted to close on one and a quarter millions of tons, valued at £5,827,000, and bringing in a revenue of £425,000 in the way of export duty.

The development of the rice trade has naturally resulted in increased value of the raw produce itself. For the three years preceding the annexation of Pegu (1849–52) the average price of "paddy" or unhusked rice was only fifteen rupees per hundred baskets of about nine gallons in capacity. On the occupation of Rangoon it rose to thirty-five rupees, and during the following three years it averaged forty rupees per hundred baskets. Now, during most years, the average price per hundred baskets ranges from about 100 to 110 rupees (£6 13s. 4d. to £7 6s. 8d.) at Rangoon and Bassein, and from 95 to 100 rupees (£6 6s. 8d. to £6 13s. 4d.) at Akyab and Moulmein. Prices are, however, always liable to fluctuations dependent on heavy speculations by local traders, on willingness of the producer to sell early or desire on his part to hold back the grain and await an advance in price, on the requirements of the rice millers, and on the various contingencies affecting all such mercantile transactions. Thus, for example, when the paddy crop of 1896 began to reach the seaports prices in Rangoon opened at 110 to 115 rupees per 100 baskets, consequent on the strong demand for India in addition to the usual export business. The harvest bringing in a bumper crop, prices fell to ninety rupees in February, but regained their former level during March.

Large quantities of grain are brought down to the seaports independently by the producers and sold to the best advantage; but by far the greater portion of the paddy required for maintaining the mills in full work is arranged for during the previous rainy season, before the rice crops have ripened. Each of the rice-milling firms has several brokers or middlemen (*Pwèza*) in their employ, to whom large advances are made. These men, proceeding up country, make advances to the cultivators on mortgage of the growing crops, securing in addition to interest on the money lent the prior right to purchase the grain at current market rates when the producer sells the paddy harvested. Formerly such advances generally carried with them conditions as to the sale of a certain quantity of paddy at a stipulated low rate per 100 baskets; but the Burmese peasants in the chief rice-growing districts are no longer so simple as formerly, and even this brokerage business is, like other mercantile operations, subject to the automatic action of the law of competition. The largest and richest firms, however, command the services of the most influential middlemen, and can consequently rely on procuring the largest supplies of paddy throughout the working season. Hence even with a growing trade still capable of enormous expansion there is the natural and inevitable tendency for the large capitalists to crush smaller firms or new enterprises out of profitable competition in the rice business.

It has been above remarked that the teak timber

business, though not yet in the healthy condition it will most likely attain in the course of the next few years, is at any rate free from the spirit of gambling with which the rice trade is tainted. As the ports of Burma lie off the beaten track of ocean tramps and sailing vessels seeking cargoes, arrangements have almost invariably to be made for chartering vessels long before the paddy begins to come down to the rice mills. At the same time forward sales of rice are also made to a great extent. If paddy be plentiful and cheap, large gains result; but if it be scarce and dear, then the shipments must still be made, although every bag of rice shipped means a certain loss to the shipper; and the fluctuations of the market for rice in Europe can easily under such circumstances convert a prospective gain into a dead loss. A rise or a fall of sixpence a hundredweight on the wholesale price of cargo rice in Mark Lane means a difference of one thousand pounds in the market value of a steamer-load of two thousand tons.

Simultaneously with the rise in the market value of the raw, unhusked rice, the area under cultivation has expanded greatly; and although the prices paid for labour and for necessities of life have risen in response to a much enhanced prosperity, yet the power of purchasing luxuries and imported articles has been continuous. Nor has this agricultural prosperity as yet anything like approached within even distant view of the ultimate limits to which the expansion of cultivation is possible. Although 6,277,678 acres are under rice in Lower Burma, or over 90 per cent. of the total area cropped (6,857,898 acres)—leaving out of consideration the rice cultivation in Upper Burma (1,818,962 acres in 1899), which is insufficient to meet all local demands of that portion of the province—yet there are still enormous tracts of land suitable for permanent cultivation as rice fields whenever population increases sufficiently, either by immigration or by natural growth, to provide labour for breaking fresh ground, because the total extent of cultivable waste amounts to 24,619,662 acres, or three-fourths of the total area of England. So far as the possibility of future supplies for export are concerned, the rice trade of Burma may still be considered as merely in a state of normal development; and the nearly two million tons now exported will increase and be multiplied according as Burma's greatest want, population, is supplied.[1] During the last twenty years the area under rice cultivation has far more than doubled; but there is still plenty of good uncleared land affording scope for further expansion at even a more rapid rate in the immediate future, though of course the first comers have already secured the best tracts within easy and cheap communication of the existing centres of the rice trade.

Without exception all the rice mills in Burma are at the seaport towns. Out of a total of 141 factories, all worked by steam, coming under the Factory Act of 1881 in Lower Burma, and employing upwards of 19,000 daily operatives, the vast majority of them are either timber or rice mills; and of these all but a few small timber mills, are situated in or near the four chief seaports. Akyab and Moulmein each draw in the surplus produce from over half a million acres, Bassein that from about a million acres, and Rangoon the lion's share from about three million acres of rice cultivation. Communications are as yet nothing like good enough to enable the surplus produce of many inland tracts to be brought to the coast. No rice mills have yet been erected in any of the inland centres of rice-producing districts, and there seems no tendency for such an innovation to be attempted either by existing firms or by fresh enterprisers.

[1] The preliminary figures for the recent census show the following results:—

Population.	1891	1901	Increase.
Lower Burma	4,408,466	5,371,328	21·84 per cent.
Upper Burma	3,362,428	3,849,833	14·49 ,,
Total, Burma Proper	7,770,894	9,221,161	18·66 ,,
Northern Shan States	} 375,691 {	319,643	—
Southern Shan States	} estimated {	809,429	—
Chin Hills	—	87,101	—
Other Hill Tribes	—	12,287	—
Grand Total	—	10,449,621	—

THE PROGRESSIVE VALUE OF THE SEA-BORNE TRADE OF BURMA DURING THE LAST TWELVE YEARS HAS BEEN AS FOLLOWS :—

Year.	Rangoon.			Other Ports.			Total for Burma.		
	Imports.	Exports.	Total.	Imports.	Exports.	Total.	Imports.	Exports.	Total.
	£	£	£	£	£	£	£	£	£
1888–89	5,326,467	3,899,400	9,225,867	891,466	1,599,734	2,491,200	6,217,933	5,499,134	11,717,067
1889–90	5,474,067	4,800,000	10,274,067	900,934	1,976,800	2,877,734	6,375,001	6,776,800	13,151,801
1890–91	5,801,600	5,964,400	11,766,000	932,400	2,279,933	3,212,333	6,734,000	8,244,333	14,978,333
1891–92	6,019,191	6,005,481	12,024,672	981,224	2,442,646	3,423,870	7,000,415	8,448,127	15,448,542
1892–93	6,209,773	6,222,316	12,432,089	1,105,924	2,160,822	3,266,746	7,315,697	8,383,138	15,698,835
1893–94	5,561,246	5,815,490	11,376,736	1,011,592	1,788,390	2,800,082	6,572,938	7,603,880	14,176,818
1894–95	4,490,516	6,283,098	10,773,614	1,060,743	2,830,749	3,891,492	5,551,259	9,113,847	14,665,106
1895–96	5,690,969	6,730,642	12,421,611	1,122,429	2,679,120	3,801,549	6,813,398	9,409,762	16,223,160
1896–97	5,508,753	7,249,477	12,758,230	1,085,216	2,465,382	3,550,598	6,593,969	9,714,859	16,308,828
1897–98	5,522,770	8,313,337	14,836,107	1,110,098	2,590,789	3,700,887	7,632,868	10,904,126	18,536,994
1898–99	6,624,640	8,081,444	14,706,084	1,162,587	2,896,386	4,058,973	7,787,227	10,977,830	18,765,057
1899–1900	6,583,182	9,656,703	16,239,884	1,807,849	2,772,260	4,580,109	8,391,029	12,428,963	20,819,992

The great bulk of this carrying trade takes place in vessels flying the British flag. Practically the whole of the interportal trade between Burma and the rest of British India, amounting in 1899–1900 to imports and exports of 2,571,926 tons, valued at £9,373,564, is conveyed in British bottoms; while of the 734,850 tons cleared to foreign countries, 629,967 were carried in British ships and 37,328 in German vessels. A good deal of the timber is carried in sailing ships, but the perishable rice cargoes are mainly conveyed in steamships.

The Distribution and the Precise Nature of such Portion of this large Volume of Sea-borne Trade as is shipped *direct* between Burma Ports and Foreign Countries can perhaps best be summarized in the following Tabular Form:—

Sea-borne Trade between Burma and	Imports, in Pounds Sterling.[1]		Exports, in Pounds Sterling.		Chief Imports.	Chief Exports.
	1898-99.	1899-1900.	1898-99.	1899-1900.		
United Kingdom	£2,265,826	£1,997,940	£1,759,555	£1,508,251[2]	Yarns and textile fabrics; iron work and machinery; liquor and provisions; miscellaneous goods.	Rice; teakwood; cutch; paraffin-wax; hides; caoutchouc.
Austria	30,653	25,983	3,742	26,164	Hardware and cutlery; cotton yarn.	Rice; teakwood.
Belgium	91,316	97,032	876	1,587	Wrought iron; hardware and cutlery; dyeing materials.	Caoutchouc only.
France	83,895	66,478	7,777	4,903	Spirits and wines; piece-goods; candles.	Teakwood; rice.
Germany	240,472	195,771	50,645	60,273	Sugar; salt; liquors; hardware and cutlery; piece-goods.	Rice; cutch; teakwood.
Holland	75,588	77,796	3,236	6,706	Cotton and woollen piece-goods; spirits.	Cutch.
Italy	397	1,727	54	8,629	Miscellaneous articles of food.	Hides; rice; cutch.
Russia	16,334	8,044	3,540	12,079	Kerosene only.	Rice only.
Egypt	2,049	1,386	2,853,703	2,685,800[2]	Tobacco.	Rice; teakwood; hides; cutch; caoutchouc (for further sailing orders only).
United States	93,264	101,205	11,148	5,172	Kerosene oil chiefly; wrought iron (for railway bridging).	Caoutchouc; cutch; hides; rice.
Ceylon	13,439	7,498	208,899	169,177	Cotton yarn; cocoanut oil.	Rice; teakwood; provisions; cutch; spices.
China	61,911	67,705	35,510	45,914	Sugar; silk (raw and manufactured).	Rice; cotton; jade-stone.
Japan	104,646	89,908	454,139	170,791	Silk piece-goods; miscellaneous articles.	Rice and cotton only.
Straits Settlements	631,968	510,691	1,734,289	1,381,886[3]	Provisions; sugar, spices, and fruits; raw silk; cotton and silk piece-goods, and apparel; matches and miscellaneous articles.	Rice; cotton; jade-stone; provisions and spices; tobacco; cutch; hides.
Other Countries	36,413	44,756	1,034,548	966,938	Miscellaneous articles.	Rice; teakwood.
Total	£3,748,166	£3,279,598	£7,816,845	£6,791,953		

[1] These do not represent the total foreign imports into Burma, but only such as are shipped *direct*. Large foreign imports are also transhipped from Bombay and Calcutta, which are shown as coasting trade. [2] Exports to Europe and Egypt (for further sailing orders) are usually larger when there is no famine in India, or elsewhere in Asia. [3] The great bulk of the trade shown as with the Straits Settlements is in reality with China and Japan, Singapore being merely an emporium and distributing centre for goods in transit.

436

THE "PADDY RING" OF 1893

A sudden and rather a serious temporary check was experienced during the year 1893 in the flowing tide of agricultural and commercial prosperity, which is indicated in the above statistical tables. About four-fifths of the whole trade of the province passes through Rangoon. There the European merchants owning the rice mills, in which the vast surplus produce of the great rice tracts of the lower Irrawaddy valley and the delta are prepared for export, combined to cause a fall in the price of "paddy" or raw, unhusked rice. From 92 rupees per 100 baskets in 1891, the market rate rose to 127 rupees, and even stood as high as 138 rupees in April, 1892, in consequence of competition among the merchants and of heavy shipments to Europe, where the market stood high. By the end of 1892, when the rice crop was ready for market, prices in Europe had already fallen, and the rice millers of Rangoon, in order to obviate the risk of loss, had entered into a combination not to pay above an average of 77 rupees per 100 baskets for the different classes of rice throughout the approaching shipping season. Prices consequently ruled between 76 and 79 rupees per hundred baskets in Rangoon, and the market rates there regulated the course of prices at the other seaports. Such a combination had been tried fourteen or fifteen years before in Moulmein, but collapsed when a suspension of work at the mills was threatened through the cultivators keeping back their rice till prices advanced. During the first half of 1893, however, the Rangoon rice millers held together and maintained their compact, with the result that, in spite of the low rates ruling in Europe, they were able to carry on an exceedingly lucrative export business. Now, the vast majority of Burmese agriculturists take advances early in the year at high rates of interest, which they clear off after selling the surplus paddy grown on their lands. As rice is rather a perishable commodity in such a hot, damp climate as that of Lower Burma, the struggle between the merchants and the cultivators was altogether an unequal contest. As the merchants happened on this occasion to keep faith with each other, the paddy had ultimately to come to the rice mills on the buyers' own terms. The consequence was that the rice millers cleared a net profit of four annas, or fourpence, on every basket of rice milled, and some of the larger firms were for some time milling 80,000 baskets a day, and making a clear profit of £1,333 daily. Under these exceptionally favourable conditions firms that were considered rather shaky at the end of 1892 retrieved a very sound position in 1893, and those that were previously flourishing made enormous gains. But the cultivators suffered a very serious reduction of income, and the effect of this became at once noticeable in a depressed state of general trade. Exports of rice decreased largely, and there was a considerable diminution in imports of metals, hardware, and woollen goods. Heavy losses were incurred by the import merchants, for the sudden fall in the value of paddy seriously affected the power of the people, throughout the richest and most populous tracts in the province, to buy luxuries. After the first season the merchants' combination collapsed. Certain of the firms insisting on having as their share a larger percentage of the paddy purchased than was under the previous arrangement allotted to them in the spring of 1893 ; but this new proposal was not consented to by the wealthier firms, who had then had the lion's share of the raw grain. With this collapse of the " paddy ring " the law of supply and demand came into natural play again in 1894, although it was some little time before the trade of the province recovered entirely from the depressed state into which it had suddenly been thrown by the rice millers' combination.

Long before the grain ripens, as soon as calculations seem justified, an official forecast is made, which is modified from time to time if necessary, as to what the total yield of the coming harvest will probably be, and as to the surplus which may be expected to become available for export. Expressed in terms of the rupee, a sixteen-anna crop means that the average quantity may be expected per acre, while a twelve-anna crop would mean that only three-quarters of the usual yield may be anticipated.

Next in importance to rice and teak timber among the

exports to foreign countries is cutch, a very dark-coloured solid extract obtained from boiling chips of the *Sha* tree (*Acacia Catechu*), which grows abundantly throughout all the tracts still under forest in the central dry zone. Its finest and most vigorous development is obtained, however, in the Thayetmyo, Prome, and Tharrawaddy districts of Pegu. It is thus a tree characteristic of the areas of comparatively light rainfall, for Burma; and as cutch-boiling has been habitually resorted to by the peasantry during the years of scarcity, which have been of frequent occurrence of late, the supply of mature cutch trees capable of yielding the extract in remunerative quantities has in portions of the cutch tracts become temporarily diminished. Besides excessive production, other causes have also been simultaneously operating to affect the export trade, but the value of cutch as one of the best of known dyeing stuffs will probably always secure for it a favourable market at remunerative rates. Of late years the reputation of Burma cutch has sunk considerably on account of adulteration with other wood and bark extracts (from various *Terminalia* and other trees), but measures have recently been taken by the Government which should operate successfully in effecting the discontinuance of such fraudulent practices by the cutch-boilers. . Cutch dyes a rich dark brown, and is extensively employed in dyeing canvas, fishing nets, yarn, etc. As yet no aniline products have been discovered which can be used as cheaper and at the same time effective substitutes. From 7,827 tons, valued at £223,000, in 1895–96, the export sank very considerably during the following years; but it is beginning to revive again, 6,301 tons, valued at £162,274, having been exported in 1899–1900, and the trade is capable of considerable expansion in future.

Another article of minor forest produce suffering from temporary depreciation is caoutchouc or india-rubber, the sun-dried milky sap of the *Ficus elastica*. This tree is only to be found growing indigenously in the dense moist subtropical forest tracts to the north of Myitkyina, Mogaung, and Indawgyi, and in the similar tracts in the upper portion of the Chindwin drainage. It is collected

BURMA UNDER BRITISH RULE

by the wild Singpho or Kachin tribesmen, from whom it
is purchased locally by Chinese pedlars, and brought
down to Bhamo or Mogaung on the Irrawaddy side, or to
Kindat on the Chindwin, for collection of the Government royalty before being further transported to Rangoon.
The trade in this commodity, now in great and increasing
demand in Europe, has also, like that in cutch, decreased
owing partly to unrestrained over-tapping of the trees
and partly to adulteration. The Chinese pedlars, who
go up trading into the Kachin tracts, swindle the wild
Kachins with false weights, while the latter try to over-
reach the pedlars by putting stones, earth, and bits of
bark in the balls of rubber to make them heavier. Of
late years, too, a large proportion of the inner part of the
rubber, which is rolled up like cordage into balls of about
seven or eight inches in diameter, has usually been made
up of "root-rubber," lighter in colour and inferior in quality
to the rubber obtained from the stem and branches. As
the tapping of the roots at the same time speedily leads
to the exhaustion of the tree, endeavours are being made
to stop this pernicious practice by cutting open every ball
on its arrival at the forest revenue station and charging an
enhanced rate of royalty on such proportion of the contents
as clearly appear to be root-rubber. At the same time
large forest reserves are being formed for the special protection of the india-rubber tree, and plantations will be
commenced so soon as such reserves have been legally
secured to the control of the Forest Department. During 1899–1900 the total exports of caoutchouc were 291
tons, valued at £80,562, including rubber of all descriptions. The stock of *Ficus elastica* is much more limited
in Burma than in the adjoining province of Assam, and
there is little prospect of increased supplies becoming immediately available. There are, however, various climb-
ing members of the *Apocyneae* family of plants common
throughout the forest tracts of Pegu and Tenasserim,
whose sap yields caoutchouc, or a substance almost
identical with it. From one of these, *Kyetpaung*
(*Chavannesia esculenta*) or " Tenasserim caoutchouc "
used to be collected and sold in the Shwegyin bazaar
more than twenty years ago, while *Talaingno* (*Parameria*

glandulifera), common in the tracts still under jungle to the north of Rangoon, also yields a similar substance. In view of the demand now existing for caoutchouc, these possible new sources of supply seem well worthy of attention.

To meet the requirements of the future, and to make revenue from them, large rubber plantations have recently been made in Lower Burma by the Forest Department. There can be little doubt that if any wealthy syndicate were prepared to form further extensive plantations of this kind they would yield very handsome returns within eight to ten years, while the Local Government are probably prepared to offer facilities for such enterprise by giving land on liberal terms to suitable parties.

The export trade in raw hides and horns is one that flourishes and shows signs of continuous expansion. During the last twenty years it has almost trebled in value, and now sometimes amounts to nearly half a million hides, and close on 250 tons of horns, aggregating nearly £140,000 in value. When the Shan States, and particularly the Southern Shan States, are more opened out by the expansion of the railway system, this trade should become much enhanced in volume.

Raw cotton is also an article of export which, already extensive, should develope considerably in future years. Unfortunately the cotton produced in Burma is short in the staple, and therefore unsuited for the production of the finer classes of twist and yarn ; but it is largely exported to Japan, and also into western China by way of Bhamo. The cotton-fields are situated in the heart of the central dry zone of Upper Burma. The chief centres of the industry are the tracts lying between Meiktila and Myingyan, and the area situated to the north of the Chindwin river near its confluence with the Irrawaddy. As both of these land-locked areas have recently been opened out by railways, this should give a stimulus to the trade in raw cotton by bringing the produce within easy reach of trading centres. Besides this, cotton for home consumption is grown on the hill-clearings all over the province. The cotton-seed is sown along with the rice, and the crop is collected after the grain has been harvested. What is thus grown, however, is entirely consumed in the jungle districts for weaving waist-cloths and other articles of personal and domestic requirement. In 1899–1900 the export of raw cotton to foreign countries amounted to 4,386 tons, valued at £140,052.

Hitherto the cotton export business has been conducted in the most primitive manner imaginable. No mill existed in any part of the cotton-producing districts till an enterprising Chinese firm established one at Mahlaing, about halfway between Meiktila and Myingyan, in 1898. The cleaning of the crop was done by hand-gins worked by women and girls, the right hand being employed to turn the handle while the narrow wooden rollers were fed with the left hand.

The cotton trade is almost entirely in the hands of Chinamen. Advances are made through their agents to the cultivators during the spring, and the latter bind themselves to deliver during the autumn, after the harvesting and ginning operations have been completed, fixed quantities of clean raw cotton at stipulated rates. From personal inquiries made on the spot during the autumn of 1896, I found that for every hundred rupees advanced in spring the lender obtained during the following November and December raw cotton to the value of about one hundred and seventy rupees. He thus secured interest amounting to seventy per cent. within less than a year, leaving out of consideration the trade profit which would accrue to him from the sale of the produce thus bought. Even though rainfall be precarious and uncertain in the main cotton-producing tracts, yet this business is on the whole safe as well as highly lucrative. If bad debts are sometimes made, there is really very little risk in the long run. The recent opening up of the Meiktila-Myingyan and the Sagaing-Âlôn tracts by branch railways ought to bring very apparent advantages to the cotton growers, while leading to possibilities of improvements in the quality of the cotton produced, if the use of Egyptian and American seed be encouraged. It seems rather surprising that this cotton trade has not yet succeeded in attracting the attention of

PARAFFIN ; JADE ; PIECE-GOODS

European firms. After making the personal inquiries in 1896 I brought the subject up in conversation with a partner in one of the large European firms in Rangoon, but was astonished to hear that, even with the profits attached to it, the cotton business was thought not to be worth their attention.

A large and expanding export trade is also carried on in paraffin and wax manufactured in refineries at Rangoon from the " earth-oil " drawn from the wells in the Myingyan and Minbu districts. This petroleum is said to contain a larger percentage of paraffin than any of the mineral oils of Russia or America, and is therefore of great technical value as a lubricant for machinery. The exports of lubricating oil and paraffin wax amount to £114,159 in value, while large quantities of refined oil are used locally for illuminating purposes. But the existing oil-wells of Burma are unable to supply the demands of the country in the latter respect, for since 1896 over two million gallons of kerosene are annually imported, chiefly from America, for this purpose.

The only other article of export on any considerable scale is jade, from the jade mines north of Mogaung, which is annually shipped to Singapore and China to the extent of about 200 tons, valued at more than £47,500. This trade is entirely in the hands of Chinamen, and is of rather a speculative nature ; for there is nothing on the exterior of the rough blocks to indicate the quality of the jade in the heart of the stone.

Of the imports, amounting in 1899–1900 to £8,391,029 in value, less than one-half consists of direct shipments from foreign countries, the bulk arising from the British Indian coasting trade.

By far the largest of the direct foreign imports are cotton, silk, and woollen piece-goods, which amount to about one million pounds a year, while cotton, twist, and yarn average over £300,000. Manufactured silks are imported to the extent of over £200,000, besides raw silk to the value of over £100,000. During the last few years silks of Japanese manufacture have gradually been supplanting English silks in a marked degree. Silk is also grown to a fair extent in the country of a strong though rather coarse fibre, silkworms being principally cultivated by tribes calling themselves *Yabein*, which are scattered over the hilly tracts of the central portion of Lower Burma. As the taking of life involved in the process of getting the silk from the cocoons is offensive to the principles of the Buddhist religion, these *Yabein* are considered an outcast race. Silk-weaving by hand-looms is still largely carried on near Mandalay, the finest productions being from the looms of Amárapura, though this industry has been languishing ever since the fall of the kingdom and court of Ava. The yellow robes worn by the priesthood are still mostly made of native silk dyed by means of boiling with chips of the jack-tree (*Artocarpus integrifolia*); but for by far the greater part, and especially in the more thickly populated districts near the seaports, the silk articles of clothing now mostly worn are the cheaper, gaudier foreign machine products specially made for the Burma trade.

Among minor imports matches amount in value to over £50,000 a year. Formerly Swedish matches were to be found in general use, and would be met with away far up in the hill jungles when one had even got beyond the range of coming across empty beer bottles used for holding oil and regarded as household treasures; but now the cheap fire-producing "Taendstickor" have been in turn supplanted by similar and even cheaper articles of Japanese manufacture.

In the trade with this portion of Britain's own territory British goods are being undersold by those of foreign manufacture. Most of the glassware, lampshades, etc., are made in Austria. Practically the whole of the many hundreds of thousands of small wax candles, burned in enormous numbers before sacred shrines and during religious festivals, are imported either from France or Belgium; and in any bazaar, if one takes up teacups bearing in gold letters inscriptions like "Forget me not" or "Remember me," the stamp below, enforced by the Merchandise Act, will show that they have been "Made in Germany." In Burma, as in most other parts of the world, British trade in small miscellaneous articles is being supplanted by foreign countries, which give more atten*ion to petty details calculated to attract the purchaser and to readily suit his convenience or his peculiar taste.

For the rice trade large quantities of gunny bags are requisite, which are all imported from Calcutta, as jute is not grown in Burma. Though the obtaining climatic and other physical conditions throughout the Irrawaddy delta are suitable for its cultivation, yet the scarcity and the high price of labour as compared with Lower Bengal would hardly yet make any enterprise in jute remunerative. The same drawbacks operate against the production of various other commodities for the growth of which the soil and the climate of the province are otherwise well adapted. Thus sugar-cane grows well, and is cultivated to a certain extent in the Amherst and Thatôn districts of Tenasserim ; but endeavours made about a quarter of a century ago to work sugar-mills by steam at Amherst and Martaban resulted in failure. The cane is crushed in wooden presses and the juice boiled down and formed into *Kyantagá* or cakes of brown sugar, very much like coarse, inferior toffee in appearance, which are sold throughout all the local bazaars in the country. Wild indigo grows freely in most of the *Pônzo* or weedy jungles, which spring up on all temporary hill-clearings after the rice crop has been harvested, and indigo is cultivated to a trifling extent for domestic use in dyeing silk and cotton yarn. The use of indigenous dyes and yarns is, however, being restricted through cheap imports coloured with gaudy aniline dyes. Salt-boiling is still carried on all along the coast and at various places in Upper Burma, but large imports from Europe and India are required to satisfy the demand. Within the last twenty years the import duty on salt has increased from £3,300 to over £80,000 a year. Tobacco of excellent quality is largely grown on the rich alluvial deposits left in the shape of mud-banks thrown up on the inner bends of streams when the water falls after the summer flood season. But the art of curing is not properly understood ; and for the manufacture of cheroots large quantities of tobacco leaf, inferior in quality to what could be grown locally, are annually imported from Madras. The future possibilities of these industries, and of others for which the soil and climate of Burma are equally well suited, at present remain undeveloped because of the scantiness and the high cost of labour. These are drawbacks to commercial development which cannot be obviated or removed merely by the influx of capital into the province, while at the same time they operate very strongly against attracting it.

If sound measures could only be devised for importing large quantities of labour at fair rates, there would then be no reason why tea and coffee gardens under European supervision should not be opened out with good remunerative prospects on the Shan hills, or why Burma should not also have a share in the expanding export trade to Europe in these commodities now almost confined to Assam and Ceylon. Coffee of excellent quality is produced at Thandaung, near Toungoo, at an elevation of about 4,200 feet. Great quantities of *Letpet*, or "pickled tea," consumed largely by the Burmese, are produced by the Shans at Pasé and other places on the northern Shan hills. Hitherto this has been conveyed by coolies and bullocks to Mandalay, but henceforth this carrying trade will fall to the new railway line. Within easy reach of this Mandalay-Kunlôn railway—as, for example, around Pyaunggaung—there are large tracts of high lands very suitable, so far as soil and climate are concerned, for tea production ; while perhaps even better sites for the growth of finer qualities of tea are obtainable further south on the range of lofty hills, within a short distance of the base of which the Rangoon-Mandalay line of railway runs parallel.

As pursued on the Shan hills at present, this industry is followed in the most uneconomical manner. The shrubs are annually stripped of leaves to an excessive extent without being manured or tended : hence they are mostly in a chronic state of enfeeblement, the branches and twigs being often thickly covered with lichens and beard-mosses whose production is favoured by the cool elevation and the damp foggy climate during a great part of each year.

The following extract from the official diary of the

forest officer in charge of the Southern Shan States Division may perhaps convey a good idea as to the suitability of some of the available highland tracts for tea cultivation under resident European supervision:—

23rd April, 1898.—Moved camp to Mene Taung village, at an altitude of 5,800 feet. This village is situated on the high range to the west of Pindaya, and is only seven miles from that place. It was reported on by Lieutenant Pottinger some years ago as being a very suitable place for a sanatorium, and our short experience there confirms his opinion. It was most delightfully cool up there, so much so that we sat out in the sun till midday.[1] There is no lack of water, and to the south there is any amount of level ground. The uncleared portions are covered with high dense evergreen forests of oaks, chestnuts, magnolias, laurels, the *Súbo* (dwarf *Zizyphus*) *Cedrela Toona*, and a great many other trees. The hill-sides are clothed with wild strawberries and violets, and two species of roses are also very common. Ivy is found growing on the stems of most of the trees, and two or three varieties of it were noticed. The inhabitants of this village are Taungthus, who live chiefly by indigo cultivation ; but to the north are several Palaung villages, some of them at an elevation of 7,000 feet. The Palaungs go in chiefly for poppy cultivation (opium). There is a nice substantial *Zayat* (native rest-house) here, and a good *Pôngyi kyaung* (monastery). Mene Taung is situated on what used to be the old trade route into Burma viâ the Natteik pass, and it is only forty miles from the railway. To the north of the village the hills gradually get higher and higher till they culminate in the Momachôt Taung at an altitude of 7,800 feet, some four miles from Mene Taung.

The inland trans-frontier import and export trade with Siam, Karenni, the Shan States, and Yunnan, registered at nineteen stations in Upper Burma and nine in Lower Burma, amounted to £2,047,314 in 1899–1900. Improved communications by road from Myitkyina, Bhamo, and Namkhan into Yunnan, the growing prosperity of the Shan States under peaceful administration, and the construction of the Mandalay-Kunlôn railway, all point to the certainty of a continuation of the expansion of trade in these directions, although the possibilities of such expansion must, of course, be confined within far narrower limits than may ultimately be prescribed for trade in the staple products of Burma itself.

The caravan routes between Burma and Yunnan are

---

[1] April is the hottest month in Burma. *Taung* means a hill, a mountain.

the northern tracks by Momein (Tenyuehfu) and Talifu, and the southern track by Namkhan, and thence viâ Sawadi, Mansi, Maingma, and Lunghin to Yungchang. The old established route to Momein was from Bhamo, up the Taiping river, navigable for about 120 miles, to Mamo (Sikaw), and thence viâ Manwaing; but, with the recent extension of the railway line to Myitkyina, a new track has now been opened out by way of Sadôn. Though shorter, this new track is reported to be steeper; and, in any case, there is little probability of the traffic down the Taping river to Bhamo being extinguished by total deflection to Myitkyina. In 1889—1900 the total trade with Yunnan amounted to about £290,000.

Previous to the annexation of Upper Burma, and for two or three years after that, the chief import into Bhamo from Yunnan was opium. This is the staple product of Yunnan, and with it that province was accustomed to pay for the whole of its imports. After the annexation the transport and sale of opium were absolutely prohibited in Upper Burma, but in 1888 the Opium Act was introduced to provide for the requirements of Chinese and natives of India, and to regulate the traffic in this drug amongst the non-Burmese permitted to use it. The Excise Act was also applied to Upper Burma in the same year. Between 1886 and 1888 the sale of opium, except to Chinese, its transport in quantities of more that three *tolas* (of 180 grains each), and the keeping of opium shops were prohibited, while the licensing of excise shops was permitted only where a real necessity existed for liquor to be consumed by Europeans, Indians, or Chinese. After the introduction of these Acts no excise licenses or opium shops were allowed in any place where the non-Burmese portion of the population was not considerable, and reasonable measures were taken to restrict the sale of intoxicants to Burmese. The import of opium from Yunnan was permitted on payment of a duty of thirty rupees per *viss* of 3·65 lb., which was enhanced by two rupees a *viss* in 1896-97, and a purchaser might buy ten tolas of opium, whereas in Lower Burma only three are obtainable by a single purchaser. Imports of Chinese and Shan-

Chinese opium soon, however, became supplanted to a large extent through Government imports of the Bengal drug of better quality ; but a considerable amount of smuggling no doubt takes place on the part of the trade caravans. Handwoven silks were also brought down in small annual quantities from Yunnan, but this too has been gradually driven back by the cheaper sea-borne supply. At present the chief articles of import are mules, cordage, fruits, honey and wax, iron, brass, and copper articles, tea, leaf-gold and orpiment ; while the exports consist mostly of raw cotton, salt, piece-goods, jade, betel-nuts, cutch, and petty articles like matches, soap, and candles. The trade is in the hands of Yunnanese or Shan-Chinese, a fine stalwart race of rosy-cheeked men, picturesquely clad in coarse light-blue cotton clothing, but usually filthy to a degree, who would probably provide excellent raw material for troops if found amenable to soldierly discipline. The caravan trade to Bhamo and Myitkyina is carried on with mules and bullocks.

Trade with the Shan States is entirely in the hands of Shans, and is carried on by means of pack bullocks and ponies. The imports consist mainly of cattle, ponies, hides, leather and metal articles, large-brimmed flexible straw hats, pickled and dry tea, stick-lac, black varnish, gums, ginger, cigar leaves, chillies, limes, and til-seed ; and the exports include twist and yarn, piece-goods, petroleum, salted and dried fish, salt, tobacco, oranges, betel-nuts, matches, candles and the like.

Except as regards the import of teak timber, the trans-frontier trade with Siam is of much the same minor class as with the Shan States. Trade with Siam amounted in 1899–1900 to about £355,000 ; but in considering this, as also the trade with the Southern Shan States and Karenni (£211,000), it must be recollected that the statistics include the value of teak timber imported into Moulmein by the Salween river, and that this ranges from £250,000 to £300,000 in value annually.

The greater portion of the inland trans-frontier trade is with the Northern and Southern Shan States, respectively amounting to £616,667 and £575,556 in

449   G G

BURMA UNDER BRITISH RULE

1899-1900, which are British possessions ; and it is there
that the best prospects exist of extending commerce by
means of opening up the country with railways. The
relative merits of the Southern Shan States and Yunnan
in this respect have, however, been elsewhere discussed
(*vide* chapter ii. vol. ii.).

The management of affairs connected with the port of
Rangoon is in the hands of a Port Trust, consisting of
merchants elected by the Rangoon Chamber of Commerce and of officials nominated by Government.
Apart from the Chamber of Commerce, there is no
general or special organization for the conduct of
business affairs. There is no central mart or exchange,
even in Rangoon. Commercial transactions are mostly
conducted by brokers of different nationalities who go
about from office to office ascertaining how they can
most advantageously place orders they have received for
the purchase or sale of produce of all kinds. To obtain
a proper knowledge of the import business and to keep
in touch with its pulse, it is essential that merchants and
their assistants should maintain themselves *au courant*
with what passes in the "bazaar," the eastern equivalent
of "the city" in its mercantile sense. This is a very
comprehensive term, including not merely the municipal
and other local bazaars for the retail vend of articles of
every description, but also the whole of the business
quarter of any town.

The petty bazaar trade of the country is still largely
in the hands of Burmese—and more especially of Burmese women, who are endowed with very keen trading
instincts. Most Burmese women keep a stall in the local
bazaar at some time of their lives, where they trade in
commodities suited to the capital they can command,
and varying from cheroots and petty articles of food up
to costly silks and satins. But at all the large centres of
trade Burmese women have now to undergo a very keen
competition from Parsis and other natives of Upper
India from Bengal to Bombay. Burmese men would
have no chance against the latter. Above all other
things the Burman loves *dolce far niente*, and principally
in the form of smoking and sleeping. For such lazy,

450

PETTY BAZAAR TRADE

inert male competitors the subtle, watchful, greedy and alert Bengali,—the *Graeculus esuriens* of the East,—the Parsi, or the Mogul is far more than a match : but the Burmese girl or woman holds her own, and will still hold it for some time yet, in the bazaar arts of persuasion and of bargaining for the sale of her goods.

Except in so far as concerns brokerage and dealings in up-country produce, with regard to which their intimate knowledge of and relations with the producers give them peculiar advantages, the Burmese are gradually but surely being ousted from trade by natives of India and by Chinese. Both of these latter show great business capacity, and both intermarry very largely with Burmese girls. The children of Indian and Burmese unions, termed " Zerbaddi," are a handsome, sharp-witted race, but the purely Mongolian offspring of mixed Chinese and Burmese parentage is physically superior. Between them, however, Indians and Chinese are bound in course of time to rake into their hands most of the bazaar trade which is still held by the Burmese in the seaport towns.

Among the European merchants changes have also been gradually going on during the last twenty or thirty years, and the most notable of these is the manner in which German firms have sprung up and secured a very large share in the commerce. In many respects they have supplanted the old class of Scottish merchants, who were the great pioneers of eastern trade in former days.

This invasion of British seaports and this conquest of a large and influential share in their trade are not confined to Burma, for a precisely similar state of affairs is also distinctly observable in Calcutta and Singapore; but it is unmistakable at all the four chief ports of Burma, and more particularly with regard to the export business in rice, the great staple product of the province. The chief reason for this seems to be that the assistants in the German firms come out better equipped for their work, and are more assiduous in their duties, than the young lads who are sent out to join the English and the Scottish firms. These latter are fond of cricket, tennis, riding, boating and other outdoor sports, and are naturally very pleased whenever, their daily task being completed, they can leave office or mill-yard to join in these healthy pastimes; whereas the young German assistant is invariably ignorant of cricket, generally bad at tennis, and only learns to ride, after a fashion, on his arrival in Burma. But, from the moment of his advent in the province, each young German assistant at once takes the interest of a prospective partner in the affairs of his firm, and thinks much less of amusement and of outdoor exercises than of business.

Which of these views of life may be the preferable when looked at from the broad human standpoint is entirely beside the question; but there can be no disputing the fact that these essential differences with regard to their assistants are most probably the chief causes which have enabled German firms in Burma to acquire a preponderating influence that seems disappointingly strange in a British possession.

Some of these German merchants, after having been local partners in the Burma firms for a given time, return to the Fatherland, while the services of others, selected for special business capacity, are transferred to the head offices in London. The German rice firms of Burma consequently become and remain English houses of business; but the home partners, the local partners, and assistants are all Germans—and they remain so, unless they happen to be selected for settling down permanently in London as partners of the head firm controlling and directing business affairs.

It is marvellous how ignorant the great majority of the merchants and their assistants are about Burma and the Burmese in general. Very few of them ever travel throughout the country, except along some of the main routes of railway or river communication; and comparatively few of them would be able to make their way into the interior without an interpreter, or to make personal inquiries or obtain information affecting even their own particular line of business. At all the trade centres commercial transactions are usually arranged through the medium of the English or the Hindustani language, and a colloquial knowledge of Burmese is hardly any longer essential. But it of course stands to reason that if merchants could, and would, equip themselves efficiently in this respect, and would take the trouble to travel about acquiring a personal knowledge of the possibilities of the country and the requirements of the people, this would naturally lead to the probable expansion of trade at a quicker rate than will otherwise in any case be bound to accrue.

But even in this matter the young German distinctly excels his English and Scottish competitors. Though not naturally more gifted with linguistic ability than the average Englishman, by sheer assiduity he acquires an earlier and often a better acquaintance with Hindustani, and sometimes also of Burmese to an extent useful for business. Hence he obtains success, as he deserves to, because he works hard to achieve it.

Both financially and commercially Burma is in a thoroughly sound position, and is developing in a healthy and normal manner. Despite the Bay of Bengal —that curse of Burma, cutting it off from direct touch with the supreme Government in Calcutta or Simla—the province is already one of the brightest jewels in the Imperial diadem of India; and its lustre will increase in proportion as inducements are offered for the influx of the capital and the labour necessary for more rapid development in the immediate future. And through the recent fixation of the rate of exchange the first and main step has been taken towards encouraging the inflow of capital required for developing the rich natural resources of the province.

APPENDIX

Summary of the last thirty-five sections of the Prime Minister's *Attasankhepa Vannaná Dammatháṭ*, or Institutes of Burmese Law (1882), referred to in chapter vii., page 190 (*q.v.*) :—

The seven kinds of wives are [1]—

    a wife like a murderess, who is liable to be divorced although she may have borne many children ;

    a wife like a thief, who is liable to be divorced although she may have borne many children ;

    a wife like a master, who is liable to be divorced although she may have borne many children ;

    a wife like a sister, who should be cherished throughout her life;

    a wife like a mother, who should be cherished throughout her life ;

    a wife like a slave, who should be cherished throughout her life;

    a wife like a friend, who should be cherished throughout her life.

Of the three kinds of wives that may be put away and the four kinds of wives that may be cherished, the one that is like a slave is the most excellent.

The wife who should not be put away.

The wife who respects her husband and looks after his material comfort, shall not be put away, although she may be laid up with illness for a length of time.

The six kinds of blemishes of a woman are—

    taking intoxicating drinks ;

    failure to take an interest in household affairs and in her duties towards her husband, and idleness;

    finding fault or quarrelling with the husband ;

    frequenting the houses of others ;

    intimacy with another man ;

    habitually sitting in the doorway of the house and looking at other men.

The five kinds of improprieties of a woman are [2]—

    impropriety with regard to property ;

    impropriety with regard to dress ;

    impropriety with regard to other men ;

    impropriety with regard to looking ; and

    impropriety with regard to food.

---

[1] Other details have already been given on page 182.

[2] See also the fuller details already given on page 186.

APPENDIX

The four kinds of pride of a woman are—
    pride of connexion ;
    pride of birth ;
    pride of property ; and
    pride of beauty.

Treatment of a wife possessing any of the six kinds of blemishes five kinds of improprieties, or four kinds of pride—

If the wife possesses any of the six kinds of blemishes, five kinds of improprieties, or four kinds of pride, the husband shall not divorce her, but shall continue to live with her, checking her conduct with instruction according to law.

The five kinds of wives who may be put away—

If a man and wife have lived together eight or ten years and have no children, the wife is a barren woman, and the husband may put her away, but their conjugal relations need not be discontinued. They may live together as usual, but, for the sake of offspring, the husband may take a lesser wife. If the wife wishes to separate, let her take all the property she brought to the marriage ; but, if there be no such property, let the wife take one-tenth of the jointly acquired property together with her wearing apparel. Let the husband take the remainder and let them separate. A wife, who has had eight or ten female children and no son, may be put away. She may not be put away by the discontinuance of conjugal relations : their status as man and wife may continue, but, for the sake of male issue, the husband may take a lesser wife. If they wish to separate from each other, let the animate and inanimate property be equally divided between them.

If a man, knowing a woman to be afflicted with leprosy, takes her to wife, let him have her cured, and perform the rites of burial in a proper manner on her death. If the husband wishes to divorce the wife, let her take all the property that is in his possession. If the leprosy, through her ill-fortune, appears after their marriage as first husband and first wife, and not before, and if the wife wishes to separate, let her take a suitable amount of property and separate. If the husband wishes to separate, let him give her one-half of the property. If a wife commits adultery, the husband may put her away in disgrace and may retain all the animate and inanimate property. If a woman sullies the good name of her family, the husband may take all the property and put her away in disgrace.

The eight kinds of husbands whom the wife has the right to abuse are—
    one who is excessively lascivious ;
    one who is ill for a length of time ;
    one who is very poor ;
    one who is very stupid ;
    one who is infirm ;
    one who is very old and sluggish ;
    one who is very lazy ;
    one who is physically incapable.

If the wife loses patience and abuses or reviles any of the said kinds of husbands, let her have the right of doing so.

The three kinds of husbands who may be put away are—
    a man of bad or immoral character ;

APPENDIX

a man who is very lazy; and

a man who is mad or imbecile.

If the wife loses patience and puts away any of such husbands, let her have the right of doing so.

The two kinds of husbands whom the wife has the right of putting away are—

one who is afflicted with leprosy, and

one who is frequently incontinent with the wives of others.

If the wife loses patience and desires to put away any of such husbands, she shall have the right of doing so, but she shall not have the right of taking the property.

The obligatory duty which a man and wife should specially observe is—

If either husband or wife is very ugly in appearance, or is afflicted with leprosy, or has been ill for a length of time, he or she shall be tended and supported by the other. The failure of such duty shall be punished with forfeiture of property and three months' imprisonment. If the wife has been ill for a long time, and the husband wishes to enjoy the society of a lesser wife, he shall first ask permission of his invalid wife, who must accede to his request.

The twelve qualifications of a good wife are—

skilfulness in cooking;

skilfulness in preparing betel and tobacco;

skilfulness in washing the clothing of her husband in time;

skilfulness in house-keeping;

skilfulness in weaving;

getting up from bed before the husband;

retiring after the husband;

eating after the husband;

communicating all matters to the husband;

suavity and affability in speech;

not visiting the houses of others without cause; and

obedience to her husband's commands.

The husband has no right to beat or abuse the wife who possesses these twelve qualifications; if he does so, he shall be liable to undergo a heavy punishment. But those who do not possess these twelve qualifications, may be corrected by beating or abusing them within the hearing of the public.

The five qualifications of a good husband are—

striving to increase his wealth;

providing a good house;

tending and maintaining the wife with care and tenderness;

looking after the cattle with care; and

supporting the relations of both husband and wife without distinction.

The wife has no right to abuse the husband who possesses these five qualifications; if she does so, she shall be liable to undergo a heavy punishment. But the wife has the right to abuse the husband who does not possess these qualifications.

*   *   *   *   *

APPENDIX

The law of separation, with mutual consent, between a husband and wife of the ruling class neither of whom has been married before—

If the husband and wife separate from each other with mutual consent, let the wearing apparel of the wife be taken by her, and let that of the husband be taken by him. Should the wearing apparel of one party be more valuable than that of the other, let the former pay to the latter the difference in value.

Further, as regards the three kinds of property, namely, property brought at the time of marriage, property given by the King, and property acquired through one's own skill or industry, let the party who brought or acquired it take two shares, and the dependant one share ; but, if the relative position of husband and wife in the acquisition of such property be equal, let the said three kinds of property be equally divided between them.

The debts shall be liquidated in the same proportion.

With regard to the children, let the father take the sons, and the mother the daughters, and let each parent have the right of selling the children thus obtained by an award at the time of separation. If a son be sold by the mother, let her give half the proceeds to the father, and if a daughter be sold by the father, let him give half the proceeds to the mother. But the mother has the right of selling the son on the death of the father, and, on the death of the mother, the daughter may likewise be sold by the father.

If, after separation, the parents contract another marriage and incur debt for their subsistence, each of them may sell the children of the former marriage who were allotted to him or her at the time of separation, provided that there are no children of the second marriage.

If there are children of the second marriage, and if the son (of the former marriage) is sold by the mother, let the share which the step-father would have received be given to the natural father; and, if the daughter is sold by the father, let the share which the step-mother would have received be given to the natural mother.

The law of separation between a husband and wife of the ruling class, neither of whom has been previously married, when only one party consents to the separation—

If either husband or wife desires to separate from the other, let the party wishing to separate take only his or her own wearing apparel, and any property given by the King (*Thinthi*), and let him or her also bear the law expenses. The other party not wishing to separate shall enjoy all the property other than that mentioned above. If there be no debt and no other property than property given by the King, the party wishing to separate shall give to the party not so wishing compensation, according to the status of such other party. With regard to any property given by the King, let the receiver of the gift retain it.

The law of separation between a husband and wife of the ruling class, neither of whom has been previously married, when either of them is guilty of a (matrimonial) fault—

If separation between the husband and wife takes place owing to the commission of adultery by the wife, she shall be sent away with only the clothes on her person, after being made to pay her husband the price of her body and damages in the sum of forty ticals of silver for

457

H H

APPENDIX

the offence committed; all the debts contracted shall be borne by her, while the property, animate and inanimate, which belonged to both, shall be enjoyed by the husband alone.

If separation occurs owing to the husband taking a lesser wife or concubine, all debts contracted shall be paid by him, and he shall be sent away with only the clothes on his person, while all the animate and inanimate property which belonged to both, shall be enjoyed by the wife alone.

It does not necessarily follow that a decree for separation should be given on account of a single act of ill-treatment of the wife by the husband; on the contrary, they should continue to live together as man and wife, a definite bond being executed by the husband to abstain from the repetition of such ill-treatment. But if the wife refuses to continue to live with her husband, let separation take place as in the case of mutual consent. On the other hand, if, after their re-union, upon the execution of the bond above-mentioned, the wife is dissatisfied with her husband, and again desires to separate, let separation take place as in the case of mutual consent. If, however, the husband refuses to be bound by a bond and desires to separate, let separation take place in accordance with the law of separation governing the case where the husband is the offender. So too, if, after the re-union upon the execution of the bond, the husband fails to abide by its conditions, let there be separation in accordance with the law of separation governing the case where the husband is the offender.

The three kinds of laws of separation between a previously married couple of the ruling class—

If there is separation, with mutual consent, between a previously married couple of the ruling class, let the property originally brought to the marriage be taken by the party who brought it; and let the jointly acquired property and debts be made into three portions, and let two be assigned to the worker for enjoyment and liquidation, and one to the dependant. If their relative position as worker and dependant is equal, let an equal division be made. If there are children, let the sons be taken by the father, and the daughters by the mother.

If, however, only the husband or the wife desires separation, let the original property brought to the marriage be taken by the party who brought it, and let the party wishing to separate take his or her wearing apparel together with the *Thinthi* property given by the King, and let him or her pay the debts contracted by both and also bear the law expenses. Let the party not wishing to separate, take all the jointly acquired property. If there is only property given by the King and no jointly acquired property, let the property given by the King be retained by the receiver of such gift. Let the party wishing to separate also pay the other party, not so wishing, compensation according to the status of such other party.

The law of separation between a previously married couple of the ruling class, when either of the parties is guilty of a matrimonial offence, is as follows—

If the separation takes place because of the wife's adultery, let the property originally brought to the marriage be taken by the party who brought it, and let the husband take the jointly acquired property

APPENDIX

together with property given by the King, and let the wife pay all the debts contracted by both. Let her also give her husband the price of her body as well as damages for the offence o adultery. If the separation takes place because the husband takes a lesser wife or concubine, let all the debts contracted by both be paid by the husband, let the property originally brought to the marriage be taken by the party who brought it, let all the jointly acquired property, together with property given by the King, be taken by the wife, and let the husband leave the house with only the clothes on his person.

The law by which the three kinds of property are distinguished, showing which is original property and which is jointly acquired—

The three kinds of property are as follows—

(1) original property brought to the marriage by the husband or the wife ;

(2) property given to either of them by the King (*Thinthi*) ; and

(3) property inherited by them during married life.

These three kinds of property are original property, and property accruing therefrom is acquired property.

A previously married man, not long after his marriage with a maiden, divorces her before any property has been acquired—

If a previously married man, not long after his marriage with a maiden, desires to divorce her before any property has been acquired, let him give her as compensation the value of a pair of earrings because of the deception on his part. This rule applies when the status of the husband is inferior to that of the wife. If the status of the husband and wife is equal, all the bridal presents and gifts made at the time of marriage shall be taken by the wife. Should there be no such property, let the husband give her one slave as compensation. Should the wife be pregnant, let the husband give her one male and one female slave. Should he be related by blood to the wife, let him give her one male and one female slave, whether she is pregnant or not.

A previously married woman, after her marriage with a man who has not previously been married, divorces him—

If a previously married woman, after her marriage with a man who has not previously been married, divorces him, let her give him a suit of clothes and a slave. If they separate before any property has been acquired, let them do so with mutual consent.

*   *   *   *

The law of divorce between a husband and wife who have set up house—

If a husband and wife who have set up house separately (from their parents) have effected a divorce, and if the wife does not return to the house of her parents, but continues to live in the same house, she may be treated as having no guardian, and the husband has the right of resuming conjugal relations with her provided that he has obtained her previous consent. If, on the other hand, the wife does not remain in the house of her husband, but returns to her parents, let him not have the right of resuming conjugal relations with her, even with her consent, unless permission has been previously obtained from her parents, because she has again passed under their guardianship.

APPENDIX

A man says to a woman having a husband, or a woman says to a man having a wife, " Divorce your husband or wife, and I will marry you "—

When a man says to a woman having a husband, or a woman says to a man having a wife, " Divorce your husband or wife, and I will marry you," and the promisee, relying on the word of the promisor, does so, but the promisor breaks the promise and refuses to marry, then all the law expenses shall be borne by the party who so refuses.

The law forbidding the transfer of the property of one wife to another—

It is improper to transfer the property of the chief wife to the lesser wife, or that of the lesser to the chief wife, or to mix up the property of both. He, who does so, shall be punished, and the property that has been transferred shall be restored to the rightful owner.

Marriage having been contracted between a previously married couple, the law declaring the right to give away, without permission, to whomsoever he or she pleases, the property which he or she has brought to the marriage—

Marriage having been contracted between a previously married couple, each party is entitled to give away, without the permission of the other, to whomsoever he or she pleases, the property which he or she has brought to the marriage. But this right shall not be exercised in favour of a concubine or paramour, and shall not extend to the whole of the property. Such right may only be exercised when the portion given away is of reasonable quantity. *The husband is, however, the lord of the wife, and the wife is the mistress of the house, and the most satisfactory way is for one to give away such property, in reasonable quantity, only with the consent of both.*

Butler & Tanner, The Selwood Printing Works, Frome, and London.

BURMA

English Miles